Ius Doni

Christian H. Kälin

Ius Doni

The Acquisition of Citizenship by Investment

IDEOS

New York · London · Zurich · Hong Kong

Abdruck der der Rechtswissenschaftlichen Fakultät der Universität Zürich vorgelegten Dissertation.

Imprint of the dissertation presented to the Faculty of Law of the University of Zurich.

ISBN: 978-0-9935866-3-7

Patria est, ubicumque est bene[1]

1 *Cicero,* Tusculanae disputations, citing the first legendary King of Troy: *itaque ad omnem rationem Teucri vox accommodari potest: »Patria est, ubicumque est bene.«*

Contents

1 **Introduction** 1
- 1.1 Overview 2
- 1.2 Challenge 10
- 1.3 Definition of the research question 24

Part I THE CONCEPT OF CITIZENSHIP AND THE ACQUISITION OF CITIZENSHIP **27**

2 **Historical Lines of Development and Modern Citizenship Concepts** **29**
- 2.1 Ancient Greece 30
- 2.2 Roman law 32
- 2.3 Middle Ages, Renaissance and Absolutism 33
- 2.4 Enlightenment and the American and French Revolutions 37
- 2.5 Criticism of Marxism; Nationalism and Totalitarianism 40
- 2.6 Post-war era and European integration 42
- 2.7 Modern economic immigration and citizenship concepts: import of talent and capital 52

3 **Citizenship vs. Nationality and the Concept of Citizenship** **57**
- 3.1 Citizenship as membership in a political community 62
- 3.2 National citizenship law 63
- 3.3 International and European law 64
- 3.4 Legal nature and the legal classification of citizenship 66
- 3.5 Definition on the basis of the law within the meaning of Article 9 TEU and Article 20(2) TFEU 70
- 3.6 Human dignity and its relevance to the allocation of citizenship 71
- 3.7 No obligation on the national legislature to follow a traditional understanding of citizenship 74
- 3.8 A new understanding of citizenship under the conditions of globalisation and transnationalism 77
- 3.9 Multiple citizenship 79

4 The Functional Significance of Citizenship 87

4.1 Overview and differentiation 88

4.2 Domestic functions 88

4.3 External functions 96

4.4 Additional non-State functions 100

4.5 Functions of modern citizenship concepts 102

5 The Constitutional and Political Dimensions of Citizenship 105

5.1 Citizenship law as a prerogative of nation States and expression of national sovereignty 106

5.2 Definition of a nation State 108

5.3 Nation State discretion in the area of citizenship 113

6 Principles of Citizenship Acquisition 117

6.1 Immigration and emigration countries 118

6.2 Types of citizenship acquisition 120

6.3 Acquisition at birth or original acquisition of citizenship 123

Part II ACQUISITION OF CITIZENSHIP BY NATURALISATION 127

7 Naturalisation Principles 129

7.1 Ordinary naturalisation 130

7.2 Frequent criteria for ordinary naturalisation 138

7.3 Citizenship as a formal or material point of connection 148

8 Analysis of Naturalisation Principles in Selected States 151

8.1 Overview 152

8.2 The UK 153

8.3 France 166

8.4 Switzerland 177

8.5 Canada 186

8.6 Austria 194

8.7 Comparative law of citizenship acquisition by naturalisation 202

Part III NATURALISATION THROUGH ECONOMIC CONTRIBUTION TO THE STATE **207**

9 Historical Examples of Citizenship-by-Investment **209**

10 The Grant of Citizenship in the National Interest **215**

11 The Economic Theory of Clubs **221**
11.1 Spectrum of opinion 222
11.2 Critical reflection 227

12 Blocked Exchange vs. Market Approach **231**
12.1 Spectrum of opinion 232
12.2 Should citizenship be governed by market values? 234
12.3 The ethics of the queue 238
12.4 The political membership aspect of citizenship 240

13 Applicable International Law and Principles with Regard to Citizenship **243**
13.1 Universal human dignity 244
13.2 Other potential international legal barriers 261
13.3 EU citizenship as a new supranational dimension to citizenship and limitation of national citizenship law 265

14 Evaluation of Citizenship-by-Investment – *ius doni* **279**
14.1 Issues, Background and Objectives 280
14.2 Definition of ius doni 280
14.3 Arguments against ius doni 289
14.4 Arguments in favour of ***ius doni*** 302
14.5 Definition of international standards and best practices 325

15 ***Ius doni* in selected reference States** **343**
15.1 Austria 345
15.2 Montenegro 359
15.3 St. Kitts and Nevis 367
15.4 Malta 377

16 Conclusions and Theses **391**

Bibliography **415**
Legal Sources **455**
Abbreviations **461**
Index **467**

1

Introduction

1.1 Overview

The different languages and religions,[2] cultures and societal conventions require a decentralised world order and its organisation into various individual states. There is a primal human need for units of solidarity smaller than the species,[3] and individual states represent the main political subdivision.[4] The realisation of a global State, which would ensure law and order around the world, or the notion of a global citizenship to parallel state citizenship, is practically impossible,[5] although the idea has persisted in human thought since ancient times.[6] On the contrary, the breakup of colonial empires and the collapse of the USSR and the many nationalist secessions all over the world have led to a proliferation of new sovereign states in recent times: whereas in 1945 there were 74 independent countries, today there are about 200.[7]

The Charter of the United Nations (UNC),[8] which codified values in an attempt at a "global constitution",[9] merely represents a minimum consensus. Bearing in mind the painful experiences of two world wars, it seeks to achieve a reasonably peaceful coexistence between the interdependent but sovereign national societies.

The decentralised organisation of the world is made particularly manifest in citizenship law, which draws connecting links between individuals and particular States. Every State needs a territory and a constituent body of citizens for it to claim its existence.[10] The citizen is publicly

---

2 *Kant*, in describing nature states of its two means of dividing nations: language and religion, KANT (1995)
3 HOLLINGER (1998) p. 85
4 Parts of this introduction are based on KÄLIN (2015)
5 cf. KANT (1795); KOLLER (1996)
6 cf. HEATER (2002)
7 ALESINA/SPOLAORE (2005)
8 The Charter of the United Nations of 26 June 1945 came into force on 24 October 1945, last amended by Decision of 20 December 1971, which came into force on 24 September 1973, published online at http://www.un.org/en/documents/charter/intro.shtml and http://treaties.un.org/doc/Publication/CTC/uncharter.pdf, both last accessed on 21 September 2012
9 For discussions on a "global constitution" cf. EMMERICH-FRITSCHE (2003)
10 JELLINEK (1976); WEIL (2004); cf. also *Klusmeyer* in ALEINIKOFF/KLUSMEYER (2001)

legally linked with the State through his citizenship, which is the political and legal point of reference.[11]

The legal concept of citizenship is "*one of our major practices of drawing lines*",[12] a "*Janus-faced*" phenomenon[13] that exists in the tension between (internal) inclusion and (external) exclusion,[14] as the freedom of the citizens of a State can only be guaranteed by the curtailment of the freedoms or access of individuals not belonging to that State (alien, foreign person).[15] The welfare, policies and culture of a community are protected through the restriction of access by individuals who do not belong to this community.[16] In fact, a person's right to live and work in a given country are a critical determinant of that person's lifetime opportunities, and passports and visas are among the most important instruments of global social inequality, as they determine the opportunities of international mobility.[17] These borders within which we happen to be born, and the documents we are entitled to, are no less arbitrary than other characteristics such as skin colour, gender or the genetic makeup we are endowed with.[18]

A child born in Laredo, Texas, is able to avail itself of all of the social and economic benefits of the American welfare state, is an American citizen and as such can seek employment opportunities throughout the United States (the US), and can enjoy wide visa-free travel around the world. A child born in the adjacent town of Juarez, Mexico, is entitled to none of these things. Through no doing of their own, the two children will have very different life prospects simply because of their place of birth.[19]

---

11 VON MÜNCH (2007); JELLINEK (1976), TOPAL (2010)

12 *Walker*, cited in NYERS (2009) p. 1

13 MAATSCH (2011) p. 4, with further references

14 BRUBAKER (1992); cf. also BLOEMRAAD/KORTEWEG/YURDAKUL (2009)

15 BOSNIAK (2006); cf. also *Kukathas* in SMITH (2011), HOWARD (2009) and CARENS (1995)

16 WALZER (1983) p. 34 et seq.

17 SHACHAR (2003); cf. also SADIQ (2009)

18 BENHABIB (2004) pp. 94–95, referring to *Carens*; cf. also CARENS (2000); KOCHENOV (2012); PASKALEV (2014); and in particular regarding citizenship as a "birthright lottery", cf. SHACHAR (2009)

19 SANDEL (2010) p. 230

The distinction between citizens and aliens is now relevant more than ever before as an important instrument, in particular for affluent nations, for excluding people from other countries – except for temporary access for tourists, students or business travellers, or where the labour or capital investments of aliens are in demand – and the issue of the regulation of access to state territories, labour markets and social benefits is crucial both for individuals and states.[20] It is revealing of the qualities a society values in others and seeks to incorporate, to observe who is fast-tracked in access to residence and citizenship and who is pushed to the back of the line or denied access altogether.[21] The control of this access is the preserve of immigration and citizenship laws.[22]

Regulating citizenship traditionally falls under the exclusive competence of individual states, which have broad creative discretion within public international law in this area,[23] and thereby control transnational migration, promote labour market policy requirements or – which is examined further in this work – stimulate direct investments and increase direct capital inflows to the country. It is in this regulation that states also display the limitations of their creative political powers, as in other areas of commercialisation of state sovereignty. Countries naturally undertake a range of activities and initiatives designed to enhance the welfare of their citizens by making some aspect of the country more attractive to foreign investors:[24] from foreign investment incentives, free zones, tax breaks, to establishing credible enforcement of contracts. Citizenship as a tool to attract foreign direct investments and talented entrepreneurs and investors to contribute to the country is nothing new, in fact it is as old as the concept of citizenship itself.[25]

---

20 BRUBAKER (1992)

21 SHACHAR/HIRSCHL (2014)

22 cf. JOPPKE (2010)

23 cf. e.g. Permanent International Court of Justice, 7 February 1923, published online http://www.icj-cij.org/pcij/serie_B/B_04/Decrets_de_nationalite_promulgues_en_Tunisie_et_au_Maroc_Avis_consultatif_1.pdf, last accessed on 28 July 2015

24 SLEMROD (2008)

25 cf. *infra*

Citizenship has long been an important concept, not only in law but also in sociology[26] and the political sciences.[27] Indeed, the idea of citizenship figures *"centrally in constitutional theory, in political philosophy, in social theory, in cultural studies, and in legal studies"*.[28] Citizenship is without doubt a complex institution with various dimensions,[29] and it is now central to the intellectual projects across disciplines.[30] Its conception and definition ultimately depends a lot on the political viewpoint and is intimately linked to the kind of society and political community we want.[31]

The debate on the primary reasons for the acquisition and the need for more restrictive or more liberal naturalisation provisions is as old as the concept of citizenship itself, which is not only a legal concept but also a sociopolitical phenomenon, touching upon fundamental policy issues and always affecting people's personal lives.[32] Much of the current major socio-political debate in modern Western societies is, in essence, concerned with citizenship.[33]

For most people today, citizenship above all means having a passport[34] or national identity card, which are now generally only issued to actual citizens[35] and have thus become a direct expression of the corresponding benefits, rights and obligations of citizenship.[36] Most people acquire their citizenship without having to think about it, without tests, without a minimum duration of stay in a territory, without application but simply and automatically at the moment of birth.

---

26 JOPPKE (2010) p. *vi*; cf. also MACKERT/MUELLER (2000) p. 9
27 MAGNETTE (2005) p. 1; cf. MILLER (2000)
28 BOSNIAK (2006) p. 17
29 JOPPKE (2010) p. *vii*
30 BOSNIAK (2006)
31 SANDEL (2012) p. 11 and p. 203; cf. also MOUFFE (1992)
32 VON MÜNCH (2007)
33 MACKERT/MÜLLER (2007) p. 9
34 VON MÜNCH (2007)
35 There are exceptions, such as those still existing in Panama, where passports are issued to a particular category of residents, who settled in Panama as not employed, under certain conditions, or in Malaysia, where specially marked national identity cards are also issued to non-nationals. From 1982 until 1984 Tonga used to issue "Tongan Protected Person Passports", which confer neither citizenship, nor residence rights in the country, nor visa-free entry. Many countries refuse entry to Tongan Protected Passport holders; cf. VAN FOSSEN (2007)
36 STILLER (2011)

The view on citizenship from the perspective of developed, well-established states as expressed in this study should consider that in many underdeveloped states, and even in some developed states that have weak institutions, citizenship often functions in the reverse,[37] with membership of the State being muddled and the causal connection between status and rights being blurred and sometimes inverted, and where a seamless transition between illegal immigration and full citizenship status is not uncommon.[38]

Although the word "nation" and the idea that humanity is naturally divided into "nations" is an ancient concept,[39] the nation state as we know it today is a relative young phenomenon. Its direct historical development can be traced back to the Reformation, when prominent personalities such as *Martin Luther* propagated a new perspective on the position of the individuals with respect to state authority, to the first codifications of constitutions and constitution-like declarations, such as the *Bill of Rights* (*An Act declaring the Rights and Liberties of the Subject*)[40] in the United Kingdom (the UK) dating back to 1689, the Constitution of the US of 1787 and the French Constitution of 1791,[41] right through to their heyday in the nineteenth and twentieth centuries. Given its history, and as its common structural feature is the gradual extension of the freedom of the individual with respect to the public authorities as significantly expressed in electoral law, citizenship should not only be viewed as the formal link between the individual and state authority, but also as being rooted in the now universally[42] recognised concept of human dignity – despite this not being equally codified today in all democratically constituted nation states[43] – and in nationality and above

---

37 SADIQ (2008) pp. 7–8; cf. also JOPPKE (2010)

38 cf. SADIQ (2008), who refers to this phenomenon as documentary citizenship, emphasizing the role that documents play in acquiring citizenship, "*...whether the documents are legal or not and whether the newly admitted citizen is a legal immigrant or not*", SADIQ (2008) p. 8

39 MAGNETTE (2005) p. 7; cf. also WEIL (2011) and KLUSMEYER (1996)

40 cf. POHANKA (2009)

41 cf. http://www.verfassungen.eu/f/fverf91-i.htm, last accessed on 21 September 2012

42 For the universal significance of human dignity cf. FORSYTHE (2012); *Günther* in COUNCIL OF EUROPE (2011), SOYSAL (1994) and MCCRUDDEN (2014)

43 For the basic parameters of democratic constitutions cf. *Bellamy* in COUNCIL OF EUROPE (2011).

all in nationalism ,[44] and historically considered as an "institution of the nation State",[45] all of which today directly affect the theory and practice of citizenship law worldwide.[46]

The gradual development of citizenship from a more formal structure to a subjective right can be illustrated through the French Revolution,[47] where a paradigm shift was brought about in France through the Revolutionary Constitution, culminating in the *Code Civil* (CC)[48] in 1804.

To bind the subject to the royal dynasty and thereby cement its absolute power, citizenship had emerged under the *Ancien Régime* at the place of birth or on the territorial principle of *ius soli*: French was he who was born on French soil. Whosoever, like the Huguenot emigrants in the seventeenth century, left France "*sans esprit de retour*", lost their citizenship.[49] Article 4 of the French Revolutionary Constitution of 1793 then gave the status of citizen to every adult, including foreign persons who had lived for one year in France, and conferred upon them the active rights of a citizen![50]

Guided by the ideas of some of the pioneers of the European Enlightenment, such as *Jean Jacques Rousseau*[51] and *Francois Marie Arouet*

---

44 cf. GOSEWINKEL (2003) pp. 278–327

45 GOSEWINKEL (1995)

46 BRUBAKER 2004; KOOPMANS/STATHAM/GIUGNI/PASSY (2005); BLOEMRAAD/KORTEWEG/YURDAKUL (2009)

47 For the development of the French Citizenship Act since the abdication of the *Ancien Régime* on 14 July 1789: NOIRIEL (1988), BRUBAKER (1992); SCHATTLE (2008); *Weil* in HANSEN/WEIL (2001); WEIL (2004), for relevant discussion on the principle of collective and individual self-determination as an expression of the natural law of the sovereignty of the people cf. *Steiger* in FISCH (2011)

48 Code Civil Francais (CC), last amended by Act No. 2006-399 of 4 April 2006, published online at http://www.legifrance.gouv.fr/affichCode.do?cidTexte=LEGITEXT000006070721, last accessed on 21 September 2012

49 TRIEPEL (1929)

50 Article 4 of the French Revolutionary Constitution of 24 June 1793 stipulates: "*The following are admitted to exercise the rights of French citizenship: Every man born and domiciled in France, fully twenty-one years of age; Every foreigner, fully twenty-one years of age, who, domiciled in France for one year: And lives there by his labor, Or acquires property, Or marries a French woman, Or adopts a child, Or supports an elderly person; Finally, every foreigner who is considered by the legislative body to be deserving of being treated humanely.*"

51 On *Rousseau's* advocary of distinctive civic identity, see *Rousseau* (1835), translated by *Willmoore Kendall* (1985)

(*Voltaire*),[52] the transition from *ius soli* to *ius sanguinis* was then enshrined in the CC: descent from individual members of the same national community came to be regarded as a higher priority: he whose parents were French was also henceforth French.[53] Citizenship as a concept developed out of *Rousseau's* notion of self-determination.[54]

This transition from the birth-right principle (*ius soli*) to the principle of descent (*ius sanguinis*) which originated in France and ultimately extended to all of Europe, represented a paradigm shift which, however, occurred at a time when the predominantly economically induced transnational migration movement was less pronounced than it is today. Even the historical observation that classical immigration countries such as Canada, the US[55] or Australia, as well as the UK to some extent, traditionally rely or relied on citizenship laws which follow the *ius soli*, and through this sought or seek to strengthen particularly the affinity to their domestic communities or the British Empire, in response to an immediate need to improve underdeveloped areas, underscores the realisation that the national development of citizenship laws can always be viewed with respect to both social and in particular economic requirements.

The aforementioned findings will ultimately be underscored by the design of the citizenship laws governing States such as Austria, Malta, St. Kitts and Nevis, as discussed here, but also Cyprus, Croatia and several other Eastern European countries, or many Latin American countries,[56] illustrating the possibility of acquiring citizenship through exceptional (economic) contribution to the domestic community and in so doing, contributing to the welfare, advancement and (economic) development of the country. Where legal provisions specifically target economic contributions as the main basis for the grant of citizenship, this is most often referred to as Citizenship-by-Investment,[57] or what I shall call *ius doni*, as the investment in this context is

52 For meticulous analysis on Voltaire's views, see ROWE (1968)
53 cf. WEIL (2011)
54 HABERMAS (1995)
55 For the US specifically cf. ZOLBERG (2006)
56 cf. EUDO Citizenship databases on citizenship acquisition laws, http://eudo-citizenship.eu/
57 Alternatively, *Economic Citizenship* or, with a view on the passport as its most important element for applicants, *Passports of Convenience*, cf. VAN FOSSEN (2007)

generally more of an economic contribution than an investment *sensu stricto*. This is even true with Citizenship-by-Investment programme options that require private sector investments, e.g. in real estate or a business, because in contrast to normal foreign direct investment, where investment decisions are based on competitive rates of return and provide for a certain level of economic efficiency, investors in Citizenship-by-Investment programmes are generally willing to invest at less favourable rates or may acquire assets for more than their intrinsic value as the result of the inclusion of the passport asset in their investment decision.[58]

Is this a sell-out of sovereignty at a time when almost everything can be bought and sold[59] and which cannot be reconciled with the purported anchoring of citizenship law in democracy and human rights?[60] Is this a possible violation of the "*blocked exchange*" between the monetary and political spheres?[61]

Or is Citizenship-by-Investment, *ius doni*, regardless of the amount, just one way among others to gain access to citizenship, as there may not be any reason to distinguish between financial and human investments after all?[62] Is *ius doni* an idea and modern concept of citizenship whose time has come?

Is it a legitimate path which leads to welfare gains through additional external investments and economic contributions at zero cost to society, which benefits the general population, and through which the fundamental objectives of citizenship law and of achieving the largest possible withdrawal of State intervention and thereby the strengthening of individual freedom can be attained?

---

58 cf. XU/EL-ASHRAM/GOLD (2015)

59 SANDEL (2012) pp. 10–11; cf. also KUTTNER (1998)

60 Elmar Broak – a CDU European representative, even spoke of "modern day human trafficking", at the time of the introduction of the Citizenship program in Malta in autumn 2013, see http://www.faz.net/aktuell/politik/europaeische-union/verkauf-der-staatsangehoerigkeit-malta-betreibt-menschenhandel-12667559.html, last accessed on 30 March 2016

61 cf. OKUN (1975) p. 19 who speaks of "bans on exchange"; cf. also WALZER (1983) and more recently SANDEL (2012)

62 cf. BERTON (2014)

This work first examines the historical evolution of citizenship law, examining citizenship functionally and normatively, as well as from a comparative law perspective, on the basis of representative reference countries (the UK, Switzerland, Austria, France and Canada). Canada and the UK (where an official citizenship has only existed since 1981),[63] which number among the classical *ius soli* States and which have a traditionally more liberal citizenship law, are examined on one hand, then turning to countries such as Switzerland and Austria, which traditionally follow the descent principle and whose citizenship laws are traditionally restrictive,[64] and beyond that considers France, which has been viewed since the 1789 Revolution as a model nation by the Western *avant garde* – instituting *ius sanguinis* in the 1804 CC, but reintroducing *ius soli* in 1889 and applying a "double *ius soli*" which has come to be regarded the bedrock of French citizenship law. The concept of Citizenship-by-Investment is looked at critically, in view not least fundamental considerations of human dignity and distributive justice, of the Economic Theory of Clubs and the theory of Blocked Exchanges vs. a market-based approach to allocating citizenship access, and international legal aspects and possible barriers. A careful discussion and evaluation of the concept is followed by an examination of the legal and institutional frameworks and experiences of four States which have adopted the *ius doni* concept: Austria, Malta, Montenegro, and St. Kitts and Nevis.

1.2 Challenge

1.2.1 The three-element theory as a basis

Georg Jellinek's traditional three-element theory of the constituent elements of a state differentiates between the constituent people, the authority of the State and the national territory.[65] The State is in any case formed by the people, for which citizenship is required to define the constituent people and thus constituting the State. Since the emergence of the nation States in the eighteenth and nineteenth centuries, not much

---

[63] cf. *Hansen* in HANSEN/WEIL (2001); FRANSMAN (2011)
[64] See HOWARD (2009) for details
[65] JELLINEK (1976); for national territory cf. LOWE (2007)

has really changed,[66] despite some authors now wanting to identify the beginning of a post-national era.[67]

Referring to the "Montevideo Convention"[68] of 1933, the active extension of external relations to other States can be added as a further State-justifying element, which however has not gained general recognition in constitutional jurisprudence. A corresponding addition would appear to be that citizenship is closely related to the territorial sovereignty[69] of the State to which the citizenship refers, to limit access to the latter in external relations with other subjects of public international law.

The philosopher and political theorist *Jean-Jacques Rousseau* associated the members of a constituent people with the function of participating in the development of the collective will in the sense of an active citizenship (*citoyen*), and on the other hand, to be subject to this collective will (*sujet*).[70] *Rousseau* thus anticipated the differentiation between "*status activus*" and "*status negativus*", which is one currently commonly drawn in constitutional theory. This distinction illustrates the close interrelation between legal subjection and the granting of protection, which ranks among the typical structural features of democratic-liberal constituted States:[71] Those who rule also owe protection and assistance.[72]

The differentiation between the constituent people and the authority of the State according to the three-element theory, and the requirement for an internal order of the (State) common will, suggests that a merely

66 JELLINEK (1976); BENHABIB (2004); TOPAL (2010)

67 *Inter alia* SOYSAL (1994); ONG (1999); HOWARD (2009)

68 Convention on rights and duties of States of 26 December 1933 (Montevideo Convention), published online at http://avalon.law.yale.edu/20th_century/intam03.asp, last accessed on 21 September 2012; cf. HERDEGEN (2010)

69 In general, State sovereignty can be described as the highest authority which is not derived from any other territorial entity, which for its part is not subject to any obligations. This corresponds formally with the authority of the State, by virtue of which it has the exclusive ability of legal self-determination and self-binding, cf. DIETRICH (2011)

70 ROUSSEAU (2006); cf. also JELLINEK (1976)

71 cf. HERDEGEN (2010)

72 cf. KLUTH (2011); with reference to KRINGS (2003)

disorganised or unstructured gathering of people under a common dominion without the quality of a nation does not meet the minimum requirements of national community.[73] In that sense, citizenship requires some commonality among its individual elements, so that they can be linked to form a national unit capable of being perceived as a state unit outwardly by other nations, and speak with a unified "voice".

In the course of economic globalisation we can however increasingly observe the phenomenon of the "migration state", which in addition to capital and goods also admits and targets specific people, according to selection criteria such as ability to invest capital, professional qualifications, demographic considerations etc.[74]

To critically discuss and to evaluate citizenship based on these considerations, this contribution is concerned with identifying criteria for its contextual ascertainment in a material sense, which play a role and are used by the receiving States in the granting of citizenship, especially within the context of the practice of Citizenship-by-Investment (existing in particular in Antigua and Barbuda, Austria, Bulgaria, Cyprus, Dominica, Dominican Republic, Grenada, Malta, Montenegro, Seychelles, St. Kitts and Nevis, and Vanuatu)[75] to obtain foreign direct investment by attracting investors who are (primarily) interested in citizenship rights, and in view of the demands of international mobility, economic, business, cultural and social globalisation,[76] and demographic shifts.

Selection criteria such as language, basic knowledge of the host country and its history, or evidence of a regular minimum income from gainful economic activities generally act as filters in the control and containment of social and other conflict in the host country, which could also

73 cf. JELLINEK (1976)

74 cf. THRÄNHARDT/HUNGER (2003)

75 There are many more states which have provisions in their citizenship laws which effectively allow citizenship by investment (e.g. Argentina, Slovakia, Croatia, France, Canada, New Zealand to name a few); however, these countries only very rarely confer citizenship on this basis and do not have an official policy or established practice in place

76 For an authoritative treatment of the economic, social and cultural rights in the global era: *Giegerich/Zimmermann* in GIEGERICH/ZIMMERMANN (2008); BLOEMRAAD/KORTEWEG/YURDAKUL (2009); cf. also ZACHARY (2000)

result especially from insufficient "compatibility" at the horizontal level between immigrants and locals, as well as vertically between the government and the governed. These general filters are not used in the case of Citizenship-by-Investment, but other criteria, such as detailed examination of the applicant (due diligence, personal and economic background verification), proof of origin of assets, and the level of required minimum investment or contribution amounts, are used for a meaningful selection and control.

The terms citizenship and nationality are used partly interchangeably in English[77] and in other languages such as German.[78] In this work either citizenship or nationality will be used, depending on the context, since these terms can contain different content, as will be demonstrated later on.

The crystallisation of the basic conflict emerges from the debate on the abovementioned basic models, which are often combined in naturalisation practice. It is a conflict of whether the acquisition of citizenship – such as of Austria, Greece, Switzerland, Luxembourg, Denmark, Germany, and since 2003, also the Netherlands – should be interpreted more as recognition of a migrant's efforts in integrating in the host country and its society or as a means of pushing integration, as is primarily the case in the classical immigration countries such as the US, Canada, Australia and New Zealand, in Latin America but also in the UK, or now in Malta, where the concept of Citizenship-by-Investment has found one of its most radical forms: citizenship is mainly granted with the aim of not only tying investments but also investors to the country, in addition to direct capital injection in the national interest. This concept is primarily concerned with attracting talent, i.e. directly offering citizenship to talented persons from across the globe, as the Prime Minister of Malta explicitly stated at an official launch event of

77 Generally, and in particular in Ireland, cf. *Symmons* in HANSEN/WEIL (2001)

78 However, the term citizenship is more prevalent in German. In some states there are clear distinctions between these two terms, for example in Israel, where "nationality" (*le'om*) is only used for Jews in Israel (and for potential Jewish immigrants to Israel), whereas "citizenship" is used for all residents of the Israeli State including the Arabic minority; cf. BEN-PORAT/TURNER (2011)

Malta's Citizenship-by-Investment programme in London in 2013.[79] This form of programme with a mainly direct non-refundable contribution requirement also brings the largest economic benefit to the state.[80]

1.2.2 Increasing incongruence between constituent people and resident population

Economic globalisation,[81] the resulting higher international migration flows[82] and the multi-layered, cross-border affiliation of an ever-growing cosmopolitan elite[83] – as well as the digitalisation which has caused our world to be reduced to a "perceived global village" resulting from increased data transmission speeds and other technological advancements – have all led to an increasing incongruence between the benefactor of State authority[84] – i.e. in democratic States, the possessors of active voting rights (or subset of the ones who are actually actively interested in the political rights and exercise these rights) – and the governed – i.e. all the people who reside, work and go about their daily business under the national territorial sovereignty (hereinafter referred to as: the resident population).[85] Traditional notions of citizenship within national borders are increasingly being brought into question given the ever-growing number and the different places of origin of international migrants.[86] Owing to the cultural, social and ethnic plurality of society, the concept of the constituent people can no longer be equated to a political community. This

---

79 Press Release No. 2425 from the Maltese Government on 31 October 2013, published online at http://www.gov.mt/en/Government/Press%20Releases/Pages/2013/October/31/pr2425.aspx, last accessed on 30 November 2013

80 SUMPTION/HOOPER (2014)

81 Concerning the concept of globalisation in this context, cf. FAIX/KISGEN/LAU/SCHULTEN/ZYWIETZ (2006); MICKLETHWAIT/WOOLDRIDGE (2000)

82 In detail, OECD (2013); and BENHABIB (2004) p. 10 et seq.

83 VERTOVEC/COHEN (2002) p. 6

84 Unlike in the Unites States, the Swiss Confederation or France, the authority of the State in the constitutional monarchy of the UK is not based on the people, but on the British Lower House, the House of Commons (the principle of absolute parliamentary government), cf. LEYLAND (2012). Moreover, a considerable number of current States are not democratically legitimate, cf. BELLAMY (2008) pp. 3–4

85 For greater detail for Europe, SOYSAL (1994); as well as generally, BENHABIB (2004)

86 In countries such as Australia (24%), Switzerland (24%) and Canada (18%), every fourth or fifth resident was born overseas, cf. BLOEMRAAD/KORTEWEG/YURDAKUL (2009); SPIRO (2008); SOYSAL (1994); and OECD (2013)

means that some of the premises on which the definition of citizenship is founded are outdated and should be revised with respect to affiliation.[87]

In a larger collective where not all its members can know each other personally, the satisfying power of personal contact is superseded by common identification points such as a common tradition, a common culture, a common language or common ideals. The French population was thus formed into a nation State through a uniform (Catholic) religion, and the ideals of the French Revolution ("Liberty, Equality, Fraternity"), which can be classified as non-material identification points.[88] In Germany, in contrast, the common nation in the sense of a constituent people was formed more prevalently from material identification points, such as the common German language, ethnic background and tradition.[89] In Switzerland on the other hand, the nation State was built from the common interest of the people in the individual cantons ("nation of will"[90] has become a key term in Switzerland), although they are very different in terms of their culture, language and religion. Nevertheless, Switzerland has a strong national consciousness, as was already recognised by *John Stuart Mill*.[91] As *Miller* determined with reference to *Renan*, nations are in fact ultimately constituted through the common will and belief in the nation: nationality thus exists if the members of the nation believe that it exists, and the central question is not whether or not a nation share common attributes such as ethnic background or language.[92] Two further important aspects identified by *Miller* are, on the one hand, the active identity – i.e. nations which are communities that actively do things together, make decisions, achieve results – and on the other, that nations connect groups of people with a geographic location and provide them with a home. It is this territorial element which makes nations ideal to form the basis for States.[93]

---

87 cf. HERING (2011) p. 89, with reference to BENHABIB (2004)
88 cf. RENAN (1882)
89 See e.g. *Schmidt* in CORDELL (1999) pp. 92–94; see also *Gardt* in GARDT/HÜPPAUF (2004) p. 199
90 In German, "*Willensnation*"
91 MILL/WILLIAMS (1993)
92 MILLER (2000) p. 28
93 MILLER (2000) p. 29; but also cf. SPITTA (2013) on how community may be possible without identity; and in view of EU integration with regard to whether it may be possible to create a European identity, cf. SCHICK (2012)

The definition of a constituent people as the totality of active persons able (and interested) to vote, is suitable against this background for democratically constituted States such as the US, France, Malta or the Swiss Confederation, but requires a correction for undemocratically constituted States, in which the broad majority of the population, despite common identification points – which are represented in democratic States in the statutory requirements for naturalisation – is governed with limited or without reference to or even against the common will. Currently, only slightly more than 60% of States are democratically constituted such that the people with voting rights have the opportunity to participate relatively freely in the selection of who should govern them.[94] The mere fact that a dictatorial, monocratic State leadership denies active persons eligible to vote such participation (either *de iure* or *de facto*) would mean that they are thus not constituted as participants in the authority of the State – despite being connected among themselves by common points of identification – are not a constituent people and are thus not citizens in the material sense of the understanding of the democratic constitutional State.

Yet, while Article 25 of the International Covenant on Civil and Political Rights (ICCPR) of 1996 explicitly restricts political rights to citizens[95] and Article 21(1) of the Universal Declaration on Human Rights of 10 December 1948 (UDHR)[96] might be also restricted to citizens,[97] the message of the UN Office of the Commissioner for Human Rights, responsible for monitoring the implementation of the ICCPR, was clear: "*States should consider granting the right to participate in public life at the local level, including the right to vote in local elections, to long-term*

---

94 BELLAMY (2008) p. 3

95 This legal provision stipulates: "*Every citizen shall have the right and the opportunity, without any of the distinctions mentioned in article 2 and without unreasonable restrictions: (a) To take part in the conduct of public affairs, directly or through freely chosen representatives; (b) To vote and to be elected at genuine periodic elections which shall be by universal and equal suffrage and shall be held by secret ballot, guaranteeing the free expression of the will of the electors; (c) To have access, on general terms of equality, to public service in his country.*"

96 On the meaning of the UDHR for the enforcement of universal rights under the impact of economic globalisation and transnationalism: *Weiss* in SANDKÜHLER (2009); *Saage-Maass* in SANDKÜHLER (2009)

97 See e.g. *Rudan* in FORLATI and ANNONI (2013) p. 120; For rather critical approach, see *Eide* in MALLOY and MARKO (2014) pp. 33–34

non-citizen residents".[98] Many countries (including the Netherlands, Sweden, New Zealand or the Swiss canton of Jura) grant foreign citizens at least a right to vote in local elections.[99] Such a right is granted to all European Union nationals in the European Union (the EU),[100] and in most Commonwealth States, the citizens from other Commonwealth States acquire full voting rights if they are lawful residents, or after just a brief period of residence (e.g. one year), even if they are not citizens of the country of residence. In the UK for example, any citizen of a Commonwealth member country who is lawfully resident in the UK can register to vote in European parliamentary and British parliamentary elections.[101]

Questioning what it means for legitimate democratic States if millions of residents with resident permits for limited periods or totally lacking official status live and participate in these countries without ever having any prospect of legally acquiring citizenship and with the fear of deportation, is certainly also justified.[102] Approximately 30 percent of the US population born oversees and 10 percent of all migrants to Europe live without legal resident permits in their respective countries.[103] As bluntly put by *Walzer*: "*Why are they admitted? To free the citizens from hard and unpleasant work. Then the State is like a family with live-in servants.*" And: "*...the rule of citizens over non-citizens, of members over strangers, is probably the most common form of tyranny in human history*".[104]

In any case it can be argued that globalisation represents an increasing challenge for the understanding of citizenship, based on State control.[105]

The increasing incongruence between the constituent people and the

---

98 UN Office of the High Commissioner for Human Rights, The Rights of Non-citizens (2006), fn. 8; See also: European Commission against Racism and Intolerance, Second report on Austria (paras. 16-21), Second repord on Belgium (CRI(2000) 2, paras. 11-15) and Second report on France (CRI (2000) 31, paras. 15-19)

99 BAUBÖCK (2005)

100 Directive 2004/38/EC

101 See Representation of the People Act 1983, ss 4(1)(c); 4(3)(c)

102 SOYSAL (1994); BLOEMRAAD/KORTEWEG/YURDAKUL (2009)

103 KOSER (2007); OECD (2013)

104 WALZER (1983) p. 52

105 BLOEMRAAD/KORTEWEG/YURDAKUL (2009)

resident population in EU Member States is also a result of the European free movement of workers (Article 45 TFEU[106] and Directive 2008/38/ EC). In particular in border regions, especially close to the borders between the (former) Eastern and Western European States, such as between Lower Austria and the Czech Republic, or on the German-Polish border,[107] a trend towards transnational labour mobility can be detected since the fall to the Berlin Wall and the end of the interim arrangements post EU accession.[108]

Economic globalisation in many EU Member States has in addition ensured that the lifetime commitment of an employee to a company, which was more the rule than the exception in the sixties and seventies of the twentieth century, not only due to the volatility of the market, is becoming an increasingly obsolescent model. A person who wants to develop and achieve a good standard of living goes where her work is needed, and does not commit herself to a specific location. The cross-border mobility of workers can be deemed a typical phenomenon of economic globalisation, and is especially promoted in the EU.[109] In the migration literature one of the standard propositions is furthermore that economic migrants tend to be favourably "self-selected" for labour market success. Indeed there would be no economic migration if the immigrants themselves "*did not expect the benefits from moving, net of the costs and risks inherent in the migration, to exceed the benefits from remaining in the place of origin*".[110]

---

106 Treaty on the Functioning of the EU, consolidated edition of the Treaty establishing the EU of 25 March 1958 as amended by the Treaty of Lisbon of 13 December 2007 (OJEU C 306 of 17 December 2007), as amended by the Proclamation of 9 May 2008, OJEU C 115 of 9 May 2008

107 After the expiry of the interim arrangements, from the perspective of Germany, approximately 100,000 mostly low skilled workers from Poland and the Czech Republic were expected (initially), while highly qualified workers can hardly be expected from these countries, especially considering that Poland and the Czech Republic are also affected by a shortage of specialist workers as their economies grow (forecasts of economic growth for April 2011: Poland 3.8%, Czech Republic 1.9%) while the population shrinks, cf. STRUNDEN/PASENOW (2011)

108 On the impact of this cf. STRUNDEN/PASENOW (2011)

109 cf. EUROPEAN COMMISSION (2013)

110 CHISWICK (2005) p. 199

1.2.3 The nation State as anachronism?

In view of the forgoing considerations as social phenomena and the fact that through the opening of the international markets, various economic regions have become much more connected with each other, the question arises as to whether or not nation States will survive under conditions of economic globalisation and transnationality.[111] Should affiliations with States be linked exclusively to individual States, or can such concepts also be promoted across State borders, so that a cosmopolitan or transnational life can be facilitated for people?[112] *Bauböck*[113] thinks, for instance, that with the ever-growing mobility and the increasing "permeability" of the State borders, in particular in Europe, citizenship should be claimed wherever one is located. However, in reality cosmopolitanism is a privilege of those who can in fact rely on a secure nation State. As *Ignatieff* has rightly determined, cosmopolitans are not beyond the nation, and a cosmopolitan spirit will always depend on the capacity of individual nation States to provide security and civility for their citizens.[114] National borders are protected by national border guards and those guards have guns,[115] an obvious fact but one that is easily hidden from the view of affluent citizens of Western countries.[116] In the US a Supreme Court decision found the exclusion of foreign persons a sovereign right, which was read as to effectively deny aliens any claim to due process.[117] *Ignatieff's* experience of his journeys has taught him that it is largely thanks to his Canadian passport that he is allowed to go through security checks under delicate circumstances in dangerous regions.[118]

Moreover, increasingly many people worldwide – as is explicitly verified by electoral polls surveys in almost all States where there are free elections

---

111 cf. *Isensee* in JESSE (2011); BLOEMRAAD/KORTEWEG/YURDAKUL (2009); SOYSAL (1994); ONG (1999); BENHABIB (2004); cf. also SKLAIR (2001); SASSEN (1999) and re transnational citizenship, BAUBÖCK (1994)

112 BLOEMRAAD/KORTEWEG/YURDAKUL (2009)

113 BAUBÖCK (1994)

114 IGNATIEFF (1993)

115 BEINER (1995) p. 229

116 cf. also CARENS (1995)

117 *Plyler v. Doe* (No. 80-1538) 457 U.S. 202 (1982), cf. in this regard also ROBERTSON (2010). From a perspective of equal protections see HUTCHINSON (1982) pp. 167–194

118 Cited in KUMAR (2003)

and no voting obligations – in widely developed western States[119] as well as in under-developed States or emerging nations – favour avoiding political and citizenship issues, concentrating on their careers, consuming the resulting "fruits", maintaining their private spheres and following the stock price of internationally operating companies rather than politics, attending sporting events (or sharing in the same experience, as millions or sometimes billions of spectators impressively do on television) or fostering cultural interests.[120] If the contact with the public sphere is restricted to the daily trip to and from work and the visit to the shopping centre, sports and cultural events, and if we consider that an increasing proportion of the public infrastructure, such as traffic routes, schools and kindergartens, are privately (pre-) financed and organised, this addresses the problem of whether or not the idea of a basically State-organised community and thus the idea of nationality has survived, or whether other ideas of belonging have obtained primary relevance.[121] Moreover, the question arises whether it is essential to be a citizen of the country where one lives, or if it is not simply enough to be a permanent resident with almost equal rights (but fewer obligations), and secure citizenship if possible of any well-respected country – if you do not already have such citizenship.

Given that numerous societal problems such as global warming,[122] nuclear disaster control, the protection of intellectual property or personal data protection[123] and many other areas which can no longer be managed at the national level, as early as 1992, the former UN Secretary General *Boutros-Ghali* proposed that "*the time of absolute and exclusive*

---

[119] For Europe cf. EUROPEAN COMMISSION (2013)

[120] For a sobering account of the political ignorance in modern democracies, cf. SOMIN (2013) p. 17 et seq.

[121] cf. also the considerations of WALZER (1983); and BENHABIB (2004)

[122] At the United Nation Climate Change Conference in Durban South Africa in December 2011, the extension of the Kyoto Protocol and further measures for the containment of the impact of CO_2 were named as the main concerns cf. PUTSCH (2011); regarding climate change as the driving force of transnational migratory movements cf. MCADAM (2011)

[123] Just think of cloud computing, through which the personal data of users can be propagated throughout the world over "server farms", and through which the control over personal data, i.e. the so-called information dominion, is at risk of slipping away

sovereignty ... has passed"[124] and at the World Economic Forum in Davos in 2000 *Fareed Zakaria* proclaimed the end of the Westphalian sovereignty.[125] Both these statements are valid, but neither have had virtually any impact in the field of citizenship law.

Rather, there is strong evidence to suggest that the nation State remains far from landing on the garbage dump of history,[126] but will continue with its diversity and complexity of institutional and normative traditions.[127] Despite globalisation and transnationalism, the fact remains that the nation states preserve a monopoly on the legitimate use of force and remain the most important actors on the world stage, and "*the issues that concern them most will be the same as they have always been: protecting their interests and preserving a balance of power*".[128] This applies particularly to citizenship. *Arendt* aptly put it: "*A citizen is by definition a citizen among citizens of a country among countries ...*"[129] and "*Nobody can be a citizen of the world while he is the citizen of a country*".[130] The question of whether national sovereignty and thus national citizenship have survived cannot reasonably be discussed today nor in the foreseeable future, since it is not apparent what they can be replaced by. Thus the debate in citizenship studies as to whether we are witnessing the demise of "national" citizenship is rather odd.[131] In fact most recently, for example, various European states have reformed and begun "renationalising" access to citizenship and the status of citizens, at the very point where some scholars were identifying an international

124 Preventive diplomacy, peacemaking and peace-keeping. Report of the Secretary-General pursuant to the statement adopted by the Summit Meeting of the Security Council on 31 January 1992, published online http://www.un-documents.net/a47-277.htm, last accessed 5 July 2015; cf. also *Hailbronner/Kau* in VITZTHUM (2010); concerning the question of whether, and to what extent, the nation State is still viable as a form of collective organisation under conditions of globalisation, cf. KUHNEN (2009)

125 Cited in *Bauböck* in VERTOVEC/COHEN (2002) p. 111; cf. also http://partners.nytimes.com/library/magazine/millennium/m1/zakaria.html, last accessed on 5 July 2015, and BENHABIB (2004)

126 BRUBAKER (1992)

127 JOPPKE (2010)

128 MICKLETHWAIT/WOOLDRIDGE (2000) p. 161

129 ARENDT (1968) p. 81

130 ARENDT (1968) p. 81

131 For an interesting and recent perspective on this debate cf. e.g. KIWAN (2013)

trend toward "de-nationalizing".[132] Only the European Union (the EU) and CARICOM have shown the first signs of "*citizenship beyond the State*",[133] but ones which still do not take precedence over but are parallel to and derivative of national citizenships.

It can even be observed that nation States, owing to their loss of control over the international and increasingly integrated economy, as well as their increasingly globalized cultural life, are reasserting themselves somewhat restrictively in those areas over which they can still maintain control: this includes visa policy,[134] immigration law and citizenship law.[135]

1.2.4 Limitation on national actions through international law

No state is however totally independent in its citizenship legislation.[136] *As Kant* already convincingly argued in the closing days of the eighteenth century, the morals which apply to the relationships among individuals ought also to be applicable to the relationships between States or nations. Accordingly, the individual States are not guided in their actions solely by their goals in the pursuit of their own interests.[137] *Rawls* recently expanded the idea of the partnership agreement to the "*society of nations*" to find that the "*well-regulated societies*" must accept the principle of the "*law of nations*".[138] However, within the sphere of international relationships, contrary to the area of interpersonal relationships within a State, conditions prevail which cause compliance with the usual moral rules to appear largely impossible.[139]

With respect to citizenship law, the restrictions on individual States in their actions towards other States had already been demonstrated in

---

132 MEER/MODOOD (2013)
133 KOCHENOV (2012) p. 3
134 cf. MELONI (2006)
135 KUMAR (2003)
136 Instead of many, cf. DONNER (1994)
137 KANT (1795); KOLLER (1996)
138 Harvard University Gazette, 26.11.02 pm, cited in MONAZAHIAN (2008); cf. also RAWLS (2000); and LEAVITT (2013)
139 For an analysis of the problem of actions under the conditions of moral imperfection, cf. KOLLER (1994) and KOLLER (1996)

1929 by *Triepel*, who at that time, interestingly, argued for the regulation of international citizenship law.[140] This was still prior to the Second World War, and national citizenship laws could not completely escape the post-war globalisation, migration, cross-border direct investment and influx of refugees:[141] the narrowly State-defined form of citizenship seems to have at least partially lost some of its legitimacy, as it is increasingly limited by international law and human rights.[142] Finally, with the increasing number of sovereign States, the number of citizenship laws around the world has also increased, resulting in more segmentation of the world population rather than less, and possibly more cases of conflict of citizenship laws.[143]

1.2.5 Citizenship as a legitimate instrument for the promotion of direct investment or a "blocked exchange"?

Regardless whether the granting of citizenship to suitable foreign persons is deemed as a legitimate instrument for the promotion of direct investment, States can design their citizenship laws so that citizenship can be practically acquired in exchange for significant investment or direct contributions to the State. Whether this is desirable or whether such a possibility should be avoided as an inappropriate comingling of the spheres of money and State ("a blocked exchange"),[144] in other words an "*expansion of markets, and of market values, into spheres of life where they don't belong*",[145] is one of the fundamental questions investigated here. Indeed, one of the most striking tendencies today is the expansion of markets and market-based thinking into spheres of life that are traditionally governed by non-market norms.[146]

As the political debates in Malta and in Europe concerning the introduction of a Maltese Citizenship-by-Investment programme as well as

140 TRIEPEL (1929)
141 VON MÜNCH (2007); SOYSAL (1999)
142 SOYSAL (1999); BLOEMRAAD/KORTEWEG/YURDAKUL (2009)
143 VON MÜNCH (2007)
144 WALZER (1983); and OKUN (1975)
145 SANDEL (2012) p. 7
146 SANDEL (2010) p. 265

the academic discussions that have followed show, there are fundamental differences of opinions on this issue, both from a legal and academic as well as a political perspective.[147]

1.3 Definition of the research question

This work addresses the question – in view of the ongoing trends of globalisation, digitisation, transnational thinking, investment and mobility – of what the development of a flexible citizenship[148] would actually look like and how this could be implemented, in particular as an instrument for the simplification of the acquisition of citizenship through extraordinary economic contribution to the State, and how individual States could benefit from such instruments. It does not however look into the details of the macroeconomic impact and its strategic management following Citizenship-by-Investment capital inflows, which can be significant particularly in smaller states.[149]

Its focus is mainly on the extent to which economic criteria, such as a significant investment or monetary contribution to a national fund or a project of national importance, are suitable as the basis for the granting of citizenship and how this is dealt with by various States.

It also enquires about the essence of citizenship, what criteria its acquisition are subject to and should be subject to, and what do they constitute. Is it really essential for acquisition that a person settles for a longer period in a national community and acquires a "personal bond" with it, by residing, living and working there? Or should additional requirements be fulfilled, through which a certain degree of loyalty to the State is manifested, such as for example, command of the national language, basic knowledge of the national culture and history, or the presence of an economic livelihood, whose existence can be used as a definite indication of the achievement of a

147 See http://www.europarl.europa.eu/news/en/news-room/content/20140110IPR32392/html/EU-citizenship-should-not-be-for-sale-at-any-price-says-European-Parliament, last accessed on 18 January 2014, SHACHAR/BAUBÖCK (2014)
148 ONG (1999) p. 112
149 XU/EL-ASHRAM/GOLD (2015)

certain level of integration? Alternatively to these traditional requirements, in the acquisition of citizenship can it be at least partially sufficient to display extraordinary economic abilities, in particular by way of investments or gifts for charitable or public interest purposes?

Closely related to the above issue is the question of the fundamental objective of modern citizenship law. What takes priority when defining an ethnic-national identity – preserving the domestic peace among the individuals living within the confines of a national territory, obtaining the greatest possible integration of cultural and ethnic minorities, or securing an efficient control of the inflow of migration and investments? Which objectives can be pursued legitimately by recourse to citizenship law while respecting public international law? What limitations are there to national law and public international law by virtue of the nation State design of its citizenship law? In light of advanced globalisation and transnationality, can citizenship law contribute to the control of demographic, social and economic issues and to counteracting structural deficits to promote direct investment through targeted incentives? Are there normative arguments in favour of the simplification of naturalisation for direct investors?

The answers to the above questions will be explored in the analysis and discussion of the relevant nation State, as well as on European and international legal bases. This will particularly concern considering the situation in various States which practice the granting of citizenship based on extraordinary economic contribution, and comparatively to analyse and assess how citizenship regulations can be designed to promote direct investments by virtue of such granting of citizenship on the basis of extraordinary economic contribution to a given State.

PART I

The Concept of Citizenship and the Acquisition of Citizenship

2

Historical Lines of Development and Modern Citizenship Concepts

When we discuss States as the point of reference for citizenship today,[150] we are speaking of the nation State, and citizenship from an historical perspective is an institution of the nation State.[151] Citizenship and citizenship law based on today's definition has only been in existence since the formation of the modern nation States in the eighteenth and nineteenth centuries (*"Citizenship developed out of the modern State"*),[152] and in particular since the French *Code Civil* of 1804, even though its historical origins[153] – at least from the perspective of the Western countries dealt with here – extend from ancient Greece[154] and through Roman law, medieval feudalism with the European Free States, the Renaissance and the Peace of Westphalia, to the French Revolution and the resulting nationalism.[155] The development of citizenship has not followed a single trajectory as it has played out very differently in different states.[156]

2.1 Ancient Greece

From a Western perspective, the concept of citizenship originates in ancient Greece.[157] So does the concept of cosmopolitanism or global citizenship, where *Diogenes* rejected the status of a *polites*, a citizen, advocating in favour of that of a *kosmopolites*, a citizen of the universe; it has been argued, that unlike his contemporary *Aristotle*, *Diogenes* has not seen man as a political animal, but as a "multicultural animal",[158] and all wise men formed a single moral community, a city of the world.[159] The stoics, starting with *Zeno*, provided a long line of philosophical support for the cosmopolitan idea, including one of the most crucial concepts

---

150 VON MÜNCH (2007)
151 GOSEWINKEL (1995)
152 GOSEWINKEL (2003) p. 11
153 A study of other historical lines, e.g. from a Chinese or Indian point of view, has been omitted here, especially because the modern design of citizenship laws in virtually all States follow Western models
154 MAGNETTE (2005) pp. 10–19
155 MACKERT (2006); KLUSMEYER (1996); MAGNETTE (2005), for the very intersting development of German citizenship cf. GOSEWINKEL (2003) pp. 11 and 278 et seq.
156 BELLAMY (2004)
157 MAGNETTE (2005) p. 10, for a detailed view see MANVILLE (1990)
158 HEATER (2002) p. 27
159 *Fine/Cohen* in VERTOVEC/COHEN (2002) p. 138; cf. also HEATER (2002)

of Natural Law,[160] which we find again in the modern human rights and human dignity discussions and codifications such as the *Universal Declaration of Human Rights*.

The fundamental elements of the conception of citizenship in ancient Greece was the separation of an autonomous civil public sphere from those of the family and clan.[161] This can be traced back to the reforms of *Solon* in the early sixth century BC,[162] but the decisive moment was likely to have been at the time of the reforms of *Cleisthenes* in around 500 BC, which introduced the *deme* (village or "neighbourhood") as the smallest unit of political organisation, and assigned each ethnic citizen to a *deme* on the basis of his place of residence.[163] Furthermore, the myth of a common Athenian origin was created, and with it newcomers were assimilated. The "common origin" is a structure that is almost always based on fiction, or as *McNeil* remarked: "*Only in remote and barbarous lands did ethnic homogeneity prevail*".[164]

The reforms of *Cleisthenes* were an exception with regard to the inclusion of immigrants. In contrast, Athenian citizenship developed much more restrictively, a trend that led to the reforms of *Pericles* (circa 450 BC). Whereas previously, the male offspring of an Athenian father could acquire citizenship at adulthood, *Pericles* demanded that both parents be citizens.[165]

In ancient Greece, the citizenship rights in Athens and in other city States was reserved only for free-born men in the *polis*, and was thus extremely exclusive,[166] representing the highest form of societal participation.[167] The majority of the population was excluded from citizen status, which hugely restricted their participation.[168]

---

160 HEATER (2002)
161 KLUSMEYER (1996)
162 MANVILLE (1990); MAGNETTE (2005)
163 KLUSMEYER (1996) p. 10
164 Cited in KLUSMEYER (1996) p. 11
165 KLUSMEYER (1996) p. 11
166 MACKERT (2006); STILLER (2011)
167 ARISTOTLE/SCHÜTRUMPF (2012); DYNNESON (2001)
168 HEATER (2004); KLUSMEYER (1996)

In the view of the Greek philosopher *Aristotle*,[169] since a right in the political sense of a fundamental requirement for a national community is only possible for the free, the political theory of ancient Greece limits the phenomena of the State and thus citizenship to people who are free.[170] Moreover, there was no connection between the ancient city State and the citizen beyond the State's borders.

Aristotle understood citizenship (at the level of the people with this privilege) as a political concept and as a participatory-republican ideal: "*He who has the power to take part in the deliberative or judicial administration of any state is said by us to be a citizen of the state; and, speaking generally, a state is a body of citizens sufficing for the purposes of life*".[171] This participatory concept influenced the Western idea of citizenship until the present day, and is thus of great importance.[172]

2.2 Roman law

In contrast to *Aristotle's* view of citizenship as a primarily political concept, the Roman jurists developed citizenship as a legal status, with various public and private rights and obligations.[173]

The now popular term, citizenship, goes back in all Latin languages and in English to the Latin *civis*, which referred to the free inhabitants of a city. The Roman *ius civile* was originally the law of the city of Rome, which applied exclusively to its citizens.[174] In contrast, *natio*, the Roman goddess of Birth and Origin, refers like *gens* and *populus* to peoples and tribes not yet organised in political associations,[175] and thus unlike *civitas*. Nations are communities of people of the same descent who are

---

169 Among the most important of Aristotle's insights in the field of politics and political science include in the present context, the position of the person who lives as a natural social being in the body politic, cf. ARISTOTLE, Cambridge University Press edition (1996)

170 cf. JELLINEK (1976); ARISTOTLE,Cambridge University Press edition (1996)

171 ARISTOTLE, Cambridge University Press edition (1996) p. 63

172 KLUSMEYER (1996)

173 KLUSMEYER (1996) p. 20; for an authoritative and comprehensive view on Roman citizenship cf. SHERWIN-WHITE (1973)

174 KLUSMEYER (1996)

175 *Habermas*, Citizenship and National Identity, in BEINER (1995) p. 258

integrated geographically.[176] In ancient Roman political theory the State was understood as a community of citizens whose identities were very soon not necessarily linked to their place of residence.[177] The need to include diverse people in the expanding Roman Empire led to the development of citizenship as a legal concept of the State, in which the citizen is considered a subject of the State,[178] and citizens and non-citizens were distinguished accordingly, during the process of the granting of so-called citizenship rights (*civitas Romana*).[179] The Roman Republic also began to develop a relatively flexible naturalisation process, so that the new subjects could very quickly be integrated into the Roman Federation and remain colonially loyal, to the great benefit of the Republic.[180] During the Imperial Era this cosmopolitan character of the Roman civil right was further extended, with Roman Emperors granting citizenship for extraordinary acts of value to the State, among other things.[181]

The *Constitutio Antoniniana* of 212 AD, a pioneering act of the modern citizenship concept and the culmination of the extension of the Roman civil rights,[182] granted all free residents of the Roman Empire Roman citizenship[183] regardless of their origin or culture and without being bound by conditions or obligations to Rome.[184] With this declaration, a preliminary cosmopolitan peak was reached in citizenship law, marking the invention of extensive territorial citizenship.[185]

2.3 Middle Ages, Renaissance and Absolutism

During the Middle Ages – the historical epoch extending approximately from late antiquity in the sixth century AD to the beginning of the modern era in the fifteenth century – the predominant perspective lacked the idea

176 HABERMAS (1995)
177 cf. JELLINEK (1976); MAGNETTE (2005)
178 BLOEMRAAD/KORTEWEG/YURDAKUL (2009); DYNESSON (2001)
179 KASER (1971); KASER/KNÜTEL (2008); SPIRO (2008)
180 For extraordinary contribution to the State, which could also be economic in nature
181 KLUSMEYER (1996) p. 18
182 MAGNETTE (2005)
183 KASER (1971); SHERWIN-WHITE (1973); KASER/KNÜTEL (2008)
184 MAGNETTE (1996)
185 *Michael Mann:* The Sources of Social Power (1986), cited in JANOSKI (2010)

of national unity and by extension the strict differentiation between private and public law. The individual appears, for instance in Germanic legal circles, as possessing rights not derived exclusively from the State. The customary law of the place of residence (domicile) was to be decisive of which rights would be engaged.[186] Kingdoms were "*based on personal loyalties and not on loyalty to abstract concepts such as the 'nation' or to ideologies or impersonal institutions*",[187] such as the (modern) state. Medieval society in general was basically "*made up of civically inactive persons, of nonparticipants*".[188]

Citizen status in the medieval free cities, however, was somewhat different and underwent an extension, at least in contrast to the ancient *polis*, insofar as that even craftsmen and later also tenant farmers were included.[189] There continued to be no relationship between the city and the citizen beyond a medieval city's borders.

With the Latin translation of *Aristotle* and the renewed interest in Roman authors in the late Middle Ages and the Renaissance in Italy, the classical ideals of participatory citizenship were revived, for example through *Niccolò Machiavelli* (1469–1527).[190] *Jean Bodin* in turn then introduced the concept of State sovereignty,[191] forming the basis of the resulting modern State system, which was also based on the territorial character of the Peace of Westphalia.

The time of absolutism – a synonym for the epoch spanning the French invasion of Italy in 1494, the religious wars of the sixteenth century and the revolutions of the late eighteenth century, characterised by autocratic

---

186 BERMANN/KORTH (1989)
187 JACOBSON (1996) p. 18
188 JACOBSON (1996) p. 18
189 STILLER (2011)
190 The citizenship practice theory was largely influenced by a civic republicanism tradition which has its roots in Greek democracies described by *Aristotle* and *Thucydides*. According to these philosophers the participations of citizens in politics was essential compmonent of creating a community neccessary for political life. Citizenship therefore was not to be seen simply as a legal status but consisted of a number of practices between states and citizens. The duty of political participation was then promoted by *Cicero*, and later, by *Machiavelli*. See the historical background in GRAY (2012) p. 118 et seq.; See also KLUSMEYER (1996) pp. 21–27
191 *Jean Bodin*, Les six livres de la république (1576), cited in DONNER (1994) p. 2

centralist leadership and extensive claims to sovereignty[192] in the style of kings such as *Louis XIV* (*"L'état c'est moi"*)[193] – turned, in contrast, again to completely dispose of individual agency and authority.[194] The roughly three centuries of absolutism also witnessed the consolidation of several large states, including France, the UK, Spain and Russia. Religious and cultural affiliations provided the basis for a protonationalism, instilling an identification with French, English etc. nationalities.[195] Nationhood during the periods of Renaissance and Enlightenment was a cultural, not a political attribute.[196]

In view of its historical development from the Middle Ages to the eighteenth century, the *ius soli* of Europe was the dominant criterion for citizenship on the Continent[197] and in England:[198] as one of the formative features of Feudal society and the absolutist sovereignty State of the *Ancient Régime* in Europe, people were relegated to the role of subjects and were subjected to their respective feudal lord, who owned the soil of the country in which they were born.[199] This ownership on the Continent (for example France) and in England, was connected to the feudal idea of subjection, and generally excluded foreigners from the acquisition of property.[200] Until the Naturalisation Act of 1870, foreigners in the UK, for example, could neither acquire nor inherit, could neither assume guardianship nor public office.[201] According to earlier law, the assets of a foreigner were at the discretion of the Crown, which generally led affluent foreigners to naturalise. There were in England, for example, a large number of German and German-Russian merchants, who acquired

192 cf. JELLINEK (1976)
193 "I am the State"
194 cf. WESEL (2006)
195 JACOBSON (1996) p. 20
196 HEATER (2002)
197 On 23 February 1515, the *ius soli* was introduced by the *parlement de Paris* into the French law, cf. WEIL (2004)
198 The precursor to *ius sanguinis* in The UK was the law of 1351 *"De natis ultra mare"*, which however only concerned the foreign-born children of kings and the nobility. cf. DUMMET/NICOL (1990)
199 cf. WEIL (2012); SAHLINS (2004)
200 BRUBAKER (1992); DUMMET/NICOL (1990)
201 SCHULTE BEERBÜHL (2007) p. 42

citizenship for merely economic reasons, and not to settle in England:[202] Such practice bears a close resemblance to the *Citizenship-by-Investment* concept.

Following the Peace of Westphalia of 1648, the then resulting sovereign nation States which replaced the power of the church and the Holy Roman Empire considered that each monarch retained the right to form its own autonomous sovereign State, and furthermore that every sovereign State can regulate its internal affairs without external interference, and that the common characteristics of the citizen of each State are sufficient in order to justify a nation.[203] With that was laid one of the most significant foundations of the concept of the modern nation State and public international law. There was a virtual recognition of the independent status or sovereignty of the parties at Westphalia, and the Dutch Republic and the Swiss Confederation were formally admitted into the family of nations.[204] Most striking was perhaps the enunciated principle of international relations following Westphalia – *cuius regio, eius religio* – to each region its own religion. This anticipated the principles of sovereignty and national self-determination.[205]

The legal principle of non-intervention in the internal affairs of individual States in this new system of nation States was then established by *Christian Wolff* in 1764, and as noted by *Lauterpacht*, "*There is, in international law, no right (and no corresponding duty) more absolute, more rigid or more formal than freedom from external interference*".[206]

This non-intervention referred and refers in particular and at its core to citizenship law or the question of who qualifies as a citizen of the individual nation States, how this citizenship is acquired or conferred, and how this is regulated by domestic law.[207]

---

202 SCHULTE BEERBÜHL (2007) pp. 21 and 45
203 Cited from STILLER (2011)
204 JACOBSON (1996) p. 20
205 JACOBSON (1996) p. 20
206 LAUTERPACHT (1977) p.290
207 cf. DONNER (1994)

Citizenship was firstly codified as "subject property" by the Josephinian Code of 1786 in Austria, in which a distinction was made between "foreigners" and "subjects", whereas the latter was defined as all people who live united in the hereditary lands under the authority of the provincial nobility.[208]

2.4 Enlightenment and the American and French Revolutions

The Enlightenment saw the propagation of the model of the watchman State, which was restricted to the maintenance of law and order, the securing of property rights and national defence. Due to this minimalistic model, no general theory of citizenship developed.[209] There were two approaches to affiliation to a political system: the "contractual" one put forward by *John Locke* (1632–1704),[210] which emanates from the idea of a "*social contract*" under which the State is based on a contract among the citizens, and an instrumental approach emanating from the self-interest theory proposed by *Adam Smith* (1723–1790).[211] Individuals are motivated by self-interest to participate in a State, since they see the benefits of being subjected to a common sovereign authority,[212] or in line with *John Rawls'* theory - the nation state as founded upon the idea of a social contract is based on the self-interest of its participants.[213]

Jean-Jacques Rousseau (1712–1778) therewith defined participatory citizenship anew, as a joint exercise of sovereignty. Whereas *Locke* and *Smith* propagated limited models of State machinery, *Rousseau* believed that Republican governance in the interest of the common good could demand a great deal from the citizens. In the years preceding the French Revolution, the idea of citizenship was increasingly discussed, and *Rousseau's* ideal of a democratically governed community of active

208 Austrian Collection of Laws 591, 2. Main part, section 3, cited from STILLER (2011)
209 KLUSMEYER (1996) pp. 29–37
210 LOCKE, Cambridge University Press edn (1988)
211 SMITH (1759) Dover Philosophical Classics edn (2006)
212 KLUSMEYER (1996) p. 30
213 RAWLS (1999); RAWLS (2001)

citizens, forming a State with a common will and equally united before the law, offered the revolutionaries a rich source of inspiration.[214]

Perhaps even as early as the Dutch Revolt (1568–1648) and the establishment of the Dutch Republic in the seventeenth century, the idea evolved that sovereignty resides with the people rather than with the monarch.[215] Emanating from the American Revolutionary war[216] and following the Declaration of Independence in 1776, US citizenship – grounded in the natural rights of mankind and guarded by a written constitution – marked a "*new beginning in the world's long experience with civic membership*".[217]

The French Revolution starting in 1789 then laid the actual foundation for the concept of citizenship in a modern sense, even though the term citizenship first gained its legal sense somewhat later in the *Code Civil* (CC) of 1804.[218] More extensive efforts towards the legal codification of citizenship law were made after the French Revolution, which ultimately resulted in the publication of the CC in 1804. Nonetheless, the French Revolutionary Constitution had already regulated who was French within this new nation State and who should be deemed a foreigner and not be granted citizenship[219] in its declaration of human and civil rights of 26 August 1789, which is often regarded as the birth of modern citizenship[220] by reference to the idea that the French Revolution accomplished the unification of people, nation and State.[221] A truly accurate determination is of course not possible, since at that time the French did not even speak one common language and did not do so until the late nineteenth century,[222] while *Vattel* on the other hand was already speaking of citizenship in 1758.[223]

---

214 KLUSMEYER (1996)
215 JACOBSEN (1996)
216 1775 to 1783
217 KESLER (1998) p. 3
218 cf. KIMMICH/HOBE (2008); SCHÄTZEL (1960); WEIL (2004); and *Sahlins* in FAHRMEIR/FARON/WEIL (2003)
219 Title II, Section 2 of the French Revolutionary Constitution of 3 September 1791, cf. WEIL (2004)
220 cf. STILLER (2011)
221 cf. HABERMAS (1992)
222 cf. KLUSMEYER (1996)
223 VATTEL (1959); STILLER (2011)

The abdication of the *Ancient Régime* was accompanied by a sociopolitical paradigm shift, which led to fundamental changes, in particular to local citizenship law, whose basis had been until then the close ties with the union of Kingdom, Crown and State, and was primarily based on birth in the national territory.[224] For *Hegel*,[225] just as later for *Marx*, the new concept of citizenship was revolutionary: it has generalised and individualised society and destroyed the former individual bonds of the feudal world.[226]

With the *Code Civil* of 1804 – and against the will of *Napoleon* – France opened the era of modern citizenship law.[227] From then on citizenship law was clearly regulated and was based on the person: a person is or was a citizen because she descended from a citizen, a status which was conferred in a similar manner to the family name and which could not be lost if the person moved abroad.[228]

The groundbreaking developments in France in the eighteenth century extended beyond its State borders, and increasingly to almost all States with the mindset of the Revolution made "*le tour du monde*".[229]

The Kingdom of Prussia was also affected by this development. The Prussian law of 31 December 1842 was a first step towards a common understanding of citizenship, determined by to whom obedience was owed and therefore a continuation of the idea of "subject". This law is considered the first modern law regulating citizenship, applying an idea of codification which not only regulated citizenship but also its associated laws which was ultimately propagated worldwide.[230] Despite the specific differences in the legislation adopted in individual States, the national laws in these early days primarily introduced the *ius sanguinis*, in contrast to the prevailing *ius soli* principle of the *Ancien Régime*. Other ethnic populations in Germany no longer received citizenship automatically at birth.[231]

---

224 *Weil* in HANSEN/WEIL (2001); WEIL (2004); SAHLINS (2004)
225 HEGEL (2004)
226 cf. DAHRENDORF (1974) p. 673
227 WEIL (2004)
228 WEIL (2004)
229 LIPOVANO (1935); cf. also WEIL (2004); STILLER (2011); BRUBAKER (1992)
230 MAKAROV (1962); STILLER (2011)
231 TOPAL (2010)

The French Revolution also brought a closer tie between citizenship and the territorial unity of the States, which created a clear demarcation between citizen and non-citizens. This demarcation from the outside world created by modern citizenship resulted in the promotion of domestic homogenisation,[232] modern nationalism and the nation State,[233] which continue to affect the theory and practice of citizenship today.[234]

2.5 Criticism of Marxism; Nationalism and Totalitarianism

Karl Marx is considered the strongest and most influential critic of the republican idea of citizenship and the Declaration of 1789. *Marx* and *Friedrich Engels* argued that in modern civil societies, individuals are only held together by market forces. The central question concerns the exploitation of the workforce through capital,[235] and the revolution merely created an imaginary political community which treats all people equal on paper, but in action and reality in the material world of society, one class dominates all others.[236]

The nineteenth century was however above all the century of nationalism. During this time, an increasingly ethnicised understanding of the nation developed, as expressed in the writings of *John Stuart Mill* and others. National symbols, traditions and theories of origin were adapted from the respective dominant cultures or simply invented.[237] *Mill* was of the view that the nationality concept creates an affiliation which deviates from previous membership concepts.[238] Membership limitations could be clearly defined with the concept of nationality. In doing so, *Mill* effectively merged *demos* and *ethnos*,[239] two different terms for people: sovereignty lies in *demos*, whose members are constituted from

---

[232] MACKERT (2006); MILL (1993)
[233] cf. GOSEWINKEL (1995); MACKERT (2006); STILLER (2011)
[234] BRUBAKER (2004)
[235] cf. MARX (1971)
[236] KLUSMEYER (1996); MARX (1971)
[237] HOBSBAWM/RANGER (1983)
[238] MILL (1861), Chapter 16
[239] LEPSIUS (1990); KLUSMEYER (1996); and HABERMAS (1992)

the common political association, while *ethnos* refers to the members who are defined through a common culture, history and a shared sense of identity. *Klusmeyer* thought that through the unification of these two concepts of the nation, the basis for an exclusive understanding of the membership in the national community was created and meant that individuals with varying *ethnos* could not have a full and equal membership in a nation.[240] However, only very briefly did the democratic nation-state forge a close link between *ethnos* and *demos*[241] and the concept of citizenship was never conceptually tied to national identity.[242]

The further development of nationalism eventually led to the First World War, by which time states became much more centralised, also as a result of industrial growth. "*Wars make states*" is a famous phrase to describe the emergence of Europe's nation states.[243] Before the First World War, "*a sensible, law-abiding Englishman could pass through life and hardly notice the existence of the state, beyond the post office and the policeman*".[244]

With the First World War states had to expand their role to ensure a regular supply of soldiers fit enough to fight.[245] Nationalism became increasingly expressive in international conflict, and "*as laws on citizenship were tabled and strict immigration control followed, the nation-state reached full fruition*".[246] New passport requirements were strictly enforced (and not even waived for personages as prominent as *Vanderbilt*), and even President *Wilson* needed a passport to travel to Versailles at the end of the First World War – apparently the first US president to be issued a passport.[247]

The Second World War and totalitarian forms of government followed – especially Stalinist-Leninist Russia and the Soviet Union and National Socialist Germany – which brought *ad absurdum* the concepts

---

240 KLUSMEYER (1996)
241 LEPSIUS (1990) p. 247 et seq.
242 BEINER (1995) p. 259; cf. also HABERMAS (1995)
243 TILLY (1975)
244 TAYLOR (1965) p. 1
245 DOWNING (1993)
246 JACOBSON (1996) p. 21
247 cf. ROBERTSON (2011); with further references

and norms developed until that point in parts of Europe and elsewhere in the world, from a societal, political and legal perspective (and of interest here, also and not least relating to citizenship).[248] Citizenship law and immigration law became instruments of power of totalitarian States,[249] whereby the sovereignty of these States was eventually also expressed and strongly asserted. *Hannah Arendt* (1906–1975), who in her writing about the development and dangers of totalitarian State forms lastingly shaped the thinking of the post war era, after her immigration to the US was herself expatriated by the national socialist regime in 1937 and was stateless until 1951, when she acquired *US* citizenship.[250] The same fate was met by many immigrants from Germany and the Soviet Union, Greeks and Armenians during the formation of the Turkish Republic, or many ethnic Chinese in Malaysia during that State's independence from the UK.[251] Without a doubt, as countless people discovered during this period, statelessness is "a condition of infinite danger".[252]

2.6 Post-war era and European integration

After the Second World War, fundamental new public international law norms and conventions were introduced which increasingly engaged with national sovereignty, particularly for the protection of human rights. Citizenship rights or the right to citizenship[253] were included in the General Declaration of Human Rights: "*the right to have rights*"[254] was recognised as a general rule. These rights primarily originated due to the injustice in the great wars: "*human rights come from human wrongs*".[255] The rise of a world-spanning human rights culture after the Holocaust

---

[248] cf. WEISS (2000); and GOSEWINKEL (2003)

[249] And has remained an instrument of power of totalitarian States to this day

[250] http://de.wikipedia.org/wiki/Hannah_Arendt, accessed on 24 July 2013

[251] There remain many people living in Malaysia today who have not been granted Malaysian citizenship

[252] WALZER (1983) p. 32

[253] Article 15(1) UDHR

[254] Chief Justice Earl Warren in *Perez v. Brownell*, 356 US 44, 64 (1957); cf. also ARENDT (1968)

[255] DERSHOWITZ (2004)

and decolonisation[256] has led to human rights norms being increasingly viewed as universally applicable principles.[257]

In liberal theory however the tension between universal rights and status in a particular country is rarely addressed. *Rawls*[258] for instance considers free movement only as a basic right of citizens within a state which is otherwise a closed society of citizens. The significant questions associated with the issues of inclusion and exclusion through citizenship status and immigration laws are largely left unasked and unanswered.[259]

Meanwhile, in America, a large part of the American people was deprived of the most fundamental rights because based on race, ethnicity or gender, they were barred from the fundamental freedoms of citizenship. In South Africa, under the Apartheid regime, black people were systematically deprived of their dignity and fundamental rights until even more recently. One of the most oppressive embodiments of the control exercised over the black population was the pass laws, which required black people at all times to carry a document that denoted permission to be in a particular place for a specific purpose, which came to symbolize the viciousness and pettiness of apartheid, and many hundreds of thousands of black South Africans were arrested every year for violating these laws.[260]

Kant's postulation,[261] that no person should be refused the right of access (or "entry") when life or limb is endangered has been established in the UN Convention on Refugees with the *non-refoulement* principle.[262] While asylum is recognised as a human right for refugees, the obligation to grant asylum remains reserved as a sovereign privilege to the

256 JOPPKE (2005)
257 BENHABIB (2004) p. 2 – 12
258 RAWLS (1999)
259 CASALINI (2004), with further citations; *Bauböck* thinks that these are relevant questions from a global justice perspective, but not from an internal democratic perspective, cf. BAUBÖCK (2014)
260 *Cameron* in MCCRUDDEN (2014) p. 470
261 KANT (1795)
262 UNITED NATIONS (1951); cf. also BENHABIB (2004)

individual States, exactly as with the immigration rights.[263] The right to limit the influx of people remains a feature of the right of self-determination of communities,[264] and is vigorously enforced, in particular against undesired refugees. This is practiced particularly strikingly, for example in Australia, where refugees are intercepted and flown to third countries if possible, before they are able to seek asylum, and are placed in detention camps where the living conditions are worse than those in the refugees' countries of origin.[265]

However, the following will continue with a particular focus on developments in Europe after the Second World War, and especially on the European Community and its effects on the national sovereignty of the EU Member States, as it constitutes a unique new development in how citizenship is viewed beyond the individual states. Citizenship beyond the nation-state is now a reality in Europe,[266] although the legal meaning of EU citizenship is profoundly contested.[267]

The Maastricht Treaty of 1992,[268] which entered into force on 1 November 1993, was the first to allude to Union citizenship as an objective of the EU, although it was clearly established from the outset of the Treaty on EU that this would only complement but not replace national citizenship.[269] It is "*out of the field of free movement that the concept of citizenship in the EU context largely emerged.*"[270] In any case, Union citizenship created a strong demarcation from those States and citizens not in possession of this status.[271]

263 BENHABIB (2004)
264 WALZER (1983)
265 For a summation of many reports, cf. MOGELSON (2013)
266 Instead of many others cf. WALTER/GÄRDITZ (2015) pp. 140 et seq.; KOCHENOV (2013), and very detailed SCHÖNBERGER (2005)
267 KOCHENOV (2013)
268 OJEU, 92/C 224/01, 31 August 1992
269 cf. for example OJEU 2002 C 325/1, OJEU 2007 C 306/1, and OJEU 2010 C 83/47
270 Shaw (2000), cited in WIENER (2007) p. 22
271 BENHABIB (2004)

2.6.1 Legal subject status of the EU and sovereignty of the Member States

On the basis of previous perceptions, the State is constituted according to *Jellinek's* three-element theory, from the State territory, the State authority and the constituent people. Against the background of the two world wars, the totalitarian State system and mindful of the historical understanding that the intensive economic interdependence between States could be an effective means for sustainable stabilisation of world peace, the European nations after 1945 formed a community on the basis of the Treaty of Rome 1957, which was initially the European Community for Coal and Steel (ECSC). The ECSC later became the European Community (EC) with the inclusion of additional Member States, culminating in today's EU (EU) with the Treaty of Lisbon (Article 1(3) of the Treaty on the EU – TEU).[272] Despite developments in European civil rights, which in their cooperation occasionally seemed to be a precursor to a political union in the model of the United States of America,[273] and although being endowed with full legal personality[274] and not being a typical international organization given its supranational features,[275] the European Union does not have the status of a State. It is rather a supranational association of countries or a supranational entity.[276] This is reflected in particular in the area of citizenship, where the individual Member States remain autonomous, and it is left up to the individual Member States to determine who may bear its citizenship. This was also expressed in a declaration on the occasion of the Treaty of Maastricht 1992:

272 Treaty on the EU of 7 February, 1992 (OJEU C 191 of 29 July 1992 as amended by the Treaty of Lisbon of 13 December 2007 (OJEU C 306 of 17 December 2007)

273 In the wake of the Second World War, *Winston Churchill* called for the United States of Europe in 1946 and intended the creation of a European Federal State to which all nation States would belong, and which as the new "sovereignty", would be responsible for overall policy. cf. DIETRICH (2011)

274 Confirmed with the Lisbon Treaty, Article 47 TEU

275 For meticulous analysis see SCHÜTZE (2009)

276 cf. for greater detail SCHOENBERGER (2005)

"Declaration on Nationality of a Member State

The Conference declares that, wherever in the Treaty establishing the European Community reference is made to nationals of the Member States, the question whether an individual possesses the nationality of a Member State shall be settled solely by reference to the national law of the Member State concerned. Member States may declare, for information, who are to be considered their nationals for Community purposes by way of declaration lodged with the Presidency and may amend such declarations when necessary."[277]

This was ultimately implemented into the Treaty of Lisbon in Article 20(1) of the Treaty on the Functioning of the EU (TFEU).[278]

The CJEU (then ECJ) has also had the opportunity in the case of *Micheletti* to express itself on this issue and has concluded that:

"The determination of the requirements for the acquisition and loss of citizenship is subject under international law, to the individual Member States. This responsibility should be exercised in observance of the Community law. It is however not the matter for the legislations of a Member State to restrict the effects of the granting of citizenship by another Member State, in that an additional requirement for the recognition of this citizenship with regards to the exercising of the intended fundamental freedom intended in the Treaty".[279]

In the *Rottmann* case,[280] on the contrary, the ECJ concluded that it is in violation of Community law, "*if the citizenship of a person who acquired the same through deception, is revoked*", if the acquisition of the citizenship of the Member State in question lead to this person having lost his original citizenship and thus being rendered stateless. In this respect,

[277] Final Act of the Conference, 7 February 1992, Declaration No. 2, cited by FRANSMAN (2011) p. 10

[278] OJEU 2010 C 83/47

[279] ECJ C-369/90 (1992) ECR I-4239

[280] ECJ C-135/08 (2010)

Community law protects (EU) citizenship if this was once acquired,[281] and can at least in this way impact on the national sovereignty of the relevant individual Member States. This is a key innovation, as EU citizenship is shaping the material scope of EU law, and the "*ability to guarantee the rights of EU citizens in this supranational capacity by automatically acquiring jurisdiction where such rights are infringed... moved EU citizenship closer to a citizenship in the Arendtian sense: a 'right to have rights'.*"[282] Furthermore, this seems to render the ECJ "*the final arbiter*" in citizenship cases,[283] as "*not to leave the EU any possibility to protect the status of EU citizenship from encroachments of the Member States would be to leave it entirely to the Member States to decide who EU citizens are, even when such decisions are taken in breach of the core principles of EU law*".[284] Although the Member States remain free to decide who their citizens are, they are bound to take EU law into account, and at least legally speaking, it is impossible that any one Member State could have a "better nationality" within the EU.[285]

2.6.2 Independent constitutional law protection through the EU Charter

The EU Charter guarantees an independent constitutional law protection at the European level, which is in principle comparable with that at the national level, in which every person can invoke the fundamental rights and freedoms under the EU Charter against the actions of the EU. This is stipulated in Article (6)(1) TEU, that the Union recognises the rights, freedom and principles set out in the Charter on Fundamental Rights of the European Union.[286] Moreover, the EU Charter is an integral part of EU primary law, and enjoys the same binding legal character as the EU

281 In a very different, yet in a way somewhat similar case like in the USA in *Trop v. Dulles* 356 U.S. 86 (1958) where Chief Justice Warren held that depriving someon of their citizenship involves "*the total destruction of the individual's status in organized society.*"

282 KOCHENOV (2013 II) p. 7; cf. also ARENDT (1986) and Chief Justice Earl Warren in *Perez v. Brownell* 356 US 44, 64 (1957)

283 *Davies* (2011), cited in KOCHENOV (2012) p. 23

284 KOCHENOV (2012) p. 23

285 KOCHENOV (2012)

286 Charter of Fundamental Rights (7 December 2000, Nice) OJ C 364, 1 (as originally adopted), as amended at Strasbourg (12 December 2007) OJ C 303, 1

Treaties.[287] Article 51 of the EU Charter defines the scope of this legal instrument, providing that its provisions are "*addressed to the institutions and bodies of the Union … and to the Member States … when they are implementing Union law*". Hence, the EU Charter should, in principle, have direct effect – just as Treaties do – where a provision is clear, precise, and unconditional,[288] In fact, the CJEU has already confirmed the vertical effect[289] of the EU Charter allowing its provisions to be successfully invoked to challenge EU law[290] or national law.[291]

2.6.3 The principle of conferral of powers

Despite this functional comparability, it cannot be ignored that the EU[292] – unlike the US – is not a federal State in the sense of being a federally organised political union, but a supranational union, built on the basis of Member States, whose power to act is not based on any original democratic mandate – regardless of the European Parliamentary elections which have been held since 1979 – but is based on the principle of limited individual authority by conferral of powers (Article 5(2) TEU). According to this the Union may only act within the limits of the responsibilities which the Member States have transferred to it in the Treaties for the realisation of the objectives stipulated therein. This principle is also reflected in that the EU Commission is not a "super national government" based on a parliamentary mandate, but is instead recruited by the States and Heads of Governments of the EU Member States, unlike the Heads of Government[293] of the individual

[287] Article 6(1) TEU

[288] The general test was described in the Opinion of AG *Trabucchi* in the Case 43/75 *Gabrielle Defrenne v. Société anonyme belge de navigation aérienne Sabena* [1976] ECR 455 as follows: *"(u)nder the criterion established by the case law of the European Court a Community provision produces direct effects so as to confer on individuals the right to enforce it in the courts, provided that it is clear, precise in its content, does not contain any reservation and its complete in itself in the sense that its application by national courts does not require the adoption of any subsequent measure of implementation either by the States or the Community."* (p. 486)

[289] As for the possible horizontal application of the EU Charter, see CRAIG/BÜRCA (2015) p. 196-198

[290] See e.g. Cases C-293 and 594/12 *Digital Rights Ireland v Minister for Communications et al* EU:C:2014:238

[291] See e.g. Case C-617/10 *Åklagaren v Hans Åkerberg Fransson* EU:C:2013:105

[292] On the current developmental trends and crises in the EU, cf. HABERMAS (2012)

[293] Or in Switzerland, the entire Federal Council

States themselves, for example. With a view to closing this separation from a mandate (though potentially undermining the principle of the conferral of powers) the author of a popular study by the *Heinrich Böll Foundation*[294] proposed that future Heads of the Commission should be named by the European Parliament.

Citizenship or at least the acquisition of citizenship[295] thereby remains one of the areas totally reserved to the Members States. Recently, the European Commission, in response to a question regarding the Citizenship-by-Investment programme in Malta, legally correctly stated in October 2013 that it is the exclusive prerogative of the individual Member States to whom and under what conditions they grant their citizenships.[296]

Regardless, there is a creeping encroachment of citizenship by EU law, which is seemingly without legitimisation,[297] as is shown in more detail *infra*.[298]

2.6.4 No EU competence-competence ("implied powers")

Based on *Georg Jellinek's* three-element theory, the EU's lack of State status is also expressed in the fact that its supranational authority cannot be attributed directly to a constituent people. The EU institutions (Article 223 TFEU et seq.) exclusively possess those powers which are granted to them on the basis of the international treaties between the EU Member States. Competencies which are not expressly granted on the basis of international treaties do not exist. Article 5(2) TEU thus stipulates that any responsibilities that have not been explicitly transmitted in the treaties remain with the Member States, and this includes responsibility in citizenship matters. In other words, the EU in the sense of the theory of "implied powers" does not have any competence-competence, i.e. no

---

294 HEINRICH BÖLL FOUNDATION (2012); cf. also KAMANN (2012)

295 cf. the abovementioned case *Rottmann*, ECJ C-135/08 (2010), regarding the loss of citizenship, and KOCHENOV (2013 II)

296 *"Member States have full sovereignty to decide to whom and how they grant their nationality"*. Report in http://euobserver.com/justice/122101, last accessed on 1 December 2013; cf. also CARRERA (2014)

297 cf. *Gärditz*, in WALTER/GÄRDITZ (2015) pp. 150 et seq.

298 cf. 14.4.4. where this issue is discussed with regard to the Maltese citizenship program

independent competence to create new responsibilities for itself. The absence of a competence-competence is based on its lack of State status, and is directly a result of the democratic principle. [299]

2.6.5 Safeguarding the principle of subsidiarity

The transfer of competence from the nation State level of the EU Member States to the supranational level of the EU, as a crucial (State organisation) decision, must be supported by a democratic mandate, or in any case must be intended under constitutional law.[300] For example, in the Federal Republic of Austria, Article 9(2)(1) of the Austrian Constitution stipulates that individual sovereign rights can be transferred to other States or to inter-State institutions through law or through an approved State treaty in accordance with Article 50(1) of the Austrian Constitution.

In terms of a barrier to competence transfer, the subsidiary principle enshrined in Article 5(3) TEU allows for action by the EU in areas which do not fall under its exclusive jurisdiction, if and insofar as the objectives of the measures proposed by the Member States cannot be sufficiently achieved either centrally or at regional or local level, but are better achieved by the EU because of the scale or effects of the proposed act. This is not applicable to citizenship law.[301]

The principle of subsidiarity as a controlling and simultaneously limiting fundamental principle in the transfer of competence rests on the one hand in the realisation that certain actions of transnational significance, such as environmental protection or peacekeeping, can only be inadequately fulfilled at nation State level. On the other hand, it also acknowledges the

---

299 In the Federal Republic of Germany, for example, the Democratic Principle is subject to the "guarantee of permanence" of Article 79(3) Constitution. An amendment to the Constitution, by which the principles laid down in Articles 1 and 20 are affected is therefore inadmissible. Counted among these principles is mainly that all State authority emanates from the people (Article 20(2)(1) Constitution) – a principle which would have been breached by the creation of competence-competence for the EU to the extent that its actions in the adoption of regulations and directives would be functionally comparable to a nation State's legal acts with respect to the extent of its freedom to act

300 Fundamental to the transfer of sovereign rights from the national to the supranational level: *Schneider* in COUNCIL OF EUROPE (2011)

301 FRANSMAN (2011) p. 9

practical realisation that the decentralized execution of a task or the decentralised implementation of a central decision can be comparably efficient and limits the distance between the recipient of State decisions and the responsible executive, counteracting the alienation between them, and in so doing confronting the widespread phenomena of political frustration.

Following from the above, the principle of subsidiarity can be seen to contribute to the "grounding"[302] between State authority and the constituent people. It helps preserve the national identity of the Member States as the basis of an organically developed Europe, which is observed by the EU and in which the fundamental political and constitutional structure, including regional and local self-governance, is expressed (Article 4(2)(1) TEU)[303] – especially concerning citizenship. The protection of national identity crystallises the principle of subsidiarity as a barrier to the transfer of competence from the Member States to the Union level, which interpreted objectively, already includes the characteristics whereby the Member States define themselves and their fundamental values, resulting from their history, culture, religion, language and legal system – all of which are values which can be considered as connecting factors in the material definition of the concept of citizenship. Democratic citizenship does not therefore need to be rooted in a particular country's national identity.[304] As fundamental political and constitutional structures within the meaning of Article 4(1) TEU constituting and substantiating national identity, the principles of democracy, social welfare, the separation of powers, the rule of law and the subjection to constitutional law are common characteristics to all States in the Western world.[305] Or, as *Habermas* formulated it "*... notwithstanding the diversity of the various cultural lifestyles... it required the socialisation of all citizens in a common political culture*".[306]

---

302 The constant feedback between the governing and the governed is underpinned through the formation of a democratic relationship. Thereby "*all State authority emanates from the people*"

303 For the definition of a European identity cf. HEINRICH BOELL FOUNDATION (2012); for the European, French and German perspectives, cf. WALTER (2012)

304 HABERMAS (1992); cf. also COHN-BENDIT/SCHMID (1992)

305 cf. *Vedder* in VEDDER/HEINTSCHEL VON HEINEGG (2012)

306 HABERMAS (1992) p.17

2.7 Modern economic immigration and citizenship concepts: import of talent and capital

Countries which are unable to address the economic deficit resulting from an investment or labour deficit[307] or a similar suboptimal matching between demand and supply for labour and capital, steadily lose economic power, growth and prosperity, or stagnate at best. Within the scope of operation of a functioning pricing mechanism,[308] such conditions result in the constant increase in the prices of goods and services. Internationally, a place loses competiveness and declines in country rankings – to the detriment of the people who reside, live and work there.[309] Among the steps that lend themselves to better coordination between the opposite sides of the market – in addition to improved educational programmes, in particular in the MINT occupations (occupations in the areas of mathematics, informatics, natural sciences and technology) – is the specific recruiting of overseas workers, such as that conducted using the "blue card",[310] which also indirectly brings the

[307] On the immigration of skilled workers, see CHISWICK (2011); on the correction of the skilled workers deficit in Germany through the specific control of immigration cf. BORSTEL/WISDORFF (2011); STRUNDEN/PASENOW (2011)

[308] At the centre of principles from which a market economy is constituted (private ownership, liability, consistency of the economic policies, contractual freedom, primacy of the economic policies, and last but not least – open markets) there must be a functional pricing system, which controls the market power of the individual players, steers the limited resources in efficient directions and fulfils essential social functions, cf. HORN (2010)

[309] As in other European States, there is a shortage of qualified skilled workers in Germany. This finding has prompted the presiding German Federal Government to lower the minimum income required for a residence permit from the previous EUR 66,000 to EUR 33,000 for "MINT" occupations and to EUR 44,000 for other occupations cf. BORSTEL/WISDORFF (2011)

[310] The "blue card" based on EU Directive 2009/50/EC includes evidence provided by one of the 28 EU Member States, on the legal residence of relatives from third countries for the purpose of gainful occupation in one of the 28 EU Member States. Although the European Blue Card Directive is mainly aimed at qualified migrants, and usually target those who earn a comparatively good income, the European resettlement program and the German Labour Migration Control Act (labour market Act on the adequate control of the immigration of highly qualified persons and the modification of further residence legislation of 20 December 2008 – ArbMigrG – announced in Volume 2008 No 63 of 24 December 2008) are approaches to an overall liberal immigration right in Europe and Germany, as an example, cf. EICHENHOFER/HÖRICH/PICHL (2011); The relevant text of the Directive is published online at http://eurlex.europa.eu/LexUriServ/LexUriServ.do?uri=OJ:L:2009:155:0017:0029:DE:PDF (last accessed on 21 September 2012); regarding "Blue Card" cf. also BORSTEL/WISDORFF (2011)

reform of the citizenship law into play. This reform would move away from the traditional criteria such as descent (personality principle or *ius sanguinis*)[311] or birthplace (territorial principle or *ius soli*)[312] and instead focus more on the naturalisation and integration[313] of the individual person, but also on economic criteria. The blue card as an instrument for the targeted control of transnational (economic) migration[314] flows is intended to harmonise and simplify the migration of suitable skilled workers throughout Europe.[315] In countries such as the Federal Republic of Germany,[316] a switch from *ius sanguinis* to *ius soli* could contribute to the better integration of future generations of migrant workers into society – especially once many no longer have the centre of their lives in their homelands.[317] Furthermore, targeted economic stimulus programmes could be established under a Citizenship-by-Investment programme and simultaneously talented and affluent persons worldwide could be attracted and retained by a country - even such as Germany. As *The Economist* wrote in 2012, *"the world's most valuable resource is talent. No country grows enough of it. Some, however, enjoy the colossal advantage of being able to import it"*.[318]

To attempt to correct the lack of coordination between supply and demand in the labour market through targeted control of the migration

---

311 On *ius sanguinis* as a connecting factor of the original citizenship acquisition through birth cf. HERDEGEN (2010); *Stern* in STERN I (1977)

312 The "*ius soli*" is linked to the birthplace of a natural person and is one of the dominant principles of the citizenship law of classical immigration countries such as The UK, the United States, Canada and Australia. To some extent it is also found in Brazilian citizenship law cf. SAMTLEBEN (2009); In France, a "double *ius soli*" is a core element of citizenship law, cf. *Weil* in ALEINIKOFF/KLUSMEYER (2001)

313 On the meaning of citizenship law within the context of integration of migrants: REICHEL (2011) pp. 83–100; STADLER (2010)

314 cf. TRACHTMAN (2009)

315 cf. *Kahanec/Zimmermann* in CHISWICK (2011), BORSTEL/WISDORFF (2011), OECD (2013); on the development of a migration-related law on citizenship in Europe cf. USLUCAN (2012)

316 On the immigration laws in the Federal Republic of Germany: *Reinhard* in KLUTH/HUND/MAASSEN (2008)

317 cf. MASING (2001)

318 The Economist, 13 October 2012

movements[319] is not a specific phenomenon of the internet age. With a stronger emphasis on economic integration in decisions about the criteria for citizenship, the resulting increased economic integration of a natural person motivated in particular by the availability of his own earned income will also cause his cultural and social integration to increase as well. Deficits in the area of economic integration can lead to welfare losses for a society, because overcoming this shortfall usually becomes a matter for the national authorities, for example in the form of special language programmes in schools, targeted social work or – following the inevitable conflicts caused by a lack of integration – an increase in police involvement. In contrast, it is a different matter for cosmopolitan investors who do not necessarily want or have to live in the country, and who also create no political integration problems due to their comparatively small numbers and cosmopolitan nature.[320]

Better coordination between the opposing sides of the market, supported by citizenship law informed by the background presented here, could lead to an improvement in welfare for all concerned. Under the premise of achieving controlled immigration, it can create employment.[321] This is even clearer in the case of immigration on the basis of investments (*investor immigration*)[322] and even more so for the direct granting of citizenship based on investment (*Citizenship-by-Investment*).[323]

Considering that the successful settlement of investors and the integration of skilled workers from overseas into the labour market of a

---

319 On the targeted control of transnational migration flows through citizenship law cf. ANGELI/KOLB (2011); ALTMEIER (2010); BAUBÖCK/ERSBØLL/GROENENDIJK/WALDRAUCH (2006); EICHENHOFER/HOERICH/PICHL (2011); MASSING (2001); PARUSEL/SCHNEIDER (2011), regarding skilled workers ("high-skilled immigration") cf. CHISWICK (2011)

320 KÄLIN (2014)

321 The "Green Card" initiated by the German Government in 2000 is an example of the successful recruitment of overseas skilled workers – a principle comparable to the "Blue Card" recruitment program – directed especially at IT specialists, within the framework of which 17,931 specialists from non-EU States were allowed to move temporarily to Germany. Each of the recruited specialists has contributed to the creation of an average of 2.5 jobs in other segments of the labour market, cf. STRUNDEN/PASENOW (2011)

322 WARE/FORTIN/PARADIS (2010), regarding the United States of America: STONE (2014)

323 KÄLIN (2014)

host country will not only lead to an increase in welfare, but that this is also beneficial to balancing its social budget[324] and supporting the State in its core efforts, one can speak in this context of a "privatisation of economic, social, and cultural organisation": the targeted promotion of direct investment or the control of immigration support the model of a self-sustaining civil society and the practical realisation of subsidiarity. To achieve this, sufficient specific, transparent and comprehensible criteria to enable migration flows to be navigated are necessary, for example based on the point system model practiced by Canada[325] – whose investor immigration component made an economic contribution of about CAD 2 billion per year to the Canadian society[326] – or the Citizenship-by-Investment programme practiced by St. Kitts and Nevis since 1984, with which significant direct investments has been attracted into the country, especially since the reform of the programme in 2006/2007, and with which the country has already been able to halve its national debt from more than 200 percent of GDP in 2010 to below 100 percent within two and a half years.[327] These are very remarkable figures and show how such programmes can have significant beneficial impact on countries, both large countries and small countries alike.

What this also shows is that we are in the midst of a global trend of transformation of citizenship. Citizenship is ceasing to be a straightforward relationship between an individual and a nation-state, and also the implied contract between state and citizen weakens as states are now less able to protect their own citizens, for example from negative impacts of the global financial markets and dominance of multinational companies and NGOs.[328] The concept of citizenship in the twenty-first century will be very different.

---

324 cf. CHISWICK (2011)

325 On a State's possibilities and limits in the control of immigration and integration cf. *Luft* in JESSE (2011)

326 WARE/FORTIN/PARADIS (2010)

327 cf. KÄLIN (2014), http://www.treasury.gov/resource-centre/international/int-monetary-fund/Documents/SKN.pdf, last accessed on 20 January 2014; SCHIPKE/CEBOTARI/THACKER (2013); INTERNATIONAL MONETARY FUND (2014); and XU/EL-ASHRAM/GOLD (2015)

328 HEATER (2002)

3

Citizenship vs. Nationality and the Concept of Citizenship

Citizenship, one of the essentially contested concepts,[329] which can be viewed as the legal counterpart of the socio-political concept of nationality,[330] is not legally defined in the majority of States and its meaning is "*inherently far from clear*".[331] From a legal perspective, citizenship (and previously the term "subject") is mainly a classification criterion: it classifies natural persons as belonging to a particular State.[332] State and citizens complement each other: citizens form the constituent people, one of the constitutive components of the State according to *Jellinek's* three-element theory.[333] As a legal institution, citizenship therefore precedes the national law and is established as a component of the States themselves.[334]

From a functional-teleological and similar genesis perspective, citizenship can be defined as a legal bond drawn between a domestic natural person and the State or the domestic legal system. In the democratic states of Western Europe in particular, citizenship is primarily defined in terms of rights,[335] and this approach has played a key role in citizenship studies since *Marshall's* seminal work.[336]

There have also been many other attempts to arrive at a definition of the concept of citizenship,[337] and international courts have coined varying definitions of citizenship in judgments relating to citizenship. In the place of this plethora, I will quote from the widely known ICJ's *Nottebohm* judgment: it is "*a legal bond having as its basis a social fact of attachment, a genuine connection of existence, interests and sentiments, together with the existence of reciprocal rights and duties.*"[338]

329 GALLIE (1955)
330 cf. MACKERT/MÜLLER (2000) pp. 9–19, although in modern legal English citizenship and nationality are usually used synonymously
331 KOCHENOV (2009)
332 JELLINEK (1976); MAKAROV (1962); IPSEN (2004)
333 JELLINEK (1976)
334 KNOCKE (2005) p. 66; cf. also THEDIECK (1989)
335 STUURMAN (2004)
336 MARSHALL (1950)
337 For a good overview see KNOCKE (2005)
338 ICJ judgment of 6 April 1955, ICJ Rep. 1955 (*Nottebohm*)

Citizenship is either connected with a person's birth[339] – either based on the citizenship of the parents (*ius sanguinis* or *citizenship by descent*) or birthplace (*ius soli*, *citizenship by birth* or *birthright citizenship*)[340] – or derived through marriage, naturalisation or acquired through conferral. As formulated by *Joppke*, the concept of *birthright citizenship* is the comparatively simplest way to localise the world's population.[341] A *ius sanguinis* citizenship concept is not infrequently attributed to an ethnic conception of the nation State,[342] which derives from the most natural and closest relationship between persons, that between parents and child.[343]

Nationality on the other hand, although often and traditionally used in the English versions of international instruments as a synonym for citizenship, including in the *European Convention on Nationality*,[344] refers more to the connecting characteristic of an ethnicity based on descent,[345] which originated from the ideal of the nation as a nation State.

Nationality can in principle only be inherently acquired if it is understood as an ethnic-cultural affiliation to "a nation", "a people", as the provenance of a person. In many States these terms are however distinguished, sometimes also internally and especially in multi-ethnic and larger States with multiple subnational entities. In Eastern Europe in particular, various nationalities are often referred to but within one common citizenship which brings them together. This is the case in Russia, for example, where ethnic affiliation (nationality or ethnicity, Russian natsional'nost' [национальность] – for example Chechen, Tatar etc.) and citizenship (grazhdanstvo [гражданство] – citizen of the Russian Federation) are

339 cf. *Ellenberger* in PALANDT (2012)

340 For greater detail on birthright citizenship cf. ALEINIKOFF/KLUSMEYER (1952)

341 cf. JOPPKE (2011)

342 cf. WEIL (2012)

343 VON MÜNCH (2007)

344 Article 2(a) *"For the purpose of this Convention: a 'nationality' means the legal bond between a person and a State and does not indicate the person's ethnic origin."* – The wording of this article shows in itself that when using the term nationality, we need to clarify to what extent a person's ethnic-cultural background comes into play: the extent of belonging to a "nation"

345 According to *Kant, "that group which recognizes itself as being gathered together in a society due to common descent shall be called a nation (gens)"*, cited in HABERMAS (1995)

differentiated. Citizenship therefore grants a person a legal status (or legal relationship)[346] essentially independent of the "nation"[347] but in relation to or as status within a particular sovereign State.

The US maintains an old status of US "nationality" that provides fewer rights than those who have US "citizenship". All US citizens are US nationals, but not all US nationals are US citizens. US nationals who are not US citizens are those who are from American Samoa, and they enjoy the same rights as US citizens except that they cannot vote in elections and cannot hold elected offices. This distinction between an American "citizen" and a "national" originally distinguished desirable races from undesirable ones - an outrageous concept today, yet still practiced in one of the leading countries in the world.[348]

In other parts of the world, for example in many Asian countries such as the Kingdom of Thailand, the concepts of "nationality" and "citizenship" are further differently understood. For example, the notion of "citizen" used in that country covers all residents in the Kingdom who are registered into the civil registration system, regardless of whether or not they possess Thai "nationality".[349] In the multi-ethnic Union of Myanmar, three categories of citizens are distinguished according to its current citizenship laws.[350] Myanmar recognizes as citizens only certain ethnic groups, referred to as "nationals": Chapter II Article 3 of the Citizenship Act of 1982 determines as citizens "*nationals such as the Kachin, Kayah, Karen, Chin, Burman, Mon, Rakhine or Shan and ethnic groups as have settled in any of the territories included within the State as their permanent home from a period anterior to 1185 BE.*"

A general commonality throughout the world however seems to be the meaning of nationality to be more associated with belonging to a particular (ethnic, cultural) "nation", whereas citizenship is more designating

---

346 Regarding differentiation between legal status and legal relationship, see section 3.4
347 cf. also HABERMAS (1992)
348 MORRISON (2013)
349 KHAOCHAN (2009), with further references
350 http://www.refworld.org/cgi-bin/texis/vtx/rwmain?docid=3ae6b4f71b, last accessed on 7 January 2015

the legal status in relation to a State including political rights. The following examples help to further illustrate those differences between nationality (ethnic-cultural affiliation) and citizenship:

In the Kingdom of Spain, the Catalans are deemed a nation without state:[351] they have their own language and culture, a largely autonomous self-governance within Spain, but have no independent State – they are citizens of Spain. In Canada the Inuit are a nation within the Canadian state, as are the other native Indian nations in Canada and the USA. The English are also a nation without a state: they cheer for England in the World Cup but are citizens of the UK.[352] The Kurds, also a nation with its own language and culture but "without a State", are distributed in the States of Turkey, Iran, Iraq and Syria, and based on local affiliation are citizens of one (or more) of these States. Moreover, these Nations in many respects, are suppressed in these States, especially in Turkey.[353] Like the Catalans and Kurds, there are a large number of nations worldwide who do not have their own States.

In Germany, on the other hand, which has received many immigrants from Turkey over decades, the phrase "Turk with a German passport" has become known for many of the more than 250,000 persons of Turkish descent who have been naturalised in Germany.[354] They are, however, German citizens. The same applies in Turkey: not only all ethnic Turks but all other Muslims (Kurds, Bosnians etc.) are viewed as "Turkish", while all non-Muslims (especially Christians, typically Greeks and Armenians) are not viewed as Turkish, even if they speak Turkish and were born there.[355] The same applies to French citizens of Moroccan descent in France, even though this country does not recognise the concept of national minority: "*The principle of all sovereignty resides essentially in the nation. No body nor individual may exercise any*

---

351 cf. CASTELLS (1997)
352 TOMBS (2015); cf. also England; "A once and future realm. The making of the English was a funny business", The Economist, 13 December 2014
353 cf. STROHMEIER/YALCIN-HECKMANN (2010)
354 KASTORYANO (2006)
355 cf. CAGAPTAY (2006)

authority which does not proceed directly from the nation."[356] This list could include many more examples from around the world.

Even though these terms are often used as synonyms in modern legal English, we can see that there is in fact a significant difference between the terms nationality and citizenship, which would of course not be problematic in the case of congruence of one's nationality and citizenship (for example German citizens of ethnic German descent). Since an ethnically pure nation State where all citizens belong to the same nation is a fiction, these terms must be differentiated. For practical purposes, the term citizenship is mainly used in this paper, and is conceptually understood simply as a classification of natural persons belonging to a particular State.

3.1 Citizenship as membership in a political community

Citizenship as membership in a State is certainly a polyvalent concept with a great deal of content which varies depending on perspective. Membership in a political community possibly represents the "*oldest, most basic and most prevalent meaning*".[357] According to *Hobbes* humans create an artificial structure, the State, for their orderly and otherwise dangerous co-existence, which mutually protects the individual citizens from the otherwise unavoidable authority which would exist between them.[358] As *Joppke* explained very well, the reference to politics, the political community is always a reference to authority and protection from authority.[359] If citizenship means membership in a particular political community[360] then this membership is the most important thing for the people since it provides elementary security and protection.[361] Citizenship as membership in a sovereign state also formally assigns a

---

356 Article 3 of the Declaration of the Rights of Man and of the Citizen. See in this respect the speech of SCHREINER in the Parliamentary Assembly: Official report of debates, 2006 Ordinary session, Fourth part, 2-6 October 2006, p. 942

357 Smith (2011), cited in JOPPKE (2010) p. 1

358 HOBBES OF MALMESBURY (1651)

359 JOPPKE (2010) p. 3 et seq.

360 Smith (2011), cited in JOPPKE (2010) p. 3

361 JOPPKE (2010) pp. 3–4

particular person to a particular sovereign state. As *Sadiq* has shown, in many countries however such membership is blurred by what he refers to as documentary citizenship,[362] and is undermining the sovereignty over a state's territory and people, an essential organizing feature of modern international relations.[363]

Immigration policy *per se* is less significant than the separation of the "rights" from the "belonging", of membership of a State from membership in the nation, or of the national home from the State.[364]

3.2 National citizenship law

National citizenship law is comprised of the legal norms which regulate citizenship, i.e., which regulate the acquisition and loss of citizenship, or which are otherwise involved with citizenship.[365] The individual States use various legal instruments in doing so, but almost everywhere, the basics are regulated at the constitutional level and the details at the legislative level, as well as in governmental orders (implementing regulations, ordinances, etc.).[366] Whereas in some States, constitutional changes are required to alter the citizenship norms,[367] in others extensive regulation by government order is possible,[368] supported by corresponding enabling legislation in citizenship enactments.

Bilateral and multilateral Treaties concluded among States are also part of citizenship law in a broader sense, as far as they apply to citizenship in a particular State.

Uniquely in the EU, Part II of the EU Treaty in conjunction with the rather progressive jurisprudence of the ECJ creates a novel, further level of citizenship law: citizenship law beyond the individual sovereign State.[369]

---

362 cf. *supra*, footnote 36
363 SADIQ (2009) p. 172
364 PICKUS (1994); HAMMAR (1990); and Gidon (1993), cited in JACOBSEN (1996)
365 KNOCKE (2005), where other authors are cited as well
366 cf. BERGMANN/FERID (2005)
367 For example in the Bahamas
368 In many European States
369 Instead of many, cf. KOCHENOV (2009)

3.3 International and European law

In addition to defining a constitutional term for citizenship, it is sometimes necessary to also define an international term. It is especially necessary to have an international definition of citizenship, because there can be no uniformed term for citizenship, given the large number of different national citizenship laws.[370] International law as mere law between the States of course cannot independently establish citizenships.[371] The term citizenship, however, cannot be established in domestic law in isolation (which State?) or in public international law, but in this context is more a legal institution which is based on individual domestic law but which joins both legal areas to certain legal consequences due to the interdependency of different States.[372]

In light of the fact that for countries such as the UK, France, Malta and Austria – the four EU Member States considered in this work – a new dimension was opened in the EU with the introduction of EU citizenship in 1992, the international and European law will be more closely examined. A legal definition of the term citizenship can neither be ascertained from relevant legal sources of international nor European primary law. A person's citizenship represents a general legal term which describes the legal relationship of a person to a State.[373]

One definition can in any case be taken from Article 2 of the *European Convention on Nationality* (*ECN*)[374] of 6 November 1997, which defines citizenship as the legal bond between a natural person and a State, without referring to the person's ethnicity (Article 2(a) Convention on Nationality). This Convention not only defines the principles and regulations regarding the citizenship of natural persons, but it also includes provisions regarding

370 See MAKAROV (1962); HOKEMA (2002)

371 WEIS (1962); STILLER (2011)

372 HOKEMA (2002)

373 KIMMINICH/HOBE (2008); *Hailbronner* in VITZTHUM (2010)

374 European Convention on Nationality of 6 November 1997 (ECN), published online at http://conventions.coe.int/treaty/ger/Treaties/Html/166.htm, last accessed on 21 September 2012. This stipulates principles and regulations regarding the citizenship of a natural person, as well as regulations regarding the regulation of conscription in the case of multiple citizenships, with which the domestic law of the Treaty States must comply (Article 1 of the Convention on Nationality)

conscription in the case of multiple citizenships, with which the domestic law of the Treaty States must comply (Article 1 *Convention on Nationality*). The current 28 Member States have adhered to its binding provisions in the design or adaptation of their respective citizenship laws.

Article 15(1) UDHR is particularly relevant internationally. According to this, everyone has the (subjective) right to a citizenship (Article 15(1) UDHR). No one may be deprived of his citizenship or be refused the right to change his nationality (Article 15(2) UDHR). A legal definition of the terms can neither be found in the UDHR nor in Article 20 of the TFEU, from which we can only determine that a Union citizen is one who possesses the citizenship of one of the Member States (Article 20(1)(2) TFEU).

Both the ECJ[375] and the European Commission have made it clear that the acquisition of citizenship is in principle exclusively a matter of domestic law. The European Commission recalled that *"Member States have full sovereignty to decide to whom and how they grant their nationality"*,[376] in response to Malta's new Citizenship-by-Investment programme,[377] but also that *"the principle of sincere cooperation, which is inscribed in the EU Treaties (Article 4.3 of the Treaty on EU), should lead Member States to take account of the impact of decisions in the field of nationality on other Member States and the Union as a whole"*,[378] even though it was also clearly established in the European Parliamentary debates that citizenship law remains a matter for individual Member States. Indeed, the Malta IIP discussions with the EU Commission represent a first direct incursion of EU institutions in a previously exclusive terrain of competence of the EU Member States, when *"one of the most sacred of cows in the division*

375 ECJ C-369/90 (1992) I-4239 (4262)

376 Report on the position of the European Commission regarding Malta, published online at http://euobserver.com/justice/122101, last accessed on 1 December 2013

377 cf. http://www.europarl.europa.eu/news/en/news-room/content/20140110IPR32392/html/EU-citizenship-should-not-be-for-sale-at-any-price-says-European-Parliament, last accessed on 18 January 2014

378 European Commission: SPEECH/14/18: Citizenship must not be up for sale, speech by the Vice-President of the European Commission Viviane Reding of 15 January 2014, published online at http://europa.eu/rapid/press-release_SPEECH-14-18_en.htm, last accessed on 18 January 2014

of competences between the Member States and the EU is the entitlement to control citizenship laws."[379] EU Member States have always been and also remain free to even establish special nationalities for their overseas regions or to create special groups of citizens upon whom they do not confer the right of abode.[380] To what extent the EU law affects the national sovereignty of the EU Member States in the area of citizenship law is one of the most interesting questions in modern citizenship law and a "*true revolution in the modern understanding of citizenship*".[381]

3.4 Legal nature and the legal classification of citizenship

There is a general disagreement about whether citizenship in its legal nature should be classified as a legal relationship[382] between State and citizens[383] or merely as a legal status or a legal capacity which a citizen can be granted by the State,[384] or something in between.[385]

3.4.1 Legal relationship

Under the premises presented here, that citizenship should be closely related to universally protected[386] human rights (according to which no one may be reduced to being a mere object of a State's actions – potentially placing them in a position of complete helplessness, defencelessness or redundancy for not able to help themselves) it would appear logical to qualify citizenship as a legal relationship.

Generally, a legal relationship can be defined as a special relationship

---

379 CARRERA (2014) p. 1
380 KOCHENOV (2011)
381 KOCHENOV (2009) p. 171
382 For a qualification of citizenship as a legal relationship: BERBER (1975); HERDEGEN (2010); KIMMINICH/HOBE (2008); MAKAROV (1962); *Renner* in HAILBRONNER/RENNER/MAASSEN (2010)
383 MAKAROV (1962)
384 MAKAROV (1962); *Renner* in HAILBRONNER/RENNER/MAASSEN (2010)
385 VON MÜNCH (2007)
386 Such as according to the second sentence of the Preamble to the European Convention on Human Rights

between two persons or respectively between one person and a thing, or a person and an institution such as the state, which result via a public legal norm from a specific situation defined at the level of public law.

According to this view, citizenship is not first constituted at the level of basic legal rights through the classification of specific subjective rights, in the sense of the individual legal power to require certain behaviour from a public authority (action, tolerance or refraining from action) and being able to enforce this before the courts. Rather, these rights are already inherently acquired with the birth of a natural person. It is an entitlement based on descent. The ordinary legal right merely substantiates this but does not constitute it. In the sense of a connected relationship between the citizens and "their" State, which could be described as "welfare versus loyalty", and which has found its way into the French legal theory, whose protagonists define the connecting link between individuals and the State community as a political and legal relationship (*lien politique et juridique*),[387] with the participants entitled and obliged.

3.4.2 Imminent status

Under Roman Law, which understood a differentiation between Romans and non-Romans (*status civitates*), which today correspondingly finds itself for example in the *Code Civil* of France's Fifth Republic, the State embodies an authority over a certain territory whose constituent people must be granted a certain legal status as their personal substrate.[388] Against this background, it seems on the other hand possible to qualify citizenship as an imminent status.[389] Membership of individual States is expressed in citizenship. This specifically means that the subjective rights typically linked to citizenship do not inherently originate at birth, but originate because a natural person – immediately after birth – is allocated

---

387 cf. MAKAROV (1962)

388 cf. MAKAROV (1962)

389 cf. JELLINEK (1964); *Kimminich* in BK, Article 16, MN 3; LABAND (1911); cf. also *Federal Constitutional Court,* judgment of 8 December 2006, L.C. 2 BvR 1339/06 (Lexetjus.com/2006,3388), MN 18, last accessed on 21 September 2012; *Federal Constitutional Court,* judgment of 21 May 1974, L.C. 1 BvL 22/71/1 BvL 21/72, Federal Constitutional Court 37, pp. 217, 239

legal rights through the State by being e.g. a descendant of a domestic person. There is at least a logical or legal instant between the moment of birth and the acquisition of the unabridged legal position of citizen.

Under this imminent relationship, the rights which are typically linked to citizenship can only exist if other ordinary legal norms are tied to citizenship.[390] The qualification of citizenship as a legal relationship can be illustrated using the example of "citizens" of the German Democratic Republic (GDR) who crossed the border into the Federal Republic of Germany prior to 3 October 1990. By crossing the German domestic border, "GDR" citizens *ipso jure*, i.e. without the interposition of State measures – would fall under the subjective laws of the Federal Republic of Germany[391] and acquired the rights of citizens, such as the right of movement within the country, the right to freely reside or the freedom of expression. In its landmark decision regarding the basic Treaty between the Federal Republic of Germany and the German Democratic Republic, the Second Senate of the German Federal Constitutional Court[392] emphasised that the status of Germans cannot be changed or reduced through any measures – deducing this from the homeland's obligation of protection which is inseparably linked to the status of citizen.

3.4.3 Exclusive and indivisible fiduciary and obligatory relationship

There is another view qualifying citizenship as a legal relationship,[393] under which the legal relationship is one of a fiduciary duty, and which interprets citizenship in the sense of an umbrella relationship which the State cannot divest itself of through exercise of its legislative power. Ultimately, it seems possible to interpret citizenship in terms of a

---

390 cf. DE GROOT (1989); THEDIECK (1989)

391 cf. *Federal Constitutional court,* judgment of 21 October 1987, 2 BvR 373/83, published online at: http://www.servat.unibe.ch/dfr/bv077137.html, last accessed on 21 September 2012

392 cf. *Federal Constitutional Court,* Judgment of the Second Senate of 31 July 1973, L.C. 2 BvF 1/73, published online at http://www.servat.unibe.ch/dfr/bv036001.html, last accessed on 21 September 2012

393 For German Citizenship Law: *Becker* in MKS, Article 16, MN 3; *Randelzhofer* in M/D III, Article 16, MN 8

combination of legal relationship and imminent status, meaning that when considered formally, it is a synonym for a legal relationship brought about by a link with a particular political community and in material terms, an incarnation of a sphere of public rights and obligations.

3.4.4 Discussion

Regardless which of the method of qualification shown here you ultimately choose to apply, it is important to note that when legislating for citizenship, the legislature is confined within the limits of public international law, arising in particular from the UDHR and the UN, which means that it is preferable that citizenship is defined in such a way that it derives as a constituent element of a demographic order, from the legal relationship for belonging to a State constituted by the people as such, and conferring those rights and obligations that follow on the basis of that membership.[394]

For citizenship to be really qualified as a legal relationship this requires that the State's powers be derived from citizenship; however, the constituting force in democratic States is typically derived from the constituent people and not vice versa. The constituent people constitute the State's authority, not the State authority the constituent people. Citizenship is the connecting thread between the domestic legal system and the constituent people as the source of all domestic authority and functions also to assist in the guarantee of the universally protected human dignity against manipulative actions by mere statutory law. This comprehensive protection seems guaranteed only when classified as a legal relationship. Classification as a legal relationship appears most effective in relation to the qualification as an imminent status, because the latter is also linked historically with the idea of being a "State grant", of the constitutional rights typically associated with the citizenship and – last but not least – the associated political rights and obligations intended to make the State transparent.[395]

394 cf. *Hailbronner* in HAILBRONNER/RENNER/MAASSEN (2010)
395 cf. *Hailbronner* in HAILBRONNER/RENNER/MAASSEN (2010)

However, it is important to note that while academically of interest, any distinction between legal relationship and imminent status is "*without any legal consequence*"[396] and citizenship in all cases has the same scope.[397]

3.5 Definition on the basis of the law within the meaning of Article 9 TEU and Article 20(2) TFEU

In assembling content for a definition of the concept of citizenship, Article 9 TEU and Article 20(2)(2) TFEU – which identifies certain rights likely to apply to citizenship and which are in view of Article 9 TEU and Article 20(1)(1)(2)TFEU constitutive of the EU citizenship – should also be included, given the regulatory relationship between Article 20(1)(2) TFEU and Article 20(2) TFEU, since they provide a direct or, in any event, an indirect equivalent in the law of the reference States studied here that are EU member states. On closer analysis, the rights set out in Article 9 TEU and Article 20(2)(2) TFEU can be deduced from the three-element theory, in that they are situated in the sphere encompassing the constituent people as sources of the democratic State authority, the State authority and the State territory – such as the active and passive right to vote (Article 20(2)(b) TFEU), the right to diplomatic and consular protection in third countries (Article 20(2)(c) TFEU), and the right to petition (Article 20(2)(d) TFEU).

Although no legal definition of citizenship can be found within the provisions of Article 20(2) TFEU, it can be deduced from the common "tenor" that the defining essence of citizenship is represented in a special close relationship between the individual and the community. This relationship can be, in the view of the subjective rights enumerated in Article 20(2) TFEU, situated in the triangle between the principle of democracy, the guarantee of human dignity and the specific freedoms such as the protection of personal freedom (Article 12 UDHR) or free movement (Article 13 UDHR), which in turn have a close functional relationship to human dignity (Article 1(1) is directly deducible from these).

---

396 cf. Thienel (1989), cited in STILLER (2011); and GRAWERT (1973)
397 STILLER (2011)

At the heart of the aforementioned triangle is on the one hand the subjective-individual position directly connected to the individual human right to self-determination ("*status negativus*").[398] There is also the individual right to protection by the State community which emerges particularly in the right to diplomatic and consular protection[399] or the right to petition the Parliament ("*status positivus*").[400] Given that citizenship determines the individual assignment of rights and obligations – most States differentiate between "national rights" and "everyman's rights" – this would appear to require a further coordinate which is not only an appropriate differentiation, but also the summary of a spatially random coincident which serves the majority of people as a justification for citizenship and to some extent acts as a connecting "link".

3.6 Human dignity and its relevance to the allocation of citizenship

Human dignity has deep roots in history, philosophy, politics, religion and law, and it is a multi-layered concept.[401] The same universal human rights which have been won over centuries in national constitutions have attained a new significance, in particular in the post-war era.[402] The philosophical concept of human dignity seems to have been in currency since ancient times, going back at least to the early *stoics*, and are popular since *Kant's* currently accepted version, but has only found its way into the texts of public international law since the end of the Second World War.[403] The Universal Declaration of Human Rights, where the word 'dignity' is not only quoted but *"given pride of place in the first sentence of the Preamble"*,[404] was critical in popularizing the

398 For the authoritative work on the *status negativus* as one of the essential constitutional law functions: cf. JELLINEK (1976)

399 cf. AMERASINGHE (2008)

400 For the authoritative work on the *status positivus* as one of the essential constitutional law functions; cf. also JELLINEK (1976)

401 *Dupré* in MCCRUDDEN (2014) p. 114

402 For greater detail SOYSAL (1994); cf. also LUHMANN (1965) and MCCRUDDEN (2014)

403 HABERMAS (2012) p. 14

404 *Costa* in MCCRUDDEN (2014) p. 393

use of dignity or human dignity in human rights discourse.[405] Today, many legal systems include the constitutional value of human dignity, and a number of constitutions recognize the constitutional right to it.[406] After the traumatic events of that war and the massive abuse of human rights and human dignity during the National Socialist period, the Federal Republic of Germany constitutionally guaranteed human dignity explicitly[407] and absolutely (i.e. as an absolute right):[408] moreover, with its "eternity clause"[409] it has even raised it to a special constitutional status and alteration of the guarantee of human dignity it expressed is impossible.[410]

The sources of rules for the guarantee of human dignity are not only found in the constitutions of our various nation States, but also in numerous supranational legal sources, such as in Article 1 EU Charter, Article 26 of the Revised European Social Charter or Article 1, first sentence UDHR.[411] If one ceases to view human dignity as a nation State-specific value, but as a universal value, namely as the individual's subjective right of defence against any form of State authority and simultaneously as a recognition of individual self-determination and personal responsibility, citizenship could in any case be developed by the liberally constituted States by bringing people together towards a consensus to achieve peace and individual development within the community as far as possible, i.e. to achieve this outside of the government sphere in the service of the community. Integration and pacification in the social sphere can only be permanently realised in the absence of a directed State involvement,

---

405 *McCrudden*, cited by *Gearty* in: MCCRUDDEN (2014) p. 161

406 *Barak* in MCCRUDDEN (2014) p. 378

407 "*The dignity of man is inviolable. To respect and protect it shall be the duty of all State authority.*", Article 1(1) GG

408 cf. in this regard Grimm in: MCCRUDDEN (2014) pp. 386–388, with further references

409 Article 79(3) GG

410 This is also an illustrative example of *Dershowitz's* theory that law arises from injustice, and this applies in particular to the development of human rights and the guarantee of human dignity. cf. DERSHOWITZ (2004)

411 European Convention for the Protection of Human Rights and Fundamental Freedoms of 4 November 1950 (ECHR), as amended by Protocol No. 11 (ETS No. 155), which entered into force 1 November 1998, available online at http://www.echr.coe.int/NR/rdonlyres/F45A65CD-38BE-4FF7-8284-EE6C2BE36FB7/0/CONVENTION_GER_WEB.pdf, last accessed on 21 September 2012

insofar as citizens are connected by a minimum level of community to each other as a group. As *Habermas* formulated it:

> *"The guarantee of human rights only generate the status of citizens, as subjects of equal rights, having the prerogative to be respected in their human dignity."*[412]

Although the bounds of nation State action probably exceed the scope of the citizenship law and can amount to the violation of public international law[413] if the acquisition of citizenship is subject to an unacceptable differentiation criterion such as on religion, language, political preference or ethnicity, the nation State meets the boundaries set by human dignity, including the obligation to exercise the discretion it enjoys within its national sovereignty to implement connecting criteria which are chosen to ensure lasting peace within its national territory, to assist the State in its original core tasks and ultimately reflect the core content of the guarantee of human dignity. This can, and absolutely should include linking factors such as investment in the territory, or other exceptional contributions to the State. It includes on the other hand an obligation of the State to control migration flows using suitable factors so that disturbances in the domestic social peace are prevented or at least kept to a minimum. *Ius doni* complies with this principle. Citizenship law understood in this manner would enable a self-sustaining civil society, which observes universal human dignity – at least within its borders.

"Within its borders" is the crucial point in the argument with regard to human dignity (as well as with regard to questions of distributive justice): even *Rawls* considers questions of how goods should ideally be allocated, and what is the result of such allocation, only within a particular society, a particular state – a state which is protected from other states and their citizen's intrusion by the exclusionary nature of its citizenship laws,

---

412 HABERMAS (2012) p. 21; "*Die Gewährleistung dieser Menschenrechte erzeugt erst den Status von Bürgern, die als Subjekte gleicher Rechte einen Anspruch darauf haben, in ihrer menschlichen Würde respektiert zu warden.*"; translation by the author

413 On international and public international law *ius cogens* cf. LOWE (2007)

immigration laws, and the border police and other state authorities that provides enforcement. The focus here is about the access to citizenship of a particular state, and any questions of human dignity or questions of distributive justice about the merits of allocation of citizens on the basis of investments that they have made in the state are necessarily to be viewed on the same level of how such allocation of citizens compares to the allocation of citizens on the basis of birthright, marriage, or lengthy periods of residence. If arguments of human dignity are to play any role with regard to allocation of citizenship, then we would need to avail ourselves of *Rawl's* "veil of ignorance"[414] for the entire world society,[415] which would necessarily lead to very different ways of allocating the privileges of citizenship among the world's population than the current citizenship allocation system we know today, for *Rawl's* tenet that *"[s] omehow we must nullify the effects of specific contingencies which put men at odds and tempt them to exploit social and natural circumstances to their own advantage"*[416] would require entirely different ways of allocating citizenship, because accident of birth is obviously one of the world's most relevant and most blatantly unjust contingencies that, moreover, allow people to exploit it to their own advantage, with equally obvious dramatic consequences to human dignity. And how can we justify "...*giving free access to those whose need to be admitted is weakest, while submitting others to a needs test or excluding them altogether...?*"[417] What is it worth to discuss universal human dignity if we at the same time support systems of exclusion and a global legal framework that perpetuates the suffering and undignified life of hundreds of millions of people who just happen to be born in miserable places under brutal or indifferent governments?

3.7 No obligation on the national legislature to follow a traditional understanding of citizenship

It would appear impossible to anyone who is aware of the basic and generally accepted functions of citizenship to associate any static content to

414 RAWLS (1999)
415 BEITZ (1999), who argues that principles of distributive justice should apply globally
416 Ibid., p. 118
417 *Bauböck* in SMITH (2011) p. 375

this concept. In short, the function of citizenship as understood here is to take an indeterminate group of people with a common culture and a common set of values by reference to a legal system, connect that commonality to the idea of a nation, form them into a self-sustaining civil society and – if possible without (much) State intervention – permanently satisfy them, while considering that they will at all times be subject to many influences, such as that of the mass media or new information and communication technologies – which can only be controlled by the State to a limited extent at best, and ideally should not be controlled at all.

The national legislature is not bound to a traditional understanding of citizenship in the execution of its internationally recognised freedom. As representing a State and underpinned by the principle of proportionality, the Government of a freely constituted society is required to identify processes of social change, to analyse them in terms of their regulatory needs and in the case of a positive finding, to propose and support where necessary the legislature to adopt appropriate measures, which will in turn ensure that the abovementioned objectives of the citizenship law can continue to be achieved, even and in particular under changed social conditions.

Not only can the social conditions change as a result of altered values, but also against a background of demographic change – as an expert from the *World Bank*[418] concluded – where the number of workers in Europe, possibly even as early as in the first half of the twenty-first century, will fall by around a million annually: i.e., from the current 325 million to 275 million. The determining factors of this development can, in addition to the falling birth rates in general, be identified in the aging population and the labour market policies of many EU Member States.

By including citizenship in its plan for action in response to one of the aforementioned social changes, the national governments and legislatures can mitigate its societal, social and economic impacts and in

[418] cf. *World Bank*, "Golden Growth: How the European economic model gets its shine back" in KAISER (2012)

particular counteract the wealth erosion that would be connected in the final analysis, not only with an increase in government transfer payments, but also with an increase in intra-societal conflicts. This is or ought to be actually one of the primary objectives of citizenship law, to reduce the latter to the extent possible, by the early identification, evaluation and mitigation of the fundamental social changes which result in particular from economic and cultural globalisation and demographic challenges, through appropriate legal regulations and a transformation of the citizenship law itself. Here, the concept of the granting of citizenship based on special contribution to the State, including of an economic nature, such as direct investments or contributions to a national development fund, find their place in modern citizenship legislation.

Although the national legislature, as shown here, is not bound by a historically received understanding of citizenship, boundaries are however drawn, which notably result from the precept of constitutional certainty, the requirement of consistency, the requirement to ensure greatest possible protection of legitimate expectations, and the prohibition of contradictory behaviour. The latter specifies the general principle of good faith, which is considered a universally valid principle of law[419] not only horizontally between private parties, but also vertically between the State and private persons.

The principle of good faith represents a principle which is not limited to the area of civil law, but is a fundamental principle which is equally valid in all areas of law and whose function it is to objectively avoid or limit in any case, unreasonable results in particular, which could result from the strict application of the positive law in individual cases.

Given that the citizenship law as an expression of the territorial sovereignty of a State is not limited internally, but this territorial sovereignty in an external capacity is limited to other subjects of public international

---

[419] cf. WIESE (1994); or for Switzerland, cf. Article 5(3) Swiss Federal Constitution which expressly states this principle: "*Government agencies and private persons act in good faith.*", and reiterates it again in Article 9: "*Each person has the right to be treated by State authorities without arbitrariness and in good faith*"

law, the requirement of good faith in the form of the consistency principle is also subjected to external barriers. Each UN Member State is thus shown the limits of its political contractual freedom upon its accession to the United Nations, to which its territorial sovereignty is subjected as a UN Member State. Should it decide to act contrary to that, a UN Member State would violate its legal obligations under Article 2(2) of the UN Charter. In addition, objections could be asserted against it for inadmissible contradictory behaviour (*venire contra factum proprium*), which as a concretisation of the recognised customary principles of good faith in public international law has a supranational binding effect.[420]

As an expression of the consistency principle, the national legislature could decide in future to make new rules in the area of the citizenship law to address the social changes discussed, within the scope of its political freedom. It is however not allowed to intervene with genuine retroactive effect in private arrangements and to subject them to new regulation (prohibition of genuine retroactivity of legal regulations, as is the case in many jurisdictions and logically should simply apply as a universal principle, which in reality is unfortunately not the case) because any regulation requires the confidence of the addressees, which is basically worthy of protection not only from a loyalty point of view.

3.8 A new understanding of citizenship under the conditions of globalisation and transnationalism

In particular, the phenomena of economic globalisation and transnationalism, but also the large waves of emigration in the nineteenth and twentieth centuries and the subsequent expansion of the citizenship laws of some emigrant countries in Europe, have contributed to the fact that the members of a State are no longer gathered only within the limits of the national territory, but are distributed increasingly on different continents to various countries, and increasingly many people are gathered within the limits of a territory who are not nationals but temporarily

---

[420] cf. WOLFRUM/PHILIPP (1991)

or permanently settled.[421] The free movement of workers and services (Article 45 TFEU) has contributed to this in Europe. The cultural, social and ethnic plurality of society can no longer be placed visibly in accordance with a political community.[422] Citizenship and nationhood are no longer woven together or linked in defining political identity and origin in the international context.[423]

From a legal point of view, in the EU, the free movement of workers, self-employed and financially independent EU citizens should be guaranteed (Article 45(1) TFEU). The movement of workers entails the abolition of any discrimination based on citizenship between workers of the Member States as regards employment, remuneration and other working conditions (the principle of national treatment, Article 45(2) TFEU). It provides – subject to limitations justified on grounds of public policy, public security or public health – workers with subjective rights to compete in Europe with one another for vacant jobs, freedom of movement in the territory of the Member States, to reside in a Member State and, in accordance with the applicable State laws, regulations and administrative provisions to take up employment and to remain after having been employed in the territory of a Member State under conditions determined by the Commission by direct regulation.

Although the national legislature is in principle bound by the *ultra vires* doctrine not to use its control and power inappropriately – here again the precept of legal determination applies, in particular of intervention – it cannot totally ignore the common good, but must respond to the changing social conditions. Within the scope of the requirement for clarity and definiteness, the principle of consistency and the *ultra vires* doctrine, the granting of citizenship can be and is regularly linked to economic criteria such as the availability of a regular minimum income from gainful economic activities. Those who work in the domestic market pay taxes, thereby contributing to the financing of the general government functions

---

421 For key detail, SOYSAL (1994); and ONG (1999); cf. also from an American perspective SPIRO (2008)

422 *Benhabib*, cited in HERING (2011) p. 89

423 cf. JACOBSON (1996)

and through their daily interactions with colleagues, are more familiar with the domestic community and its culture than a recipient of public aid, who may not contribute to any community work and even merely render himself a ward of the State. The link between the acquisition of citizenship and economic criteria can, in light of economic globalisation and increasing transnational investment and worker migration, contribute to attracting more foreign investment, contribute to improved matching of labour demand and supply as well as investor and investment demand and supply, and thereby secure the foundations of domestic prosperity, which in the foreseeable future – if one believes the *World Bank* study mentioned – especially in Europe but also in other parts of the world, may otherwise be undermined by demographic developments. As legitimate and desirable the demand for a "national culture"[424] in the face of cherished (though nonetheless cultivated) conventions and traditions may be, the national legislature should not prevent the development of a modern citizenship law from reasonably taking into account changing circumstances and the changed understanding of citizenship and nationality. Also from this point of view, the targeted promotion of foreign direct investment and thus job creation in the domestic market through the granting of citizenship to qualified investors from abroad, is a suitable instrument to respond to these changing conditions.

3.9 Multiple citizenship

These changed conditions certainly also include the phenomenon of multiple citizenship,[425] which has acquired a wider impact in the wake of globalisation and the expansion of human rights in international law,[426] but also due to the new realities of dramatically increased availability of improved transportation and communications technologies, which make it increasingly possible and realistic to pursue one's life in more than one country.[427]

---

424 For this concept, cf. *Joppke* in ISIN/TURNER (2002/2011)

425 Also referred to as dual citizenship or plural citizenship; for a comprehensive overview on multiple citizenship, cf. FAIST/KIVISTO (2007)

426 cf. RITTSTIEG (1990)

427 BOSNIAK (2006)

Multiple citizenship was once an unacceptable situation, since – during periods in history when countries had large-scale standing armies and military service obligations and were regularly in conflict with each other – it was assumed that a person could have a relationship and corresponding loyalty only to one State. As US Attorney General *Jeremiah Sullivan Black* stated in 1859:

> *"[N]o government would allow one of its subjects to divide his allegiance between it and another sovereign; for they all know that no man can serve two masters."*[428]

Theodore Roosevelt described the "theory" of multiple nationality *"a self-evident absurdity."*[429] Indeed, *"[s]ingular affiliations inherently have greater meaning than nonexclusive relationships."*[430]

However, increased international marriages and family ties, increased migration, but also and in particular the professionalisation of the military and the diminished relevance of compulsory military service in many States – one of the main problems arising from multiple citizenship – as well as a prolonged phase of general world peace since the Second World War, has meant that today, multiple citizenship is recognised or tolerated by an increasing number of States,[431] and currently more than half of all states allow if not embrace multiple citizenship.[432] Even in countries which still oppose (albeit to different extents)[433] multiple citizenship, it is increasingly tolerated. In Germany for example, public officials must be German citizens but there is no requirement that they

---

428 Cited in SPIRO (2008) p. 61
429 Ibid.
430 SPIRO (2008) p. 59
431 *Triadafilopoulos* in FAIST/KIVISTO (2007) p. 27, and pp. 34–35
432 FAIST (2001), and JOLY (2004)
433 There are numerous instances where dual citizenship is allowed by the German Nationality Act, including, since 28 August 2007, to nationals of EU Member States and Switzerland, and since 20 December 2014, dual citizenship extended to persons born in Germany to foreign parents who have: a) lived in Germany for at least eight years by the time of their 21st birthday; b) who have attended six years of school in Germany; or c) who completed schooling or occupational training in Germany. See (ss 25, 29, Nationality Act of 22 July 1913 (Reich Law Gazette I p. 583 - Federal Law Gazette III 102-1), as last amended by Article 1 of the Second Act Amending the Nationality Act of 13 November 2014 (Federal Law Gazette I p. 1714))

are *only* German citizens; thus, even in core areas of public authority, Germany does not regard multiple citizenship as an issue.[434]

With this trend, gaining an additional citizenship and passport in an affluent and rule of law country "*no longer extracts a potentially prohibitive cost (from the emigrant's perspective) of severing her membership ties with the country of origin. She can hold both, simultaneously*".[435] Even in countries where dual citizenship is formally rejected, e.g. in China, *de facto* toleration of dual citizenship is common.[436]

The political attitude to multiple citizenship has also changed, as more than half of the countries in the world allow multiple citizenship and every year more states follow in a clear trend: for example, Belgium in 2010, Haiti in 2011, Niger in 2012 and Sri Lanka in 2015.[437] Today multiple citizenship is valued for its potential capacity for international influence,[438] as expressed by French Senator *Joëlle Garriaud-Maylam*, who declared: "*The two and a half million French citizens living abroad, half of whom are binationals, constitute a rich and varied network of entrepreneurs, project managers, importers and exporters, consultants and teachers who are indispensable to our external trade and our soft power.*"[439] Beyond migration, this global trend is driven by geopolitical, economic and technological factors. Fears over the loyalty of citizens – the main argument used against dual citizenship – faded after the Cold War ended and increased international political cooperation calmed international relations. Unlike earlier migrants in the eighteenth and nineteenth century, who had little contact with those they left behind them, twenty-first century migrants communicate with their families on a daily basis, by phone, internet,

---

434 *Gärditz* in WALTER/ GÄRDITZ (2015) p. 138, fn 297

435 SHACHAR/HIRSCHL (2014) p. 231

436 *Triadafilopoulos* in FAIST/KIVISTO (2007) p. 35, with further references, and *Preston/ Siemiatycki/Kobayashi* in FAIST/KIVISTO (2007) p. 208

437 BREVILLE (2014)

438 BREVILLE (2014)

439 *La Tribune*, Paris, 17 June 2011. See also "Gone but not forgotten", about the growing importance of diasporas for countries, The Economist, 27 June 2015, p. 51, and generally re *soft power*, NYE (2005). Re the Chinese view that "*in practice, one cannot count on the loyalty of overseas Chinese, only on their desire to make a profit*" cf. ONG (1999) p. 61, with further references

email, they visit them for holidays and return home for retirement.[440] A new class of "global citizens" has furthermore emerged which truly have multiple homes and bases and for whom multiple citizenship is the norm.[441] Yet, multiple citizenship is still prohibited in many countries, while some only tolerate it in certain cases.

Selected countries which prohibit dual citizenship

Brunei	Kazhakstan	Malaysia	Netherlands	Singapore
China	Kenya	Mauritius	Norway	Solomon Islands
Indonesia	Kiribati	Myanmar	Papua New Guinea	Venezuela
Japan	Kuwait	Nepal	Saudi Arabia	

440 BREVILLE (2014)
441 KÄLIN (2014)

Selected countries which allow dual citizenship

Austria[1]	Cyprus	Germany[2]	Italy	New Zealand	Spain (only in certain cases)	United States
Australia	Denmark	Greece	Jordan	Pakistan[3]	Sri Lanka	Vietnam
Bangladesh	Dominica	Grenada	Latvia	Peru	St. Kitts and Nevis	Western Samoa
Belgium	Ecuador	Hungary	Lebanon	Philippines	Sweden	
Belize	Egypt	Iceland	Lithuania[4]	Poland	Switzerland	
Brazil	El Salvador	Iran	Macedonia	Portugal	Syria	
Canada	Fiji	Iraq	Malta	Romania	Thailand	
Chile	Finland	Ireland	Mexico	Russia	Turkey	
Colombia	France	Israel	Montenegro	Serbia	United Kingdom	

1 Generally not allowed; except for persons who obtain two citizenships at the time they were born. The exceptions to this rule are stated in s 28 of the Austrian Citizenship Act; additionally Austria allows dual citizenship if Austrian citizenship is acquired under § 10 (6) of the Austrian Citizenship Act

2 Dual citizenship is allowed in numerous circumstances (s 12 of the German Nationality Act) which have recently extended with the amendments of the German Nationality Act of 2014 (ss 25 and 29)

3 According to Chapter 14, Annex J-Article 6* of 1951 Pakistani Nationality Law and the amendments 1952,1972,1973 and 2000, holding dual citizenship was not permitted. But now the government of Pakistan recognizes and allows its citizens to also hold citizenships of 16 countries, including Australia, Belgium, Canada, France, Iceland, New Zealand, Sweden, Switzerland, the United Kingdom, the United States, and others

4 Only under limited circumstances, cf. http://www.dualcitizenship.com/countries/lithuania.html; https://usa.mfa.lt/usa/en/travel-and-residence/consular-issues/citizenship-of-lithuania

Macklin points out that from a state perspective dual citizenship has also become more attractive because it allows a state more easily to take away one's citizenship without making a person stateless as a result. Thus dual citizenship enables citizenship revocation without rendering the person stateless, who can then be deported to the other country of citizenship.[442] A most recent example of this are the latest amendments to the Canadian Citizenship Act, which allows under certain circumstances the withdrawal of Canadian citizenship if the person in question also holds another citizenship, effectively introducing two classes of Canadian citizens: those with single Canadian citizenship, and those who also hold other citizenships.[443]

Viewed from the perspective of the individual, or of "consumer citizenship"[444] which is seen to flow from neo-liberal premises regarding the subjectivity of the new citizen,[445] multiple citizenship reflects the commodification of citizenship itself, and instead of merely accumulating material goods, the international consumer citizen collects access rights: citizenships and passports.[446] There are many advantages for individuals to holding dual or multiple citizenships. The status is beneficial as it provides them with additional options: an alternative country in which to live and work (or, in the case of citizenship of any of the 28 EU member countries, it means an additional 28 countries to choose from), an additional locus and source of rights and community ties, more visa-free travel and thus better personal mobility, and more personal security in the face of global terrorism directed very often at citizens of large, powerful countries such as the US, the UK or Germany.[447]

A person who has more than one citizenship is in most cases more privileged than a person with only one, and can in many cases freely chose

---

[442] MACKLIN (2007) pp. 42 et seq., *Faist* in FAIST/KIVISTO (2007) p. 10
[443] Canadian Citizenship Act (R.S.C., 1985, c. C-29), last amended by Bill C-24 on 19 June 2014, which has come into effect on 29 May 2015, published online at http://www.parl.gc.ca/LegisInfo/BillDetails.aspx?Language=E&Mode=1&Bill=C24&Parl=41&Ses=2, last accessed on 30 June 2015
[444] *White*, cited in STASIULIS/ROSS (2009) p. 99
[445] Regarding neo-liberal citizenship in general, cf. HINDESS (2002) pp. 127 et seq.
[446] STASILIUS/ROSS (2009) p. 99
[447] cf. KÄLIN (2014); also see PICKUS (1998)

the more advantageous of two passports, two legal systems and two or more[448] places of residence.[449]

The question has been raised of whether multiple citizenship is compatible with the principle of equality before the law – a fundamental right that can be found in almost all constitutions in the world – which arises in the context of visa requirements, the need for a work permit or the right to acquire real property.[450] However, this principle is generally considered only in terms of the group of persons who are already citizens[451] and can therefore be left out of consideration here, at least with regard to naturalisation.

With regard to citizenship granted in the national interest – such as the granting of citizenship on the basis of extraordinary contribution to the State – it is actually desirable in most cases and also mostly unavoidable that the previous citizenship be retained. This has been recognised even in Austria, which generally still strictly requires the renunciation of previous citizenships as a condition of naturalisation, but in the case of naturalisation pursuant to Section 10(6) of the Austrian Citizenship Act, i.e. the acquisition of citizenship due to extraordinary contributions to the State - including economic contributions - interestingly allows the retention of previous citizenships.

Multiple citizenship has undoubtedly eroded the strong bond between the individual citizens of a particular country and lead to the decoupling

---

448 In case of EU citizenship, 28 countries

449 cf. KÄLIN (2014)

450 VON MÜNCH (2007)

451 CARENS (1995) While concerns may be raised in this respect under Article 14 ECHR providing for prohibition of discrimination, that legal provision is not self-standing but must be linked to another ECHR right. This is not only explicitly mentioned in Article 14 ECHR itself (*"The enjoyment of the rights and freedoms set forth in this Convention shall be secured without discrimination on any ground..."*), but it has been also long-standing ECtHR case law (e.g. ECtHR, *Burden v. the United Kingdom* (Grand Chamber), 29 April 2008 (Appl.no. 13378/05), at para. 58). Yet, ECHR does not give a guarantee of equality before the law and neither does Protocol 12 which extends the Convention to "'any right set forth by law"', although mentioning equality before the law in its Preamble. Furthermore, it should be also emphasized that Article 14 prohibits such discriminatory measures which have no objective and reasonable justification rather than every difference in treatment (ECtHR, Case "Relating to certain aspects of the laws on the use of languages in education in *Belgium" v. Belgium*, 23 July 1968 (Appl.no. 1474/62, 1677/62, 1691/62, 1769/63, 1994/63, 2126/64), at para. 10)

of citizenship status from the effective nationality. Having several citizenships means more options for the individual and a kind of citizenship of convenience: depending on the situation, one or the other passport can achieve the objective best (e.g. no visa is required to travel, faster entry at border checkpoints for instance for EU citizens entering from outside of the EU etc.). This does not mean however that you cannot also maintain a meaningful relationship with several states, and indeed, with increased mobility and the transnational lives of global citizens, having multiple ties in different countries and even on different continents has become much more commonplace.[452] It is no longer controversial that "*individuals hold multiple social identities*"[453] and people can feel a sense of belonging e.g. to Europe, their nation-state(s), their gender, and so on.

---

452 cf. KÄLIN (2014); RISSE (2010)

453 RISSE (2010) p. 40; and SPIRO (2008) p. 126

4

The Functional Significance of Citizenship

4.1 Overview and differentiation

Given its fundamental importance, particularly for containment of the nation State's scope for action in the area of citizenship and for the interpretation of indefinite legal terms, the coherent representation of its functional features seems necessary.

The classical legal, economic and the sociological or political functions of citizenship can be distinguished.[454] It would appear sensible given the diversity in political ideas circulating around the concept of citizenship and what it should contribute through (economic, but also cultural) globalisation and advanced information technology driven societies, to deduce that the relevant functions of the basic parameters of the nation State, which in view of progressive international investors, labour mobility and demographic change, impose a comprehensive territorial responsibility for the welfare not only of "own" nationals but all resident persons.[455] With regard to their protective responsibilities a distinction can be made between domestic and external functions, and between traditional state functions and additional non-state functions.

4.2 Domestic functions

4.2.1 Limitation and control of a State's population

The traditional functions of citizenship can be differentiated between domestic and external ones. However, a closer look reveals the constitutive characteristics of citizenship which links citizenship, from an objective State-organisational perspective, to domestic persons through domestic law. As a prerequisite for the creation of a corresponding relationship, it helps isolate the constituent people as the source of State power. *Jellinek's* three-element theory[456] draws a link between the domestic legal system and the constituent people which in turn forms

---

[454] cf. the Typology by *Marshall* in MARSHALL/BOTTOMORE (1992), which follows the well-known legal classification (HABERMAS (1992)); as well as MACKERT/MÜLLER (2000)

[455] cf. SCHEUING (2003)

[456] cf. Section 1.2.1.

the personal substrate of the organised community called a nation State. Regardless of whether this bond (*genuine link*) is physical (taking up residence, permanent residence etc.), ethical (proof of a moral code), intellectual (knowledge of the sociocultural norms of the national community etc.) or – last but not least – is of a financial nature (independence from government transfer payments, investment in the host country)[457] it justifies as such not only a right of residence but creates a (comprehensive) integration and fiduciary duty on the State towards its citizens.[458] The latter forms the equivalent for citizens of the not uncontroversial duty of allegiance and loyalty.[459]

The comprehensive territorial responsibility of nation States has meant that all the people who reside within the limits of a territory must be granted protection – as evidenced in most Western democracies in the distinction between the constitutional rights of residents and all others – standing as often the only essential obligation equally applied to both own citizens and non-citizens, and in complete contrast with the distinctions drawn as regards access to the labour market and housing market, where active and passive voting rights define access to other protections.[460] By controlling the provisions of their citizenship laws, nation States can limit and control such access and the corresponding level of social protection and privileges. In all countries this inevitably leads to internal discrimination.

4.2.2 Creation of a consistent community of values

The wake of the recent debt crisis[461] revealed that increasingly many countries among EU Member States are reaching the limits of the possible political responses in the face of overwhelming public debt. The demand for low taxes and comprehensive freedom in all areas of life is

457 cf. the corresponding differentiation in DZANKIC (2012)

458 cf. *Becker* in FS SCHEUING (2011), with reference to the *Nottebohm* decision of the ICJ

459 The loyalty and the duty of loyalty are, for example, expressed in military service; cf. also WEIL (2004)

460 cf. *Becker* in FS SCHEUING (2011)

461 On the also relevant recent crisis in the EU in the light of the constitutionalisation of public international law, cf. HABERMAS (2012) p. 39 et seq.

not compatible with nearly ubiquitous expectations on the State for all aspects necessary for daily life, including services at the lowest possible prices, job opportunities and so on. The former US President *John F. Kennedy* at the beginning of his term in the early sixties of the last century offered the famous words of warning to his people not always to ask what the State can do for them, but what each individual can do for their State.

In particular, volunteering provides individuals with civil society engagement through the immediately practical services they render, thereby satisfying *Kennedy's* admonition. Especially in view of the fact that the central tenet of the democratic principle that all State authority emanates from the people is crystallised in this and other forms of civic engagement, the minimum required consensus on corresponding values is inconceivable outside of the State community in the Western democratic tradition, even if the rule of law and the welfare State in the absence of democracy are possible in principle.[462]

The constitutional rights as a constitutive part of national policy from which the essential functions of nationality derive – according to various views – and which in the case of the *status negativus* are directed to secure each person a minimum of individual freedom, create the basic premise for this civic activism and help support the State's community in accordance with the subsidiary principle, which can itself consequently focus on its core tasks (education, transport infrastructure, police and judiciary etc.). This mechanism, however, can only work if there is a minimum consensus of shared values among the guardians of constitutional law. Citizenship functionally contributes to binding groups of people together by being a prerequisite of granting central constitutional rights such as freedom of assembly and freedom of association, thus making the commitment to civil society practically possible. It is the starting point of a consistent – that is, consistent within itself – and thereby stable community of values which presupposes these values are held in common.

---

[462] cf. HABERMAS (1992)

4.2.3 Ensuring the greatest possible congruence between the State and the constituent population

That a certain correspondence is required between the holders of democratic rights and those who are permanently subject to State rule in the sense of subordination should ideally rank among the determinants of the democratic principle.[463] To underline this, several studies from renowned organisations such as the *Konrad Adenauer Stiftung*[464] have found that the granting of citizenship significantly influenced the willingness of migrant people to integrate and willingly participate in their host country's political and civic responsibilities. With regard to a fundamental objective of the citizenship law, to achieve substantial withdrawal of government intervention and self-sustaining peace among the domestic population, these findings appear essential and contribute, at least in theory, to the requirement for the greatest congruence possible between the State population, i.e. those with active and passive electoral rights, and the resident population, i.e. the people with permanent or temporary residence or usual abode in the State. This is not to say, however, that states cannot – *per se* – attract investors and workers if they offer no prospect to acquire citizenship, to which the example of the United Arab Emirates, and especially Dubai, testifies.

If integration is interpreted as a fundamental function of citizenship law – less in the static sense of integration into a particular cultural state, and more in a dynamic sense of gradual development, above all being the mastery of the local language and traditions – then the domestic origin of the parents provides the strongest guarantee for cohesion within a nation. This is probably also the real reason why the principle of descent (*ius sanguinis*) in all States is overall the most important principle for citizenship acquisition virtually worldwide.

Achieving the greatest possible congruence between citizens and the resident population promotes intra-societal peace, especially given that

---

463 cf. *Böckenförde* in ISENSEE/KIRCHHOF (2005); MASING (2012) p. 24; *Stern* in STERN I (1977)

464 KONRAD ADENAUER STIFTUNG (KAS), Turks in Germany (2002), published online at http://www.kas.de/wf/doc/kas_201-544-1-30.pdf?040415180309 last accessed on 21 September 2012, p. 5 f.

the different "characteristics" of the aforementioned groups with respect to their subjective (public) rights are always justified on the grounds of difference. If two groups in a country are at least equally involved in social life and achieve comparable income levels, they are more likely to willingly participate in the payment of taxes and similar charges (fees, charges and special taxes), to help ensure that the general government functions can be financed. Citizenship law allows the divergence between citizens and the resident population to be controlled and minimised, because the granting of citizenship in most States is still decisive for the access to public facilities and other social benefits, despite there also being a trend discernible to move in the opposite direction.[465]

4.2.4 Controlling access to public offices and functions

The special connection of domestic individuals with the national community is demonstrated by the fact that many States restrict access to public offices and functions to own citizens. The "bond of loyalty" this implies between the State, its institutions and its citizens, is in itself a guarantee of the continued proper fulfilment of public functions, which is usually not assumed in the case of non-citizens.

Although this loyalty to the State, even in a republican State such as France, is felt not capable of being implied in a foreigner, it should not be forgotten that citizenship from today's perspective does not serve the purpose of drawing a line between people, but is primarily interpreted as a bond of belonging to a organically grown consistent political and social community.[466] Citizenship in itself actually provides no guarantee of the proper and loyal fulfilment of sovereign functions, often looks anachronistic, given its historical roots in the Absolutist State and in Europe should be revised in the light of existing EU law.[467]

At the European Union level, the "public authority exception" of Article 51 TFEU provides that the chapter on the freedom of establishment in

---

[465] cf. SOYSAL (2004); BAUBÖCK (2005)
[466] cf. FORTMANN (2005)
[467] Article 51 TFEU

the EU does not apply to activities which are connected, even occasionally, with the exercise of official authority in a Member State. Those who exercise public authority, must have the opportunity to make use of special rights, privileges and sovereign coercive powers over the citizens.[468] However, the scope of the exception within the meaning of Article 51 TFEU is not placed in the hands of the Member States, as the concept of public authority is determined solely in accordance with the European primary law.[469] The legal framework of the free movement provisions and the Union principles of subsidiarity[470] and proportionality not only provide a functional[471] and activity-based definition, but favour a restrictive interpretation of Article 51(1) TFEU. Public authority is accordingly exercised to the extent that the subordination[472] between a public authority and a private entity exists, in a sense that the addressee cannot avoid triggering concrete legal consequences in the mandatory enforcement of a sanction that results from a legally binding instrument.[473]

4.2.5 Integration through empowerment to participate in active policymaking

The laws of most States provide the right to vote exclusively to citizens, although some countries have also granted foreigners the right to vote in local elections (such as the Netherlands, Sweden and New Zealand, in the UK for Commonwealth citizens, in some cantons of Switzerland, as well as across the EU for resident EU citizens).[474] Citizenship acts in particular here as an instrument of integration, it controls the ability to

---

468 cf. *Broehmer* in CALLIESS/RUFFERT (2007); *Schlag* in SCHWARZE (2009)

469 The concept of "official authority" under Article 51 TFEU (then 45 TEC) was defined by the AG Mayras in his Advisory Opinion in Case 2/74 *Jean Reyners v Belgium* [1974] ECR 631, in the following terms: *"Official authoritiy is that which arises from the sovereignty of the State, for him who exercises it, it implies the power of enjoying the prerogatives outside the general law, privileges of official power and powers of coercion over citizens."* (p. 664). Yet, Article 51 TFEU has to be narrowly construed, or as noted by the Court in the above case: it applies only to activities which have *"direct and specific connection with official authority"* (para. 45)

470 cf. *Müller-Graff* in STREINZ (2008)

471 cf. PREUSS (2008); PREUSS (2005)

472 cf. *Federal Constitutional Court*, decision of 18 June 1986, Case 1 BvR Federal Constitutional Court 73, pp. 280, 293

473 cf. PREUSS (2005)

474 cf. BAUBÖCK (2005)

participate in active policymaking. The integrative effect of such rights may largely result from their creating a sense of "belonging", of being "needed" and the belief that individuals can achieve something positive in the immediate living environment by taking political responsibility, i.e. not to be mere subject-recipients of orders handed down from the rulers, but to take action with regard to the important political decisions affecting their lives. Here again emerges the close factual proximity of citizenship and human dignity, which prohibits degrading individuals to being mere recipients of political decisions and thereby provides incentives for the engagement of individual experience, knowledge and ability in the service of the political community. In liberal democracies at least, citizenship increases the individual's access to political rights, such as the active and passive right to vote, which by virtue of their mention in Article 21 UDHR should be considered as universal and place individuals in a position of being able to help shape their own communities.[475] In this context, the regulation in St. Kitts and Nevis is remarkable, according to which new St. Kitts and Nevis citizens who have become citizens under the local Citizenship-by-Investment programme acquire political rights only after five years of residence in the country.[476] The neighbouring State of Antigua and Barbuda, which has adopted an almost identical Citizenship by Investment programme since August 2013, does not have this rule, and thus foreigners naturalised under their programme acquire full political rights,[477] which in the light of the above explanations however is unlikely to be of importance: the vast majority of applicants under these programmes are not interested, as global citizens, in political participation, and thus would also not have any or much integrative effect.

4.2.6 Final point theory versus incentive theory

Although having domestic parents is the strongest guarantee of integration in the domestic polity and promises immediate, interference-free communication between governors and governed, the objectives pursued

---

475 According to UDHR Article 21(1)(1) everyone has the right to take part in the public affairs of his country, either directly or through freely chosen representatives

476 Section 3(5) SKN-CA

477 There are simply no restrictions in this respect in Antigua and Barbuda law

by the nation State in its design of citizenship law and its functions must conform to those boundaries set particularly by the constitutional principle of legality and the prohibition of arbitrary rules, which necessitates that if nationality is to be understood as the formal recognition of successful integration and the culmination of the adaptation and assimilation process (final point theory)– as it does e.g. in Denmark,[478] Germany,[479] Luxembourg,[480] Austria,[481] Greece,[482] Switzerland,[483] and since 2003 also in the Netherlands[484]; and on the other hand in e.g. United Kingdom, Ireland, Belgium, Italy, Spain, Portugal, Sweden and Finland as well as the traditional immigration countries like the USA, Canada, Australia etc. where granting in particular improved access to public goods in the host country, it should act as an incentive to increasingly integrate into the host society (incentive theory).[485]

Citizenship law creates a link to the extent necessary between a domestic natural person and the national legal order. It acts as a filter for access to social and other services which are monopolised by the State as public goods.[486] Its ability to function appears to be elementary to the continued existence of a State order which is committed to the principle of

---

478 Denmark has been tightening its nationality legislation in the 2000s, introducing new requirements for loyalty and allegiance to the country, *"reinforc(ing) the idea of citizenship as a reward for a complete successful integration into Danish society"*: MIDTBØEN (2015) 7

479 For analysis of the roots and development of the "integration before naturalisation" principle in Germany, see Brenner in GÖKTÜRK/GRAMLING/KAES (2007) p. 176 et seq.

480 With regard to the amendments of the Luxembourgish law in this respect, see Horner in HOGAN-BRUN/MAR-MOLINERO/STEVENSON (2009) p. 117

481 For an extensive analysis see WALLACE GOODMAN (2014)

482 See e.g. the analysis of *Markou and Parthenis* in CATARCI/FIORUCCI (2015)

483 For the further tightening of the Swiss law in this respect and beyond, see ACHERMANN/D'AMATO/KAMM/VON RÜTTE, EUDO Citizenship Observatory Country report: Switzerland (revised 2013)

484 For the "New Style" integration policy of the Netherlands, introduced in 2003, and beyond, see DE VRIES, Chapter 3

485 The term assimilation is commonly defined as the adaptation of one group to the norms of another as a one-sided process, and contrasts to integration, which requires both groups to adapt, and for which responsibility generally flows back to the State for the maintenance of cohesion in the system, cf. REICHEL (2011)

486 Public goods are defined in financial theory as: firstly, those characterised by a lack of substitution in consumption; and secondly, those to which the exclusion principle is not applicable. Public goods are therefore not dependent on direct payment and nor is the extent to which benefit is derived dependent on the price paid cf. BECHTHOLD (2008); GRAF (2005); ZIMMERMANN (1999)

subsidiarity and which is sustained by civil commitment. The relevant State monopoly helps control access to these uneconomic goods and thereby fulfils its obligations arising from human dignity and other constitutional principles.

4.3 External functions

4.3.1 Clear and unambiguous assignment of rights in international and transnational issues

Citizenship requires the clear demarcation of the domestic legal system at the national level, based on the mapping of individual rights in relation to other subjects of public international law, to help ensure the clear and unambiguous assignment of rights. This is particularly significant when it comes to understanding the welfare function of the State of residence, which to some extent requires the equivalent of the loyalty of citizens for the national community, concretised especially in the granting of consular and diplomatic protection.[487] The separation between national and State functions beyond citizenship corresponds to that between the internal and external sovereignty of a State. The latter describes a subject's independence from other States and defines its position with respect to the outside world in the sense of public international law.[488]

4.3.2 Diplomatic and consular protection

The granting of citizenship aims to ensure that protection claimed extraterritorially from the home State works as seamlessly as possible. Even though most citizens never need diplomatic protection, the question of what constitutes diplomatic protection[489] does arise, especially in extreme cases such as in the international law-violating conditions in *Guantanamo Bay*, or in the problematic situation of stateless persons.[490] The passport of a respected and in particular of a powerful State like the US offers

487 cf. FELTHAM (2006), regarding diplomatic protection in respect of statelessness cf. SILENT (2011)
488 cf. DIETRICH (2011)
489 cf. JOPPKE (2010); AMERASINGHE (2008); and DENZA (1998)
490 STILLER (2011)

its owner even a certain amount of *de facto* protection against arbitrary treatment abroad.[491]

The value of diplomatic and consular protection has, however, greatly reduced in view of the ever-increasing importance of universal human rights and international law. Until the early twentieth century diplomatic or consular protection was practically the only protection against the misuse of State power encountered abroad.[492] Today, human rights provide universally recognised standards which are protected or asserted in various conventions and international institutions.

4.3.3 Avoidance of statelessness

The award of at least one nationality is an essential basis for granting extensive rights, as is exemplarily demonstrated by the differentiation between resident and non-resident constitutional rights. Citizenship is for the individual the primary way to gain standing in public international law – or even in law at all:[493]

> *"...citizenship is man's basic right for it is nothing less than the right to have rights."*[494]

Arendt also speaks of the fundamental importance of "the right to have rights", and this is as *Benhabib*[495] also points out, why it is essential for humanitarian reasons that: "*the State itself is the critical mechanism in advancing human rights.*"[496] It is also the polity's basis of access to welfare. It shows the close factual proximity of citizenship and human dignity, including at the European level within the scope of the Lisbon Treaty through the Article 1(1) of the German Constitution, which has produced

491 cf. SALTER (2003)
492 SPIRO (2008); DENZA (1998)
493 STILLER (2011)
494 Chief Justice Earl Warren in *Perez v. Brownell*, 356 US 44, 64 (1957); cf. also *Afroyim v. Rusk*, 387 US 253 (1967), which prevented the government from revoking citizenship against the will of the person concerned
495 cf. BENHABIB (2004) pp. 49–129
496 JACOBSON (1996) p. 15

the so-called "object formula",[497] prohibiting the treatment of a person as a mere object of State action, including by rendering the person defenceless and applied as such not only by German courts but also by the ECtHR.[498]

The risk that individuals become defenceless before State law appears particularly acute if it cannot be determined definitively which country (the country of residence, the country of origin or the country of employment) is committed to providing welfare from among several relevant States. The case of homelessness is an effective illustration of where timely assistance should be effectively exercised by State authority but can be brought into question by failures related to citizenship. Conflicts of jurisdiction and civic issues such as the right to vote or the obligation to pay personal income tax, and humanitarian issues such as legal proceedings for the granting of extraterritorial assistance or extradition to the country or origin,[499] all complicate cases where excessive delay in offering assistance can amount to an existential issue for the person in need.

Article 15(2) UDHR provides against this background that no one shall be deprived arbitrarily of his nationality. The objective is the avoidance of "statelessness",[500] which from a purely logical point of view – considering *Jellinek's* three-element theory according to which the constitutive people forms the basis of organised law – seems barely conceivable, but which can and does result from the international heterogeneity in nationally-oriented citizenship law, especially from the aforementioned intergovernmental conflicts of jurisdiction, and as unpleasant as the consequences of statelessness for individuals may be, they are not illegal.[501]

4.3.4 Ensuring cross-border family ties

Citizenship also includes as one of its function the fostering of sustainable peaceful social relations within a community, by setting appropriate

[497] For extensive explanation on the object-formula see BRATILOVEANU
[498] See, for instance: ECtHR, *Tyrer c. Royaume-Uni*, 25 April 1978 (Appl. no 5856/72) para. 33
[499] cf. FORTMANN (2005); In this context, just imagine yourself in the refugee camps in North France Pas de Calais or between North Africa and Italy
[500] cf. *Blitz/Lynch* in BLITZ/LYNCH (2011)
[501] STILLER (2011)

incentives and stimulating civic engagement, permitting the State within the meaning of subsidiarity to retreat to its original core activities (schools, homeland security, transport etc.) and to enabling the increase in individual liberty for all people.

To achieve the aforementioned objectives, it is particularly necessary to support the cohesion of families as the foundation of a free society – in the sense of enabling family members to live together in one place to support each other,[502] and in particular to establish livelihoods that permit independent economic existence beyond State benefits. In light of that, Article 16(3) UDHR provides that the family is the natural basis of society and is entitled to protection by society and the State. Although Article 16(3) UDHR thus still does not constitute an individual-subjective right to family reunification and the issue of entry permits remains at the discretion of the host country, what can be derived from Article 16(3) UDHR in conjunction with the general prohibition of discrimination in Article 12(1) UDHR – that no one shall be subjected to arbitrary interference with his family – is an obligation to respect the common family life of foreigners, if a family member has already been lawfully resident in the host country.[503] A national law on the basis of *ius soli* reduces this problem because a person born in the host country *ipso iure* acquires local citizenship directly or for example if one parent was lawfully resident in the host country and meets the applicable minimum time criteria.

There was interesting debate on the guarantee of cross-border family ties in the context of the 1990 reform to the Citizenship Law of the Federal Republic of Germany, which adopted a paradigm shift in its stronger emphasis on *ius soli*[504] motivated by the concern for the intergenerational family ties of the families of "guest workers", i.e., the support labour recruited for the reconstruction of Germany in the nineteen-sixties, which remained and found other livelihoods. This shift in emphasis to *ius soli* does not only find its binding expression in Article 16(3)

502 For greater detail on the problem of family reunification in Europe: WALTER (2009)
503 cf. WALTER (2009)
504 cf. VON MÜNCH (2007); and MASING (2001)

read with Article 12(1) UDHR, but also Article 33 Paragraph 1 EU Charter, which provides for the legal, economic and social protection of the family. The nation State design of citizenship law does not preclude family reunification within the scope of the EU. In Switzerland, however, such a shift in emphasis remains outstanding and it is uncertain whether Switzerland will move in this direction in the foreseeable future.

4.3.5 Effective suppression and sanctioning of violations of public international law by individuals

Under public international law, one of the basic requirements for State sovereignty emanating from the State people to be exercised effectively by special organs of State power, is that violations of State law are sanctioned consistently. The fundamental requirement for the international recognition of an organised community as a State is the unambiguous definition of its territory and its ability to effectively exercise control over this area.[505] A State under public international law is only sovereign if it has a functioning monopoly on authority and the use of violence, to echo the social scientist *Max Weber*,[506] is respected by its nationals, and determines violations of public law consistently. The State's duty of care remains irrespective of the location of the person in question, following from of the spatially unlimited effect of nationality corresponding to the extent of the State's duty of action and intervention when its nationals violate norms of public international law.

4.4 Additional non-State functions

Economic globalisation has increasingly led to comparison being drawn between legal systems: what can emerging economies (e.g. Brazil, Russia, Turkey, India, Indonesia or China) do better than established industrialised countries? With respect to settlement, there is far more to compare than the juxtaposition of economic conditions, such as the lowest tax rates, the most liberal corporate regulation or the best possible protection of intellectual property. In view of the fact that the granting of citizenship

---

505 cf. *Hailbronner* in HAILBRONNER/RENNER/MAASSEN (2010)
506 cf. WEBER (1972)

implies a pluralistic and decentralised structure worldwide – with only States being the primary subjects of public international law as holders of sovereign rights, the expression of organically grown traditions and cultures – the comparison of legal systems comes to encompass nationality-relevant parameters such as civic engagement, the constitution of State power by means of elections and voting, the communication and transparency of administrative processes (citizen-based management) or the granting of social rights. Constitutionally organised states – in particular along the lines of federally structured communities such as the Swiss Confederation, Canada, the US or the Federal Republic of Germany – enable comparison and support the formation of an "experimental chamber" to obtain reliable findings on which political order is the most durable and corresponds most closely to the predominant concern of citizenship, a permanent peace within a community and the greatest possible withdrawal of State intervention in the stimulation of civil society forces.

In particular, the effective protection of (ethnic, linguistic and cultural) minorities, which require the greatest possible certainty of legal norms and the prevention of demoscopic regulation, militates against material entrenchment of the concept of citizenship and for the reduction of nationality to the function of a formal connecting link between a natural person and the national legal order. State sovereignty is the spearhead of a democratic constitutional order in which the decision-making processes work from the bottom up, i.e. extend from the national to the State decision-making bodies. Nor can cultural or civic engagement be imposed from the top down in a domestic order. An example in this respect is the former Yugoslavia, where different ethnic groups were held together against their will under the umbrella of a forced State order. This example underlines the fact that the regulation of citizenship must map organically grown structures and cannot be abstracted, so that disasters like *Srebrenica* and *Sarajevo* will not repeat themselves in the twenty-first century. Enabled through the "institution" of citizenship, our decentralised world structure suggests how this can best be achieved.

4.5 Functions of modern citizenship concepts

4.5.1 Improving the coherence between labour supply and labour demand

Assuming the proper design of the citizenship laws at the level of nation States, such laws could significantly functionally contribute to improving the coherence between labour demand and labour supply. This can be observed especially within the EU, and CARICOM. To avoid repetition, the reader is referred to the analysis *supra*.

4.5.2 Controling of demographic, social and economic structural deficits

Ultimately, the endogenous factor of demographic change and the exogenous factor of transnational labour migration are likely to cause a redefinition both of the concept of citizenship and the functions it pursues. The latter not only brings about the increasing divergence between the State and the people, but also between those who speak the national language and those who do not. To clarify this: the question is not the horizontal relationship between workers and employers who in international companies already have English as the common company language, but that between the rulers and ruled, between the State and the individual.

4.5.3 Promoting direct investment

Of central interest here is the function of national legal arrangements for managing and promoting direct investment. States have since ancient times used in different ways the fact that their citizenship is a "good" that is in demand.[507] Because of this demand situation, citizenship may well acquire various other features which are in the interests of the State, for example, the recruitment of foreign military personnel for use in wars (as was common practice throughout history, and to the present day in France with the French Foreign Legion[508] or as the US generally provides[509] for the

[507] cf. the discussion on "Economic Theory of Clubs" in section 10
[508] PORCH (2010)
[509] USC. 8, cf. SPIRO (2008)

US Army) – where citizenship is provided in return for the soldiers' commitment. Another example is the recruitment of elite foreign athletes for national teams in the Olympic Games or other world sporting championships, gaining not only the privilege of competing for the State concerned in such games in return for their efforts, but also citizenship itself.[510] Similarly, citizenship can perform the function of recruiting foreign investors, who are granted citizenship for their significant direct investment or economic contribution to the country: Citizenship-by-Investment, or *ius doni*, a function on which increasingly many States are beginning to rely on.[511]

510 SHACHAR (2011)

511 cf. XU/EL-ASHRAM/GOLD (2015); KÄLIN (2014)

5

The Constitutional and Political Dimensions of Citizenship

5.1 Citizenship law as a prerogative of nation States and expression of national sovereignty

The power of a State to regulate its citizenship legislation and population movement is in theory autonomous, within certain very broad international limits as an expression of its territorial sovereignty, and is in this respect fundamental to the existence of the modern nation-state system as well as to national sovereignty.[512] Citizenship's national character and national location are treated as axiomatic.[513]

The territorial sovereignty describes the status of a national community which is not subject to direction from other authorities, except for those international legal obligations voluntarily ratified, and includes as an integral part of its territorial sovereignty the sense of authority, the effective and legal exercise of State power.[514] While this can be described as its prerogative to exercise sovereign power in a given spatial region, the territorial sovereignty of a State – *Jellinek* emphasises that the development of any State and its activities can only be on the basis of spatial development and to the spatial extent that the State requires to exist – denotes the assignment of a given area to a State and its power to possess that: territorial sovereignty determines the territory and its borders.[515]

In *France vs. Turkey* the *Permanent Court of Justice* held in a judgment in 1929:

> *"The rules of law binding upon States...emanate from their own free will... [R]estrictions upon independence of States therefore cannot be presumed".*[516]

---

512 *Zolberg*, cited in SOYSAL (1994) p. 120; cf. also DONNER (1994), and in terms of the European Convention on Citizenship as a barrier to the provisions of national citizenship law cf. KNOCKE (2005)

513 BOSNIAK (2006)

514 cf. *Vitzthum* in VITZTHUM (2006)

515 cf. ERBGUTH/MAHLBURG (2003); and JELLINEK (1976)

516 cited by DONNER (1994) p. 10

This must also require that any limitation on the right of States to design their citizenship laws be demonstrated in bilateral or multilateral treaties, to which the States submit voluntarily.[517]

According to the traditional understanding of the State, according to *Jellinek* this can be described as constituted generally from the sum of public law in the territory, the constituent people and State power (the "three-element theory", cf. *supra*). Given that the sustainable performance of a State's obligations under public international law only seems realistic under the premise of a permanent order, the national community must be able to meet its obligations under public international law sustainably, including to be able to provide a certain degree of *ex-ante* organisational stability for the permanent existence of the State order.[518] Under effective authority,[519] the constituent people must be organised within a certain territory according to the theory of *Jellinek*.[520] The three-element theory views the State as a primary subject of public international law, and which we again recall is composed of the territory, the constituent people and a unitary (effectively exercised) State authority.[521]

From the three-element theory can be deduced that a State is an association of persons necessarily exercising its powers in a certain territory.[522] State power can only be exercised lawfully in respect of public international law within the frame defined by the spatial extent of the legitimacy-creating sovereign. It is one of the fundamental constitutional achievements of the constituent people that it does not submit itself individually to State power, but transfers sovereign powers by means of the Constitution to those State organs which exercise them under the constitutional monopoly of power held in trust on behalf of the legitimacy-creating sovereign. The exercise of public authority outside the frame thus drawn cannot be based on an order of the legitimacy-creating sovereign, as it would thus violate the territorial integrity of the

517 DONNER (1994) p. 11 et seq.
518 cf. *Hailbronner/Kau* in VITZTHUM (2010)
519 cf. *Aleinikoff/Klusmeyer* in ALEINIKOFF/KLUSMEYER (2001)
520 cf. JELLINEK (1976)
521 cf. IPSEN (2011)
522 cf. IPSEN (2011)

host country and is illegal under public international law insofar as the specific conduct is to be regarded as the exercise of State power.

The three-element theory and the effective exercise of State power implies in particular that the State must be able to enter into diplomatic or foreign relations to engage with and respect public international law.[523]

Once the national territory is defined under international law, the State authority can legitimate its power through the regular holding of elections and referenda – upholding the internationally recognised democratic principles – to address directly the sovereign concerns of the constituent people. This constitutes full citizenship.[524]

5.2 Definition of a nation State

Closely linked to citizenship is the definition of nation State,[525] as the international law subject for scope of action in citizenship law. Can the essential structural features that constituted a national polity in the Greek *polis* to be found in the modern community of the twenty-first century – a relatively uncontroversial idea under *Jellinek's* three-element theory, albeit with a culturally and historically conditioned different accent – despite the nation State in the modern sense being a comparatively recent phenomenon? Ultimately, it is in the definition of the State as a nation State that an indefinite number of persons can be organised into a structured community within defined bounds that is capable of attributing to itself permanent sovereign territorial rights under the international legal order.

---

523 cf. AUST (2007); *Hailbronner* in ALEINKOFF/CHETAIL (2003); KOKOTT/DOEHRING/BUERGENTHAL (2003)

524 cf. *Epping/Gloria* in IPSEN (2004); *Hailbronner* in HAILBRONNER/RENNER/MAASSEN (2010); *Kokott* in SACHS (2009)

525 For the nation State model cf. *Brubaker* in SHAFIR (1998); *Fong* in TALANI (2012); *Ford* in ALEINIKOFF/KLUSMEYER (2011)

5.2.1 Emergence of historical development lines

So as to not repeat the already outlined historical background *supra*, only a few key aspects of important historical development lines of the nation state are outlined here.

The ideas advanced during the Enlightenment and the French Revolution in the years after 1789 – especially by *Voltaire*, *Rousseau* and *Kant*, are those most likely to act as an inspiration and pioneer a paradigm shift in the organisation of the State in this context – whose beginnings are situated in the eighteenth century. Its emergence can be explained by the growing secularisation and the waning influence of the (Roman Catholic) Church. However, also the increasing individual awareness of the individual seen in the American[526] and French Revolutions,[527] as well as that the revealed in the decline of the Holy Roman Empire and the rise of the German nation[528] in 1806, contributed significantly to this.

On closer inspection, one of the many roots of the present-day nation State, which places an ever-greater emphasis on the individual and has accompanied his democratic maturity from subject to citizen, already dates back to 1517, when *Martin Luther* nailed his 95 theses against Roman Catholic authority to the door of the Castle Church in Wittenberg, at the heart of which was the assertion that belief in God is direct and did not require mediation by any secular or ecclesiastical authorities. The strengthening of individual awareness was thus promoted into German from Greek or Latin by Luther's translation of the New Testament, which he completed at the Wartburg[529] near Eisenach. From then on the people were also able to obtain information about State and civil law without the intervention of religious and secular authorities

526 cf. ZOLBERG (2006); PICKUS (1998)

527 For a nation State conception of France cf. *Brubaker* in SHAFIR (1998); and WEIL (2004)

528 The Holy Roman Empire of the German Nation extended from around the 10th Century after Christ until the year 1806 and found its culmination in the Congress of Vienna in 1815, and the conception of the nation State of Germany cf. *Brubaker* in SHAFIR (1998)

529 The Wartburg in Thuringia has a symbolic power for the awareness of the Germans as a unified nation that can hardly be overestimated which results not only from the person Martin Luther, but can also be explained by the Wartburg Festival of 1817, where the national colours of black, red and gold, which at that time were officially banned, were shown publicly for the first time in German history.

to interpret the essential tenets of Western jurisdictions. The empowerment of nationals as *citoyens* requires that comprehensive information is as accessible at all times and in any place to make informed and effective decisions.

Despite the partial setbacks of the 1815 Congress of Vienna or the – failed – Assembly at St Paul's in Frankfurt am Main in 1848, *Martin Luther* will forever be intellectually linked with the reformation process, as the trigger of the development of the continental European nation State, in the face of increasing individual awareness of State and government, and with the maturation of the *sujet citoyen*, which began no later than in the nineteenth century in a "national assembly". This was to take place in France in the Paris "February Revolution" of 24 February 1848, with the abdication of the "citizen king" *Louis Philippe of Orléans* and the beginning of the Second French Republic. It also found expression in Germany in the Hambach Festival of 1832 and led in both cases to concessions being wrested from the royal houses which spelt the end of the Absolutist age.[530]

The initial mutual recognition of the sovereignty of States going back to the *Peace of Westphalia* is another of the essential origins of the modern nation State system. The international expansion of the European nation State model – through colonisation, economic interdependence, role modelling etc. – meant that this is now established worldwide and universally accepted.[531]

5.2.2 The national colours as a vehicle of national awareness

Like at the Wartburg Festival in 1817, the Hambach Festival saw the tricolour of black, red and gold – one of the predominant identifying features of the Federal Republic of Germany since 1949 – raised instead of the official State colours (black, red and white).[532] Here again, the French Constitution has played the role of "Godfather" since 1791, when

530 cf. WESEL (2006)
531 HOBSBAWM (1992); GIDDENS (1985)
532 Article 22(2) of the Basic Law ("The German flag is black-red-gold")

Article 2, paragraph 2 of the French Constitution prominently declared that the national emblem would be the blue, white and red tricolour and that the "French" would be identified as a "Grande Nation" through is essential symbols such as its language (Article 2(1) French Constitution), National Anthem (Article 2(2) French Constitution) and the Republican motto "Liberty, Equality, Fraternity" (Article 2(3) French Constitution). Their importance for the awareness of the French nation – even if they appear tainted by chauvinism or seem mundane, depending on political perspective – can hardly be overestimated, and this underlines that the Revolution of 1789 and subsequent years was a "revolution from below", i.e. a victory for individual awareness over the State. In addition to the French and German constitutions, national colours provisions are found, *inter alia*, in the Austrian Federal Constitution (Article 8a(1) ÖB-VG) and in many other countries.

5.2.3 Language as a vehicle of national awareness

Against this historical background highlighting the process of maturity of the individual to become a self-confident sovereign from a faithful subject of authoritarianism, it is clear that the nation State is not and should not be the result of authoritarian dictation, but a "bottom up" development, i.e. based on the shared core beliefs of individuals and the State power, who belong together based on a feeling or sense of solidarity from sharing (lived) traditions, common (living) culture (music, theatre, art, literature etc.) and above all a common language (for example Article 2, Paragraph 1 French Constitution, Article 8, Section 1 ÖB-VG).[533] This means that the sometimes artificial and clinical State as a political-administrative construct acquires an identity which, given the fundamental functions of citizenship laws (integration, inner peace, enabling the principle of subsidiarity to guide civil society) and the connecting factor of the legal bond, links the domestic people with their laws. The common language as an identifying feature of a nation finds its corrective in minority protection, which is underlined in France

[533] According to this provision, the German language is the State language of the Republic (Austria), without prejudice to the linguistic minorities acknowledged by federal law

by the constitutional clarification that the regional languages are part of the cultural heritage of France (Article 75-1 French Constitution), and is expressed in Austria in that the German language there is made State language of the Republic of Austria (Article 8, paragraph 1 HS. 2 ÖB-VG), only without prejudice of the linguistic minorities.

In most multilingual countries such as Switzerland, Belgium, Canada, etc., however, the language naturally plays no or only a limited role in national awareness, but rather the language-related awareness is shifted to the subnational constituents of the country (e.g. Flemish and Walloon communities in Belgium, Québécois and English-speaking Canadians, etc.)

5.2.4 The nation State in the information age

Driven by new information and communication media such as the Internet, with all its social networks, the autonomy of the individual has reached a level of development where nation State structures can sometimes seem almost redundant, and moving supranational and quasi-governmental structures to the centre seems appropriate – you need only reflect on the decline seen in the majority of EU Member States and other Western-style democracies of participation in the parliamentary elections, the calls for a greater involvement of the individual in government decision-making, or the debate on conscription in France, Germany and other countries. This can cause us to question whether the nation State continues to exist now in its established form, and whether it has a future.

Through providing regular income to their employees, multinational companies are creating increasingly large groups of people who share their corporate cultures, a common "corporate language" – given its importance as a world language, it is almost always English – and internally binding codes of conduct which increasingly seem[534] to compete with nation State cultures, becoming at their scale a "law" in addition

[534] cf. also from an American perspective SPIRO (2008)

to the law. This trend is fed and complimented by the growing dominance of social networks such as *Facebook* or *Twitter*, which for instance played a crucial role in the protests in Iran in June 2009, in the "Arab Spring" or, more recently, in Russia and Ukraine, and continues to play, to channel discontent with the State system, to help the domestic population overcome unwanted State systems and which – given the size and power of the membership of social networks – can sometimes take on State structures. *Facebook* is thus working on its own "currency" and *Bitcoin* is already established as a State-independent *peer-to-peer* currency and increasingly accepted method of payment.[535] Considering their international dimension, such trends cannot but have an impact on the nation State and highlight the importance of the organisation of global citizenship. This will also be discussed below, in considering the nature and limits of the national discretion in the area of citizenship.

5.3 Nation State discretion in the area of citizenship

The starting point for our deliberations is the background presented of the national government's discretion in citizenship matters,[536] which is recognised in the EU law,[537] as well as at the international level as illustrated among many others in the *Nottebohm* decision of the ICJ, as being directly linked to national State sovereignty and the right of each State to manage its citizenship laws autonomously, i.e. to regulate this field in statute within the limits of its territory. It is important to stress that while the ICJ did not consider that *Nottebohm* was entitled to diplomatic protection, the conferral of citizenship was in fact valid despite lacking a "genuine link".[538] The general freedom of States in terms of citizenship

535 http://bitcoin.org

536 cf. HERDEGEN (2010); *Stern* in STERN (1977)

537 As noted in by the ECJ in its judgment in C-369/90 (1992) (*Micheletti*), "*Under international law, it is for each Member State, having due regard to Community law, to lay down the conditions for the acquisition and loss of nationality. However, it is not permissible for the legislation of a Member State to restrict the effects of the nationality of another Member State by imposing an additional condition for recognition of that nationality with a view to the exercise of the fundamental freedoms provided for in the Treaty*" (para. 10). See along similar lines: paras. 19-27 of the ECJ's judgment in C-192/99 (2001) (*Kaur*), paras. 39-41 of ECJ's judgment in C-135/08 (2010) (*Rottmann*)

538 CARRERA (2014)

laws is a well established principle[539] of public international law, even if in a European context there are limits set to national citizenship provisions[540] by virtue of a multilateral agreement (the European Convention on Nationality) and following the decision in *Rottmann*,[541] restrictions for EU Member States set by the ECJ.[542]

Nation State sovereignty[543] can be assigned various functions in this context,[544] ranging from mere regulatory law on integration and immigration control to the protection of ethnic, cultural, political and religious minorities. On the one hand, nation State sovereignty defines the status of a community exclusively subordinated to public international law and thus to international law directly (so-called "internal sovereignty"), and on the other hand, underpins an obligation not to intervene in other countries out of respect for their territorial sovereignty[545] and thus for peace (so-called "external sovereignty").[546] Had the UK in its Naturalisation Act of 1870 for example granted British Citizenship to all the world's native English speakers, this would have been responded to by a declaration of war by the US:[547] the completely arbitrary grant of nationality to another State's detriment would be illegal under public international law.

---

539 cf. DONNER (1994), or also the decision of the Permanent Court of Justice in the Lotus Case (*France v. Turkey*, PCIJ (1927) A No. 10: *"International Law governs the relations between independent States. The rules of law binding upon States therefore emanate from their own free will"*

540 cf. KNOCKE (2005)

541 ECJ C-135/08 (2010), although this case should be further qualified. While the ECJ recommended that the national court takes the principles of EU law into account, it was up to the national court to apply EU law (paras. 48 et seq.), which is why *Dr. Rottmann* is now stateless. EU law, while capable in principle to defend the individual EU citizen's nationality, in practice has only a limited power to do it

542 cf. specifically SHAW (2011)

543 For greater detail on the concept of national sovereignty in the context of Europeanisation and globalisation: cf. *Burchell* in ISIN/TURNER (2002/2011); *Fong* in TALANI (2012); *Hailbronner* in HAILBRONNER/MARTIN (2011); with reference to the situation in France: *Weil* in HANSEN/WEIL (2001); with reference to the situation in Germany, see BRUBAKER (1992)

544 For greater detail on the different functions of nationality: WIESSNER (1989)

545 For more on the content of the principle of the external sovereignty of a State, especially the principle of non-interference in the internal affairs of another State and the principle of territorial integrity, see LOWE (2007)

546 cf. *Hailbronner/Kau* in VITZTHUM (2010)

547 According to TRIEPEL (1929)

As a concretisation of nation States' "external sovereignty", nationality performs the function of delineating the personal sovereignty of the States themselves.[548] If one interprets the nation State of modern design as being born out of a decision-making process that runs from the governed to the governors, and thus as a specific case of the principle of democracy in the broadest sense, national sovereignty can of course only be as far ranging as the mandate of the national legislature obtained from the votes and elections of the State people. The nation State design of citizenship is recognised by other States and subjects of public international law, insofar as it relates to applicable international conventions, customary international law and with respect to general principles of law.[549]

Within the limits of public international law and thus the precise limits of its sovereignty, each State regulates itself when and under what conditions someone acquires and loses its citizenship.[550] As set out in Article 1(1) of the Hague Convention, each State is entitled (as a subject of public international law) to determine by its laws, who should possess its citizenship.[551] National citizenship is thus one of the constituent elements of the political system, not least also of the 28 EU Member States, and falls under the protection of national identity, which is addressed in Article 4(2) TEU.[552] Accordingly, the EU must respect the equality of the Member States before the Treaties and their national identity, their fundamental political and constitutional structures, including the regional and local self-government (Article 4(2) TEU first sentence). The

---

548 cf. GOEBEL-ZIMMERMANN (2000)

549 cf. for example in Germany *Federal Constitutional Court*, decision of 28 May 1952, 1 BvR 213/51, Federal Constitutional Court 1, pp. 322, 329

550 *Federal Constitutional Court*, decision of 21 May 1974, 1 BvL 22/71 and 21/72, Federal Constitutional Court 37, pp. 217, 218

551 The case law of the German Federal Constitutional Court (Bundesverfassungsgericht) emphasises the extent to which EU Member State discretion persists in this area even under the Treaty of Lisbon, enabling differentiation on the basis of nationality, see *Federal Constitutional Court*, judgment 30 June 2009 – Case 2 BvE 2/08, 2 BvE 5/08, 2 BvR 1010/08, 2 BvR 1022/08, 2 BvR 1259/08, 2 BvR 182/09 – published online at http://www.servat.unibe.ch/dfr/bv123267.html, last accessed on 21 September 2012, the Europeanisation of immigration law under the validity of the Treaty of Lisbon cf. HECKER (1970)

552 cf. HAILBRONNER (2011)

national discretion to regulate citizenship is thus the primary expression of national sovereignty.

6

Principles of Citizenship Acquisition

6.1 Immigration and emigration countries

A preliminary comparative rule appears to be that the development of the modern citizenship law of a country is mostly correlated with whether the migration flows were predominantly inward in recent history – in which case we are talking about immigration countries (or settler countries)[553] – or outward – in which case we speak of emigration countries. The term immigration country is represented here especially by those countries whose populations increased markedly through immigration of people from other countries, and historically whose populations were mainly composed of immigrants or in which immigrants represent a substantial part of the population. In addition to Canada and the US,[554] almost all other States in Central and South America, as well as South Africa, Australia and New Zealand are classic immigration countries.[555] The UK had actually become an immigration country before the great waves of migration to the New World.[556]

Classic immigration countries such as the US of America, Canada, New Zealand and Australia, as well as many of the Latin American States, are particularly characterised as such by the fact that they were founded by immigrants and have populations, the majority of whom were drawn from immigrants or their descendants; "emigration countries" in contrast, are primarily shaped by their traditional populations, consisting to a considerable extent of sedentary people who have comprised the majority constituent "core population" in an area for centuries, and maintain connections with members of their group who become immigrants elsewhere.[557] This includes most European States.

---

553 The term immigration countries or "*settler countries*" (JANOSKI 2010) is understood here as those States whose population originated through immigration from other countries or where immigrants represent a substantial part of the population

554 cf. ZOLBERG (2006); cf. also AMRHEIN/LINDQUIST/YALE-LOEHR/DANIELSON (2011) for a good explanation of what has defined the US as a nation of immigrants from all walks of life, from all corners of the world

555 Also partly Russia during the eighteenth and nineteenth centuries

556 SCHULTE BEERBÜHL (2007) p. 1 et seq.

557 cf. WEIL (2012)

In its most classic form, immigration countries traditionally follow the principle of territoriality (*ius soli*). They bind the acquisition of citizenship primarily to birth in the country and only secondarily to the citizenship of the natural or adopted parents.[558]

Emigration countries, however – this includes historically almost all European countries (previously Ireland, Italy and Poland and other Eastern European States)[559] but also India, Pakistan, Japan, China, many African countries and almost all others which emerged from the recent colonial States – primarily follow the principle of descent (*ius sanguinis*), which ensures that the emigrant populations do not lose their citizenship but transfer this to the next generation where they have settled. Many of these countries also suffer from a significant brain drain, i.e. mass migration of top-level manpower from underdeveloped countries to wealthy countries.[560]

Furthermore, classic immigration countries such as, in particular, the US and Canada are characterised, at least today, by a pronounced multi-cultural society. They arrived at this now dominant principle of "source-country universalism",[561] according to which immigrants are selected as individuals and not as representatives of particular ethnic groups or countries and regions, only after having very significantly violated it, in the form of racially exclusive immigration policies in force for most of the late nineteenth and well into the latter half of the twentieth century.[562] More than 100 different languages are spoken, for example, in the Canadian province of Ontario. Although Canada is by area the second largest country in the world, it is characterised by substantial regional differences resulting from the cultural traditions of its provinces and territories, and especially by the differences in the penetration of technological and cultural developments. Canada has been for many

---

558 Concerning the United States, see SPIRO (2008)
559 See in regard to the European States RANDALL/WEIL (2001)
560 HUNGER (2003) pp. 58–60, BARNHILL (2012) p. 143 et seq.; cf. also ADAMS (1968)
561 SCHUCK (1991); and JOPPKE (2005)
562 JOPPKE (2005)

years regarded as the model country[563] among the immigration countries. The multicultural citizenship of Canada was portrayed as a role model for other countries in this regard; recently however, previous steps toward liberalisation and multiculturalisation in immigration policies have again been reversed by many countries, including Canada.[564]

6.2 Types of citizenship acquisition

A fundamental first distinction can be drawn between the acquisition of citizenship at birth (of origin) and acquisition after birth.

The types of acquisition at birth are distinguished into the *ius sanguinis* at birth and *ius soli* at birth. The types of acquisition after birth can be distinguish into *ius sanguinis*[565] or *ius soli*, acquisition based on family relations, by affinity (e.g. ethnic or religious affiliation) and naturalisation, including Citizenship-by-Investment.

The following table according to *Waldrauch* gives a comprehensive overview of the various possible types of acquisition and the systematic, detailed division into groups and subgroups.

Of particular interest and examined in greater detail below, are the original acquisition types (acquisition at birth) and the acquisition by naturalisation, in particular naturalisation by extraordinary (financial) contributions to the State.

[563] On the relevant requirements and challenges cf. *Kymklicka in* SHAFIR (1998); on the immigration policy of Canada cf. *Soysal* in SHAFIR (1998); and SCHMIDTKE (2003)

[564] WINTER (2013)

[565] Which still should be considered as an original acquisition

Typology of Citizenship Acquisition Modes

Group of Modes	*Sub-group*	*ID*	*Mode of acquisition of Citizenship*
Birthright-based modes of acquisition at birth	*ius sanguinis* at birth	A01	Acquisition by persons born to citizens of C1
	ius soli at birth	A02	Acquisition by person born in C1 (except those classified under mode A03)
		A03	Acquisition by persons who are foundings, by persons born in C1 of unclear citizenship or persons born in C1 who would otherwise be stateless
Modes of acquisition after birth	Birthright-based modes	A04	*ius sanguinis after birth: acquisition by persons whose relevant parent was a C1 citizen at the time of their birth*
		A05	*Ius soli after birth: acquisition by persons born (or assumed to have been born) in C1*
	Basic residence-based modes	A06	Residence-based acquisition by persons with a certain period of residence in C1 with no other special status
		A07	Socialisation-based acquisition by persons raised (while minors) in C1
	Family relation-based modes	A08	Transfer of citizenship to spouses of citizens of C1 (spousal transfer)
		A09	Transfer of citizenship to children of persons who are now, but were not citizens of Cl at the time of the child's birth, or whose citizenship at that time is irrelevant (filial transfer)
		A10	Transfer of citizenship to adopted children of citizens of C1
		A11	Transfer of citizenship to other relatives of citizens of Cl
		A12	Transfer of citizenship to relatives (spouse, child, grandchild) of former or deceased citizens of C1
		A13	Extension of acquisition to spouses of foreign citizens who acquire citizenship of Cl (spousal extension)

Group of Modes	*Sub-group*	*ID*	*Mode of acquisition of Citizenship*
		A14	Extension of acquisition to children of foreign citizens who acquire citizenship of Cl (filial extension)
		A15	Extension of acquisition to other relatives of foreign citizens who acquire citizenship of C1
Modes of acquisition after birth	Affinity-based modes	Al6	Reacquisition by former citizens of Cl
		A17	Acquisition by special citizens with restricted citizenship
		A18	Acquisition by persons with citizenship of C2
		A19	Acquisition by persons with cultural affinity to Cl (special ethnicity, mother tongue or religion)
		A20	Acquisition by persons who acted as citizens of Cl in good faith and/or were presumed C1's citizens for some time
		A21	Acquisition by persons with other special connections to Cl
	Other targeted inodes	A22	Acquisition by recognised refugees
		A23	Acquisition by stateless persons or persons of unclear citizenship
		A24	Acquisition by persons with special achievements for Cl
		A25	Acquisition by persons in the public (military or non-military) service of Cl
		A26	Acquisition by persons with special financial assets and/or persons who invest money in C1
		A27	Other modes of acquisition

Notes: Cl = States whose rules for the acquisition of nationality are being described; C2 = foreign State subject to special rules, such as EU Member States, Member States of the other groups (e.g. the Nordic countries), countries with whom bilateral or multilateral agreements have been concluded. Adapted by the author from *Waldrauch* in BAUBÖCK/ERSBOLL/ GROENENDIJK/VALDRAUCH (2006), Vol. 1. Highlighted at (A26) is the author's own.

6.3 Acquisition at birth or original acquisition of citizenship

6.3.1 Ius soli: Territoriality and place of birth

According to the territorial principle, or *ius soli*,[566] which is a fundamental principle in the US, Canada and most Latin American countries, a natural person acquires his or her citizenship by birth in the respective territory. Its historical development is set out *supra*.[567]

The overriding concern of *ius soli* is to promote a high degree of congruence within a nation – meaning between the people who are actively and passively fully eligible to vote, and the domestic population as the totality of individuals with domestic residence or permanent place of habitual abode – and beyond this, to support integration in the sense of internal social cohesion in order to mobilise – according to the principles discussed above – the forces of civil society that allow the State to focus on its core tasks. The perspective of the French Revolution, where the territorial principle notably served to preserve the power of the ruling feudal monarch and to aid him in the reliable recruitment of the human military resources required to enforce his claim to power, becomes obsolete under the terms of transnational citizenship, economic globalisation and increasing penetration and interconnection of civil societies with the new digital media such as the Internet.

6.3.2 Ius sanguinis: principle of descent

The principle of descent or *ius sanguinis*[568] directs that the citizenship is transferred through direct blood relationship, i.e. through the natural parents of a child as the product of a long-term cohabitation between a man and a woman in the context of marriage or other consensual union. As detailed above, the principle of descent aims within the meaning of

---

566 For *ius soli* cf. HERDEGEN (2010); WEIL (2012); *Weil* in KÄLIN (2014); *Janoski/Gran* in ISIN/TURNER (2002/2011); *Margiotta/Vonk* in TALANI (2012); with respect to the United States, SPIRO (2008)

567 cf. section 2

568 For ius sanguinis cf. HERDEGEN (2010); WEIL (2012); *Weil* in KÄLIN (2014); *Smith* in ISIN/TURNER (2002/2011); *Zarnetske* in TALANI (2012)

subsidiarity primarily to the decentralised cohesion of smaller social units and, in particular, of families within a State polity. It was enforced in all European countries after the successful culmination of the French Revolution in 1789 and subsequent years. As the birthplace of a person frequently results by chance[569] and the closest relationship between people is that between parent and child, the *ius sanguinis* would in the past have been preferable to the *ius soli*, if one had to choose between the two.[570] Today there is a wide convergence in both directions: most countries use a mix between *ius soli* and *ius sanguinis*.[571] Only Austria and Switzerland are considered pure *ius sanguinis* countries among European States.

The objective of the principle of descent is primarily at guaranteeing both domestic and in particular the cross-border family ties and at promoting the identification with the established traditions and conventions of a State community against the other processes of assimilation. Given its historical development, the principle of descent, however, is also directed at strengthening the family in the sense of creating the necessary permanent coexistence or connectedness required as an essential component of the private authority of a social polity against the State authorities. From this perspective, *ius sanguinis* strengthens the defensive effect of a universally acknowledged and nationally concretised human dignity, whose essential purpose is to ensure that the individual as a free person is not degraded to a mere object of State force – at least within state borders. Given the increasing fragmentation of social structures in many European and non-European States, which results partly also from the increasing transnational mobility of workers and increasingly relativises the value of the family in the classical sense, however, the aforementioned basis for validity of the descent principle is also weakened. It therefore comes as no surprise that in all of Europe today, only Austria – the last remaining relic of the multi-ethnic State of Austria-Hungary resulting from the Habsburg Monarchy – and the directly democratic Switzerland apply the principle of descent as the absolutely dominant principle in their respective citizenship laws.

---

[569] Critical to this SPIRO (2008)
[570] VON MÜNCH (2007)
[571] For greater detail WEIL (2012); and *Weil* in KÄLIN (2014)

A particular variety of the principle of descent is the so-called "*law of return*", which is recognised in Israel, and which provides that every Jewish person is allowed to "return home" to Israel at any time and immediately acquires Israeli citizenship upon immigration to Israel.[572] In Germany, similar provisions are contained in Article 116(1) of the Constitution, which defines the term "German" and German "national", and grants refugees and displaced persons of German origin special legal status under certain conditions ("repatriated German").[573]

In some Eastern European countries and in Italy, it is also possible for people who can prove their descent to obtain the corresponding citizenship.[574] In Croatia, a country with a large diaspora both in Europe and overseas (America, but also Australia and New Zealand) for example, it is possible if Croatian descent can be shown to regain Croatian citizenship immediately.[575]

Ireland, which relative to its size has experienced in the past one of the largest mass emigrations in history, also has a very generous principle of descent, one of the most liberal in the world, which allows anyone who has at least one grandparent born in Ireland to regain Irish citizenship.[576]

6.3.3 Ius soli vs. ius sanguinis

When comparing the principle of descent with the territorial principle, it is evident that both systems have their advantages and disadvantages. The problems inherent to both is reflected in practice mainly by the fact that around the world, neither of the two principles has established itself as the primary one, and instead there persists an unharmonised coexistence of different principles bridged only partly by a number of international conventions.[577]

---

572 "Law of Return" 5710-1950 of the State Israel of 5 July 1950; cf. also SHAFIR/PELED (2002)

573 cf. VON MÜNCH (2007); TERNES (2011)

574 For example, in Poland (up to the third generation), Croatia, Romania and Bulgaria

575 Article 11 in connection with Article 8 of the Croatian Citizenship Act 2001 (Official Journal issues 53/1991, 70/1991, 28/1992, 113/1993, 4/1994, 130/2011)

576 cf. *Symmons* in HANSEN/WEIL (2001)

577 VON MÜNCH (2007); WEIL (2012)

PART II

Acquisition of Citizenship by Naturalisation

7

Naturalisation Principles

In the following, particular emphasis will be laid on the acquisition of citizenship by naturalisation. This type of acquisition will be analysed in greater detail, in particular the acquisition by ordinary naturalisation, which, systematically speaking, represents the actual basis for the extraordinary naturalisation through investment or other economic contributions to the State (Citizenship-by-Investment or *ius doni*) and naturalisation by other extraordinary contributions to the State (these could also be related to culture, sports, science, national politics or other), since for these exceptions, it is precisely the usual criteria or requirements of the ordinary naturalisation which are being waived because of the qualified investment or other extraordinary contributions to the State. Citizenship-by-Investment or *ius doni* is therefore not comparable to any other type of acquisition but is a *sui generis* type based on ordinary naturalisation, where the usual conditions such as residence, language skills etc. are waived or rather replaced by the requirement of investment (or more generally by the extraordinary contribution to the State).[578]

7.1 Ordinary naturalisation

To those denied access to a citizenship by birth or adoption, only the route through naturalisation is open.[579] Citizenship acquired by naturalisation forms a complement to the acquisition of citizenship by virtue of *ius soli* or *ius sanguinis* and is not linked to birth but requires a foreign citizen to actively apply,[580] and it can also unilaterally result directly from legal actions, such as marriage or the acquisition of immovable property.[581]

Further requirements for the acquisition of citizenship by naturalisation in the liberal nation State almost always include a certain minimum length of stay. Such a length of stay, which varies greatly depending on the State (e.g. two years in Singapore, all the way up to 10 years in Switzerland, 20 years in Brunei, and 30 years in Liechtenstein and the

578 cf. KÄLIN (2014)
579 BLOEMRAAD/KORTEWEG/YURDAKUL (2009)
580 VON MÜNCH (2007)
581 This occurred for example in Peru in the nineteenth century, cf. DONNER (1994)

UAE)[582] is the least controversial requirement, being an expression of the basic idea that the applicant should have lived for some time in the country in which she wants to become naturalised.[583]

Another prerequisite often required is language skills in the official language of the State where naturalisation is sought. In Europe, for example, only Belgium, Ireland, Italy and Sweden refrain from such requirements. Citizenship tests are amongst the other common requirements. While the traditional immigration countries – the USA, Canada, Australia and New Zealand – have all had naturalisation tests in one form or another for some time, citizenship tests in Europe are a rather recent phenomenon.[584] An important exception is Switzerland, which has long been familiar with such tests and where persons seeking naturalisation, depending on the canton and municipality, have had to endure some very far-reaching and detailed naturalisation tests.[585] Nevertheless, other States including Germany, France, the Netherlands and Denmark, now have introduced such naturalisation tests.

The success of EU citizenship however is a strong argument against these practices and puts them in a very interesting perspective. For example, if a Romanian citizen is good enough to be embraced by British society as equal, then subjecting a Moldovan citizen to any kind of tests is illogical, as the arguments of the protection of culture, language etc. are irrelevant when more than half a billion EU citizens are exempt from them.[586]

Ethnic or religious criteria have and are also being contrived by States as citizenship requirements, such as the *Law of Return* in Israel, which, in addition to the otherwise (at least formally) neutral Israeli Citizenship Act, provides special provisions for Jewish people. This allows all the Jews throughout the world to immediately and without the usual requirements

582 BREVILLE (2014)
583 HAMPSHIRE (2010) p. 75
584 HAMPSHIRE (2010) p. 77
585 STUDER/ARLETTAZ/ARGAST (2008); or also ACHERMANN/GASS (2003), and historically cf. ARGAST (2007)
586 KOCHENOV (2014)

directly acquire Israeli citizenship upon "return" to Israel.[587] Another interesting example is the Liberian Law of 8 February 1922, Section 69, which permits naturalisation exclusively for black Africans ("Negroes"): the naturalisation of other people is "unauthorised and void".[588] Also military service frequently gives access to privileged naturalisation: The US grant citizenship to foreigners in peacetime who have served for a year in the US armed forces, or in times of war, including since 11 September 2001, already at the point of recruitment and in which case, even the *Oath of Allegiance* is waived in the US.[589] This extraordinary naturalisation option serves as an incentive and reward to perform military service and risk of one's life. And sometimes, nothing of the above applies, as the example of former world chess champion *Bobby Fischer* shows, who was naturalised in Iceland to escape custody prior to extradition in Japan, after an alien's passport issued by Iceland was not recognised to secure his passage to Iceland.[590] In Denmark, a country which has one of the most restrictive naturalisation regimes today and since 2001 only naturalises people who can speak Danish and know the history and values of Denmark, the bride of *Crown Prince Frederik*, the Australian *Mary Donaldson*, received Danish citizenship as an engagement gift.[591]

Since antiquity, non-citizens were in some cases naturalised by decisions of the authorities or the relevant councils of the city States, principalities etc., or as practised in the Roman Empire, entire peoples were awarded Roman citizenship after a victorious conquest. However, the naturalisation by *lettres de naturalité* of the French king *François I* can be regarded as the beginning of a "modern" naturalisation practice in the modern era,[592] where non-French persons were systematically declared French by decree.

The rate of naturalisations relative to population varies very significantly. By controlling the number of naturalisations of course the political

[587] BEN-PORAT/TURNER (2011); DIECKHOFF (2006)
[588] Quoted in DONNER (1994)
[589] SPIRO (2008)
[590] VON MÜNCH (2007)
[591] VON MÜNCH (2007)
[592] cf. WEIL (2004)

authorities of a country are effectively choosing the make-up of the population. the US for example grants about 600,000 naturalisations a year for a population of some 300 million. Senegal, with a population of 12.5 million has granted only 12,000 naturalisations over the last 50 years. China, according to the 2010 census, had a population of 1.3 billion, but only 1,448 naturalised citizens.[593]

Meanwhile in Europe, in 2010 over 800,000 naturalisations and other grants of citizenship occurred in EU Member States.[594] Since 1990, millions of people from all over the world have been granted EU citizenship, and, as the following table shows, the numbers vary widely between the individual states.

---

593 BREVILLE (2014)

594 http://ec.europa.eu/eurostat/statistics-explained/index.php/Migration_and_migrant_population_statistics, last accessed 16 February 2015

Citizenship Acquisition in Europe

Country	*1990*	*1991*	*1992*	*1993*	*1994*	*1995*
Austria	9,198	11,394	11,920	14,402	16,270	15,309
Belgium	8,657	8,457	46,368	16,376	25,787	26,129
Czech Republic	n.a.	n.a.	n.a.	n.a.	n.a.	n.a.
Denmark	3,028	5,490	5,118	5,136	5,767	5,266
Estonia	n.a.	n.a.	5,421	20,370	22,474	16,674
Finland	899	1,236	876	839	651	668
France	64,976	72,213	71,595	73,164	92,484	58,988
Germany	101,377	141,630	179,904	199,443	259,170	313,606
Greece	n.a.	n.a.	n.a.	n.a.	n.a.	n.a.
Hungary	n.a.	n.a.	n.a.	8,857	n.a.	10,695
Iceland	n.a.	161	129	136	200	198
Italy	4,045	4,148	4,395	5,065	6,613	7,445
Latvia	n.a.	n.a.	n.a.	n.a.	n.a.	984
Lithuania	n.a.	n.a.	n.a.	n.a.	n.a.	n.a.
Luxembourg	748	n.a.	n.a.	n.a.	664	770
Malta	n.a.	246	187	249	237	277
Netherlands	12,794	29,112	36,237	43,069	49,448	71,444
Norway	4,757	5,055	5,132	5,538	8,778	11,778
Poland	n.a.	n.a.	n.a.	n.a.	n.a.	n.a.
Portugal	n.a.	n.a.	n.a.	12	144	30
Slovakia	n.a.	n.a.	n.a.	66,384	22,005	2,289
Spain	n.a.	n.a.	n.a.	n.a.	n.a.	6,756
Sweden	n.a.	n.a.	n.a.	n.a.	n.a.	n.a.
Switzerland	8,658	8,757	11,133	12,898	13,739	16,790
United Kingdom	n.a.	n.a.	n.a.	45,791	44,033	40,516
Total	219,137	287,899	378,415	517,729	568,464	606,612

Country	*1996*	*1997*	*1998*	*1999*
Austria	16,243	16,274	18,321	25,032
Belgium	24,581	31,687	34,034	24,196
Czech Republic	n.a.	n.a.	n.a.	7,309
Denmark	7,289	5,487	10,277	12,478
Estonia	22,773	8,124	9,969	4,534
Finland	981	1,439	4,017	4,730
France	n.a.	n.a.	n.a.	n.a.
Germany	302,830	271,773	283,604	241,972
Greece	n.a.	n.a.	n.a.	n.a.
Hungary	9,913	10,136	6,516	7,046
Iceland	270	239	305	234
Italy	8,823	9,787	12,013	11,334
Latvia	3,016	2,992	4,439	12,427
Lithuania	n.a.	n.a.	n.a.	n.a.
Luxembourg	874	629	743	612
Malta	318	239	221	133
Netherlands	82,687	59,831	59,173	62,093
Norway	12,237	12,037	9,244	7,988
Poland	n.a.	n.a.	n.a.	n.a.
Portugal	147	153	512	584
Slovakia	1,343	935	934	1,266
Spain	8,432	10,311	13,177	16,384
Sweden	n.a.	n.a.	n.a.	n.a.
Switzerland	19,159	19,169	21,277	20,363
United Kingdom	43,069	37,010	53,934	54,902
Total	564,985	498,252	542,710	515,617

Citizenship Acquisition in Europe[595]

Country	*2000*	*2001*	*2002*	*2003*	*2004*	*2005*
Austria	24.645	32,080	36,382	45,112	42,174	35,417
Belgium	61,980	62,982	46,417	33,709	34,754	31,512
Czech Republic	6,436	6,321	4,532	3,410	5,020	2,626
Denmark	19,323	11,892	16,662	6,583	14,976	10,193
Estonia	3,425	3,090	4,091	3,706	6,423	7,072
Finland	2,977	2,720	3,049	4,526	6,880	5,683
France	141,455	121,631	122,834	139,930	165,121	151,861
Germany	186,688	178,098	154,547	140,731	127,153	117,241
Greece	n.a.	n.a.	n.a.	n.a.	1,425	1,711
Hungary	5,446	8,590	3,369	5,261	5,432	9,822
Iceland	286	352	356	463	671	726
Italy	9,555	10,380	10,682	13,443	11,945	19,266
Latvia	14,900	10,637	9,844	10,049	16,064	19,169
Lithuania	n.a.	507	504	389	610	435
Luxembourg	692	474	826	721	848	995
Malta	587	1,190	783	589	584	562
Netherlands	49,968	46,667	45,321	28,799	26,173	28,488
Norway	9,517	10,838	9,041	7,867	8,154	12,655
Poland	1,436	1,070	1,186	1,634	1,937	2,866
Portugal	1,142	956	1,136	2,043	1,413	1,655
Slovakia	4,526	2,978	3,770	4,042	4,344	1,537
Spain	11,999	16,743	21,810	26,556	38,335	42,829
Sweden	43,474	36,399	37,792	33,222	28,893	39,573
Switzerland	28,700	27,583	36,515	35,424	35,685	38,437
United Kingdom	82,210	90,295	120,148	124,313	140,790	161,780
Total	711,367	684,473	691,597	672,522	725,804	744,111

596 *Source: European University Institute/EUDO Citizenship Observatory, 2015*

Country	*2006*	*2007*	*2008*
Austria	26,259	14,041	10,268
Belgium	31,860	36,063	n.a.
Czech Republic	2,346	1,877	1,837
Denmark	7,958	3,646	5,770
Estonia	4,753	4,228	2,124
Finland	4,433	4,824	6,682
France	145,315	n.a.	n.a.
Germany	124,566	113,030	94,470
Greece	1,962	3,921	n.a.
Hungary	6,172	8,442	8,060
Iceland	844	647	914
Italy	35,766	38,466	39,484
Latvia	16,439	6,826	3,004
Lithuania	467	370	240
Luxembourg	1,084	1,311	1,129
Malta	474	553	644
Netherlands	29,089	30,653	28,229
Norway	11,955	14,877	10,312
Poland	1,060	1,542	1,715
Portugal	7,662	n.a.	n.a.
Slovakia	1,050	1,390	646
Spain	62,339	71,810	84,170
Sweden	51,239	33,629	30,461
Switzerland	46,711	43,889	44,365
United Kingdom	154,085	164,635	129,375
Total	775,888	600,670	503,899

7.2 Frequent criteria for ordinary naturalisation

7.2.1 Residence

While the criteria for the original acquisition of citizenship turn out to be comparatively straightforward, the derivative acquisition criteria can diverge significantly from State to State. Due to the considerable freedom that countries enjoy, these are not only subject to the prevailing traditions, conventions and values, but above all to political expediency as it appears to the respective government officials. It may therefore be sufficient in one country for the applicant to remain in the host country for a long time and find a personal link to the local community in which he/she lives and works (keyword: acquisition of citizenship by factual, social and economic integration), while other host countries such as Austria, known among the EU Member States for its restrictive naturalisation policy (which however simultaneously permits direct naturalisation without antecedent residence for extraordinary – even economic – services to the State under Section 10(6) of its Citizenship Act) require that a degree of loyalty to the polity can be shown, such as command of the national language, basic knowledge of the national culture and national history or through the establishment of the person's sufficient economic livelihood, the existence of which may indeed be taken as an indicator of the achievement of a certain degree of integration.

If the naturalisation law of a State requires a closer actual relationship in the sense of a certain attachment of a natural person to the domestic legal order, which in general, in addition to a spatial-physical element such as taking up residence or permanently lawfully staying within the territory, also requires a certain connection to the national polity manifested inwardly and outwardly, its content should be determined not only by the central functions of citizenship law, but by considering the general socio-demographic and socio-structural situation of the nation.[596]

---

[596] Regarding the naturalisation laws of the Federal Republic of Germany, which is not treated in this work as a reference State, but which is of interest here in this context, the German *Constitutional Court* (*Bundesverfassungsgericht*) held in 1952 that nationality is to be conferred by a state only to persons having actual connection to it – see Decisions of the Federal Constitutional Court, (1992) Vol. 1, pp. 322, 329; other German federal courts have considered arbitrary granting of citizenship without regard to generally accepted connecting

In general, a State's population can be defined as those individuals residing within the limits of the national territory. However, the residence element within the meaning of permanent (normal) place of abode and the centre of life under a given address is not congruent with the basic assumption that the permanent component of a national polity requires a certain minimal cultural consensus, which cannot be achieved merely by taking up residence. The increased mobility that we enjoy today internationally also reduces the likelihood that our physical residence guarantees a long-term commitment to our host country.[597]

Nevertheless, residence is still the most important criterion used for ordinary naturalisation in almost all countries, and is also historically the most important point of orientation in this respect.[598]

7.2.2 Self-employed basis or own earned income

Those States, such as Cyprus, which link the acquisition of citizenship to the applicant investing substantially in the economy of the country under the model of Citizenship-by-Investment (Cyprus makes the relevant acquisition citizenship dependant, among other options available, on the corresponding company of the applicant having contributed at least EUR 500,000 per year in the form of tax payments, sales tax or by purchasing professional services within the Cypriot economy in the three years preceding the application) can at least conceptually be connected to the Canadian system for acquisition of Canadian citizenship under the "Skilled Worker Programs" (see below). However, France, Austria (Section 10 ACA) and Germany[599] (Section 10(1) (3) dStAG) also base the acquisition of citizenship on the fact that the applicant should be able to show a steady income from gainful economic activity.[600]

---

factors as contrary to public international law – see *Hailbronner* in BAUBÖCK et al. (2006) p. 59; See also *Epping/Gloria* in IPSEN (2004); *Kokott* in SACHS (2009)

597 SPIRO (2008)

598 SPIRO (2008)

599 Like Canada's "Skilled Worker Program", which is particularly concerned with the emigration of skilled workers, during the boom in the new economy in 2000–2001, so-called green cards were issued in Germany which allowed temporary legitimate residence locally – with quite a significant impact on the German labour market. cf. in particular *Kahanec/Zimmermann* in CHISWICK (2011)

600 According to this rule, naturalisation in Germany is possible if the applicant is in a position to earn a livelihood for himself and his dependent family members, without

The Canadian "Skilled Worker Program" bases the right of residence (which after three years can lead to the acquisition of Canadian citizenship) on achieving a certain minimum number of points which can be influenced by submitting evidence of a binding job offer, or even by practical experience in one of officially specified occupations, and indispensably requires that an independent financial livelihood can be demonstrated.

7.2.3 Payment of taxes and other contributions

Exceptional economic criteria should also be considered as indicative of a special relationship with the domestic polity and, given the key objectives of citizenship law (integration, internal social peace, and the realisation of subsidiarity between public and private spheres) in principle can justify the granting of citizenship. Considering that the sovereignty of a State polity is only permanently guaranteed under the premise of sufficient financial resources, which is particularly bound up in sufficient tax revenue, it does not seem unreasonable to base the discretionary decision on the granting of citizenship (naturalisation) on economic criteria, such as the payment of taxes or a one-time contribution to the State, or of investments leading to one-time as well as permanent revenue for the State.

You could take the principle of "no representation without taxation"[601] as an inversion of the guiding principle of "no taxation without representation", rooted in the US American War of Independence, which translates as "no taxation without (elected) political representation" and refers back to the fundamental critique put forward by the apologists for independence that the 13 British colonies were required to pay taxes to the British Crown but were not represented in the Parliament in Westminster by their own elected members. On closer inspection, this maxim can be attributed to the *Petition of Rights* of 1628[602] adopted

---

claiming benefits under the Social Code or by exception recourse to such benefits is due to conditions beyond his or her control: Nationality Act of 22 July 1913 (Reich Law Gazette I p. 583 - Federal Law Gazette III 102 - 1), as last amended by Article 1 of the Second Act Amending the Nationality Act of 13 November 2014 (Federal Law Gazette I p. 1714)

601 cf. SCHAEFER (2011)

602 Published online at http://pinkmonkey.com/dl/library1/ahis02.pdf, last accessed on 21 September 2012, the Petition of Right cf. SCHICK (1996)

in the UK, where it was hailed as a foundational part of English constitutionalism.

7.2.4 Language proficiency

Given that the deeper meaning of citizenship can still be closely associated with the phenomenon of the nation State, which not only consists of the inner pacification of an indeterminate plurality of persons, but also of enabling its efficient self-management to reduce the State to certain fundamental core tasks, which pursue incidental deficiencies in the social and political spheres in as decentralised a manner as possible, taking the future development of the polity, national language or languages into account would also appear to be significant.

On the vertical plane,[603] between the State's population and State power, a common language can significantly contribute to ensuring that the laws and related administrative decisions – which are themselves an expression of the shared values and common culture – are understood and respected both in terms of language and content. It thus creates a good but not necessary[604] condition for the foundation and maintenance of a domestic order.

On the horizontal plane between the members of a State's population this domestic order also paves the way for the practical implementation of the subsidiarity principle, which is of such relevance to most liberal States. This authoritative principle of social structure is derived from a Catholic encyclical and is enacted at national level in the interaction between the EU and its Member States (Article 5(3) TEU)[605] States,

603 The distinction made here between the will of members of the State's population among themselves (the horizontal plane) and the relationship between the State's people and the State power (the vertical plane) corresponds to the distinction drawn particularly by *Jellinek* of the State as a cooperative association, which is linked to a State's incorporation in a federation, cf. JELLINEK (1976)

604 Take the example of the Swiss Confederation, which has three or four different languages and very distinct cultural areas, and yet because of their common history and federal structure, can exist as a nation of consensus

605 For the application of the subsidiary principle between the EU Member States and the supranational EU cf. *Langguth* in LENZ/BORCHARDT (2010), Article 5 TEU; *BVerfG*, judgment of 30 June 2009 – Case 2 BvE 2/08, 2 BvE 5/08, 2 BvR 1010/08, 2

providing that recourse should be had to a higher level of administration (e.g. family over the individual family member, Federal State over State, supranational association of States over the individual nation State) only when the lower level is unable to take the right action itself. The subsidiary principle not only applies to the relationship between citizens and the State, such as in the social sector, but in all possible areas between the EU Member States and the EU. [606]

Both current and potential conflicts which naturally arise from people's coexistence in the same place, and whose settlement appears necessary to achieve internal peace within the social unit, should be settled in as decentralised a manner as possible at the respectively lowest level, as a decentralised conflict resolution is not only usually more effective, but also takes into account the responsibility of the individual, which accords with the guarantee of human dignity. For a conflict resolution understood in this way to be practically possible, it usually requires a common national language or languages, without which an autonomous conflict resolution within the law is impossible.

In any case, in those States such as France or Germany which are not characterised by language pluralism – i.e. where a variety of regional languages are spoken (in India, for example) – and which recognise a universal official language, requiring command of the common national language as a unifying condition appears to be a decisive criterion in their concretisation of citizenship. In countries which lack language pluralism, the domination of the national language is not only regarded as a fundamental prerequisite for achieving intra-community order, but can be identified as an essential requirement of intra-community peace – both at the vertical level between the individuals of the State polity and the institutions of State power, as well as on the horizontal level between individuals.

Where there is no actual or possible guarantee of either the laws and administrative decrees or interference-free communication between individuals,

---

BvR 1022/08, 2 BvR 1259/08, 2 BvR 182/09, published online at http://www.servat.unibe.ch/dfr/bv123267.html, last accessed on 21 September 2012

606 cf. HERZOG/GERKEN (2007)

there is an imminent likelihood of conflicts of various kinds, as transpired recently for instance in the problem districts of metropolitan areas in America, England or France. This is one of the underlying reasons why all of the reference States, including Canada, used in this work link the acquisition of citizenship to the command of at least one of their national languages. This is also a decisive reason why the citizenship laws of the Netherlands have undergone a paradigm shift, not least in the wake of the assassination of the film producer *Theo van Gogh*, understanding the acquisition of citizenship since 2003 as the conclusion of successful integration.

If we consider a traditional element of citizenship as being a minimum canon of shared values, cultural beliefs and conventions, which a State is ultimately ready to defend, the importance of a common language in many countries is also illustrated by the performance of military service whose defining principle is one of inner leadership ("command and obedience") and which, without a common language, would be rendered inoperable. Those committed to the values which make up the nation State polity at its core, must also be ultimately prepared to defend the State's "constitutional" values.

7.2.5 Identification with fundamental national values

Given that another important objective of citizenship law - at least for liberal democracies - is to ensure adequate minority protection, for example, by allowing immigrants to participate in government decision-making when choosing their active central abode, one must always bear in mind that with respect to cultural criteria being defined as prerequisites for the acquisition of citizenship, these can pave the way to demoscopic lawmaking. Under no circumstances will international law countenance that the acquisition of nationality be linked to improper criteria such as homeland and origin, race, sexual identity, ideology, political creed or faith.

However, many national legal systems, such as those of the US,[607] Canada,

[607] On the oath of allegiance in the United States see *Jackson* in ALEINIKOFF/KLUSMEYER (2001) pp. 164–166, also cf. ALEINIKOFF/KLUSMEYER (1952)

Malta or Austria, provide for the taking of an *Oath of Allegiance*,[608] in which the applicants are required to solemnly commit themselves to thenceforth identify with the core values of the respective community. It is questionable whether such oaths make any sense in this day and age.[609] Civil societies in many modern States have transnationalised themselves: many national civil organisations are connected to international umbrella organisations which determine the ultimate policy, for example regarding environmental protection, women's rights, human rights etc. Professional organisations, churches and businesses are also increasingly active on an international and transnational level. As *Spiro* illustrates neatly:

> *"Take an American who is also a member of Greenpeace, Amnesty International, and the Catholic Church, is an employee of Toyota, and is a woman...(and) is also a citizen of, say, the Dominican Republic. That is not an exceptional profile, the substantial transnational elements included. Can we say of this person that her 'largest and most inclusive group' remains American?"*[610]

A binding State "culture" is mostly not provided in the constitutions of liberally constituted States. Given the objectives of citizenship law and its factual proximity to the guarantee of human dignity as explained below, a "leading culture" in whatever shape can only arise from the traditions, conventions and values that are prevalent in the population. Under the premise that the recognition of the individual as a person is the foundation of all political legal relationships, the State's will is also always the human will.[611]

If mutual exchange of care and loyalty is considered as a basic content of citizenship, as it is expressed for example in the payment of taxes and duties (fees, contributions and special levies etc.) and the assumption

608 Fundamental to the oath of allegiance: ALEINIKOFF/KLUSMEYER (1952); BLOEMRAAD (2006); FAHRMEIER (2000); *Hansen* in HANSEN/WEIL (2011)
609 cf. SPIRO (2008)
610 SPIRO (2008) p. 126
611 cf. JELLINEK (1976)

of political responsibility or military service – with military service in particular demonstrating the willingness, if necessary, to enforce and defend basic national values by military means to its ultimate extent – a gradual paradigm shift from the *status negativus*, i.e. the sphere of constitutionally secured individual freedom, to the *status passivus*, i.e. based on individual demand for public goods of general interest, can be observed recently (entitlement mentality). Increasingly often the public discourse concerns what the State is doing for individuals, without these demands being reflected in any significant effort attributable to the individual.

With compulsory military service – in the sense of the citizen in uniform – lying at the core of national identity in the modern nation state, the question arises of what still remains at the core of national identity in those countries such as France or Germany, and many others, which have suspended military service. With the paradigm shift towards an understanding of the State as a comprehensive provider, in particular of social services, in which the equivalence between giving (loyalty) and taking (welfare) is no longer ensured at all, the question arises whether the nation State still has legitimacy in this regard as a consequence of citizenship, especially since the aforementioned services do not all reflect the original core functions of the State, but in some cases could well be provided privately.

Nevertheless, in terms of ordinary naturalisation, most States still apply extremely diverse conditions or requirements on the applicant's identification with national values which, although they seem largely anachronistic, represent at least in part, significant practical hurdles for the respective applicant.[612]

7.2.6 "Genuine link" or "genuine connection"

As early as its 1955 ruling on the *Nottebohm*[613] case, the International

[612] For example, Switzerland, which provides particularly high demands internationally, cf. HELBLING (2008); historically ARGAST (2007)

[613] ICJ judgment of 6 April 1955, ICJ Rep. 1955, p. 4 ff. (*Nottebohm*)

Court of Justice called for taking account of essential actual points of connection in the justification of citizenship: the individual's habitual residence, his centre of interests, his family ties, his participation in public life and the affinity with the country transferred onto his children. Consequently, citizenship was qualified as a legal bond which, according to the ICJ, comprises the fact of social belonging, a genuine connection of existence, interests and sentiments, as well as the existence of reciprocal rights and responsibilities as its basis. Therefore, an objective element, the presence of which suggests that a natural person chose a specific place as the centre of his/her personal interests and a subjective inner or voluntary element, which must manifest itself outwardly and whose presence in the sense of loyalty suggests an inner connection with a specific polity, must coincide. In *Nottebohm* the ICJ used the term "genuine connection". As the ICJ elaborated, the exercise of the right to diplomatic protection requires a "*real and effective citizenship*". The "genuine connection"[614] as demanded by the jurisprudence of the ICJ, requires – considering the purpose of citizenship law – more than the one-off appearance at a competent national registration authority to register as a member of the national community, i.e. it requires the fulfilment of material criteria along with a merely formal criterion. Citizenship should reflect ideally a certain closeness and actual proximity of citizens to their country, which is reflected in particular by permanent settlement, work or marriage, owning of property, investments in the country, so that a sufficiently close connection to the host State required for naturalisation can be assumed, just as when someone has been living there for a long time and has her centre of life there.[615]

As pointed out *supra*, it is important however to highlight that while the ICJ did not consider that *Nottebohm* was entitled to diplomatic protection, the conferral of citizenship was in fact valid despite lacking a "genuine connection".[616]

---

614 Or "genuine connection of existence, interests and sentiments, along with the existence of reciprocal rights and duties", ICJ judgment of 6 April 1955, ICJ Rep. 1955, p. 4 ff. (*Nottebohm*)

615 cf. LAEMMERMANN (2011)

616 CARRERA (2014)

With regard to legal practice after the *Nottebohm*[617] ruling, some national courts and the practice of various States have made reference to the "*effective citizenship*" in the event of collisions with multiple nationalities, which can be interpreted either as the nationality of the country with which the person concerned may be assumed to have the closest connection (according to the Secretary of State for Justice of the Netherlands)[618] or France's official position that priority is always given to the State in which the person with multiple nationalities in question lives.[619] The view has also been expressed that the *Nottebohm* ruling, even though it very clearly relates specifically to the diplomatic protection aspect of citizenship only, requires the existence of a recognised objective connecting point in addition to an application for naturalisation.[620]

Though a State may probably not choose the connecting points of citizenship completely arbitrarily, this does not mean that that the principle of effectiveness of the *Nottebohm* ruling can be used to justify the acquisition of citizenship under international law.[621] Indeed, a principle of effectiveness does not exist in general international law.[622] It can only be engaged to resolve factual issues where the question concerns diplomatic protection in the context of collisions of multiple citizenship, such as was the case with *Mr. Nottebohm*.[623] Now also national courts employ these criteria ("*genuine connection*", "*effective citizenship*") when multiple nationalities require a prioritisation.[624]

As part of its autonomy and decision-making discretion, the individual State is left at a national level to set the criteria for the acquisition of citizenship, and no further requirements are introduced in terms of international law by the effectiveness or "*genuine connection*". On the contrary, public international law demands less than a "*genuine connection*" for

617 ICJ judgment of 6 April 1955, ICJ Rep. 1955 (*Nottebohm*)
618 https://zoek.officielebekendmakingen.nl/dossier/26675/kst-26675-3?resultIndex=17&sorttype=1&sort order=4, last accessed 27 July 2015
619 DONNER (1994)
620 cf. DAHM/DELBRÜCK/WOLFRUM (2002); VERDROSS/SIMMA (1984)
621 cf. HOKEMA (2002)
622 DAHM/DELBRÜCK/WOLFRUM (2002); SALAHELDIN (2012)
623 RANDELZHOFER (1997); HOKEMA (2002)
624 cf. DONNER (1994)

the acquisition of citizenship, but of course does not forbid any State to imposing higher standards.[625] However, any further additional requirements or criteria beyond the formal act of State following a voluntary application filed by a foreigner as a declaration of intent, are not required by international law, and provide a sufficient connection for the purposes of international law for the granting of citizenship.[626]

This answers a central question of this work: in the formal application for naturalisation, in addition to a clear declaration[627] of intent by the applicant, is a significant investment or any other prerequisite as determined by a State's legislature, sufficient to be considered as a connecting factor for citizenship? This question can thus be answered in the affirmative.

Furthermore, in the European context in particular, the logic of free movement within the area of freedom, security and justice is antithetical to the "genuine connection" idea, and cannot allow EU member states not to recognise the (EU) citizenship of other EU member states nationals using their free movement rights, as this would introduce uncertainty in the application of Community law and making its uniform application throughout the EU member states impossible.[628]

7.3 Citizenship as a formal or material point of connection

With particular regard to the possibility of taking economic criteria into consideration, the question of whether the legal essence of citizenship is of rather a formal nature (could it for example suffice for the acquisition of citizenship if it is linked to nothing more than a simple declaration of intent to the competent national authority) or, beyond this, also of material nature, i.e. a commitment to the nation manifested in certain external criteria (political or social engagement, command of the national language, or basic knowledge of the country, including

625 cf. HOKEMA (2002)
626 HAILBRONNER/RENNER/MAASSEN (2010); DUBOIS (1955); HOBE (2008)
627 cf. RANDELZHOFER (1997)
628 KOCHENOV (2009)

its history and culture, or owning property or holding investments in the country, etc.). In the latter case, the question arises as to what the essence of the nation is – is it a cultural nation or an ethnic nation or liberal nation State?

Is it legitimate and does it lie within the limits of nation State discretion as recognised by customary international law to regulate citizenship law, if a State directs investment and migration flows by means of economic regulation, and confronts economic structural deficits and sets relevant incentives with its citizenship legislation? This is, in any case, indicated by the economic success achieved by special recruitment programmes[629] and which, ultimately, presents a benefit for all parties. The migration of individuals of high potential, and in the case of Citizenship-by-Investment this includes also part of their capital, which may be assessed as negative from the perspective of their country of origin, [630] can be assessed as positive in an economic sense as it ultimately contributes to international economic, technological and cultural experience, and, moreover, to consistent market discipline. I agree with *Kochenov* that there is no real negative brain drain in the world if properly put in perspective.[631] History also teaches us "*that 'brains' will move no matter what public policy is in place*".[632] The same is true of capital.

Moreover, there are many historical and current examples where citizenship was, and is, awarded purely formally and recognised internationally. The conferral of citizenship for entering the civil service was formerly common in many States (*Adolf Hitler*, as a grotesque example, only became a German national by [pro forma] employment in the German State of Brunswick

629 In particular in Canada, which operated the largest investor immigration programs in the world, adding about CAD 2 billion to the Canadian economy annually (see WARE/FORTIN/PARADIS (2010)), or St. Kitts and Nevis, where the local Citizenship by Investment Program is one of the governments most important economically productive actions (see KÄLIN (2014), enabling this small State in recent years to reduce its significant external debt of over 180% of gross domestic product to below 100%

630 Less developed countries may argue against that instead of compensating them for their investment loss in human capital, they are being drained of their much needed investment funds *and* their human capital, cf. BORNA/STEARNS (2002)

631 KOCHENOV (2012): "*treating the world of knowledge as divided into states is simply wrong*". Of a different view, BARNHILL (2012) p. 143 et seq.

632 BORNA/STEARNS (2002) p. 195

civil service).[633] The citizenship of the Vatican City State, in turn, cannot be tied to birth: consequently, only those entering the service of the State receive this citizenship,[634] which is nonetheless recognised internationally.

It can therefore be concluded that the legal essence of citizenship is of a rather formal nature and consequently its acquisition may, at the discretion of the relevant State, be linked to nothing more than a simple formal declaration of intent to the competent national authority, and the acceptance of such intent by the competent national authority.

633 VON MÜNCH (2007)
634 VON MÜNCH (2007)

8

Analysis of Naturalisation Principles in Selected States

8.1 Overview

The following is a representative selection of citizenship acquisition rules in a number of States – the UK, France, Canada, Switzerland and Austria – which were chosen for their different histories and the distinct characteristics of their jurisdictions in terms of the principles they support and the foundations from which they developed, to provide a meaningful overview in terms of the historical and contemporary design of legal citizenship norms and the spectrum of regulation this establishes, with particular attention to the acquisition of citizenship by naturalisation.

The UK was chosen as its citizenship provisions follow a long and curious tradition based on the British monarchy and the *British Empire*, which resulted in British citizenship only being defined for the first time in 1981, and differing greatly from the traditions in continental Europe. Furthermore, while France, the actual birthplace of the modern idea of citizenship, was selected and will also be examined in greater detail below, two other representatives, Switzerland and Austria, will be discussed. Switzerland was chosen because it is today[635] one of the most restrictive countries in the world in terms of naturalisation, and is only surpassed in this respect by some Islamic, African and Asian countries; and Austria, because while having a very restrictive Citizenship Act which is similar to the law in Germany and Switzerland and even – and in this it goes further than Switzerland – prohibits multiple citizenship in principle, also reveals an astonishing pragmatism, in particular (and especially relevant to the present work) enabling the acquisition of Austrian citizenship due to extraordinary contributions to the State, including specifically economic contributions. Strikingly, as a culmination of Alpine pragmatism, this latter route to the acquisition of Austrian citizenship is also an exception to the rule which otherwise prohibits multiple citizenship, permitting the retention of the previous citizenship. Canada is presented here because it represents the "New World" as a

[635] This was however not always the case: prior to the First World War, naturalisation required an average of only two years of residence. cf. *Diggelmann* in WALTER/GÄRDITZ (2015) p. 166

classic immigration country whose citizenship regulations have traditionally focused on the integration of immigrants since the early days of the Canadian State, and are thus designed far more historically and fundamentally liberal than in the emigration countries of Europe.

In this context, different aspects of specific interest to this work are highlighted depending on the State, and comparisons with other States are drawn, particularly with the Federal Republic of Germany (which of course has a very interesting history with respect to citizenship law)[636] and the US (another classic immigration country).

8.2 The UK

8.2.1 State structural parameters

As one of the founding members of the Commonwealth of Nations[637] and the *North Atlantic Treaty Organisation* (NATO) as well as being a permanent member of the UN Security Council,[638] the UK has also been a member State of the EU since 1973. Its membership in the Commonwealth of Nations, emerging from the *British Empire*, can be classified as part of the constitutional doctrine of the UK.[639] The UK has had a lasting influence on large parts of today's world as the last great

---

636 Germany will not, however, be presented in its own a section here, as the countries with a Germanic legal tradition, Austria and Switzerland, are already exemplified

637 The Commonwealth of Nations, which up to and including 1947 was called the *British Commonwealth of Nations*, is a voluntary association of sovereign States, composed mainly of the UK and its former colonies, and formed around their common language into a Commonwealth (a hobbesian term meaning Common good or common prosperity) to attain common objectives as a loose political community. The term Commonwealth is derived from the Latin *republica* and is an expression of a political philosophical tradition, which follows an intergovernmental idea, cf. LEYLAND, p. 21 ff. In addition to Canada, currently Australia, India, New Zealand, South Africa and of course the UK number among its 54 Member States

638 With its current 15 members (Article 23(1)(1) UNC), the United Nations Security Council (UNSC) currently has primary responsibility for world peace and international security (Article 24(1) UNC). As sovereign subjects of public international law, the UN Member States agree to accept and carry out the UNSC's resolutions in accordance with the UNC (Article 25 UNC), in principle achieving binding effect which extends directly to the relationship between the UN Parties and their contracting States

639 For the British Commonwealth as part of British constitutional law, see LEYLAND (2012), FRANSMAN (2011) pp. 59–89

colonial power, both culturally-linguistically as well as constitutionally-legally. The UK had also long been an immigration country, before the great migration waves of the eighteenth century reached America.[640]

In the UK, citizenship law developed from English law and must, therefore, actually be considered as English rather than British law. It is only since the Union with Scotland in 1707 that we can speak of a British citizenship and the evolution into a British nationality.[641]

This is decisively due to the nature of the *British Empire* as a constitutional monarchy.[642] It is for example reflected in the fact that the State's authority, unlike in most democratic nation States, is not bound by a written constitution and formally emanates not from the people – the democratic mandate is only made manifest through elections to the *House of Commons*[643] – but by the *King* or *Queen* in *Parliament* or from the Parliament itself (principle of absolute parliamentary rule).[644] To some extent, as the legislative chamber of the British system of government, Parliament represents the highest legislative power (the principle of parliamentary sovereignty) and is constituted from the British *House of Commons,* and the *House of Lords,* an upper house composed of 90 members of the hereditary aristocracy, a handful of bishops and many hundreds of political appointees.

Furthermore, the political system of the UK is decisively shaped by the fact that – in contrast to the other countries reviewed here – it has no written constitution[645] to determine the relationship of the individual to the State and delineate the State's exercise of power. The British Citizenship Act, as well as the entire legal system of the British Empire, is thus characterised on the one hand by uncodified customary law

---

640 SCHULTE BEERBÜHL (2007) p. 1 et seq.

641 SCHULTE BEERBÜHL (2007) p. 39; cf. also HARRIS (2004)

642 Concerning the role of the UK as a constitutional monarchy cf. LEYLAND (2012)

643 The House of Commons joins the Crown and the House of Lords to form the British Parliament. It possesses wide-ranging powers and is the politically crucial chamber, cf. LEYLAND (2012)

644 For meticulous analysis see ALLAN (2013)

645 For an explanation of the hierarchy of norms in the UK see AUST (2007)

(*Common Law*)[646] concretised judicially by binding precedent (*Case Law*), and on the other hand, an increasingly relevant body of *Statute Law*, which adds an element of commonality with the codified legal systems.

Similar to the constitutional system of other Commonwealth countries such as Canada, India, Australia, New Zealand, Singapore or St. Kitts and Nevis, and unlike e.g. France, Austria, Switzerland or Germany, it is not the State population, but Parliament – a triumvirate formed of two chambers under the Crown (Monarch, House of Lords and House of Commons) – which is sovereign in the sense of being the State's source of authority, and the monarch retains a representative role through the two chambers, and political power lies almost exclusively with the House of Commons and the Prime Minister (*Westminster System*).[647] Theoretically, the *King* or *Queen in Parliament* is the unconditional owner of all State authority.

8.2.2 Citizenship statistics

In the years between 1990 and 2008, the UK granted citizenship (by naturalisation and by registration) to between 37,010 and 164,635 persons per year, a total of more than 1.6 million and an average of about 89,000 per year.[648] The naturalisation/registration to population ratio is however low at 0.15% per year.

646 For common law as part of the British constitutional law: cf. LEYLAND (2012), FRANSMAN (2011); fundamental to the legal system of the Common Law: BLUMENWITZ (1998); MAUCH (2007); REIMANN (1997)

647 cf. http://www.verfassungen.eu/gb/, last accessed on 21 September 2012

648 cf. country database of citizenship acquisition for the UK on http://eudo-citizenship.eu, last accessed 26 January 2015

Naturalisation in the UK - Selected Countries of Origin[649]

Country	1990	1991	1992	1993	1994
Azerbaijan	n.a.	n.a.	n.a.	n.a.	n.a.
Russia	n.a.	n.a.	n.a.	n.a.	n.a.
Serbia and Montenegro (former)	n.a.	n.a.	n.a.	n.a.	n.a.
Turkey	n.a.	n.a.	n.a.	n.a.	n.a.
Algeria	n.a.	n.a.	n.a.	n.a.	n.a.
Angola	n.a.	n.a.	n.a.	n.a.	n.a.
Congo, Republic (Congo-Brazzaville)	n.a.	n.a.	n.a.	n.a.	n.a.
Congo, Dem. Rep. (Congo-Kinshasa)	n.a.	n.a.	n.a.	n.a.	n.a.
Egypt	n.a.	n.a.	n.a.	n.a.	n.a.
Ghana	n.a.	n.a.	n.a.	n.a.	n.a.
Kenya	n.a.	n.a.	n.a.	n.a.	n.a.
Morocco	n.a.	n.a.	n.a.	n.a.	n.a.
Nigeria	n.a.	n.a.	n.a.	n.a.	n.a.
Sierra Leone	n.a.	n.a.	n.a.	n.a.	n.a.
Somalia	n.a.	n.a.	n.a.	n.a.	n.a.
Sudan	n.a.	n.a.	n.a.	n.a.	n.a.
Guyana	n.a.	n.a.	n.a.	n.a.	n.a.
Jamaica	n.a.	n.a.	n.a.	n.a.	n.a.
Afghanistan	n.a.	n.a.	n.a.	n.a.	n.a.
Bangladesh	n.a.	n.a.	n.a.	n.a.	n.a.
China	n.a.	n.a.	n.a.	n.a.	n.a.
India	n.a.	n.a.	n.a.	n.a.	n.a.
Iran	n.a.	n.a.	n.a.	n.a.	n.a.
Iraq	n.a.	n.a.	n.a.	n.a.	n.a.
Kazakhstan	n.a.	n.a.	n.a.	n.a.	n.a.
Lebanon	n.a.	n.a.	n.a.	n.a.	n.a.

[650] *Source: European University Institute/EUDO Citizenship Observatory, 2015*

Country	*1995*	*1996*	*1997*	*1998*	*1999*
Azerbaijan	n.a.	n.a.	0	1	2
Russia	n.a.	n.a.	244	356	392
Serbia and Montenegro (former)	n.a.	n.a.	0	9	0
Turkey	n.a.	n.a.	1,118	2,154	2,913
Algeria	n.a.	n.a.	233	332	376
Angola	n.a.	n.a.	13	48	25
Congo, Republic (Congo-Brazzaville)	n.a.	n.a.	1	1	55
Congo, Dem. Rep. (Congo-Kinshasa)	n.a.	n.a.	49	86	102
Egypt	n.a.	n.a.	231	364	334
Ghana	n.a.	n.a.	1,152	1,909	1,951
Kenya	n.a.	n.a.	342	566	586
Morocco	n.a.	n.a.	440	595	485
Nigeria	n.a.	n.a.	2,144	3,550	5
Sierra Leone	n.a.	n.a.	171	345	413
Somalia	n.a.	n.a.	955	1,617	1,333
Sudan	n.a.	n.a.	136	324	472
Guyana	n.a.	n.a.	140	211	195
Jamaica	n.a.	n.a.	732	1,370	1,437
Afghanistan	n.a.	n.a.	96	139	116
Bangladesh	n.a.	n.a.	1,931	3,316	3,383
China	n.a.	n.a.	894	1,429	1,438
India	n.a.	n.a.	3,259	5,741	5,055
Iran	n.a.	n.a.	1,147	1,708	1,714
Iraq	n.a.	n.a.	736	1,180	1,609
Kazakhstan	n.a.	n.a.	0	6	6
Lebanon	n.a.	n.a.	325	518	540

Country	*1990*	*1991*	*1992*	*1993*	*1994*
Pakistan	n.a.	n.a.	n.a.	n.a.	n.a.
Philippines	n.a.	n.a.	n.a.	n.a.	n.a.
Vietnam	n.a.	n.a.	n.a.	n.a.	n.a.
Yemen	n.a.	n.a.	n.a.	n.a.	n.a.

Naturalisation in the UK - Selected Countries of Origin

Country	*2000*	*2001*	*2002*	*2003*	*2004*
Azerbaijan	7	15	30	65	40
Russia	635	790	1,185	1,160	1,390
Serbia and Montenegro (former)	9	15	1,670	4,850	5,280
Turkey	4,875	4,050	8,045	4,910	4,885
Algeria	629	705	1,345	1,145	1,255
Angola	77	190	375	475	730
Congo, Republic (Congo-Brazzaville)	130	650	970	1,010	845
Congo, Dem. Rep. (Congo-Kinshasa)	155	235	555	855	1,200
Egypt	487	425	705	535	585
Ghana	2,935	3,195	3,080	3,525	3,250
Kenya	870	1,040	1,085	1,390	1,645
Morocco	721	710	800	745	610
Nigeria	5,594	6,290	6,480	6,300	6,280
Sierra Leone	675	845	980	1,165	1,305
Somalia	2,586	5,500	7,490	8,550	11,185
Sudan	1,785	1,270	1,605	1,135	910
Guyana	297	265	275	270	305
Jamaica	1,882	2,070	2,025	2,795	3,180
Afghanistan	313	375	875	1,610	4,080
Bangladesh	5,380	5,395	5,745	6,145	5,810

Country	*1995*	*1996*	*1997*	*1998*	*1999*
Pakistan	n.a.	n.a.	3,275	5,562	6,348
Philippines	n.a.	n.a.	609	1,113	1,065
Vietnam	n.a.	n.a.	671	756	715
Yemen	n.a.	n.a.	155	245	230

Country	*2005*	*2006*	*2007*	*2008*
Azerbaijan	150	130	215	160
Russia	2,235	1,830	1,885	1,380
Serbia and Montenegro (former)	9,800	7,550	3,485	1,865
Turkey	6,765	5,590	4,710	4,640
Algeria	1,485	1,015	1,170	955
Angola	870	945	1,200	1,070
Congo, Republic (Congo-Brazzaville)	670	550	470	280
Congo, Dem. Rep. (Congo-Kinshasa)	1,810	1,910	2,100	1575
Egypt	785	595	730	485
Ghana	3,305	2,990	3,375	3,135
Kenya	2,320	2,380	2,235	1,405
Morocco	705	495	510	500
Nigeria	6,615	5,875	6,030	4,530
Sierra Leone	1,740	1,660	2,195	1,270
Somalia	8,305	9,050	7,450	7,165
Sudan	1,000	965	735	570
Guyana	295	240	240	210
Jamaica	3,515	2,525	3,165	2,715
Afghanistan	4,950	3,400	10,555	5,540
Bangladesh	3,640	3,725	2,250	3,635

Country	*2000*	*2001*	*2002*	*2003*	*2004*
China	1,966	1,590	2,535	2,020	2,045
India	8,135	8,190	10,005	10,780	13,540
Iran	1,904	1,450	2,850	1,820	2,250
Iraq	2,340	1,835	3,455	2,245	2,340
Kazakhstan	12	15	40	35	65
Lebanon	1,013	775	1,275	515	500
Pakistan	8,631	10,160	10,940	12,795	14,125
Philippines	1,361	1,385	1,345	1,610	2,015
Vietnam	1,116	590	500	400	390

8.2.3 Selected structural features of British citizenship law

The UK is of particular interest in relation to citizenship law because such law was not developed in its modern form[650] until after the Second World War, and was traditionally geared to the British concept of "*subject*" (subject, not: "*citizen*").[651] In fact, "*subject*" had been the culturally preferred term for centuries.[652] The (State's) citizen was not defined in British law before 1948, where with the Nationality Act 1948, the UK introduced an extraordinarily generous citizenship concept which practically covered the entire *Empire*, a large part of the global population at that time, some 800 million people worldwide (see *infra*). It was not until 1981 that British citizenship corresponded to some extent to the actual community of the UK of the British Isles (England, Wales, Scotland and Northern Ireland), and to date there has been no consistently defined concept of citizenship and domestic nationality.[653]

650 British Nationality Act 1948

651 cf. on this and the following FRANSMAN (2011) and *Hansen* in HANSEN/WEIL (2001); concerning the term "subject" see in particular *Cole* in CALDER/COLE/SEGLOW (2012)

652 HARRIS (2004)

653 DUMMET/NICOL (1990)

Country	*2005*	*2006*	*2007*	*2008*
China	2,545	2,880	3,455	2,965
India	14,160	15,125	14,490	11,825
Iran	3,525	3,285	4,425	2,200
Iraq	3,260	4,125	5,480	8,895
Kazakhstan	115	95	120	80
Lebanon	630	515	625	320
Pakistan	12,615	10,260	8,140	9,440
Philippines	3,800	8,840	10,840	5,380
Vietnam	205	190	305	290

The "*allegiance to the Crown*" is a central concept in British citizenship law: while in modern Western States, the affiliation relationship occurs between State and citizen, the allegiance of citizens in the UK is still based on the Crown. However, this is no longer about a personal relationship between monarch and subject, as in the late Middle Ages, but "*a political relationship directed to the Crown as an institution*".[654] This was officially recognised only in 1886 in the *Isaac vs. Durant* case[655] and the Crown only definitively appears as a political institution from that time.[656]

As the founder of the *British Empire*, the UK, initially dominated by *ius soli* citizenship law, supplemented this in the course of history with elements of *ius sanguinis*, particularly in order to perpetuate the connection to their lingering extraterritorial nationals, where *ius soli* was to remain in force for so long that the UK was not significantly affected by immigration. As with other European countries of emigration, this ensured that contact with citizens residing outside the territory was not broken until their descendants renounced it.[657]

654 SCHULTE BEERBÜHL (2007) p. 39
655 DUMMET/NICOL (1990)
656 SCHULTE BEERBÜHL (2007) p. 40
657 cf. WEIL (2012)

The UK, in designing its citizenship law,[658] follows its tradition which has always been essentially *ius soli* – unlike France, for instance, but like the Commonwealth country Canada[659] or like the US[660] – wherein the status *British Subject* is primarily the status of the individual as a subject of the British Crown – comparable to the situation in France before the entry into force of the *Code Civil*.[661] The *ius soli* was formally established in common law by "*Calvin's case*" of 1608 [662] and ultimately resulted in an extension of loyalty ("*ligeance*") to the monarch, legitimising the bonding of subjects to monarchs from birth. The rights and obligations connected to British citizenship are fundamentally based on this and were expanded to the entire *British Empire*. At its widest extent in the early twentieth century, this meant that over 800 million people worldwide theoretically possessed the right to settle in the UK and assert the same rights as British-born nationals.[663]

Building on the basis of the *Act of Union of 1707*,[664] the subjects of the British king were granted only the status of *British Subject*.[665]

The long-standing status of *British Subject* underwent a gradual development in the context of decolonisation, dividing into "citizen of the UK and Colonies" and "citizen of the independent Commonwealth countries". The independent dominions were later granted their own citizenships on the basis of the *British Nationality Act 1948*:[666] their citizens, however, would continue to remain *British Subjects* and enjoyed

---

658 For the design of British citizenship law, see also *Marshall* in SHAFIR (1998); *Dummett* in BAUBÖCK/ERSBØLL/GROENENDIJK/WALDRAUCH (2006)

659 In any event, in the classic immigration countries such as the United States, Canada and Australia, the requirement for *ius soli* is less motivated by ensuring the connection of the domestic population to an Absolutist ruling monarch, but to tap into and civilize their huge expanses of land as quickly as possible, see WEIL (2012)

660 FRANSMAN (2011); cf. also WEIL (2012)

661 See section 2.4.

662 FRANSMAN (2011); as well as *Hansen* in HANSEN/WEIL (2001)

663 HARRIS (2004)

664 Union with England Act 1707, c.7, published online at http://www.legislation.gov.uk/aosp/1707/7/introduction, last accessed on 21 September 2012

665 cf. *Cole* in CALDER/COLE/SEGLOW (2012)

666 *British Nationality Act* of 30 July 1948 (GBNA), 1948 Chapter 56 11 and 12 Geo 6, published online at http://www.legislation.gov.uk/ukpga/Geo6/11-12/56/contents, last accessed on 21 September 2012

the corresponding rights, including the right of establishment in the UK itself. The term *subject* was discontinued only within the narrower area of the UK and replaced by *citizen* in 1948.[667] In 1935 the Irish Free State passed its own Citizenship Act and declared all non-Irish persons – including all *British subjects* – foreigners, and bowed out completely from the Commonwealth in 1949.[668] Canada introduced its own Citizenship Act in 1946, which was the continuation of the concept of "*British subjecthood*", but derived afresh from Canadian citizenship. Canada has remained in the Commonwealth to this day.[669]

In response to the significantly increasing immigration to the UK in the period immediately after the Second World War, mainly from the "new Commonwealth",[670] the immigration rights of citizens of the newly independent colonies was largely restricted on the basis of the *Commonwealth Immigrants Act 1962* (CwIA 1962).[671] Just as with the subsequent *Immigration Act 1971* (GBIA 1971),[672] the CwIA 1962 not only limited entry and settlement in the UK, but created other categories in the British nationality law, using "patriality" and "right of abode" to differentiate between nationals and foreigners – granting citizenship solely on the basis of the premise that only a person born on British territory, or adopted or registered in the preceding five years was an inhabitant of the UK.[673] The CwIA 1962 is also noteworthy in the extent to which it interrupted the fundamental relationship between "nationality" and citizenship rights. From 1962 to 1981, a British passport did not represent guaranteed access to civil rights, but depended on which authority issued the passport and under

---

667 FRANSMAN (2011); DUMMET/NICOL (1990)

668 cf. *Symmons* in HANSEN/WEIL (2001)

669 Canadian Citizenship Act, s. 28

670 The Indian subcontinent, East Africa and the Caribbean, in contrast to the "*old Commonwealth*", which refers to Canada, Australia, New Zealand and sometimes South Africa. Migration from the "*old Commonwealth*", initially populated by a white people of European descent, was never an issue, cf. *Hansen* in HANSEN/WEIL (2001)

671 Commonwealth Immigrants Act 1962 (CwIA) 10 & 11 ELIZ. 2. CH. 21, published online at http://www.britishcitizen.info/CIA1962.pdf (last accessed on 21 September 2012)

672 British Immigration Act 1971 (GBIA 1971), Chapter 77, Published online athttp://www.legislation.gov.uk/ukpga/1971/77/pdfs/ukpga_19710077_en.pdf, last accessed on 21 September 2012

673 FRANSMAN (2011); WEIL (2012)

which conditions. Millions of British subjects (largely of non-European descent) worldwide still had "*British nationality*", but without actually having the associated rights: they were British nationals "*in passport but not in right*" and were *de facto* rendered stateless.[674] With these provisions, effectively introducing several different levels of nationality, the UK was in a different category to the rest of Europe or North America.[675]

A clear differentiation and codification of British citizenship was performed with the *British Nationality* Act which received Royal Assent in 1981, a move which was significantly affected by the accession of the UK to the EU in 1973, by which a uniform *British Citizenship* was created for the first time which, today is considered to be British citizenship in the more specific sense.[676] While being significantly amended since 1981, the *British Nationality Act 1981* (BNA 1981)[677] is still an authoritative source of law. Nevertheless, a differentiation remained between the inhabitants of the mother country (*British Citizens*), the dependent territories (*British Dependent Territories Citizen, BDTCs*) and those who did not fit into either of these first two categories following the enactment of the BNA 1981 (*British Overseas Citizens, BOC*).

In all, the 1981 legislation has resulted in a written and uniform British citizenship for the first time in the history of the UK: for those born under British territorial sovereignty as descendants of British citizens or to non-UK residents, *ius soli* enabled the acquisition of "Britishness" to those whom, prior to its entry into force, had been inhabitants of Britain with an uninterrupted stay of 10 years. The Act further stipulated that British citizenship was transmitted through the *ius sanguinis* readily to

674 KOCHENOV (2011)

675 FRANSMAN (2011) and *Hansen* in HANSEN/WEIL (2001); other European countries had special arrangements for people from their colonies, but in general these mean that if citizenship was acquired, all the rights associated with it were granted (as in the Netherlands) or if not, another nationality was granted (as in France). Latvia distinguishes between "citizens" and "non-citizens": "non-citizen" status effectively amounts to "functional Latvian nationality" (KOCHENOV (2011)) and is reserved for ethnic minorities

676 cf. http://www.ukba.homeoffice.gov.uk/britishcitizenship/aboutcitizenship/, last accessed on 21 September 2012

677 *British Nationality Act 1981* of 30 October 1981 as amended.

the first generation born abroad.[678] The unrestricted freedom of movement to and from the UK is reserved today to the possessor of British citizenship in the strict sense.

8.2.4 Acquisition of British citizenship: a modified *ius soli*

The centrepiece of current British citizenship law is a modified *ius soli.* Accordingly: firstly, British citizenship is granted to those people born in the UK and who either have a parent with British citizenship or a permanent place of abode in the UK, and secondly, the children of British citizens are awarded the opportunity in certain circumstances to register as "British" abroad.[679] The descendants of citizens of the UK must in principle settle in the UK to avoid the loss of their British citizenship.[680] Comparable to the applicable citizenship law in the US, all the subjects of the British Empire were, before the current citizenship law entered into force, equally required to swear an *Oath of Allegiance*[681] to the British Crown. It was worded as follows:

> *"I swear (or affirm) that I will be faithful and bear true allegiance to Her Majesty Queen Elizabeth the Second, Her Heirs and Successors, and that I will faithfully observe the laws of the United Kingdom and fulfil my duties as a British citizen."*

Those born under British territorial sovereignty could apply to acquire British citizenship through their local consulate.[682]

Regarding the minimum periods of residence in the UK, spouses can acquire British citizenship after three years of legally valid marriage while other naturalisations require a five year residence period and the absence of final convictions for offences.[683] However, a relatively strict

---

678 cf. WEIL (2012)
679 For the relevant UK minimum stay periods cf. FRANSMAN (2011)
680 cf. FRANSMAN (2011); WEIL (2012)
681 For more detail on the oath of allegiance: ALEINIKOFF/KLUSMEYER (1952); BLOEMRAAD (2009); FAHRMEIER (2000); *Hansen* in HANSEN/WEIL (2001)
682 cf. FRANSMAN (2011), WEIL (2012), *Hansen* in HANSEN/WEIL (2001)
683 cf. WEIL (2012), see also the presentation of the effects of marriage on nationality in selected States by ALEINIKOFF/KLUSMEYER (1952)

physical presence requirement applies: those seeking naturalisation must not have resided more than 450 days outside the UK in the five years preceding the application, and not more than 90 days outside the UK in the year immediately prior to the application.

All the citizenship standards of the UK in the domain of naturalisation are subject to a non-justiciable discretionary decision by state officials. Rejection of an application for naturalisation cannot generally be challenged.[684]

8.2.5 Multiple Citizenship

Multiple citizenship has been tolerated in the UK since time immemorial.[685]

8.3 France

8.3.1 State structural parameters

As the traditional opponent of the UK and the "*Grande Nation*" of the European continent (at least, in the eyes of the French themselves) citizenship in France[686] (*droit de la nationalité française*) continues to be influenced decisively by the ideas of the French Revolution of 14 July 1789[687] and subsequent years, which were initially expressed in the first French Constitution on 3 September 1791[688] and remain today as part of the Fifth Constitution of the Republic of France (French Constitution):[689] "*Liberté,* égalité, *fraternité*" (liberty, equality, fraternity),

684 *Hansen* in HANSEN/WEIL (2001)

685 cf. WEIL (2012)

686 Fundamental on the Citizenship Act in France: WEIL (2004), BRUBAKER (1992); *Weil* in HANSEN/WEIL (2001); *Weil/Spire* in BAUBÖCK/ERSBØLL/GROENENDIJK/WALDRAUCH (2006); see also the official presentation of the French government under http://www.botschaft-frankreich.de/spip.php?article1611 last accessed on 21 September 2012

687 For the development of French citizenship law from the abdication of the *Ancien Régime* on 14 July 1789: NOIRIEL (1998), BRUBAKER (1992); SCHATTLE (2008); *Weil* in HANSEN/WEIL (2001); WEIL (2004); *Weil/Spire* in BAUBÖCK/ERSBØLL/GROENENDIJK/WALDRAUCH (2006)

688 cf. TORPEY (2000)

689 Constitution of the Fifth French Republic 4 October 1959 (French Constitution), as last amended on 21 July 2008 by Constitutional Act No. 2008-724

Article 2(4) French Constitution, and with the philosophers *René Descartes* (1596–1650), *Jean Jacques Rousseau* (1712–1778) and *Francois Marie Arouet (Voltaire)* (1694–1778) came the renowned French pioneers of European enlightenment and the liberation movement. Their ideas not only took root in the Revolution of 1789 and subsequent years but – despite their secular French nature (Article 1(1)(2) French Constitution) – also influenced numerous European and non-European constitutions.

The abdication of the *Ancien Régime*[690] in France occurred with a fundamental, sociopolitical paradigm shift which led to radical changes, especially for French citizenship law[691] which until then had enjoyed a close association with the kingdom and crown, but from then also granted citizenship to people of Jewish faith, to non-whites and to slaves.[692] One particularly noteworthy change is that the definitive principle of *ius soli* which, until that moment, had served to preserve the power of the French monarchy, was replaced with citizenship laws characterised by *ius sanguinis* (*nationalité d´origine*): France proved itself to be in the sociopolitical *avant-garde* as the first country in the whole of Europe to give effect to the principle of descent. Today, the *droit de la nationalité d´origine* continues to be the norm for French citizenship.

The consensus surrounding the validity of the principle "*nationalité d´origine*" was already in place in 1801, before the official commencement of the CC on 21 March 1804. The formation of the CC through the decisive participation of jurists *Jean-Étienne-Marie Portalis* (1746–1807), *François Denis Tronchet* (1726–1806), *Félix-Julien-Jean Bigot de Preameneu* (1747–1825) and *Jacques de Maleville* (1741–1824) was the first codification of its kind in Europe in the field of civil law.[693] The CC was considered to be an exemplary system of laws and standards within Christian-Western majority culture and has had since then, significant influence on the legal culture of the "*Grande Nation*" for 200 years. For a considerable period it not only applied in France but also in the kingdoms

690 For the *Ancien Régime* cf. SAHLINS (2004), BRUBAKER (1992)
691 cf. TORPEY (2000)
692 cf. *Weil* in HANSEN/WEIL (2001)
693 cf. *Noiriel* in CAPLAN/TORPEY (2001), on the later influence of Napoleon on the development of French Citizenship Act, see BRUBAKER (1992); FAHRMEIER (2000)

of Belgium and the Netherlands, as well as the current Federal Republic of Germany (in part) and Switzerland, and has been regarded as an excellent example in many other countries worldwide.

The commitment to the principle of "*nationalité d´origine*" was provided in Article 10 CC, whereby only the descendants of French parents acquired French citizenship *ipso iure* at birth.[694] This was driven by the goal of preserving French citizenship for those individuals whose descent from the nation of France was backed by the State's expectation of timely and uncomplicated integration.[695] The detail of today's citizenship law can be traced back to the decisive *Code de la nationalité française* (CNF)[696] of 1945.

8.3.2 Citizenship statistics

In the years between 1990 and 2008, France granted citizenship to between about 59,000 and 165,121 persons per year, a total of nearly 2 million and an average of about 108,000 per year.[697] The naturalisation to population ratio is low at 0.16% per year.

---

694 WEIL (2004); *Weil* in HANSEN/WEIL (2001)

695 cf. *Weil* in HANSEN/WEIL (2001)

696 Code of the nationality Francaise (FCN), consolidated edition of 22 July 1993, last amended on 1 January 1994, Published online at http://www.legifrance.gouv.fr/affichCode.do?cidTexte=LEGITEXT000006071189&dateTexte=19930722 last accessed on 21 September 2012

697 cf. country database of citizenship acquisition for France on http://eudo-citizenship.eu, last accessed 3 February 2015

Naturalisation in France - Selected Countries of Origin[698]

Nation	*Algeria*	*Morocco*	*Tunisia*	*Other*
1990	5,355	7,741	3,076	27,805
1991	6,631	10,289	4,375	31,068
1992	7,410	12,292	4,991	27,326
1993	7,909	13,131	5,370	27,428
1994	10,868	22,676	9,248	20,341
1995	9,499	12,249	4,182	13,596
1996	n.a.	n.a.	n.a.	n.a.
1997	n.a.	n.a.	n.a.	n.a.
1998	n.a.	n.a.	n.a.	n.a.
1999	n.a.	n.a.	n.a.	n.a.
2000	17,627	37,794	12,763	49,934
2001	15,498	34,922	10,251	41.023
2002	15,711	33,967	9,956	43,888
2003	20,245	36,875	11,412	51,329
2004	25,746	43,610	13,046	58,978
2005	25,435	37,848	12,012	54,060
2006	n.a.	n.a.	n.a.	145,315
2007	n.a.	n.a.	n.a.	n.a.
2008	n.a.	n.a.	n.a.	n.a.

8.3.3 Selected structural features of French citizenship law

The ideas of the French Revolution were represented in the current French Constitution of 4 October 1958 and remain in place today. Accordingly, France is an indivisible, secular, democratic and social Republic (Article 1 French Constitution). When defining citizenship,

698 *Source: European University Institute/EUDO Citizenship Observatory, 2015*

the republican polity is underlined by the fact that all French *citoyens* are liberated, equal and eligible to vote in all democratic processes without limitation, which is emphasised in the French Constitution by the terms "People" and "Nation" in Article 3(1) French Constitution.[699]

The rules of citizenship are also fundamentally applicable in France's overseas departments and regions. As listed in Articles 72-3(2) French Constitution, these are Guadeloupe, French-Guyana, Martinique, La Réunion, Mayotte, Saint-Barthélemy, Saint-Martin, Pierre and Miquelon, the Wallis and Futuna islands and French Polynesia (Article 73(1) French Constitution), which are recognised by the Republic of France as being part of French territory and sharing a common ideal of liberty, equality and fraternity (Article 72-3(1) French Constitution). Since the reform in 1993, anyone born in these territories qualifies for French citizenship without any further action, providing that both parents are of French origin. Acquisition of citizenship is otherwise by application, which will usually be refused for (significant) criminal convictions. A person born before 1 January 1994 one of whose parents was born in a former French territory prior to independence will also receive French citizenship.[700]

The French Constitution deals with citizenship in a rudimentary fashion at best, in that in Article 3 it merely states that all French citizens of legal age and of either gender, who are in possession of their civil and civic-national rights, are eligible to vote in accordance with the law. The linking of the elements of nation State and State governance is thereby underlined by the right to vote and to be voted for in the election of the President of France, to whom Article 5 French Constitution not only assigns responsibility as the guardian and preserver of the Constitution (Article 5(1)(1) French Constitution), but also as guarantor of national independence, the integrity of the national territory and the preservation of the Treaties (Article 5(2)(1) French Constitution).

---

699 WEIL (2004); *Weil* in HANSEN/WEIL (2001)

700 http://www.botschaft-frankreich.de/spip.php?article1611, last accessed on 21 September 2012

In line with a law passed on 22 July 1993, the regulations of the old *Code de la Nationalité* have been completely subsumed into the CC. Until then, the codification of French citizenship law was originally drawn from the legislative decree of 19 October 1945, which underwent comprehensive revisions from a law passed on 9 January 1973. French citizenship law, as determined under the French Constitution, acquired relatively detailed provisions in Articles 17 to 33 CC. The acquisition, award and the loss of French citizenship is regulated therein under the international treaties and agreements (Article 17 CC) ratified by the French Republic.

8.3.4 Original acquisition: the double ius soli

The main parameters of the CC include a commitment to a double *ius soli* since the French nationality law of 1889[701] As a basic rule of the CC, the acquisition of citizenship is granted at birth. According to this, a child with one French citizen parent, possesses French citizenship in any event (Article 18 CC). With the exception of the descendants of French-born diplomats or consul-generals (Article 20-5 CC), any new-born child enjoys French citizenship if it is born in French territory and, in any case, has one French citizen parent (Article 19-3 CC). In other words: children born in France get French nationality, even if only one of the parents has French nationality.[702]

As an extension of the principle, in force in one form or another since 1804, that a child with one French citizen parent is characterised as having been born in France (Article 18 CC), French citizenship by descent as provided by Article 19(3) CC is granted in terms of a double *ius soli*. Accordingly, a legitimate or illegitimate child born in France with at least one French-born parent, also has French citizenship. However, the citizenship legislation which entered into force on 1 September 1998[703] again partially shifted dominance back to the

701 For the successive development and redevelopment of this law from *ius sanguinis* in 1804 to *ius soli* due to the different migration flows to France since the late nineteenth century: BRUBAKER (1992) and WEIL (2004)

702 Article 19(3) CC stipulates: "*Is French a child born in France where one at least of his parents was himself or herself born there*" (CC translated in English by *Georges Rouhette*)

703 Law No 98-170 of 16 March 1998

territoriality principle, away from the dominant principle of descent in place since 1804.

Under these conditions, a child is considered a French citizen even if they only fulfil the legal requirements for French citizenship later on (Article 20 CC). The departure of the current French citizenship law from the originally dominant principle of descent in the CC is evident in the fact that the parentage of the child only has exceptional influence on his or her French citizenship (Article 20-1 CC).

8.3.4.1 Citizenship by ordinary naturalisation

The principle of double *ius soli*[704] which leads, without any further action, to the acquisition of French citizenship[705] in the third generation of immigrants at the very latest, is particularly emphasised in the 1993 reform of French citizenship law. Ever since, every child born in France to foreign parents acquires French citizenship upon reaching legal age, if at this time the child has had his or her habitual residence in France for a total period of five years since reaching the age of 11. (Article 21-7(1) CC).[706] The determining factor in this instance is that during this period, the place of residence and centre of vital interest must have both been in France.[707]

The five year requirement applies for adults on the condition that the person is earning her own livelihood[708] and, at the time of the deadline, has no convictions for any criminal offence. Approval of naturalisation is automatic in the absence of any express contravention of these conditions.[709] In practice, the acquisition of French citizenship is thereby already possible at the age of 16 through the presentation of a declaration

704 cf. WEIL (2004); and *Weil* in HANSEN/WEIL (2001)
705 cf. USLUCAN (2012); *Weil* in HANSEN/WEIL (2001)
706 This requirement cf. HAGEDORN, page 3 ff; KLUSMEYER/ALEINIKOFF (2002), and *Weil* in HANSEN/WEIL (2001)
707 Article 21-7(1) CC
708 For the labour market access in France as a condition of raising its own income from gainful economic activity cf. KLUSMEYER/ALEINIKOFF (2002)
709 cf. *Weil* in HANSEN/WEIL (2001)

without specific endorsements.[710] If the applicant is a member of the French armed forces, or has rendered outstanding services to the French nation in another area of the public sector in economic or cultural terms, the minimum length of stay can be reduced to two years for single persons and immediately for spouses, provided that the union has been legally effective for one year.[711]

France, as a unitary republican nation State prominently highlights that the language of the Republic is French (Article 2(1) French Constitution).[712] Although France, unlike say Austria or Canada, does not require a formalised test to be completed in which command of the French language must be demonstrated as a condition for naturalisation,[713] it can, nevertheless, be surmised from the relevant legal sources that France applies "final point" theory and views naturalisation as completed integration.[714]

8.3.4.2 Citizenship by naturalisation under special circumstances: ius doni

Of particular interest for the present study in relation to France are the provisions of the Act of 22 December 1961 which, until July 2006,[715] amended the 5 Article 21-19 CC to exempt nationals of all countries or territories whose official language or one whose official languages is French and/or who had ever been under French rule (!)[716] from the five-year residence period, enabling naturalisation to be demanded directly, as long as you resided and your centre of vital interest was France.[717] Residence and centre of vital interest in France are, however, generally only recognised in practice or in accordance with the jurisdiction of the

---

710 Among the possibilities in this respect, see also the official presentation of the French State Government at www.travail-solidarite.gouv.fr (last accessed on 21 September 2012)

711 cf. STURM (2001); cf. also http://www.botschaft-frankreich.de/spip.php?article1611, last accessed on 21 September 2012

712 For the command of the French language as a prerequisite for naturalisation see KLUSMEYER/ALEINIKOFF (2002)

713 cf. USLUCAN (2012)

714 cf. USLUCAN (2012)

715 Repealed by Act 2006-911 of 26 July 2006

716 This applies to dozens of countries and territories worldwide, see WEIL (2004)

717 cf. WEIL (2004)

Conseil d'Etat, if someone really has his family, professional interests and connections primarily in France and, according to established case-law, can prove that France has been this centre of vital interests for the previous three years. It is worth noting that top athletes, artists and "*catégories prioritaires*" are still exempted from this.[718] Even though the former provisions of the fifth Article 21-19 CC were repealed in 2006, the same continues to be provided in the sixth Article today, in that aliens who have made extraordinary contributions or whose naturalisation is in the extraordinary interest of France may be naturalised without the residence requirement being fulfilled.[719]

Furthermore, under today's legislation, the provisions of Articles 21-20 and Articles 21-21 apply, which are both of interest here. These provisions allow for a foreign person to apply for French citizenship with no residence requirement, provided that this person belongs to the "*entité culturelle et linguistique française*" and is a citizen of a State or territory where at least one of the official languages is French, provided that this person either speaks French as his or her mother tongue, or has spent at least five years in a French-language school (Article 21-20 CC). Furthermore, any foreign francophone person can be granted French citizenship on demand without a residence requirement following a proposal by the French Minister of Foreign Affairs, provided this person "*contribue par son action* émérite *au rayonnement de la France et* à *la Prospérité de ses relations* économiques *international*" (Article 21-21 CC). In other words, any foreign individual who is a "francophone" and has achieved something extraordinary for France can, on the proposal of the French Minister of Foreign Affairs, be granted French citizenship: *ius doni* par excellence, so to speak. France thus not only has far-reaching provisions concerning the extraordinary naturalisation of francophone foreigners who meet certain conditions, but also has provisions that allow the State to naturalise directly those "francophone" foreigners who have made an extraordinary contribution, including by reference to economic services

718 WEIL (2014)

719 *"Peut être naturalisé sans condition de stage:...L'étranger qui a rendu des services exceptionnels à la France ou celui dont la naturalisation présente pour la France un intérêt exceptionnel."* (Article 21-19 (6) CC)

(*"prospérité de ses relations* économiques *internationales*"), i.e. provisions that include the very concept of Citizenship-by-Investment.

When drawing a legal comparison with the other reference countries here, the citizenship laws of the Fifth French Republic are also particularly remarkable in that they place a relatively high value on individual assimilation, which is expressed in one form through the ban on the full-body veiling of Islamic women ("burqa ban").[720] Although having been married to a Frenchman for four years, in 2005 the *Conseil d'Etat*[721] rejected a Muslim[722] woman's application for French citizenship because of her full-body veiling, which could not be reconciled with the core values of the Fifth French Republic and, moreover, went against the principle in Article 1(2) and Article 3(4) of the French Constitution that women and men have equal rights. Such a decision also came to light in an earlier decision in 1989 (*"L'affaire du foulard"*).[723]

The granting of French citizenship may be refused by the State if a *defaut d'assimlilation*[724] (Article 21(4)(1) CC) can be ascertained.[725] Under the conditions specified therein, the French State can, within one year, oppose the acquisition of French citizenship on the basis of a decree[726] of the *Conseil d'Etat*. As French citizenship law continues to require the presentation of assimilation as a condition of naturalisation, it has a distinctive, unique characteristic among the reference States.[727] Where such a decision is made, it is implied by the State that the person concerned

---

720 cf.: http://diepresse.com/home/politik/aussenpolitik/398131/Frankreich_Marokkanerin-mit-Burka-Einbuergerung-verweigert?from=simarchiv last accessed on 21 September 2012

721 Judgment of the Conseil d´Etat, published online at www.conseil-etat.fr/ce/jurispd/index_ac_id0820.shtml, last accessed on 22 March 2012

722 On the opportunities and obstacles to integration by religious institutionalisation: *Bruce* in TALANI (2012): for a comparison of the French Council of Muslims (CFCM) to the German Islamic Conference

723 cf. BENHABIB (2004)

724 cf. http://www.legislationline.org/documents/action/popup/id/5587, last accessed on 21 September 2012

725 For general information on the revocation of French nationality: *De Groot* in HAILBRONNER/MARTIN (2003)

726 Naturalisation applications are initially processed in France by the locally competent prefecture and subsequently approved or rejected and decided by decree by the Commissioner for naturalisation issues

727 cf. JOPPKE (2011)

never acquired French citizenship (Article 21(4)(2) CC). If a bi-national marriage later ends in divorce, it does not, however, affect the citizenship of any of the children (Article 21-6 CC).

As in Dutch citizenship law, French citizenship law is following a social trend[728] towards greater restriction, which is inspired by critical events such as the riots in the Paris suburbs in the autumn of 2005 or the events in Toulouse[729] in southern France which are, to some extent, a consequence of the conventional citizenship law of France.[730] It therefore comes as no surprise that French citizenship is sometimes spoken of with reference to an "assimilation model", in the sense that the social upheavals of 1789–1791 refer back to the will of the nation and State affiliation, which determines its spirit and language.[731]

8.3.4.3 Citizenship by marriage

In a departure for French citizenship law, which from the end of the Second World War under *Charles de Gaulle* until 1973 held that the spouse of a French person *ipso iure* acquired French citizenship when the marriage became legally binding, marital status today is of no significance. Accordingly, French citizenship is influenced neither by marriage (Article 21-1 CC) nor by adoption (Article 21 CC).

Nevertheless, a foreigner or a stateless person who marries a French person can acquire French citizenship by declaration after two years of a legally valid marriage, so long as their partnership remains intact, is not physically terminated by separation and the spouse originally had French citizenship (Article 21-2(1) CC).[732] The two year rule, introduced in 1984, is primarily to address the concerns about "devious"

---

728 Regarding the recent development of French Citizenship Act, cf. *Weil/Spire* in BAUBÖCK/ERSBØLL/GROENENDIJK/WALRAUCH (2006)

729 The murder of seven people and including several children by the radical Islamist and Maghreb Al-Qaeda activist *Mohamed Mehra* in early 2012. The impact of the latest murders by French Islamist terrorists at the satirical publication *Charlie Hebdo* in Paris in January 2015 remains to be seen

730 cf. USLUCAN (2012)

731 cf. RENAN (1882); USLUCAN (2012)

732 cf. http://autexier.jura.uni-saarland.de/skripteca/DPFStaatsexamen/drpufr/drpufr_000023.htm last accessed on 21 September 2012

attempts to gain French citizenship through marriages of convenience. The foreign wife or the foreign husband must provide (Article 21-2(2) CC) proof of sufficient knowledge of the French language. In this respect, the minimum period is extended to three years if the foreign spouse does not prove when submitting a declaration that he/she has lived in France continuously for one year during the marriage (Article 21-2(3) CC).

8.3.4.4 Multiple Citizenship

Multiple citizenship[733] is permissible in accordance with both the provisions of the French Constitution and with those of the CC.

8.4 Switzerland

8.4.1 State structural parameters

Although the Swiss Confederation is not a member of the EU, large parts of its legislation is heavily influenced by European law in practice, due to the bilateral agreements which it maintains with all EU member States today.[734] Moreover, on 1 November 2008 it joined the Schengen area within which all internal border checks had been abolished.[735] Both the Swiss federal state and the Swiss Cantons recognise public international law by virtue of its explicit incorporation in Article 5(4) of the Federal Constitution of the Swiss Confederation (SCst).[736]

A particular distinguishing feature of the Swiss legal order is the principle of individual and social responsibility (Article 6 SCst), according to which, every resident of Switzerland takes responsibility for themselves and must, in accordance with their own capacities, contribute to dealing with the

---

733 For an authoritative view on multiple citizenship in France: *De Groot* in HAILBRONNER/MARTIN (2003); *de la Pradelle* in HANSEN/WEIL (2002) pp. 191–214

734 For the relationship between Swiss Law and European Law cf. THÜRER (1999)

735 Convention of 14 June 1985 between the Governments of the States of the Benelux Economic Union, the Federal Republic of Germany and the French Republic on the gradual abolition of checks at their common borders ("Schengen I Agreement")

736 Federal Constitution of the Swiss Confederation (Cst) of 18 April 1999

tasks of the State and society – emphasised in the strong federal, grass-roots democratic and subsidiarity-driven constitution of Switzerland. The State's purpose is to defend the freedom and the rights of the people (Article 2(1) SCst), the common welfare, sustainable development, internal cohesion and the cultural diversity of the country (Article 2(2) SCst). In ethnic terms, about 80 percent of residents are Swiss. The approximate 20 percent of foreign residents originate chiefly from Germany, Italy, Portugal, and from the former multi-ethnic State of Yugoslavia.

The cultural diversity of Switzerland is particularly expressed in its linguistic diversity. As explicitly provided in Article 4 SCst, the national languages are German, French, Italian and Rhaeto-Romanic. Although there is no kind of hierarchy in that order – all languages referred to in Article 4 SCst are formally equal, not least because Article 18 SCst explicitly guarantees freedom of language – reflecting the *de facto* balance of power again, German is the official language in 17 of the 26 Swiss cantons. Of the 8 million Swiss citizens, about 4.1 million live in cantons with German as the official language, corresponding to about 55 percent of the total population. Only four cantons (Geneva, Jura, Neuchâtel, Vaud) use French as their sole official language, and only Ticino has Italian as the exclusive language. Rhaeto-Romanic is one of the official languages only in the Canton of Grisons.

Unusual for a modern federal state, the Swiss Cantons are sovereign insofar as their sovereignty is not limited by the Federal Constitution (Article 3 SCst). They exercise all the rights that are not explicitly transferred to the Confederation (Article 3 SCst). In terms of State structure, the relationship between the Swiss cantons and the Swiss Federal State can be compared with the relationship between the EU and its 28 Member States today, which – as mentioned *supra*[737] – applies the principle of conferral. This proportion of foreign residents is surpassed only by small and microstates such as, for example, Qatar, Liechtenstein, Luxembourg or Monaco. Characterised by a concern over a successive loss of identity, and in view of the fact that about one-fifth of the Swiss population is now not

[737] cf. section 2.6.1.

in possession of Swiss citizenship, the Swiss Confederation has, for the first time in recent history, witnessed the rise of a xenophobic movement. Even the Germans who are the numerically largest group of foreigners after the Italians and who additionally commute from the neighbouring German State of Baden-Württemberg in their tens of thousands every day to Switzerland to work, are now subject to some resentment.[738] All things considered, the laws and practice of naturalisation in Switzerland are in any case designed to be very restrictive, which is also reflected in the fact that in some municipalities, the key naturalisation decision is taken at the community level – permitting, for example, a commune to practice an effective stop to naturalisation due to the country's federal and grass-roots democratic constitution, and while community authorities generally only have a formal right to review applications.[739]

Switzerland arguably has one of the world's most restrictive conditions for naturalisation,[740] only surpassed by many Asian countries, in particular Japan and China, and many African and Arab States.

8.4.2 Citizenship statistics

In the years between 1990 and 2008, Switzerland granted citizenship to between 8,658 and 44,365 persons per year, a total of nearly 489,000 and an average of 27,160 per year.[741] The naturalisation to population ratio is low at 0.34% per year.

---

738 cf. HENCKEL (2012)

739 cf. HAINMUELLER/HANGARTNER (2013); USLUCAN (2012)

740 This is however only a relatively recent phenomenon. Prior to the First World War, naturalisation required an average of only two years of residence. Between the wars this was increased to six years and in the nineteen-fifties only this was increased to 12 years. The long term effect of this recent restrictive citizenship admission practice is that Switzerland has a high percentage of foreign citizen residents, cf. *Diggelmann*, in WALTER/GÄRDITZ (2015) pp. 165–166. A new amendment, to enter into force in 2016, will reduce this residence period to 10 years, however other restrictive requirements, including tests to assess the "integration" of applicants, remain

741 Bundesamt für Statistik http://www.bfs.admin.ch/bfs/portal/de/index/themen/01/07/blank/data/01.html; Statistik, Erwerb des Schweizer Bürgerrechts nach Art des Erwerbs, 1900 -2013

8.4.3 Selected structural features of Swiss citizenship law

In the German-speaking territory of Switzerland, citizenship has long been known as the *Schweizer Bürgerrecht* (citizenship in the sense of the "Swiss civic right"): the term *Staatsbürgerschaft* or even more so *Staatsangehörigkeit* has been avoided since 1848 because it acts as too strong a reminder of a condition of being a subject.[742] The term "subject", as it was used in the UK until very recently, would be unthinkable in Switzerland. In its current configuration, citizenship of Switzerland[743] is essentially regulated under the second chapter of the SCst "Civil and political rights". Swiss citizens are those people in possession of the civic rights of a community and the civic rights of their respective Canton (Article 37(1) SCst). Swiss citizenship, as regulated in Articles 37 and 38 SCst, is then given substance by the federal Swiss Citizenship Act (SCA).[744] This tri-fold character of Swiss citizenship is rather unique. Swiss citizenship as acquired by birth or by the process of naturalisation[745] is however otherwise comparable to the other reference countries, as the legal affiliation of a natural person to Switzerland. Any associated rights connected thereto are to be derived from the overall context of the SCst. A legal definition of this citizenship cannot, however, be inferred from the SCst. According to Article 37(2)(1) SCst, no individual may be advantaged or disadvantaged because of his or her citizenship (principle of non-discrimination).

The layered Swiss citizenship model that was introduced with the founding of the modern federal state in 1848 has inspired the German Federal State citizenship between 1870 and 1934 as well as the Austrian Federal State citizenship after the end of the Habsburg monarchy in 1918. In the

742 *Rieser*, The Swiss Civil Rights (1892), quoted in SCHOENBERGER (2005)

743 Fundamental to citizenship in Switzerland: CARONI/GRASDORF-MEYER/OTT/SCHEIBER (2014); HELBLING (2008) and historically ARGAST (2007); and also cf. STUDER/ARLETTAZ/ARGAST (2008), KLUSMEYER/ALEINIKOFF (2002); *Jackson* in ALEINIKOFF/KLUSMEYER (2001); MILLER (2000) pp. 129–130; USLUCAN (2012); *Talani* in TALANI (2012); Regarding migration statistics of the Swiss Confederation cf. JOPPKE (2011)

744 Federal Act on the acquisition and loss of Swiss nationality (Swiss Citizenship Act) of 29 September 1952 as amended (status as of 1 January 2013)

745 cf. *Brubaker* in SHAFIR (1998)

continuity of this continental-European federalism the EU emerged, and is occasionally compared with the development of Swiss citizenship.[746]

Following an extensive political debate about a long needed reform of the Swiss citizenship Act, a new revised SCA was approved by the Swiss parliament on 20 June 2014 (nSCA). There was no referendum taken up against the nSCA, and this will become law in due course, however a particular date has not yet been set.[747] Hereinafter reference is therefore made to both the old and the new citizenship law, which also nicely show how citizenship law is evolving in a what is for western standards a relatively conservative country in terms of access to citizenship.

8.4.4 Ordinary acquisition of citizenship: *ius sanguinis*

The *ius sanguinis* remains the decisive legal principle for the acquisition of Swiss citizenship. This can be explained not least by the fact that Switzerland has like for example Luxembourg for years had an unusually high proportion of people born outside the Swiss territory, many of whom, in turn, are active within international organisations or multinational companies and thus contribute indirectly to the country's domestic prosperity.[748] This finds its significant expression in Article 1 SCA/nSCA. Accordingly, the legitimate child of a Swiss national acquires the Swiss citizenship at birth by the operation of law (Article 1, Section 1 SCA/nSCA). Likewise, the illegitimate child of a Swiss citizen acquires Swiss citizenship at birth if the mother is a Swiss citizen or otherwise as if he or she had already acquired citizenship at birth, upon the presentation of a declaration of paternity to the relevant authority (Article 1(2) SCA/nSCA). This also applies similarly to adoption cases (Article 7 SCA, Article 4 nSCA). Accordingly, a minor acquires the cantonal and communal citizenship of the adopter and thus the Swiss citizenship when he or she is adopted by a Swiss citizen.

---

[746] Instead of many, SCHÖNBERGER (2005) pp. 80–81, with further references
[747] As of 24 June 2015
[748] cf. JOPPKE (2012)

8.4.5 Combination of citizenship of the municipality and canton

Swiss citizenship is acquired on the basis of possessing a cantonal citizenship which, in turn, is based on citizenship in a particular municipality, and is distinctly directly democratic in form.[749] Comparable to the situation in Austria before its federal single citizenship law came into force, Article 37(1) SCst attaches Swiss citizenship to membership of a Swiss canton. It therefore again emphasises the very federal, subsidiary (Article 5(a) SCst) and grassroots democratic structure in Switzerland, as described in particular in Article 3 SCst.

A child acquires the cantonal and municipal citizenship and "Place of Origin"[750] of their parents, which emphasises the origin principle as the dominant principle underpinning citizenship in Switzerland: indeed, instead of place of birth, the Swiss passport has a field "Place of Origin" which lists the commune(s) and canton(s) of which the holder is a citizen. Multiple citizenship within Switzerland, i.e. holding citizenship of more than one municipality and more than one canton, is possible.

The pronouncedly federal and directly democratic constitution of Switzerland is slightly moderated in that the legal minimal requirements for the acquisition and loss of Swiss citizenship by origin, marriage and adoption are regulated by the Swiss Federal State (Article 38(1)(1) SCst). Also, ultimately the Swiss Federal State grants naturalisation on Federal level and thus has the final say. (Article 38(2) SCst). Nevertheless, both the federal and the directly democratic structure in Switzerland also find expression here in that the Swiss State may only provide minimum requirements for the naturalisation of foreigners by the cantons.[751]

Given that federal law only sets minimum requirements, the cantons and municipalities retain considerable regulatory scope, which is expressed in the diversity of administrative procedures, forms and conditions for

---

749 cf. *Jackson* in ALEINIKOFF/KLUSMEYER (2001)

750 "Heimatort"

751 In accordance with Article 15(a) SCA, the naturalisation process is regulated, in contrast to the definition of the substantive criteria for naturalisation by cantonal law

naturalisation provided,[752] although in the nSCA this has been somewhat streamlined. This diversity, as so often in Switzerland, results in quite significant "administrative duplication".[753] The Swiss Federal State grants Swiss citizenship within a framework of "simplified naturalisation", which concerns mainly applications on the basis of marriage to a Swiss citizen (cf. *infra*), after prior consultation at all three levels, federal, cantonal and municipal. The latter two are however jointly primarily involved in "ordinary naturalisation" under Article 38 SCst, meaning that an applicant's access to the Swiss citizenship most often falls at the hurdles on cantonal and in particular municipal level, as far more applications are rejected by the municipalities than by the cantonal or the federal authorities, respectively.[754]

8.4.6 Acquisition of Swiss citizenship by naturalisation

Based on Article 38 Section 2 SCst, while the Swiss federal state provides the overall framework,[755] the cantons are in fact responsible for the actual naturalisation of foreign persons. However, the Federal authorities must still give the final consent (Article 12 Section 2 SCA, Article 9 nSCA). The provisions regarding the ordinary naturalisation are contained in Articles 9 to 18 nSCA.[756]

Ordinary naturalisation used to require that the applicant resided in Switzerland for 12 years before application, three of which must have been completed in the five years immediately preceding the application (Article 15(1) SCA).[757] The time spent in Switzerland between the applicant's tenth and twentieth birthdays counted double.[758]

The new Citizenship Act brought about several changes. In Article 9 nSCA it is now required that the applicant must hold a permanent

752 cf. *D'Amato* in D'AMATO/GERBER (2005)
753 cf. USLUCAN (2012); STEINER/WICKER (2004)
754 HAINMUELLER/HANGARTNER (2013) p. 160 re the autonomy of municipalities; cf. Also USLUCAN (2012) and SCHÖNBERGER (2005) p. 90
755 Article 38 Section 1 SCst
756 Previously Articles 12 to 15c SCA
757 cf. JOPPKE (2012)
758 Article 15(2) SCA

residence permit (while previously any legal status was permissible), and has resided in Switzerland for at least 10 years, of which three must have been spent in Switzerland within the last five years before applying for naturalisation. The time spent in Switzerland between the applicant's eight and eighteenth birthdays are now counted double.[759] However, the effective period of residence must in any case be six years.[760]

Both the old law and the nSCA require the applicant to be integrated and not pose a threat to public security.[761]

Additionally, cantons and municipalities may provide for further, additional requirements, for example knowledge of the local language or additional residence requirements in the canton or municipality.[762] The new law will however require cantons to provide conditions within a certain framework, for example to provide for a minimum residence requirement of two to five years.[763]

The relatively strict naturalisation provisions undergo some mitigation in the so-called simplified naturalisation. Under Article 26 SCA or Article 20 nSCA, ordinary and simplified naturalisations are differentiated; the simplified naturalisations principally concern spouses of Swiss citizens, as well as a few special cases.

This process provides that if the applicant is integrated into Switzerland (Article 26(1)(a) SCA), respects the Swiss legal system (Article 26(1)(b) SCA), does not pose a threat to the internal or external security of Switzerland (Article 26(1)(c) SCA) and, after marrying a Swiss citizen, he or she may apply for naturalisation, having lived in Switzerland for a total of five years (Article 27(a) SCA, Article 21 Section 1 nSCA), having been living in Switzerland for the whole previous year (Article 27(b) SCA, Article 21 Section 1 nSCA) and having been living in marital union with a Swiss citizen for three years (Article 27(c) SCA, Article

759 Article 9 Section 2 nSCA
760 Article 9 Section 2 nSCA
761 Article 14 SCA and Article 11 nSCA; cf. also *infra.*
762 This is specifically provided for in Article 12 Section 3 nSCA
763 Article 18 Section 1 nSCA

21 Section 1 nSCA). Considered together, this means that foreign spouses will acquire Swiss citizenship after three years of marriage and five years of residence, benefiting them and their children. In terms of their legal nature, Swiss simplified naturalisation acts are considered as justiciable legal applications which must meet the federal constitutional requirements which limit the plebiscite and the grassroots democratic instruments of Switzerland.[764] They cannot be subject to direct democratic votes and are exclusively subject to written statutory law, they can be challenged in cantonal courts and be annulled following a constitutional appeal before the Federal Court.

8.4.7 Suitability for naturalisation

In material terms, the central conditions for the granting of Swiss citizenship are provided by Article 14 SCA and Article 11 nSCA and Article 12 nSCA, which state that it is necessary to determine whether an applicant is qualified for naturalisation before granting authorisation.[765] As underlined in the wording of Article 14(1) SCA (Article 12 nSCA) "in particular", the suitability criteria are not exhaustive but allow the granting authority a considerable margin of discretion based on the facts. Whether naturalisation is granted is decided on whether the applicant is incorporated into the Swiss community (Article 14(a) SCA), familiar with Swiss habits, customs and practices (Article 14(b) SCA), respects Swiss law (Article 14(c) SCA) and does not pose a threat to the internal or external security of Switzerland (Article 14(d) SCA).[766] In the new version, it is required that the applicant is "integrated" successfully (Article 11(a) nSCA, is familiar with Swiss ways of life (11(b)), and does not pose a threat to the internal and external security of Switzerland. (11(c)). Article 12 nSCA further clarifies these points and requests that

764 HAINMUELLER/HANGARTNER (2013) p. 160 and 162; cf. also ABDERHALDEN/EHRENZELLER (2008)

765 For greater detail on the historic criteria for integration in Switzerland: ARGAST (2007), which largely continue to apply in principle in the Swiss naturalisation rules even under the nSCA. In this regard also cf. CARONI/GRASDORF-MEYER/OTT/SCHEIBER (2014)

766 For greater detail on the relevant values in Switzerland under the conditions of progressive European integration: THUERER (1999)

the applicant must have at all times respected the public order and security (Article 12 (a) nSCA), respect the Swiss constitution (12 (b)), is able to communicate in one of the country's official languages (12(c)), participates in economic activity or acquires skills through education (12(d)) and assists in the integration of the spouse and/or the children for which the applicant has custody. These provisions are thus a prime example of final point theory citizenship legislation: the applicant who wishes to become a Swiss citizen really has to show that he or she is largely integrated into Swiss society.

Hainmueller/Hangartner have shown that the applicant's country of origin is effectively a decisive factor in a successful application for naturalisation in Switzerland.[767] The presupposed integration of the applicant under Article 14(a) SCA and now Article 11 (a) nSCA requires good language skills and knowledge of culture and history, which can be determined in part in a written aptitude test. Various forms of such tests are the norm in the citizenship application procedures in Switzerland.

Switzerland does not, however, have provisions in its citizenship law that come even close to incorporating *ius doni* principles.

8.4.8 Multiple Citizenship

Multiple citizenship has been allowed under Swiss law since 1992.

8.5 Canada

8.5.1 State structural parameters

The main sources of Canadian citizenship law are the *Citizenship Act, as amended* (*CaCA*),[768] the *Canadian Charter of Rights and Freedoms* (*CaCharter*)[769] and the *Immigration and Refugee Protection Act* (*CaIRPA*).[770]

---

767 HAINMUELLER/HANGARTNER (2013) p. 185

768 For greater detail on the Canadian Citizenship Act: GoCa, Canadian Citizenship Act, s.1 ff.; cf. also BLOEMRAAD (2006); *Galloway* in ALEINIKOFF/KLUSMEYER (2000); KAPLAN (1993)

769 Constitution Act, 1982, Part I: Canadian Charter of Rights and Freedoms

770 Immigration and Refugee Protection Act (S.C. 2001, c. 27), current as at 20 February

The CaCA is the main body of law regulating Canadian citizenship and was enacted by the Canadian Parliament on 27 June 1946, coming into effect on 1 January 1947. For a long time, Canada was viewed as a model nation[771] among immigration countries[772] as a parliamentary monarchy of around 35 million inhabitants, having emerged from the *British Empire*, and having been decisively influenced by these factors.[773] Accordingly, both Canadian-born and naturalised citizens continued to be considered British citizens until 1946.[774]

The *Canadian Immigration Act* was already in place as early as in 1910 and, at that time, Canada was driven by the desire to facilitate the development of the then largely unpopulated Western Canada,. The *CaCA* replaced a previous Canadian Citizenship Act on 15 February 1977 and remains in force today.

One of the objectives of the Canadian Government in recent years has been to limit citizenship by descent. On 17 April 2009, the rules for Canadian citizenship changed for persons born outside Canada to Canadian parents and who were not already Canadian citizens. Canadian citizenship by birth outside Canada to a Canadian citizen parent (citizenship by descent) was limited to the first generation born outside Canada.

The most recent amendments are contained in the Strengthening Canadian Citizenship Act (SCCA), which received Royal Assent on 19 June 2015. The provisions of the SCCA, some of which came into force on 29 May 2015 and others on 11 June 2015, have brought further significant changes to the CaCA, including stricter physical presence requirements to qualify for citizenship and the authority of the Minister of Citizenship and Immigration to revoke Canadian citizenship from

---

2012, last amended on 30 June 2006, published online at http://laws.justice.gc.ca/eng/acts/I-2.5/ last accessed on 21 September 2012

771 On the relevant requirements and challenges cf. *Kymklicka* in SHAFIR (1998); regarding Canada's immigration policy, cf. *Soysal* in SHAFIR (1998); and WINTER (2013)

772 JANOSKI (2010)

773 On the limits to the idea of the Commonwealth resulting from the self-determination the people in the case of Canada, see SCHÖNING (2011)

774 cf. GoCa, Canadian Citizenship Act: Introduction

dual citizens who are convicted of terrorism, high treason, and/or treason or espionage offences, depending on the sentence received.

In addition, the Federal Court now has the authority to revoke Canadian citizenship from dual citizens for serving as a member in an armed force of a country or an organized armed group engaged in armed conflict with Canada.[775]

8.5.2 Citizenship statistics

In the years between 1990 and 2008, Canada granted citizenship to between about 105,000 and 260,000 persons per year, a total of nearly 3.2 million and an average of about 180,400 per year.[776] The naturalisation to population ratio is low at 0.55% per year.

8.5.3 Selected structural features of the Canadian citizenship law

It would appear to be appropriate to review the content of Canadian citizenship law in the context of the fundamental rights and freedoms set out in the CaCharter. CaCharter is the bill of rights entrenched in the Constitution of Canada and contributes significantly to shaping Canada's citizenship law. In particular, consideration ought to be given to the freedom of conscience and religion (Article 2(a) CaCharter), the freedom of thought, belief, opinion and expression, including the press and media (Article 2(b) CaCharter), the freedom of peaceful assembly (Article 2(c) CaCharter) and the freedom of association (Article 2(d) CaCharter).

In terms of language, Canada is unique for having two official languages - English and French (especially in the Province of Quebec,[777]

---

775 cf. statement by the Canadian Immigration and Citizenship Ministry, published online at http://news.gc.ca/web/article-en.do?nid=981809, last accessed on 29 June 2015

776 Citizenship and Immigration Canada, External Statistical Reporting Group, individual request CR-15-0178 RE: Citizenship-Grant (Naturalization) Statistics 1990-2008, response received 12 May 2015

777 On the secessionist tendencies of this mainly French-speaking province: *Kymklicka* in SHAFIR (1998); MILLER (2000); SCHOENING (2011); *Simard* in KAPLAN (1993); *Turp* in KAPLAN (1993)

which stands out in its aspirations for autonomy,[778] the so-called "*société distinct*"). As can be seen in Article 16(1) of the CaCharter, English and French are the two official languages of Canada and have equality of status and equal rights and privileges as to their use in all institutions of the Parliament and Government of Canada.

The proportion of the population of British origin is predominant, numbering about 28%, followed by the French (about 23%) and the rest of Europe (about 15%). The group of other nationalities in Canada is large, at about 34%, and underscores the pronounced multi-cultural character of this country built upon immigration, which has significantly influenced its citizenship law and naturalisation practices.

In comparison to continental European law, which links back by no small measure to Roman law, an essential feature of the common law is the great importance accorded to judicial decisions (*case law*) and their precedential effect.[779] As with the laws of England and Wales, this also applies to Canadian law. An essential characteristic of binding precedent is that the legislation is based on judicial precedents and individual decisions: it follows the premise that the lower courts are bound by previous decisions of higher courts insofar as these decisions constitute legal precedents.[780] Compared to the legal situation in the Federal Republic of Germany, where the decisions of the Constitutional Court are law (Section 13 Federal Constitutional Court Act),[781] a binding effect applies in principle only at the level of appeal, where federal courts are bound only by the decisions of higher federal courts, and the courts of the constituent States only by the decisions of higher courts of those constituent States.[782]

---

778 For the international legal capacity of the Canadian provinces, which are even bound by international treaties and thereby justify "external sovereignty" see AUST (2007)

779 cf. KLOEPFER/MAST (1995)

780 cf. SOWADE (2002)

781 Federal Constitutional Court Act (Federal Constitutional Court). Notice of 11 August 1993, last amended by Article 1 of the law of 12 July 2012

782 cf. SOWADE (2002)

Canada's State authority is broadly similar in principle to the State authority of the UK.[783] Thus, the majority of legislation emerges almost exclusively from central government and takes the legal form of an Act of Parliament. Delegated legislation (statutory instruments) in turn is adopted as ordinances in the form of rules and orders. Ministerial direction is principally expressed in the mostly non-binding *codes of practice, guidance notes* and *circulars*.[784]

8.5.4 Acquisition of citizenship by origin: modernised *ius soli*

In principle there are two ways to acquire Canadian citizenship. A Canadian citizen is someone who has Canadian citizenship either from birth or by naturalisation. In terms of the routes to acquiring Canadian citizenship: firstly, a Canadian-born person is a Canadian citizen without any other requirement being imposed ("Natural Born Citizen"), insofar as he or she is not the descendant of a foreign diplomat[785] (Section 3(2) CaCA).

Where the person concerned does not thereby become stateless, a biological parent must in any case have Canadian citizenship, i.e. be a Canadian citizen or "permanent Canadian resident".[786] Canada citizenship law recognises a modernised *ius soli*.[787] It is regarded as a modernised *ius soli* because a person born of a Canadian citizen abroad, who, at the time of his or her birth, has one of his or her parents who is a Canadian citizen, acquires Canadian citizenship *ipso iure* (Section 3(1)(b) CaCA).

While the decisive formal criteria relating to the acquisition and loss of Canadian citizenship can be readily found in the CaCA,[788] its silence on multiple citizenship (except negatively, since the amendment which came into effect in June 2015, to allow the government to revoke Canadian

---

783 cf. MUELLER (1991)
784 cf. KLOEPFER/MAST (1995)
785 For the granting of diplomatic asylum by the Canadian Government cf. KLEPPER (2008)
786 cf. GoCa, Canadian Citizenship Act, B.: Natural born citizens
787 cf. ALEINIKOFF/KLUSMEYER (1952)
788 For the possible conditions under which Canadian citizenship can be lost: *De Groot* in HAILBRONNER/MARTIN (2003)

citizenship from persons who hold dual citizenship in some cases), the waiver of original citizenship or on the rights, responsibilities[789] and privileges connected with the status of citizenship, is almost "deafening".[790] Reference to the CaCharter is the only way of deriving the powers typically associated with citizenship, such as to be entitled to vote for the representative political bodies (Section 3 CaCharter), the right to free movement (Section 6(1) CaCharter) or the right to be educated in one of the two official Canadian languages (Section 23(1) CaCharter). In particular, the right to apply for a Canadian passport should also be emphasised.

The comparatively low level of regulation in Canadian citizenship law can be traced back to the country's roots in the Commonwealth, whose legal system is heavily influenced by the British Common Law.

8.5.5 Acquisition of citizenship by naturalisation

A non-Canadian can acquire Canadian citizenship by naturalisation,[791] on application, by fulfilling certain conditions hereinafter set forth.

First, an application for Canadian citizenship is required; second, the applicant must have reached the age of majority (at least 18 years of age); third, he or she must meet the residence requirement: applicants must be physically present in Canada for four years out of six years (1,460 days) prior to the date of application, and at least 183 days in any given calendar year must be spent on Canadian soil in each of four calendar years within the qualifying period before applying for citizenship, and, furthermore, filing Canadian income tax returns for four of the six years preceding the application for citizenship.

Time spent in Canada before achieving permanent residence status, i.e. as student or on a temporary work permit, does not count. Fourth, the

---

789 Regarding the relationship between the responsibility of nation States for their nationals and universal human rights law, see THIELE (2011)

790 cf. *Galloway* in ALEINIKOFF/KLUSMEYER (2000)

791 For the naturalisation procedures in Canada see BRUBAKER (1989); *Brubaker* in SHAFIR (1998)

applicant must have good knowledge of one of the official languages of Canada (English or French). Prior to the recent changes, adults aged 18 to 54 needed to meet the language requirements, and this has now been extended to applicants aged 14 to 64; fifth, he must have knowledge of the country (such as the political system of Canada, its geography and its history) and know the responsibilities and privileges associated with the status of citizenship. While this test was possible to do with the support of a translator in the past, this is no longer permissible and the citizenship test must now be conducted in English or French without the assistance of an interpreter; sixth, the application must not be subject to a removal order (Section 5(1) CaCA), and, finally, there must be an intent to reside in Canada once citizenship is granted.

Usually, knowledge of the political system – specifically Canada's form of government, legal system, history and geography – are tested in a written citizenship examination, which covers a wide range of different issues.[792]

The foregoing reinforces the fact that the straightforward acquisition of citizenship is not possible in Canada and is much stricter than it used to be in the past. Moreover, it is not sufficient for a person simply to reside part-time on Canadian soil, while residing for significant portions of time outside Canada as well – as millions of mainly Asian immigrants have done in the past decades – or just marry a Canadian citizen.[793]

Considered in terms of time, the naturalisation process can range from five months up to several years, and various specific factors can play a decisive role. The presentation of the certificate of citizenship is an official ceremony, culminating in an oath of citizenship (Oath), which is a promise or declaration to the Canadian monarch and a promise to abide by Canada's laws and uphold the duties of a Canadian citizen.. The Oath is sworn by any applicant over the age of 14. Despite various proposals to amend its wording since its inception, the current form of oath is as follows:

---

792 cf. HAMPSHIRE (2010)

793 cf. GoCa, Canadian Citizenship Act, C.: Citizenship by Naturalisation

> *"I swear (or affirm) that I will be faithful and bear true allegiance to Her Majesty Queen Elizabeth the Second, Queen of Canada, Her Heirs and Successors, and that I will faithfully observe the laws of Canada and fulfil my duties as a Canadian citizen."*

The acquisition of Canadian citizenship by way of naturalisation can be challenged if the applicant had been previously expelled from the country, has a criminal record, was convicted by a court of law of an indictable offence in Canada or an offence outside Canada in the four years before applying for citizenship, or who is suspected of or has been convicted of a war crime. The annulment of citizenship within a period of five years preceding the application constitutes itself an obstacle to naturalisation.

8.5.6 Exemptions and relief

Section 5(4) Citizenship Act states that, despite any other provision of the Act, the Minister may, at his discretion, grant citizenship to any person. This discretionary grant of citizenship is to alleviate cases of special and unusual hardship or to reward services of an exceptional value to Canada, including *ius doni.*

8.5.7 Multiple Citizenship

Guided by the idea that multiple citizenship could devalue the importance of Canadian citizenship, the Standing Committee appointed by the Canadian State Government criticised the 1977 Citizenship Act reform,[794] which provided that Canadian citizens acquiring new citizenship should not be required to give up their Canadian citizenship, nor should foreigners be obliged to give up their original citizenship on acquisition of Canadian citizenship – *de lege ferenda*,[795] recommending a return to the previous legal arrangements which required that adult

---

794 cf. GoCa, Canadian Citizenship Act, Dual Citizenship

795 For dual citizenship in Canada and the relevant case law ALEINIKOFF/KLUSMEYER (1942); BLOEMRAAD (2006); *Hammar* in BRUBAKER (1989); *Koslowski* in HAILBRONNER/MARTIN (2003)

Canadian citizens who willingly and observing the prerequisite formalities acquire another citizenship, would *ipso iure* lose their Canadian citizenship.[796]

Particularly in view of the practical difficulty that there are hardly any situations today in which Canadian citizens have to formally prove their loyalty to the nation – Canadian citizens are not required to vote in parliamentary elections nor do they have to support the Canadian State Government or Olympic Team, nor do they have to sing the Canadian national anthem or demonstrate respect for the symbols of national importance at formal occasions – the proposals of the *Standing Committee* left many unanswered questions and the Canadian government ultimately decided with the *Citizenship Bill* of 1998 to no longer involve itself in issues surrounding multiple citizenship in Canada.[797] Multiple citizenship therefore remains permissible.

8.6 Austria

8.6.1 State structural parameters

Due to its history, the Federal Republic of Austria and the Federal Republic of Germany are very similar in terms of State structure, [798] even though today's Austria emerged from the Habsburg multination State. With its nine Federal States (Burgenland, Carinthia, Lower Austria, Upper Austria, Salzburg, Styria, Tyrol, Vorarlberg and Vienna – Article 2(2) Federal Constitution Act (ÖB-VG)) and a population only one tenth the size of the Federal Republic of Germany – the Republic of Austria is very federal in structure, and was previously even more so. Thus, on the basis of Article 6(1) of the Austrian Constitution of 1929,[799] and until 1988, every Austrian state had its own "Federal State citizenship", whose acquisition was automatically combined with the acquisition of the Federal citizenship. The principle of

796 cf. *Galloway* in ALEINIKOFF/KLUSMEYER (2000)
797 cf. *Galloway* in ALEINIKOFF/KLUSMEYER (2000)
798 Re Germany, see GOSEWINKEL (2003)
799 For greater detail on the Austrian Federal Constitution of 1929: SCHEUNER (1929)

a single Austrian citizenship was introduced into the Austrian Federal Constitution only in 1988.[800] In terms of competence, the regulation of citizenship law is assigned to the Austrian Federal State (Article 11(1)(1) ÖB-VG), whereas, the individual states have far-reaching administrative powers and – especially in discretionary naturalisations – room for interpretation.[801]

The citizenship law in its current form, which goes back to an amendment of the Citizenship Act passed in 1985, was decisively changed in 1998 in order to flatten the federal structure of Austria to mitigate variations in law enforcement and facilitate naturalisation, which, however, at the same time – for the first time in the history of the Federal Republic of Austria – required proof of command of the German language.[802]

Although Austria has changed in recent years to become more of an immigration country – the proportion of foreigners in the total population in 2004 was comparable with that of the immediately adjacent Federal Republic of Germany at 8.9% – the Austrian Citizenship Act even in its current version does not provide any conditions expressing elements of *ius soli*: birth on Austrian territory is neither associated with the automatic acquisition of Austrian citizenship, nor does it give the children of immigrants a legal right to immediate acquisition of Austrian citizenship, for example on the basis of minority rights.[803]

The significant increase in naturalisations, which have been recorded since the mid-1990s and which have led to a tightening of the Austrian naturalisation law since the turn of the millennium, can be attributed to the fact that increasingly many former Turkish nationals, who are the third largest group of immigrants after Germans and people from the

800 cf. *Cinar/Waldrauch* in BAUBÖCK/ERSBØLL/GROENENDIJK/WALDRAUCH (2006)

801 *Bauböck/Cinar* in HANSEN/WEIL (2001)

802 cf. *Cinar/Waldrauch* in BAUBÖCK/ERSBØLL/GROENENDIJK/WOOD SMOKE (2006), but not in discretionary naturalisation pursuant to Section 10(6) ACA, cf. further below.

803 cf. *Cinar/Waldrauch* in BAUBÖCK/ERSBØLL/GROENENDIJK/WALDRAUCH (2006)

former Yugoslavia,[804] no longer have to fear any serious consequences from the renunciation of their original nationalities, and consequently routinely stay for more than 10 years continuously in Austria, thus fulfilling a central naturalisation requirement.[805]

Its citizenship law[806] follows the principle of descent (as e.g. in Denmark,[807] Greece,[808] Spain[809] and Italy[810]) and belongs to the group of European countries along with Switzerland which have the most restrictive naturalisation policies.[811] Austrian citizenship is regulated by the Austrian Federal Act on Austrian Citizenship (Austrian Citizenship Act 1985, ACA)[812] and some of its special features related to the acquisition of the Austrian citizenship by foreigners discussed further in this work.

Both the Austrian Federal Constitution, significantly influenced by *Hans Kelsen's* "Pure Theory of Law", and the authoritative legal source of citizenship law, the Austrian Citizenship Act 1985, use the expression citizenship (Staatsbürgerschaft) in place of the concept of citizenship, with respect to the localisation of its own nationals or their association with Austrian territory. This choice of terminology describes the core of the regulatory substrate more meaningfully and truly, in that the citizen is typically the bearer of legal powers such as the active and passive right to vote or the extensive right of access to public facilities, which usually pertains only to residents. Historically, an important aspect of Austrian citizenship was also the requirement of military service, which

---

804 http://www.statistik.at/web_de/statistiken/bevoelkerung/bevoelkerungsstruktur/bevoelkerung_nach_staatsangehoerigkeit_geburtsland/index.html, last accessed 17 January 2015

805 cf. *Cinar/Waldrauch* in BAUBÖCK/ERSBØLL/GROENENDIJK/WALDRAUCH (2006)

806 For greater detail on the citizenship law of the Federal Republic of Austria: *Cinar/Waldrauch* in BAUBÖCK/ERSBØLL/GROENENDIJK/WALDRAUCH (2006); FESSLER/KELLER/POMMERENING-SCHOBER/SZYMANSKI (2006): REICHEL (2011); MATZKA/BEZDEKA (1999); UNTERWEGER (2007); USLUCAN (2012)

807 cf. *Ersboll* in HANSEN/WEIL (2001)

808 cf. *Rozakis* in HANSEN/WEIL (2001)

809 cf. *Moreno Fuentes* in HANSEN/WEIL (2001)

810 cf. *Pastore* in HANSEN/WEIL (2001); GIRONDA (2010)

811 HOWARD (2009) p. 94 et seq.; cf. also JOPPKE (2011), regarding Austria in particular cf. REICHEL (2011)

812 Österreichisches Staatsbürgerschaftsgesetz, ÖBGBl. No. 311/1985, last amended by ÖBGBl. No. 111/2011

still remains in force.

As defined in Section 2(4) ACA, in the ACA the term "foreigner" is used for non-citizens.

As mentioned *supra*, no legal definition of the concept of citizenship can be found, even in the ACA. Section 2(2) ACA merely provides that "citizenship" as defined by ACA means the citizenship of the Republic of Austria. Thus nothing is gained from this.

8.6.2 Citizenship statistics

In the years between 1990 and 2008, Austria granted citizenship to between about 10,200 and 44,600 persons per year, a total of nearly 403,000 and an average of about 22,400 per year.[813] The naturalisation to population ratio is low at 0.26% per year.

8.6.3 Acquisition of citizenship by origin: strict *ius sanguinis*

At the constitutional level, citizenship is governed by Article 6 ÖB-VG. The principle of *ius sanguinis* applies strictly in Austria. While the ÖB-VG presupposes that the concept of citizenship is expressed in Article 6(1) ÖB-VG – which states that there is only one citizenship in the Republic of Austria, although, similarly like in Switzerland, one also has citizenship of an individual state depending on one's main place of residence[814] – explicit specification of two alternatives for the acquisition of citizenship are provided. Exercise of nation State discretion in the field of citizenship law is also permitted in Austria exclusively within international parameters. Article 9(1) ÖB-VG underlines the extent to which the generally recognised rules of public international law apply as part of the federal law. Following on from the aforementioned transfer of competence from the EU Member State to the EU level, Article 9(2) ÖB-VG states that individual sovereign rights can be transferred to other

813 Statistik Austria http://www.statistik.at/web_de/statistiken/bevoelkerung/einbuergerungen/index.html?ssSourceSiteId=null; Eingebürgerte Personen und Einbürgerungsrate seit 1991 nach Bundesländern

814 cf. www.ris.bka.gv.at, last accessed 17 January 2015

agencies or intergovernmental institutions by law or by an approved State treaty pursuant to Article 50(1) ÖB-VG. The passing of legislation regarding citizenship is a prerogative of the Federal Government, whereas its implementation (Vollzug) is a prerogative of the individual States (Länder).[815]

The detailed conditions for the acquisition, granting and loss of nationality or citizenship are regulated in Austria in the ACA, as last amended 2006.[816]

Austrian citizenship law is in particular distinguished by the fact that it continues to strictly follow the principle of descent even now, in the early twenty-first century. While birth in Austrian territory does not establish a right to naturalisation in favour of immigrants, the children of Austrian nationals receive Austrian citizenship even if they are born outside of Austria.[817]

A distinctive feature of Austrian citizenship law since its latest revision, furthermore, is its strict gender neutrality (gender equality). The priority given to some of the most striking principles in the Austrian citizenship law has been increasing and the Federal Government only recently pushed through various legislative measures to ensure strict equality between the sexes. Already at the constitutional level, Article 7(1)(2)(2) ÖB-VG stipulates that privileges based on sex are excluded. In its current version, the ACA underlines these altered priorities, for example, by providing that a person in possession of Austrian nationality is an Austrian citizen regardless of sex (Section 2(3) ACA). This strict gender neutrality is also underlined by Section 4(1) ACA, according to which sex and marital status are attributed no legal significance, insofar as the ACA does not expressly determine otherwise. Other key principles of Austrian citizenship law ultimately include the desire to avoid[818] situations of multiple citizenship.

815 Article 11(1)(1) ÖB-VG

816 For a good overview of the current Austrian Citizenship Act see FESSLER/KELLER/POMMERING-SCHOBER/WOLF (2006)

817 cf. *Cinar/Waldrauch* in BAUBÖCK/ERSBØLL/GROENENDIJK/WALDRAUCH (2006)

818 For an authoritative treatment of the loss of original nationality as a result of the acceptance of another nationality see TOPAL (2010)

8.6.4 Acquisition of citizenship by naturalisation

The ACA, which clarifies Article 6(1) ÖB-VG, stipulates in section 6 that citizenship can either be acquired by descent or legitimation, as further provided for in Sections 7, 7a and 8 ACA) or by grant, as further defined by Sections 10-24 ACA.

While maintaining their presupposed discretion, the competent naturalisation authorities are required to consider the integration progress of the applicant as part of its decision to allow or reject an application for Austrian nationality, in addition to the general interest and the public interest (Section 11(1) ACA). In particular, a foreigner must demonstrate knowledge of the social, economic and cultural life of Austria as well as commitment to the fundamental values of a democratic European State and society (Section 11(2) ACA). Furthermore, the applicant's work ethic or her respect for law and observance of public traffic laws can be relevant to the decision.[819] Whatever the decision, the competent authority is required to justify it.[820]

As a difficult barrier to overcome, the previous entitlement naturalisation in many cases has been replaced by a discretionary naturalisation, i.e., in Austria even with the fulfilment of the statutory minimum requirements, there is no (binding) subjective right to the Austrian citizenship, except if one has been resident in Austria for more than 30 years and in certain defined circumstances after 15 or six years of residence.[821]

8.6.5 Selected criteria for naturalisation

The main residence of a person under Austrian law is basically grounded on where he demonstrably settled or where the intention to establish his centre of vital relations can be shown from other circumstances (Article 6(3)(1) ÖB-VG). Exceptionally, under certain circumstances, six years of uninterrupted primary residence suffices.

---

819 cf. *Cinar/Waldrauch* in BAUBÖCK/ERSBØLL/GROENENDIJK/WALDRAUCH (2006)
820 cf. *Cinar/Waldrauch* in BAUBÖCK/ERSBØLL/GROENENDIJK/WALDRAUCH (2006)
821 cf. *Cinar/Waldrauch* in BAUBÖCK/ERSBØLL/GROENENDIJK/WALDRAUCH (2006)

Provided that the federal law states nothing to the contrary, Austrian citizenship can only be conferred on a foreigner if he or she resided for at least 10 years legally and uninterruptedly in the Federal State, and had established residency for at least five years (Section 10(1)(1) ACA); and if he had no binding convictions from a domestic or foreign court resulting in imprisonment (with the foreign court's conviction and sentence being authoritative in this respect regardless whether the offence was imprisonable under domestic law, provided that the conviction was established conviction according to due process under the principles of Article 6 ECHR (Section 10(1)(2) ACA).

Matrimonial children acquire citizenship according to Section 7(1) ACA at birth, if one parent was an Austrian citizen at the time (Section 7(1)(a) ACA) or if one parent who subsequently died, was a citizen on the day of his death (Section 7(1)(b) ACA). Illegitimate children acquire Austrian nationality at birth if either their mother or their father is an Austrian citizen at this time of birth (Section 7(3) ACA). If citizenship is claimed on the basis of a legally binding marriage in Austria, this must have remained in place in any case for five years.

In addition to these conditions for naturalisation after a stay of only six years, the level of integration achieved must be demonstrated. Examined after an independent, country-specific naturalisation test (in place since 2005), the applicant must in particular have knowledge of the language and country (Section 10a(1)(1) and (1)(2) ACA) and have participated in a comprehensive 300 hour long integration course. Article 8(1) ÖB-VG reaffirms the explicit commitment to the German language. According to this, the German language is, without prejudice to the rights granted to linguistic minorities by the federal law, the official language of the Republic. The linguistic minorities of the Federal Republic of Austria include Slovenian, Croatian and Hungarian. The wording "*to respect, secure, and to promote language*" according to Article 8 (2)(2) ÖB-VG, also includes the protection of these minority languages.

Furthermore, the applicant has to demonstrate basic knowledge of the democratic order as well as the history of Austria and the respective Federal States (Section 10a(1)(2) ACA).

Austria's comparatively restrictive naturalisation policy is further reflected in the fact that the applicant's ability to earn a livelihood is also taken into consideration in addition to mere petty and administrative road traffic offences – for which a court conviction would in any case prove a barrier to naturalisation (Section 10(1)(2) ACA).

Dependence on government assistance is a ground for exclusion from naturalisation (Section 10(7) ACA). What constitutes a material assurance of livelihood is set out in Section 10(5) ACA. According to this, livelihood is regarded as sufficiently ensured if the applicant's fixed and regular personal income from employment, other income, legal claims for maintenance or insurance benefits on average for the three years preceding the time of the decision allow him or her to live without recourse to social assistance, and the amounts correspond to the average indicative rates in Section 293 of the Austrian General Social Insurance Act (ÖASVG)[822] for the preceding three years (Section 10(5)(1) ACA). Fixed and regular personal income will be reduced for regular expenses, especially rental charges, credit charges, garnishments and child support payments to third parties not living in the same household (Section 10(5)(1) ACA).

Austrian citizenship can in addition be acquired for outstanding scientific, economic, artistic or athletic contribution by the applicant to Austria (Section 10(6) ACA). Under these conditions, neither proof of regular income nor the renunciation of the original nationality is required.[823] For further discussion of *ius doni* naturalisation, cf. section 14.1.

8.6.6 Multiple Citizenship

Austria is one of the few countries in Europe which still insists on the renunciation of previous citizenships if Austrian citizenship is sought (important exception is *nota bene* made in the case of discretionary naturalisation under Section 10(6) ACA) and Austrians lose their Austrian citizenship upon acquisition of a foreign citizenship.[824]

---

822 ÖBGBl. No 189/1955

823 cf. *Cinar/Waldrauch* in BAUBÖCK/ERSBØLL/GROENENDIJK/WALDRAUCH (2006)

824 cf. *Bauböck/Cinar* in HANSEN/WEIL (2001)

8.7 Comparative law of citizenship acquisition by naturalisation

Following on from the previous review of the regulations in the selected reference States, the most important aspects will now be presented below in summary from a comparative law perspective, with a particular focus on the derivative acquisition of citizenship by naturalisation. In addition to the selected reference states the regulations in other countries are partially shown for comparison.

The requirements for naturalisation vary greatly between the different countries, but there are some characteristics which most States share.

It is interesting in this context to compare different countries in terms of their overall citizenship acquisition rules using *Howard's Citizenship Policy Indicator* (CPI).[825] This measures different States by how restrictive or liberal their corresponding regulations are in terms of their citizenship laws (both by original as well as derivative acquisition). The CPI score ranges from 0 to 1.5 (restrictive), 1.5 to 4 (medium) and 4 and above (liberal). Germany, with a CPI value of 0.00 is deemed one of the most restrictive countries, followed by Austria at 0.50. At the most liberal end of the spectrum is France (4.22) and the UK (5.47), which receives the highest value in Europe, and is thus regarded as the most liberal State by this indicator.[826]

8.7.1 Minimum duration of residence

In comparative law terms, the minimum period of residence prerequisite for naturalisation in Germany is eight years, in Austria 10 years and in Switzerland 12 years. St. Kitts and Nevis, in requiring a minimum length of stay for its ordinary naturalisation procedure of 14 years, is also restrictive. In contrast, the naturalisation processes of the US (five years), Canada (three years), the UK (five years) and France (two to five years) are comparatively liberal, although for different reasons (land development and civilisation in North America against the constitutional maintenance

---

[825] cf. HOWARD (2009) p. 19 et seq.
[826] HOWARD (2009) p. 157

of power in continental Europe), and with a minimum requirement of only three years in the case of Canada (and Belgium!), exceptional. In the other classical immigration countries, Australia and New Zealand, four and respectively five years minimum stay is required.[827]

8.7.2 Language proficiency

All the aforementioned countries require mastery of the national language or one of the official languages in principle for naturalisation. Such requirement is waived in the case of naturalisation due to extraordinary economic contribution to the State in Austria,[828] St. Kitts and Nevis,[829] Malta[830] and Cyprus.[831]

8.7.3 Swearing an oath of loyalty

An oath of loyalty is required in Canada and the UK, but also in the US, Malta and Cyprus. This can seem anachronistic given current social and technological developments and advancing globalisation.[832] Anyone visiting one of these countries will also observe the presence of broad, very pronounced social stratification within their domestic polity. Although proving causality between the solemn taking of an oath of loyalty and the depth of integration is likely to be difficult, the latter may, in my opinion, certainly contribute to the individual consciousness of being a part of a nation and its destiny, this particularly in the case of direct naturalisation following the rendition of special services to the State without the prior taking up of residence (Cyprus, Malta or Dominica, where an *oath of allegiance* must also be sworn). Under this premise, the swearing of an oath of loyalty could be a positive element of engaging the loyalty of new citizens.

---

827 s 22(1) Australian Citizenship Act 2007; and s 8(2)(b) of the Citizenship Act 1977 of New Zealand as amended (Reprint as at 1 July 2013)

828 Article 10 (6) of the Austrian Citizenship Act, 1985 (as amended)

829 Part II, S 3 (5) of the St Kitts and Nevis Citizenship Act, 1984 (as amended)

830 Part IV, S 10(9)(b) of the Maltese Citizenship Act, 1964 (as amended)

831 Criteria defined in the Scheme for Naturalisation of Investors in Cyprus by Exception on the Basis of Subsection (2) of section 111A of the Civil Registry Laws of 2002-2013

832 cf. in particular SPIRO (2008)

8.7.4 Good character requirement and lack of binding conviction

A statement of good character – which is a synonym for integrity and socialisation, demonstrated by the presentation of a police certificate of good conduct, as well as a more or less comprehensive documentation of lifestyle as a rule – is required in all States as a naturalisation requirement. A binding court conviction for an offence is an obstacle to the acquisition of nationality in all reference countries; while in the US, only a conviction for a minimum prison sentence of one year would result in the rejection of an application for naturalisation.

In St. Kitts and Nevis, Antigua and Barbuda and particularly in Malta under the local Citizenship-by-Investment programme, in additional, very extensive, far-reaching investigations of the personal profile and economic background of the applicant are performed. In addition to the usual State checks with Financial Intelligence Units, Interpol etc., private companies specialising in background research are also mandated[833] to undertake a comprehensive audit and report to the government, which provides information on the applicant's past and economic background, especially with respect to whether the information provided by the applicant is also correct.[834]

8.7.5 Proof of national or historical knowledge

The demonstration of knowledge of the culture and history of the host country is currently required only in Switzerland and Canada for naturalisation purposes. In the other reference countries naturalisation will not definitively fail exclusively on this point. This is to be welcomed, because such knowledge is – given the predominant objectives of citizenship law if not totally redundant, best relegated to being a private matter for each individual. The peaceful coexistence between domestic individuals will not be called into doubt based on whether someone knows the name of the State's founder, the date on which its

[833] For example Thomson Reuters, IPSA International, Kroll etc.
[834] cf. KÄLIN (2014)

Constitution entered into force, or the name of the highest mountain in your Canton of residence.

8.7.6 Existence of a secure financial situation

Beyond Austria and Switzerland, applicants are also required to prove a regular minimum income or secure financial situation in France, and by all countries which offer naturalisation on the basis of extraordinary economic contribution. The latter condition is also very understandable, because in any case it ensures that such applicants, in addition to being able to make the economic contribution in question, are also able to provide for themselves and do not use naturalisation as a means to then burden the public system – be that in States where granting the citizenship is done on this basis, or in a third country (consider here, for example, Dominica, where people acquired citizenship under its extraordinarily "favourable" Citizenship-by-Investment Programme[835] in order to then travel to Canada and seek asylum there).

Taking the above into consideration, it seems reasonable to suggest that introducing the requirement for proof of sufficient financial means from all applicants in the *Citizenship-by-Investment* programmes would be advisable to as much as possible avoid the possibility that any third countries (particularly within the EU or CARICOM, where certain rights are acquired by the acquisition of citizenship of one member state that apply throughout the territories of the EU and CARICOM) may be negatively affected by such applicants.

8.7.7 Effects of personal status

With respect to the effects of personal status, Canada stands out on account of the fact that it has no special legal provisions for marriages: marrying a Canadian has no impact on the citizenship of the other spouse. In all other reference States there are special statutory rules

835 In Dominica (the English Commonwealth of Dominica, not to be confused with the Spanish-speaking Dominican Republic), it used to be possible for a single applicant to acquire citizenship by means of a commitment to the Treasury of USD 50,000 and other fees

on the effects of marriage to a national, combined with a minimum stay requirement for the foreigner; three years in the UK, in the US of up to five years (residence), and six years (for foreign residence and proof of close ties to the Swiss Confederation, otherwise five years) in Switzerland. A personal status-related waiting period of one year is required by the citizenship laws of France and Austria. Immediate citizenship is acquired by a person who marries a St. Kitts and Nevis citizen.

8.7.8 Multiple citizenship

Multiple citizenship renders identification requirements with the host states unreliable to a certain degree,[836] and is thus traditionally frowned upon and still not tolerated by some States. With regard to the admission of multiple citizenship, the continental European States with comparatively restrictive naturalisation also require the loss of the citizenship of the country of origin for the naturalisation process.

This is not however the case in Canada, Switzerland, France, Malta, the UK and the US, as well as in St. Kitts and Nevis and Cyprus.

In Austria, the naturalisation process is, like in Germany, restricted in that the acquisition of citizenship requires the loss of the citizenship of the country of origin. Interestingly, this otherwise strictly applied rule however does not apply in the case of naturalisation on the basis of extraordinary contribution to the Austrian State under Section 10(6) of the Austrian Citizenship Act. In that case, Austria allows multiple citizenship

836 ROELLECKE (2004)

PART III

Naturalisation Through Economic Contribution to the State

In the following, some historical examples of citizenship granted on the basis of an economic contribution to the State, hereinafter generally referred to as Citizenship-by-Investment, or *ius doni*, will first be briefly considered, then its theoretical foundations will be discussed and critically analysed, along with a review of individual States, which already pursue a corresponding naturalisation concept, and a comparative benchmarking of these States will be performed in order to ultimately arrive at empirically verifiable conclusions about the extent to which the assumptions made so far can hold.

9

Historical Examples of Citizenship-by-Investment

There are actually many examples and a very long tradition of the granting of citizenship on the basis of exceptional contributions to the State, and in particular – and of interest here – with regard to exceptional economic contribution.

As far back as in Ancient Athens and later in Ancient Rome, it was possible to naturalise deserving people. In Rome people were made Roman citizens "*for great acts in the service to the community*".[837] The Roman Empire then conducted what was probably the first actual Citizenship-by-Investment programme and sold citizenship to rich foreigners or others who could meaningfully contribute to the empire.[838] A famous account of this can be found in the *Bible,* where during the arrest of Saint Paul the Apostle the Roman commander referred to his acquisition of Roman citizenship-by-investment:

> "*The commander came and said to him, 'Tell me, are you a Roman?' And he said, 'Yes.' The commander answered, 'I acquired this citizenship with a large sum of money.' And Paul said, 'But I was actually born a citizen.' Therefore those who were about to examine him immediately let go of him; and the commander also was afraid when he found out that he was a Roman*".[839]

With the development of feudal systems in the Middle Ages, peasants and foreigners with limited property and financial resources had restricted rights.[840] However, medieval towns took on new arrivals as citizens, if this was of benefit to the city or if enough money flowed into its treasury. Citizenship in London was conferred on rich merchants from Europe, to entice them there or to integrate them, as an important part of the English economic development and later on for the global expansion of the British Empire.[841] Naturalisation was in fact an important instrument of the mercantilist policy of the UK in its competition with other States, in its progress

837 SPIRO (2008)
838 BERTON (2014)
839 Acts 22, 27–29; cf. also BELLAMY (2008) p. 39
840 DZANKIC (2014)
841 SCHULTE BEERBÜHL (2007) p. 1

towards dominance and its rise as a global trading power, and one which transformed from being a backward country into an economically thriving one.[842] The country's ascent was organised and promoted in no small measure through its new naturalised citizens – especially rich merchants from continental Europe, particularly from Germany, who became "British" through acquiring citizenship-by-investment.[843]

This lent a homogeneous social and professional profile to the people naturalised: the majority were merchant traders. Since the naturalisation costs were high, only a wealthy minority could afford this. The British State and the foreign merchants formed a community of interest, through the mutual promotion of the individual as well as the common good. From the perspective of the British State "*immigration and naturalisation of foreign economic elites serves the immediate promotion of innovation, economic progress and expansion*".[844]

Since 1695 and up to the passage of a new law in 1818, there was also a provision in the founding charter of the *Bank of Scotland* that each person who bought shares worth at least GBP 83 would be granted Scottish nationality. Since Union with England in 1707, Scots were also simultaneously British nationals and this Citizenship-by-Investment provision therefore led directly to citizenship of the UK. Naturalisation through the acquisition of shares in the *Bank of Scotland* was not only cheaper and economically more advantageous, but was also not subject to the political and economic restrictions of naturalisation,[845] such as the usual restrictions of private naturalisation acts like residential or religious requirements, and while it conveyed full political rights, it did not require any oath of allegiance. The charter of the Bank of Scotland was confirmed several times by the British Parliament.[846]

The grant of citizenship status in eighteenth century the UK (as it then was, following the Act of Union with Scotland in 1707) continued to be

---

842 SCHULTE BEERBÜHL (1995) p. 1
843 cf. SCHULTE BEERBÜHL (2007)
844 SCHULTE BEERBÜHL (2007) p. 2
845 SCHULTE BEERBÜHL (2007) p. 50
846 *Schulte Beerbühl* in FAHRMEIR/FARON/WEIL (2003)

regarded not only as a tool for signifying allegiance to the reigning monarch, but also of attracting capital to the realm. Following the revocation of the Edict of Nantes by the Edict of Fontainebleau in 1685, French protestant Huguenots lost the right to peacefully practice their religion and faced persecution at home, causing them to seek asylum in protestant states and resulting in a great flight of capital and talent from France, as well marking the end of the brief spell of religious tolerance across continental Europe which had followed the Thirty Years War.[847] Keen to gain from the potential offered by this large and comparatively highly skilled community, Parliament passed in 1708 the Foreign Protestants Naturalization Act, which expressly acknowledged that the *"increase of people is a means of advancing the wealth and strength of a nation"* and that offering the Huguenots and other Protestants the opportunities to partake *"of the advantages and privileges which natural-born subjects do enjoy"* would induce them to *"transport themselves and* their estates *into this kingdom"* (emphasis added), and which resulted in a wave of migration of greater magnitude in relation to the size of the then population than the much discussed contemporary arrival of the Polish to the UK.[848]

In the time of the French Revolution, which shaped modern citizenship law, *ius doni* was part of the citizenship law, under which French citizenship was granted to foreign supporters of the French Revolution, to anyone who contributed, materially or immaterially, to the cause of the revolution.

A striking example of citizenship being granted on the strength of individual contribution to the economic wellbeing and security of a nation was the wholesale naturalisation of German scientists and technicians in the aftermath of the Second World War under the auspices of Project Paperclip. Over 1,500 nationals from the former Axis powers were imported into the US with the promise of assured residence and eventual citizenship in order to secure for the US access to their knowledge and

847 SPIELVOGEL (2003) p. 410

848 "Poles Depart", The Economist, 28 August 2008, accessed 21 July 2015 http://www.economist.com/node/12010095

intellectual property,[849] principally for the benefit of American industry, a direct contribution to the national economy of sufficient value to be regarded on the part of the US Government as a significant contribution towards the reparations owed by Germany to the US.[850]

849 LASBY (1971) p. 152
850 GIMBEL (1990) pp. 52, 170

10

The Grant of Citizenship in the National Interest

Although formulated differently in different States, the majority of States with a Citizenship-by-Investment option require in their relevant legal standards that the monetary inflow is in their domestic (national) interest, without however specifically defining this interest. Indeed, many programmes have poorly defined goals, while other struggle to demonstrate a meaningful economic benefit.[851] However, St. Kitts and Nevis, Antigua and Barbuda, and Malta are exceptions to this, as they have fairly clear policy and possess detailed regulations to make conditions more specific.[852] Given that their nation State scope for action in the field of citizenship law can only reach as far as their sovereignty, which remains constrained somewhat by their international legal commitments, a question arises regarding the definition of the nation State interests which may justify Citizenship-by-Investment.

The central idea of the Citizenship-by-Investment approach is the attraction of foreign capital for the stimulation of domestic investment projects, which can be as investments in private projects, often in property development, "seed capital" for the establishment of other companies or as the nucleus of infrastructural development in the beneficiary territory. It is in the primary interest of each State to secure sufficient foreign direct investment for its economy. Citizenship as "consideration" for such investment is functionally a legitimate means to promote foreign direct investment and, as set forth herein and as will be further explained, is entirely within the bounds of the nation State discretion in the field of citizenship law.

The beneficiary of general naturalisation will either receive individual incentives for personal input into the host country's society, or they will receive appreciation for their integration efforts exerted and proven, or both. The main objective of such naturalisation is to recognise and strengthen their integration into the host country's society. The motives and motivations underlying this objective, can in any case remain unexamined in keeping with the proportionality test. The State naturalisation authorities have to verify whether the granting of citizenship is justified based on the overall picture acquired of the applicant.

---

851 SUMPTION/HOOPER (2014)

852 cf. for example, St. Kitts and Nevis Citizenship by Investment Regulations, 2011

In Citizenship-by-Investment the emphasis is not overly on the recognition or promotion of individual integration of a natural person, but on the commitment of capital.

In what *Ayelet Shachar* calls "Olympic citizenship" – the "*spread of the talent-for-citizenship exchange*"[853] – the emphasis is on the attraction of exceptional talent, be it in sports, culture, science or other fields. This practice is particularly prevalent in the field of sports (hence *Shachar's* choice of the term Olympic citizenship).[854] As an illustration of this widespread practice, the French sports paper, *L'Equipe*, reported on the quarter-final of the European Table Tennis Championships in October 2013 as follows: "*In the women's singles, two-time European champion Li Jiao of the Netherlands (2007 and 2011), lost to Portugal's Fu Yu. In the semi-finals, Fu Yu will meet Sweden's Li Fen*".[855] Foreign top athletes in whom Germany has a special interest are preferred for naturalisation based on an administrative directive; yet only a maximum of 10 top athletes per year have been admitted in the more recent past.[856] Other countries are more relaxed about this. At the World Athletics Championships in 2005, Qatar was represented by almost a dozen elite athletes born in Kenya and naturalised in Qatar.[857] Shortly before the 2006 Winter Olympics, President Bush signed a bill that included a special provision granting citizenship for aliens of extraordinary ability,[858] which allowed, among others, the Russian ice dancer Maxim Zavozin to represent the USA. Zavozin thereafter became a Hungarian citizen in time to represent Hungary at the Winter Olympics 2010.[859] The USA, more than any other country in the world, has gone out of its way to perfect the technique of attracting accomplished athletes by offering them citizenship in pursuit of Olympic medals.[860]

---

853 SHACHAR (2011) p. 2088; cf. also SHACHAR/HIRSCHL (2014) re this "*race for talent*"
854 For greater detail on this, SHACHAR (2011), who coined the term "Olympic Citizenship"
855 Cited in *Le Monde Diplomatique*, January 2014
856 VON MÜNCH (2007)
857 Hamburger Abendblatt of 11 August 2005, "Qatar and its Kenyan", citing at VON MÜNCH (2007)
858 Res. 2044 109th Congress (2005)
859 SHACHAR (2011) p. 2092, with further references
860 SHACHAR (2011) p. 2092

Some authors feel that Citizenship-by-Investment should be distinguished clearly from Olympic citizenship in that recipients of citizenship who are given specialized treatment on the basis of their human capital from those who gain citizenship on the basis of commitment of their financial capital.[861] Citizenship-by-Investment programs, it is further argued, link citizenship with social standing and wealth and by selecting future citizens on the basis of investment or economic contribution, and this is a departure from the "*egalitarian thrust that underlines rules of birthright citizenship as well as residence-based naturalisation*".[862] Those authors however routinely fail to show why selection on the basis of financial capacity – which very often and not least reflects the person's overall talents and abilities as an entrepreneur and investor, talents and abilities which are and should be much sought-after by states – is any less arbitrary than selection on the basis of exceptional talents such as being able to play table tennis really well and thus help the national table tennis team to excel. Both in fact immobilise the less well-off and less talented within their national borders.[863]

Thus, there can be no qualitative difference in whether citizenship is allocated on the basis of some natural talent assets or on the basis of financial assets. There can certainly be no ethical justification for the allocation of citizenship exclusively on the basis of the circumstance of one's birth and not through natural talent or private contribution, any more than can be justified the exclusive allocation of wealth and property by the same means. Or as *Armstrong* pointed out, selling citizenship is only a rather visible instance of the wider unfairness in allocating citizenship.[864] It is no less arbitrary than the granting of citizenship according to nothing further than the circumstances of birth, which represents nothing more than a "birthright lottery" as *Shachar* has convincingly demonstrated,[865] yet which is nevertheless the norm worldwide: the overwhelming majority of people are allocated their citizenship at birth based

861 For example SHACHAR/HIRSCHL (2014); or *Bauböck* in SHACHAR/BAUBÖCK (2014)
862 BAUBÖCK (2014) p. 7
863 BARBULESCU (2014)
864 ARMSTRONG (2014)
865 SHACHAR (2009)

on nothing more than where they were born and to whom. Much like inherited wealth or an innate talent for playing the piano, this is a most arbitrary and unjust allocation system and is reminiscent of the feudal bonds which we liberated ourselves from in the Enlightenment period and through a series of revolutionary wars.

Ius doni, then, with its very limited scope of application, even if to some it appears somehow repugnant, pales in comparison to many of these other inequities of ordinary transmission of citizenship.[866]

Investing money, whatever the amount, then appears more like a reasonable way to gain access to citizenship, as there is also no point, after all, to distinguish between financial and human investments.[867] Both are in the national interest. As *Okun* pointed out, "*[W]hen people differ in capabilities, interests, and preferences, identical treatment is not equitable treatment*".[868] If the requirements for naturalisation are focused on the ability and willingness to make a substantial investment (in addition, of course, to meeting stringent character requirements and undergoing strict due diligence upon application to take care of security concerns), this appears equitable and in everyone's interest, and the "traditional" functions of citizenship then simply play a secondary role, which are increasingly becoming irrelevant anyway.[869] If the objectives of Citizenship-by-Investment are expressly underpinned by the desire to accelerate domestic growth or distribute wealth to broad sections of society, i.e. national interest motives, this actually makes Citizenship-by-Investment a more attractive proposition than many other modes of acquisition of citizenship. It would also not appear to be illegitimate in Europe or the CARICOM given the relevant European provisions and the objectives of CARICOM on the economic integration. The extent to which these objectives can and should be legitimately pursued by citizenship law and policy is of course up to the individual nation states to determine.

---

866 ARMSTRONG (2014)
867 BERTON (2014)
868 OKUN (1975) p. 8
869 cf. ARMSTRONG (2014)

11

The Economic Theory of Clubs

11.1 Spectrum of opinion

For as long as we have the present global system of national citizenship regimes that determine the allocation of citizenship, we in effect also have market forces and competition, including state competition in a capitalist "world-system".[870] Citizenship has become an economic good[871] with which both States and investors improve their competitiveness.[872] It is aimed not only at wealthy people, but in the context of attracting wealthy citizens it is comparable to tax competition where likewise, both States and investors seek to improve their competitiveness. High demand for Citizenship-by-Investment programmes and the significant economic contributions and investments that interested individuals are prepared to make in return for citizenship status as well as the significant fees that such interested individuals are willing to pay are clear evidence of this.[873] This raises the question of whether nation States face similar questions and issues as associations or "clubs" do, or in other words, whether citizenship has the quality of a more or less voluntary club membership.[874]

Citizenship certainly has a value to the individual, as it represents the membership in an exclusive society and participation in an inventory of accumulated and constant newly generated "club goods".[875] Indeed, in a world of *"growing disparities of wealth and security, yet one that is more connected than ever by technology and ideas, the objective value of citizenship must further increase."*[876]

Nation states today can be viewed as institutions which provide a range of public goods, the enjoyment of which are subject to certain conditions. Naturally, nation states did not evolve like private clubs, where a few people get together jointly to "produce" a "club good", and of course nation states also do not just produce one "club good", but they (should)

870 WALLERSTEIN (2000)
871 BORNA/STEARNS (2002), SANDEL (2012); cf. also SHACHAR/HIRSCHL (2014)
872 DZANKIC (2012), KÄLIN (2014)
873 BORNA/STEARNS (2002)
874 STRAUBHAAR (2003) p.77
875 STRAUBHAAR (2003) p. 81
876 JOPPKE (2010) p. 152

produce a vast array of such goods. However, in the final analysis, the evolution of nation states can still be very effectively compared to clubs: people (originally just adult, property-owning men living in cities)[877] have agreed on common rules, which are contained in constitutions, laws, regulations, and so forth. They are willing to contribute, through taxes and administrative charges, to obtaining public goods and services (roads, utilities, hospitals, courts, defence), and they are very careful about citizenship, who may become a citizen and who should remain excluded.[878]

Indeed, migration policy must essentially fulfil two selective functions: firstly, who should be allowed admittance as a "guest" and use the country's "club goods", and at what price? In this respect, we are talking about short-term visa policy, and short and longer term immigration policy. Secondly, who should be allowed to become a "full member" (i.e. citizen) and not only use the club goods, but also benefit from additional club goods reserved exclusively for full members (e.g. a passport), become a voting member to participate in the determination of the club rules and club politics (i.e. participation in the political community). Here we are looking at the acquisition and loss of citizenship.

Considered in terms of history of economic theory, the Citizenship-by-Investment concept can be traced back to the Economic Theory of Clubs,[879] which was established in 1965 by *Buchanan*[880] and sustained by the economic hypothesis that not only private companies but – at least in welfare theory terms – also States produce "club goods" for their members and should therefore behave according to cost-benefit analysis, especially regarding the common burden on whose individual contribution each individual stands and falls. A club is a group whose members derive mutual benefit from sharing production costs, member characteristics or a good characterised by excludable benefits. Citizenship is a

---

877 cf. DAHRENDORF (1974) p. 673 - 674

878 STRAUBHAAR (2003)

879 For a good introduction into the theory of club goods, cf. CORNES/SANDEL (1996); but also see SANDLER/TSCHIRHART (1986)

880 cf. BUCHANAN (1965)

public good which is indivisible[881] (at least if not issued to new citizens in very large numbers) and whose benefits are excludable, thus belonging to the subclass of goods referred to as club goods. Against this background, the nation States should be entitled to consider, when deciding on the naturalisation of a new "member", what monetary contribution she or he brings to their community. Furthermore, additional members into the club should reduce the cost for each individual member.[882]

Following closely on *Buchanan's* theory, *Reich*[883] developed the idea that every citizen – like the employees or shareholders of a company – bears individual responsibility for the economic welfare of all, so each nation State, when embracing new "members", should avoid generating new burdens on its economy and overall welfare. The grant of citizenship as a *quid pro quo* for direct investment in the host country was discussed in this context. Particularly since the welfare contribution of an investment or direct contribution (strengthening the domestic economy, creating and preserving jobs etc.) as a rule far exceeds the costs incurred, the inclusion of new investing club members is in principle an appropriate means of optimising a country's economy, balance of payments and securing other benefits for the country and society.[884] Ultimately, this is a question of finding the right balance, where the key condition is simply that new members should be admitted so long as their "contributions" to the club are greater than the "burden" they create for the existing club members.[885] In terms of citizenship viewed as a club membership, it is important to consider that all new citizens, regardless of how they became citizens (i.e. also newborn citizens who acquired citizenship based on birthright citizenship, or spouses who married citizens etc.), pose on one hand a "burden" and on the other hand contribute (hopefully) in different ways. From this perspective, the Citizenship-by-

---

881 A good is considered indivisible when a unit of the good can be consumed by one individual without detracting from the consumption opportunities still available to others; cf. CORNES/SANDLER (1996)

882 "*[T]he bringing of additional members into the club also serves to reduce the cost that the single person will face*": BUCHANAN (1965); and WALZER (1983)

883 cf. REICH (1991)

884 cf. DZANKIC (2012)

885 STRAUBHAAR (2003)

Investment exchange through admitting new citizens who fulfil clearly stipulated membership criteria and actively contribute to the club (*ius doni*) is, from this point of view, even more logical than the traditional *ius soli* or *ius sanguinis* bases of citizenship acquisition, which constitutes a very arbitrary allocation of citizenship[886] without consideration of the burden or contribution new citizens make to society.

Carens[887] argues against the views of *Buchanan* and *Reich*, and states that the transfer of the Economic Theory of Clubs to the relationship between individuals and government communities oversteps the boundary between private and public spheres, especially also in the light that the nation States are bound by international law to treat all domestic individuals equally, and not to use the criteria for the acquisition of "their" citizenship in a discriminatory manner.

However, even *Walzer* argues that States can be imagined as perfect clubs[888] – or, as *Marshall* puts it, as "*mutual benefit clubs*"[889] – with sovereign authority over their membership conditions.[890] The benefits, which could be described as "citizenship services", vary depending on the society and time, but usually include goods such as education, medical services and social support services.[891]

Becker and *Chiswick* have argued that a large (rather than nominal) visa fee or post-immigration charge on income tax (in a way, a club entry fee) would bring reasonable compensation and greater economic benefit to the native population, and as a consequence would motivate them to favour more immigration.[892] It is also undeniable that belonging to a nation state, membership in the club – citizenship – has a value in itself, as it permits participation in the common inventory of club goods which have been built up over a long time.[893] Immigrants willing to pay

886 cf. KOCHENOV (2012); ARMSTRONG (2014)
887 cf. CARENS (1995)
888 WALZER (1983) p. 35 et seq.
889 *Marshall*, cited in WALZER (1983) p. 81
890 WALZER (1983) p. 40
891 CROUCH (2007); cf. also MARSHALL (1950)
892 CHISWICK (2005); BECKER (1997)
893 STRAUBHAAR (2003)

a substantial entry fee would automatically have desirable characteristics in this respect.[894]

Another economist, *Julian L. Simon*, even suggested auctioning admission to the highest bidder until a particular quota was filled.[895] The proposals by *Becker* and *Simon* materialised in 1990 with the still active US EB-5 immigration programme, whereby you can buy entry to the US "club" with a minimum investment of USD 500,000. You do not have to go far to extend this same logic also to the acquisition of citizenship, which represents, even more so than residency rights, "access to a club".

The economist *Thomas Straubhaar* suggested that the model of European soccer clubs ought to be considered: who cares about origin and country of birth at Real Madrid, Manchester United or Bayern München? Talented soccer players from all over Europe and the world are united to play for a particular club.[896] This is what *Shachar* refers to as *Olympic citizenship*.[897] Important only is the readiness and commitment to do your best for the club. Why should not people, independent of their place or origin, be permitted to do their best for a new country – knowing that their achievements for the club is always also one of self-interest? Likewise in reverse, if you leave a country and want to remain a member of that club (i.e. remain a citizen), you should probably have to make an annual contribution, or as *Straubhaar* suggests, an additional passport renewal fee, in order to maintain your club membership. He refers to the interesting example of Swiss citizens living abroad, who have to pay a monetary compensation for not doing military service, and remains with Switzerland as an example of a "nation by will" (*Willensnation*), with its highly democratic and decentralised structures, where citizens are quite willing to pay "club fees" (i.e. taxes) if they feel that they receive an adequate provision of "club goods" in return.[898] He contends that in large part, the actual workings of a "nation by will" corresponds to the expectations of the Economic Theory of Clubs.

---

894 BECKER (1997)

895 Julian L. Simon, Auction the Right to Be an Immigrant, New York Times, 28 January 1986, cited in SANDEL (2012) p. 62

896 STRAUBHAAR (2003)

897 SHACHAR (2014)

898 STRAUBHAAR (2003) pp. 88–89

11.2 Critical reflection

Understanding citizenship as a contract between the State and a private individual does not come without concerns. The consideration specified within the framework of a contract for exchange must be reasonable with respect to the entirety of the circumstances and must be in keeping with the factual context of authority's contractual performance. The granting of citizenship in democratic States, however, does not usually underlie any contract. When considered from a dogmatic perspective, countries such as Austria where the granting of citizenship through investment is primarily at the discretion of the apex political decision-making bodies can be described as following a two-stage process: one stage which is the mere administrative[899] (government) decision on the qualification for granting citizenship by *ius doni* which must be clearly differentiated from its actual grant, which – based on its legal nature – may be regarded either an administrative act or an administrative contract.

A distinction between acceptable and unacceptable consideration can be made using the concept of "factual connection". Creating links to contractual performance on the basis of consideration that would be deemed "unreasonable" in a one-sided sovereign action and which would be a misuse of powers are frowned upon or forbidden. Whether a performance link will be prohibited according to this reasoning, depends mainly on the statutory purposes, as well as the content and the circumstances of the specific contract.[900]

A factual connection is likely to be found between the power being exercised and the consideration offered if the consideration amounts to a resolution of legal obstacle to performance, which itself remains at the discretion of the authority, or if the consideration of the contractual party represents a kind of reimbursement of the expenses of regulatory performance.[901] A

[899] The decision on the granting of citizenship on the basis of an investment, which is at the government's discretion, could on the one a hand affect democratic policies and principles, especially since the decision-makers are bound by the written law. Until the announcement of the final decision there is however no external effect in the sense of the creation of rights and obligations for and against the investor

[900] cf. *Bonk* in STELKENS/BONK/SACHS (2008)

[901] cf. KOPP/RAMSAUER (2005)

factual connection is likely to be absent on the other hand, if a sovereign decision is bound externally without legal authorisation to such economic consideration, if the consideration does not first lawfully allow for the performance of the authority. In contrast to Austria, [902] in the Federal Republic of Germany, for example, the agreement of consideration – such as a "cultural contribution" or an "investment" – which would primarily serve to generally improve the public finances would be inadmissible, [903] because it violates the requirement of there being a sufficiently specific purpose for the consideration, and due to its undefined nature, from the outset fails to achieve a relationship to the specific legal administrative act sought.[904]

Based on the principles of the prohibition of tying arrangements, Citizenship-by-Investment programmes in States such as Malta or St. Kitts and Nevis appear however more consistent with constitutional principles – at least measured against the principles of administrative and public law of European countries – than those of Austria for instance, where, on the basis of the views expressed here, given the vague wording of Section 10(6) ACA (i.e. grant of citizenship on the basis of extraordinary [economic] contribution to the state), the required constitutional certainty is lacking. Accordingly, states should therefore tread with caution if they are to be guided by the Economic Theory of Clubs in the design of such programmes, and should create clear legal frameworks with predefined requirements for admission to citizenship under their respective Citizenship-by-Investment programmes.

Malta is exemplary in this regard; an EU country whose newly elected government and parliament in 2013 introduced a Citizenship-by-Investment programme (called the Malta Individual Investor Programme, IIP), and which includes comprehensive implementation provisions with detailed and transparent rules and institutions for the secure and exemplary operation of such a programme.[905]

---

902 cf. KLEEBER (2007)

903 See the judgment of the German Federal Administrative Court (BVerwG), Case 4 C 4/99, BVerwGE 111, § 162, 169

904 cf. *Fehling* in FEHLING/KASTNER/WAHRENDORF (2006)

905 Republic of Malta Individual Investor Programme Regulations, 2013

So long as we do not live in a world without borders and universal world citizenship, every distinction between "citizen" and "foreigner", every exclusion or inclusion, requires a selection and selection criteria. Those criteria or membership norms "*affect those who are not members precisely by distinguishing insiders from outsiders, citizens from non-citizens.*"[906] Every immigration and citizenship policy is inherently discriminatory in some way.[907] In fact, national citizenship in itself is an expression of the geo-political dimension of global social inequality.[908] It is thus naïve to think that states are exacerbating inequalities through their selective migration and citizenship policies. Instead, or in addition to random selection (e.g. *ius soli*), Economic Club Theory and with it the *ius doni* concept could help provide clear criteria, such as the ability and willingness to make an economic contribution to the State and the acceptance of the club rules established by that State.[909] This at least potentially allows all the people randomly allocated at birth citizenships that they feel are inadequate for them, the opportunity to seek actively an alternative citizenship on the basis of clear criteria. Even though it could be argued that this excludes all those who cannot afford to pay the price set by states – and even this argument does not hold, cf. *infra* – it is in fact a less random, less arbitrary and less restrictive criterion than any other criteria for the admission to citizenship.

Citizenship-by-Investment does not necessarily actually exclude the poor from becoming citizens, as the human capital which e.g. *Shachar* and *Hirschl* wish to normatively distinguish from financial capital as a basis for citizenship and thereby somewhat justify citizenship granted for the special talent which someone possesses as a person,[910] can be reflected through business and other organisations recognising exceptionally talented individuals by financing or providing investment or financial contributions for these individuals to become citizens. This then benefits all three parties involved: the talented individual; the business

906 BENHABIB (2004) p. 15
907 BORNA/STEARNS (2002)
908 FAIST (2007); cf. also SHACHAR (2003)
909 cf. STRAUBHAAR (2003)
910 SHACHAR/HIRSCHL (2014)

organisation from the new hire, for whom it would have been more difficult to travel e.g. on a passport which requires visas everywhere rather than being a citizen of a country which affords its passport holders largely visa-free access across the world; and the country which receives the economic contribution and a highly talented new citizen.[911]

---

[911] cf. BORNA/STEARNS (2002)

12

Blocked Exchange vs. Market Approach

12.1 Spectrum of opinion

As *Okun*[912] and *Walzer*,[913] and more recently *Kuttner*[914] and *Sandel*[915] have shown in detail, there are areas or spheres in human society and its legal systems in which money can play a role, and areas – domains of rights – in which money may not play a role. The latter are also referred to as *blocked exchanges*.[916] The question then arises whether access to citizenship belongs in the sphere where money or other material aspects may play a role.

Alongside administrative power, money has generally become an anonymous medium of societal integration which functions beyond the minds of the individual actors.[917]

In immigration and citizenship law, non-economic considerations drive policies more often than not: for example the anti-Asian immigration policy in the US, the "all white" policies of Australia and New Zealand, Germany's policy to grant immediate citizenship to repatriates, the Spanish law to remember the victims of the civil war and dictatorship under the *Franco* dictatorship, which grants citizenship to descendants of people who fled during that period,[918] or Israel's well-known "law of return"[919] which encourages the immigration of Jews to Israel and the granting of citizenship upon "return" to Israel, no matter how destitute, aged or unskilled those new citizens are, are some of many examples.

A fundamental question therefore relates to the theoretical discussion of the grant of citizenship based on investments or economic contributions to the state – actually citizenship for money – and whether this falls or should fall under the area of *blocked exchanges*, or whether, in the light

912 OKUN (1975)
913 WALZER (1983)
914 KUTTNER (1998)
915 SANDEL (2010); and SANDEL (2012)
916 WALZER (1983)
917 HABERMAS (1995)
918 Ley por la que se reconocen y amplían derechos y se establecen medidas en favor de quienes padecieron persecución o violencia durante la Guerra Civil y la Dictadura of 31 October 2007
919 Law of Return 5710 of 5 July 1950

of modern citizenship laws and in view of the increasing transnational financial and immigration flows and globalisation, the primary aim of having well-off citizens of the world linked to the state via naturalisation based on a significant economic contribution to the State, are or should be considered legitimate functions of modern citizenship laws.

Undoubtedly, we live in times where more than ever, money is able to buy things which previously have not been considered appropriate to be bought and sold. The right to pollute the air – which can now be bought and sold openly,[920] for example; for-profit schools and prisons; naming rights for schools, public parks and civic spaces; or the system of political campaign finance that "*comes close to permitting the buying and selling of elections*".[921] The WTO tries to introduce markets in areas which were previously governed by other principles.[922] *Sandel* is right to point out that some of the good things in life are corrupted and degraded if turned into commodities, and that we have drifted from having a market economy to being a market society: a way of life in which market values seep into every aspect of human endeavour.[923] Moreover, *Miller* assumes that "*in societies in which economic markets play a central role, there is a strong tendency toward social atomization, where each person looks out for the interests of herself and her immediate social network.*"[924]

While critics have a point that the very fact that an immaterial value like citizenship has a price tag may undermine and devalue it, however the opposite can also be true: granting citizenships and passports to highly esteemed persons can make that same citizenship and passport highly esteemed, too.[925]

---

920 The EU operates the EU Emissions Trading System, which enables companies to buy and sell the right to pollute, cf. http://ec.europa.eu/clima/policies/ets/index_en.htm, last accessed on 29 October 2014

921 SANDEL (2012) p. 8

922 In particular, the previously state-dominated education and health systems, cf. CROUCH (2007), with further references

923 SANDEL (2012) p. 8–10; cf. also HIRSCH (1976); and KUTTNER (1998)

924 MILLER (2000) p. 32

925 PASKALEV (2014)

12.2 Should citizenship be governed by market values?

At first sight, one could easily place citizenship in the sphere of goods that should be governed by non-market values. After all, it seems to be the basic status underlying a democratic state: with citizenship comes the right to vote and to take political office – membership in a political community, a most sacrosanct non-market good,[926] and a certain dignity.[927]

However, as outlined *supra,* the rights, privileges and dignity that citizenship confers are limited to within a particular society, to within a system. Thus citizenship is not universal but particular to one state. It cannot be compared, therefore, to universal values like human rights or human dignity, which clearly cannot be governed by market values (it would be unimaginable to have a market for dignity, as this is a universal concept). If citizenship were equal and universal, then it could indeed be regarded as a "sacred", non-market good that cannot be bought and sold, that should not be governed by market values. Indeed, one of the greatest achievements of the modern era, originating mainly in the American and French revolutions, is the removal of birth right privileges. Equality before the law, equality of opportunity, universal suffrage, universal rights and freedom of people and similar, are all cornerstones of modern liberal democratic societies. But there are two important areas in our modern societies which are still largely governed by birth right: the laws that govern inheritance and citizenship.[928] Citizenship is exclusionary and totally arbitrary, a birthright lottery.[929] As a result, naturalisation is needed, to keep the door open at least for worthy people to become citizens, if they happened to be born in other places or to parents of a different citizenship. Naturalisation is possible in many countries[930] based on residence and a few other criteria which are supposedly making sure that the new citizen is sufficiently suitable to be admitted. But what does this mean? If naturalisation is acceptable based on residence and other

---

926 A view expressed, among others, by *Ayelet Shachar*, cf. SHACHAR/HIRSCHL (2014)
927 cf. *Waldron* in MCCRUDDEN (2014) pp. 333 et seq.
928 SHACHAR (2009) pp. 21–43
929 SHACHAR (2009)
930 But not in several Asian countries, such as China, where according to the 2010 census, it had a population of 1.3 billion but only 1,448 naturalized citizens, cf. BREVILLE (2014)

criteria (e.g. marriage to a citizen), what would speak against it to be also acceptable on the basis of economic or other significant contributions to the state? Because of its fundamentally exclusionary and arbitrary nature, *ius doni,* i.e. citizenship acquisition on the basis of economic contribution to the State, are not any more or less arbitrary than the *ius sanguinis* or *ius soli* principles, or the commonly applied principles for naturalisation including years of residence.

Citizenship is not only unequal and non-universal, even in the reality as it exists, it is also a good which has undergone very significant transformation in recent times which, in fact, makes it even more, rather than less, unequal and non-universal.

Today, in most countries, most citizens do either not have the right to vote, have the right (or even the obligation to vote) but the elections are a farce, or in democratic states have the right to vote but do not vote, and most of those who do are often ignorant of even the most basic political facts.[931] The latter is particularly true for larger countries, whereas in smaller countries, democratic understanding and involvement tends to be a little bit better. Political philosophers have long debated the extent of knowledge that voters have to have to make democracy actually work, and today it is more than merely debatable whether knowledge levels meet the demands of democratic theory:[932] *"A citizen democracy can only work if most of its members are convinced that their political society is a common venture of considerable moment and believe it to be of such vital importance that they participate in the ways they must to keep it functioning as a democracy."*[933]

Furthermore, all countries have a socially excluded "underclass" which, regardless of their actual legal status as citizens, are effectively deprived of many of the rights of citizens and are in many ways excluded from their citizenship.[934] Thus one can hardly maintain that one of the

931 SOMIN (2013) p. 17
932 SOMIN (2013) p. 39
933 TAYLOR (1994) p. 120
934 LEUNG (2003) p. 296 et seq.

primary functions of citizenship is the membership in a political community, when most people are either factually excluded or choose not to participate.

Rather, citizenship is, for the overwhelming majority of the world's population, simply a legal status or relationship vis-a-vis a particular nation state, which grants them more or fewer rights and benefits, greatly depending on the level of development, politics and reputation of the particular State to which they are connected to via their citizenship.

A natural experiment which occurred between Bulgaria and Macedonia helps illustrate to what extent citizenship is about identity and democracy, or perhaps rather about other values.[935] The position of Bulgaria is that Macedonians are actually ethnic Bulgarians who happen to live in an artificial country because of an accident of history.[936] Macedonians are annoyed by this suggestion and strongly assert their Macedonian identity against Bulgarians. However, when Bulgaria joined the EU, thousands of Macedonians flocked to Bulgarian consulates to apply for passports. Suddenly, they were claiming that they are "of Bulgarian origin". Very few of them had any actual bonds with Bulgaria and it is rather difficult to believe that all these people had suddenly woken up to their true Bulgarian identity. For all the value we attach to the internal aspect of citizenship, this is by far superseded by its external dimension and concrete benefits it affords or denies.[937] The same occurred and continues to occur in many countries around the world, such as the provision of Hungarian passports to hundreds of thousands of Serbians and Romanians, or turning a million Argentineans into Italians. Investing in your citizenship is at least as random or as sound as investing in lawyer's fees to discover your Italian heritage to claim an Italian passport.[938]

From a formal legal point of view, the status of being a citizen is clear-cut: either you are a citizen or you are not. However that is a very different

[935] cf. PASKALEV (2014)
[936] See e.g. ROUDOMETOF (2002) p. 108; see also PESHKOPIA (2015) p. 186
[937] PASKALEV (2014)
[938] KOCHENOV (2014)

thing with regard to the normative and substantive ideas of citizenship, where there is no such precision. Citizenship as a mode of behaviour requires knowledge and understanding that must be acquired, skills that must be developed and cultivated, and a wish and will to perform the role of a citizen must be felt. To become a citizen in the true sense requires competence, which can only be acquired by education.[939] This in essence is the issue with a market-value approach: of course those aspects of citizenship cannot be bought and sold, not even for an infinite amount of money. However, the formal legal status, if considered separately, is a different matter, the granting of which can very well be subject to monetary consideration.

The question also arises of what remains of the core of national identity in those countries – such as France or Germany, to take just two examples from among many others – which no longer have a national military service requirement, an element which was originally viewed by thinkers such as *Rousseau* as one of the core elements of citizenship.[940] With the paradigm shift towards an understanding of the State as a comprehensive provider, in particular of social services, in which the equivalence between giving (loyalty) and taking (welfare) is no longer ensured in any case, the question arises whether the nation State as a consequence of citizenship and the political rights and duties of the status is still legitimate in this respect, especially since the aforementioned services do not all reflect original core functions of the State. Furthermore, the non-liberal nation states, which actually make up a large part of the world's states, have long since been mere service providers to their citizen-subjects and, at best, provide security, law and order, and certain social services, but do not allow real political participation of its citizens. The citizen is a mere consumer of rights and benefits (and some obligations). At worst, it is as an oppressive, totalitarian structure, as experienced extensively throughout history and, very unfortunately, which continues to be found today around the world. The problem is self-evident when you compare the extremes: to be a citizen is a very different thing if you are Swiss or

939 HEATER (2002)

940 cf. *supra*

North Korean. Swiss citizens probably enjoy more rights than in any other country, including the right to propose a constitutional amendment by collecting a mere 100,000 signatures of fellow citizens, whereas North Koreans are arguably at the other end of the spectrum, where any discussion of political participation and the rights of citizens and human dignity are irrelevant.

12.3 The ethics of the queue

If citizenship is considered as a status and the right to certain benefits,[941] this perspective renders comprehensible the fact that the political component of citizenship is practically to a large extent irrelevant even in liberal democratic States in the case of *ius doni,* for the reasons outlined above combined with the reality that nearly all the applicants under Citizenship-by-Investment programmes have absolutely no interest in the political participation aspect of citizenship.

Nonetheless, this still raises the question of the ethics of the queue. Applicants who pay, although they must also otherwise be suitably qualified and undergo strict due diligence procedures, can jump the queue and do not have to wait for many years to be admitted to citizenship status like other applicants do. "*First come first served*" is displaced by the ethics of the market: "*you get what you pay for*".[942] Citizenship-by-Investment is then, in essence, nothing more than a fast track procedure to citizenship access, based on the ability and willingness to pay, comparable to toll roads or fast-track lanes at airports for First and Business class passengers. But the liberal argument supporting such practices, i.e. that people should generally be free to buy and sell whatever they please, as long as they do not violate other people's rights,[943] seems to hold here: by introducing a *ius doni* option in the national citizenship legislation, there is no harm done to those who are unable or unwilling

---

941 In the context of Citizenship-by-Investment, these are primarily a passport that allows good visa-free travel, and the undeniable right – but not the obligation – to settle at any time in the country of citizenship, which both are highly valued benefits for internationally mobile investors

942 SANDEL (2012) p. 28, and generally pp. 17–41

943 cf. VON MISES (1998)

to pay the price to jump the queue, as they still enjoy the same possibility to acquire citizenship through the normal naturalisation procedures as before. The allegation that such liberalism undermines itself by favouring the wealthy or the privileged also does not hold – while Citizenship-by-Investment does necessarily imply an economic transfer of some kind to be made in return for status, there is nothing to preclude this transaction not being supported by a loan or future garnishing of income.[944] Indeed, in the US, this practice has even become relatively common, with private financial institutions offering Citizenship Loans to cover the costs of the naturalisation process. Moreover, the *utilitarian argument*, and the argument of the effective allocation of goods, i.e. that market exchanges benefit buyers and sellers alike, thereby improving our collective wellbeing or social utility,[945] also supports the case for a market-based citizenship allocation: markets are not good or bad, they are simply the most effective means to allocate resources and goods.[946] By providing an additional means to acquire citizenship, based on investment in the country or other economic contributions to the country, it improves our well-being and social utility. Everyone benefits from such practice: in addition of course to the applicant herself, who values the citizenship she obtains more than the economic cost she incurs by applying under such a programme; the State receives additional funding at virtually no costs; the country receives additional investments in the private or public sectors or direct monetary contributions (depending on how the Citizenship-by-Investment programme of the particular country in question is structured); and the country adds qualified, talented and wealthy entrepreneurs and investors to its stock of citizens. This inclusion of valuable citizens then also increases the chances that some of these new citizens will also proceed with additional activities such as further direct investments, setting up businesses in the country and thereby creating additional jobs and opportunities for other citizens living there, and spending time in the country and thereby paying taxes through their spending – which in the case of wealthy individuals

944 BORNA/STEARNS (2002) p. 194
945 MANKIV (2009)
946 cf. HAYEK (2007)

can create not only significant indirect tax revenues but also additional economic activity due to the need for the supply of goods and services, which in turn also yields more taxes, and so on. For all these reasons, *ius doni* seems to have no real negative effects[947] but actually provides many positive effects, not only for the person acquiring citizenship this way but also and in particular for the country granting citizenship. The only downside seems to be of a fundamental idealistic nature, if the political membership component or the "internal" aspects of citizenship are considered as more important than the other components which make up modern citizenship.

12.4 The political membership aspect of citizenship

It is therefore not unreasonable to reduce the essential question on whether *ius doni* should, as a concept, be admissible, to whether the political membership component of citizenship is felt to be significant enough to prevent a market-value approach. From a liberal-democratic perspective it is this component, the membership rights in the political community, the right to vote and to hold political office, which seem to hold back the acceptance of the concept of *ius doni*, i.e. the acceptance of making such membership effectively available in return for an economic contribution. This is the potentially repugnant side to this economic access-to-citizenship concept,[948] as this seems to be the aspect where money or other material factors should not play a role (a *blocked exchange*).

Assuming that there is consensus that it is this political membership aspect which is the key issue, rather than any other aspects of citizenship, the fundamental acceptance or rejection of *ius doni* therefore significantly depends on whether one views this political membership aspect as sufficiently important in today's understanding of modern citizenship to conclude, as some scholars do,[949] that it must be rejected overall, or as

---

[947] Regarding the possible macroeconomic dependencies and resource-rent implications, however, cf. XU/EL-ASHRAM/GOLD (2015)

[948] cf. SHACHAR/HIRSCHL (2014)

[949] Notably SHACHAR and BAUBÖCK

others maintain,[950] that the other aspects of citizenship in fact prevail, and thus a market-based approach is permissible.

To evaluate this question, consider this:

> *"Imagine that our country is waging a desperate war of self-defence. Just when defeat – and the collapse of our community – appears inevitable, a force of foreign volunteers enters the fray and swings the result in our favour. These volunteers have performed a tremendous service to our community – perhaps the greatest service we can imagine.*
>
> *Imagine, next, that we decide to thank the volunteers by offering them citizenship in our country. Would this be morally repugnant? Far from it: the decision would, I think, be perfectly appropriate. What, then, of rootedness, interaction, residence, or participation? If giving citizenship to our imaginary volunteers is appropriate, then those things cannot be as important as we thought. Perhaps a massive, one-off contribution to the polity can be enough".*[951]

The same applies to significant economic contributions, which is in excess of the economic lifetime contributions made by the average current citizen (current club member). The contribution and support to the polity is very significant, and, provided that good character requirements are met, such persons ought to be admitted as they demonstrate commitment to the polity that is significant enough, and more significant than in many other instances of naturalisation, to warrant their acceptance into the polity.

A more market-based approach to citizenship is a trend that will only grow stronger in the coming years as we come to realise the relative practical insignificance of political membership in a community for the majority of the population in liberal democracies, and for most parts of the population of the rest of the world, in light of the relative and increasing practical importance of the state as a service provider to its

---

950 e.g. SPIRO and KOCHENOV
951 ARMSTRONG (2014) p. 14

citizens and residents. The political membership component of modern citizenship should thus not prevent us from accepting the utility and benefits of offering citizenship to people who are able and willing to contribute significantly to society by injecting capital to the economy, and thus regard the *ius doni* concept as a positive, modern and additional access route to citizenship for progressive states. In any case, the global *"spread of the talent-for-citizenship exchange… is one of the most significant innovations in citizenship practice in the past few decades. In this emerging competitive environment, countries have come to realize that their exclusive control over the assignment of membership goods is a major draw."*[952]

952 SHACHAR (2011) p. 2088

13

Applicable International Law and Principles with Regard to Citizenship

13.1 Universal human dignity

If a right to citizenship is derived from the universal guarantee of human dignity, which is not subject to statutory reservation in most Western countries, cannot be curtailed and is not subject to the unilateral unfettered disposition of nation States, then the nation State's scope for action in the area of citizenship law cannot be unlimited.[953]

From the perspective of public international law, there is also prevailing agreement that the national citizenship legislation should be subject to certain barriers.[954] There is, however, far-reaching disagreement regarding the content and scope of these barriers.[955]

The supervision of human dignity in nation States is legitimately in the hands of the international community, because of its universality, which bearing in mind the proportionality principle and the principle of international subsidiarity, can permit intervention in the internal affairs of States, if a nation State is failing on its fiduciary duty towards its own nationals. Recent examples here include the Apartheid regime in South Africa, the North Korean state, the genocide in Rwanda, the conflict in Kosovo and the recent events in Syria, where the State regime allowed gunning down of its own nationals.[956] Universal human dignity is only confirmed declaratively in the legal systems of the nation States in which it is expressly codified. National law and public international law overlap in the international norm hierarchy in subsidiary order: national regulatory autonomy and sovereign equality end when they come up against universal human dignity. The same is true in citizenship law. Closely related to the guarantee of human dignity is the respect for individual decision-making autonomy, which is directly linked to humanity. Accordingly, no one's citizenship should be revoked against his will. Taking away a person's citizenship involves the *"total destruction of the individual's status in organized society"* and *"the American concept of man's*

953 Cf. in this context *Grimm* in MCCRUDDEN (2013) p. 381 et seq.
954 MAKAROV (1962); KANAAN (2012)
955 MAKAROV (1962); DAHM/DELBRÜCK/WOLFRUM (2002); KANAAN (2012)
956 For the conditions of one such case and similar cases of humanitarian intervention cf. *Hilpold* in FISCH (2011)

dignity does not comport with making even those we would punish completely stateless – fair game for the despoiler at home and the oppressor abroad, if indeed there is any place which will tolerate them at all." [957] *Arendt* pointed out that the rights of man were supposed to be "inalienable", but *"the moment human beings lacked their own government and had to fall back upon their minimum rights, no authority was left to protect them and no institution was willing to guarantee them."*[958] Human rights worked only for those who were citizens of a particular state, and although times have changed since Arendts observations, there is still a fundamental truth in them. But what does this mean, and how is it relevant, for the question of human dignity with regard to the acquisition of citizenship, as is relevant here? Does a *ius doni* based allocation of citizenship violate any principles of human dignity in the allocation of citizenship?

13.1.1 Respect for individual freedom of choice

Citizenship forms a legal "bond",[959] a connection, a relationship or a bridge between a natural person and a national legal order. Given that in a democracy, the national law is (more or less) an expression of the will of the State's population which can only be determined through a democratic vote, the boundaries to the nation State's leeway in the field of citizenship law are drawn on the basis of the internal relationships among the nationals and through their constitutionally guaranteed rights, among which human dignity prohibits State power being exercised to reduce the individual to a mere object of State regulation, which (also) directly links back to the principle of democracy.

If in democratic states all power emanates from the people – as suggested by the French Constitution with the phrase "*government of the people by the people and for the people*" in Article 2(5) and affirmed by the subsequent "*national sovereignty lies with the people*" in Article 3 – it would appear logically inconceivable that a State could impose limits on

---

[957] Chief Justice Earl Warren in *Trop v. Dulles*, 356 US 86 (1958), cited by *Waldon* in MCCRUDDEN (2014) p. 337

[958] ARENDT (1973) p. 268

[959] JELLINEK (1976)

the sovereignty of its citizens in the internal relationship of control by means of elections and voting. State power today, as distinct e.g. from the time of *Louis IX ("L'*état *c'est moi")*[960] – cannot develop a life of its own and cannot decouple from the will of the citizens – that would reduce them to mere objects of State power and "strip" the State's citizenry of its importance as a source of all State power.

To confirm the importance of citizens and to ensure and reinforce their role as the source and beneficiaries of all State authority, their freedom of choice is protected as the essence of a democratic constitutional State system through their constitutional rights – including through the constitutionally secured right to self-determination, which is part of the general rights enjoyed by all, regardless of the national organisation of citizenship laws and the boundaries to discretion they set. Within the limits of its scope for action, the State can regulate the citizenship law autonomously.

Within the limits of its scope for action, the State can regulate how its citizenship is allocated, including how the conditions under which a non-resident, non-citizen receives "his" citizenship by way of naturalisation, i.e. it can justify granting citizenship in favour of non-residents. Due to the link between citizenship law and universal human dignity, the principle of democracy and the constitutionally secured individual decision-making autonomy, it should however not be in the State's power to "strip" a citizen of his citizenship and thus "deprive" him of those rights to which he is entitled based on his citizenship if this would render the relevant person stateless. Citizenship as a legal property should not be withdrawn against the will of the person concerned.

The State may only define and design of those rights which are directly related to the legal status of citizenship, such as extending the electoral term to a domestic representative body from four to five years, reinstating the requirement for military service or conditioning the receipt of State benefits in connection with a job placement on proof of volunteer work.

---

[960] "I am the State"

Internally to citizens, the nation State's scope for action in the area of citizenship law is thus limited by what feeds back onto the citizens themselves, whose constitutionally protected decision-making autonomy expressing the limits to the individual self-determination of State sovereignty. A liberal polity is one in which government decision-making flows from the bottom to the top, based on the freedom of decision of the individual, in which universal human dignity is concretised and manifested. [961]

But externally, it is evident that each State is largely[962] free to decide on the modes of allocation of its citizenship, and there is definitely no limitation on the respect of individual freedom of choice[963] (imagine the world population having the freedom of choice with regard to citizenship).

13.1.2 Prohibition of discrimination based on descent, language, homeland and origin

With respect to the national scope for action in the area of citizenship in many of the reference States considered, many compelling lines have already been drawn to the effect that *no one* should be discriminated against because of her descent, language, homeland and origin. The US, France, Austria and the Federal Republic of Germany can be considered exemplary in this regard. This applies both to the entire population as well as with regard to questions of access to citizenship. Liberally constituted states shall not discriminate on these grounds.

In the case of France, the French Constitution determines that the equality of all citizens before the law is guaranteed without distinction of origin, race or religion (Article 1(1)(2) French Constitution) and the Republic of France respects all beliefs (Article 1(1)(3) French Constitution).

---

961 Of course in a large number of countries, these ideal liberal democratic conditions do not exist, and citizens are mere subjects of state authority that emanates more often than not from other sources (monarchies, "managed" democracies, military dictatorships, etc.)

962 Within the very few limitations discussed herein, e.g. within the EU for EU member states

963 As provided by Article 15(2) UDHR: *"No one shall be arbitrarily deprived of his nationality nor denied the right to change his nationality."*

In Austria the national scope for action is similarly circumscribed in that the law requires that public schools be accessible to the general population without distinction for birth, sex, race, status, class, language or religion (Article 14(6)(4) ÖB-VG).

In the law of the Federal Republic of Germany, Article 3(3) GC stipulates that no one may be prejudiced or favoured because of sex, descent, race, language, homeland and origin, faith or religious or political opinions. No one may also be discriminated against because of disability.

Other democratically constituted states have similar provisions. Again, in large parts of the world, however, outright discrimination, in particular in citizenship law, is widespread, and this is particularly so with regard to the allocation of citizenship.

13.1.3 No undifferentiated connection to political opinion, religion, race or language

One of the main achievements in particular of the European Enlightenment, which was accompanied by the formation of nation States and represents the maturation of the subject into the citizen, is the knowledge that the individual relationship of man to extra-worldly and spiritual powers is something wholly personal and not mediated by either government or ecclesiastical powers. The relationship of the individual to extra-worldly or spiritual powers is subject exclusively to his individual conviction. The principle predominant until the Absolutist era, "*cuius regio, eius religio*" ("Whose realm, his religion") – according to which the individual was unconditionally obliged to accept a religious-ideological allegiance with his ruler, if he did not wish for his rights to be revoked – is no longer applicable in the reference States we are considering here, although it is still prevalent in many countries around the world, particularly in Muslim countries.

The principle of political-ideological neutrality applies, as exemplified in Article 1(1)(1) French Constitution (*secular republic*) in conjunction with Article 1(1)(3) French Constitution (*All religions are respected*); or with respect to access to general education, in Article 14(6)(5) ÖB-VG, according to which, public schools are available generally without distinction of birth, sex, race, status, class, language and religion. In the Swiss Confederation the move away from the Absolutist maxim "*Cuius regio, eius religio*" is also supported by the fact that every person has the individual right to freely choose her religion and other convictions, and to profess this, either alone or in a community with others (Article 15(2) Cst). In the US, Congress may not pass any law designed to prohibit the free exercise of religion (First Amendment of the US Constitution).

Furthermore, in designing its citizenship laws, the liberal democratic State is prohibited from tying the granting of citizenship to the individual's political opinion, religion, race or language. The decision to believe or disbelieve in an extra-worldly power or to accept or renounce any religion is subject to individual decision-making autonomy, which, as an expression of universal human dignity, is a defining axiom of a human personality. As the example of France shows (refusal of grant of citizenship in case of a *defaut d'assimilation*), restrictions are only imposed on the ideological and political decision-making autonomy, where this autonomy impinges on other rights or legal interests of a constitutional nature, such as the public interest, criminal enforcement and the exercise of organised State power as an expression of territorial sovereignty.[964]

13.1.4 General principle of equality

Functionally, one of the essential basic ideas of the concept of citizenship is the creation of a formal bond between the individual and the national legal system in terms of a rule of law which generally respects individual freedom and different individual lifestyles uniformly: i.e., without linking it to individual characteristics such as political opinion, religion, race or language. General equality is another barrier in the national scope for action in the field of citizenship law.

Organised law in the sense of effectively exercised State authority does not include a monopoly over the definition of culture nor a claim to

964 cf. supra; Article 1(2) French Constitution; Article 7(1)(1) ÖB-VG; Article 3(1) GC.

absolute control over culture. Rather, it includes an obligation to protect cultural minorities in its citizenship law, as seen e.g. in Article 8(1) ÖB-VG which recognises the State language of Austria only without prejudice to linguistic minorities.

13.1.5 Democratic principle

One "*...can be a citizen in an absolute monarchy, but Aristotle was right to insist that 'our definition of citizen is best applied in a democracy'*"[965]. Universal human dignity prohibits any State authority from degrading the individual to a mere object of State regulation, and therefore requires, at least from the reference States considered here, that any form of State power derives from an expression of the will of the sovereign, expressed particularly in elections and votes. Only a national parliament – constituted on the basis of a corresponding declaration of intent – and not a group of experts behind closed doors away from the public eye, can decide on the design of citizenship law. To some extent there is an institutionalised hinge between the constitutive people and the organised State authority, whose conduct both internally and externally must in principle be based on a parliamentary decision. Only in this way can, for example, the government of the people, by the people and for the people (principle of popular sovereignty as the embodiment of the principle of democracy, and as stipulated in Article 2(5) French Constitution) be guaranteed.

13.1.6 Principle of certainty

Curtailing universal human dignity, which forms an unqualifiable barrier for nation States in their design of citizenship law, can also occur itself if the legal criteria for the acquisition of citizenship are either not sufficiently precise or are incomplete, so that the government's decision-makers are left with too large of a margin of discretion in determining whether an application for citizenship should be approved or declined.

---

[965] *Waldron* in MCCRUDDEN (2014) p. 340

In this context, the fact that social conditions are constantly changing should also be taken into account, as it makes it difficult to define when the integration process is complete. Instead, it would appear preferable to define minimum legal requirements that should be formulated as precisely as possible, and which must be present for the derivative acquisition of citizenship. Because of the constitutionally protected individual autonomy and constitutional minority protection, any further integration should be left to individuals, who in their efforts to further integrate simultaneously decide on what individual opportunities will be open to them, such as in the labour and housing markets in the host country, and what social receptiveness and acceptance they will engender. Their other integration efforts fall under the constitutionally protected sphere of freedom, which is respected by the State. The extent to which the government generally respect this or seek to "govern" it is ultimately a matter of political expediency.

The lack of certainty, from the perspective of the applicant, leads to unpredictable, uncertain and arbitrary State action, which, depending on how crucial the access to the relevant citizenship is, can lead to serious consequences for the applicant. It can also be as difficult from the perspective of the person concerned, if the relevant facts and legal consequences are not based on an "if, then" relationship, but in the case of discretionary naturalisation, on an "if, then maybe". In this regard the naturalisation provisions in Belgium are interesting, in that they entitle an alien to a justiciable right to naturalisation after seven years of residence,[966] an entitlement which in most States is only granted, if at all, after up to 30 years (Austria).

With the unpredictability of government decisions on the granting of citizenship, which results from indeterminacy in the content of the rules or from non-conditional linking of facts and legal consequences, individuals can become the playthings of arbitrary administrative convenience. In other words, applicants can be reduced to mere objects of State interests if the decision on the granting of citizenship is not taken

---

966 cf. KÄLIN (2014)

by a multi-member collegial body, whose decisions are subject to judicial review by State courts or independent review boards, but by individual officials, rendering naturalisation decisions subjective when they should be made objectively. The fundamental importance of citizenship, in particular as a precondition for access to essential facilities and services of general interest, requires that the legal criteria for the granting of citizenship should in general be as sufficiently clear and precise as possible, and thereby the principle be implemented, that a legal norm must be more specific in content, the more acutely the constitutionally protected positions are affected as a result of their application and enforcement.

In this regard, many Citizenship-by-Investment programmes are actually more certain for the applicant than the ordinary naturalisation processes, as in most cases they provide an "if, then" process: if you fulfil the requirements stipulated in the relevant law and regulations, including character requirements of course, and make the required economic contribution, then you will generally become a citizen. Of course, the final decision is still a discretionary one, however the process is much more transparent and certain than most of the ordinary naturalisation procedures, and thus from a legal certainty perspective of a higher quality.

13.1.7 Need for unity of citizenship

As citizenship due to its nature is closely related with the general principle of equality (principle of non-discrimination, *égalité de traitement*), it prohibits as a legal principle to discriminate within the context of citizenship according to sex, sexual identity, descent, race, language, homeland and origin, faith, and religious or political opinion. To formulate this principle differently, the status is (or normatively should be) binary: Either a person has or does not have citizenship.

Apart from quite practical difficulties which are associated with a "graduated citizenship", who or what should define the criteria "for going up a level" – i.e. moving from "citizenship-lite" to "full citizenship" – is controversial. Any deficiencies in the integration process cannot be resolved on the strength of the acquisition of citizenship through naturalisation, and should not be dealt with by citizenship law, but in the political process.

The fact that normatively no "graduation" of citizenship should exist, underlines the rather practical need to define the derivative acquisition of citizenship by way of naturalisation requirements and criteria, taking into account the current and foreseeable social development so that those conflicts resulting from incomplete integration at the time of the acquisition of citizenship remains as limited as possible.

It should however also be noted that in many countries this unity of citizenship is not complied with. Apart from the often encountered provisions which specify that the head of State must be State-born and not a naturalised citizen, for example (as in the US), or that political rights accrue only after a certain time (as in St. Kitts and Nevis, after only five years of residence), the UK offers, in particular in its recent history, the great and glaring example of a differentiated, non-uniform citizenship.[967]

Citizenship-by-Investment programmes have generally the tendency to deviate from the principle of unity of citizenship. An example is St. Kitts and Nevis, which due to its voting restriction on new citizens under its Citizenship-by-Investment effectively creates two classes of citizens (see *supra*), or Cyprus, which in its latest amendment to its Citizenship-by-Investment programme requires new citizens under that programme to at all times hold a residential property worth at least EUR 500,000 for the rest of their lives, leaving many questions unanswered (what happens in case of a divorce?) and in any case also creating a different class of citizenship. Such uncertainties should be rather eliminated.

13.1.8 Prevention of multiple citizenship?

General public international law principally recognises that each State may determine who should be counted among its nationals, and that this regulation of nationality belongs to the reserved domain – *domaine*

967 cf. *Hansen* in HANSEN/WEIL (2001); and *Harris* in BELLAMY/CASTIGLIONE/SANTORO (2004)

réservé[968] – of the individual States. This principle goes back at least to the advisory opinion of the Permanent International Court of Justice in The Hague of 7 February 1923, concerning nationality decrees in Tunisia and in a zone formerly controlled by Morocco, which States: "*The question whether a certain matter is subject to the exclusive control by a State or not, are relative based on their characteristics: it depends on the development of national relations. According to the Court in the present State of international law, the nationality principle questions falls under this reserved area*".[969]

Articles 1 and 2 of the Hague Convention also stipulate, responding to certain questions over conflict of citizenship issues current in 1930, that individual States are entitled to determine by their laws, who should have their citizenship, and emphasises the exclusive domestic jurisdiction.[970] The Council of Europe Convention on Nationality of 1997 also recognises this principle in Article 3(1), which States: "*Each State shall determine under its own law who are its nationals.*"[971]

In particular to prevent loyalty conflicts, such as in the context of military service, and to avoid conflicts of jurisdiction, which in the context of consular or diplomatic protection could be to the detriment of those affected, it follows that limiting cases of multiple citizenships is a potential barrier in the design of citizenship regulation addressed to national legislators.[972] Boundaries to the nation State scope for action in the area of citizenship law can arise here, such as from the *Council of Europe Convention on the Reduction of Cases of Multiple Nationality and on Military Obligations in Cases of Multiple Nationality* (CRCMN)[973] and from the ECN.

This view, that multiple citizenship should in principle be avoided

---

[968] cf. MAKAROV (1962)

[969] Permanent International Court of Justice, 7 February 1923, published online http://www.icj-cij.org/pcij/serie_B/B_04/Decrets_de_nationalite_promulgues_en_Tunisie_et_au_Maroc_Avis_consultatif_1.pdf, last accessed on 28 July 2015

[970] Text of the Hague Convention, see HECKER (1970)

[971] European Convention on Nationality, CETS No. 166, http://conventions.coe.int

[972] cf. HOKEMA (2002); as well as TOPAL (2010); and KANAAN (2012)

[973] Convention on the Reduction of Cases of Multiple Nationality and on Military Obligations in Cases of Multiple Nationality (CRCMN) of 6 May 1963

or prohibited, goes back to the *Institute du Droit International*, when it was recognised in 1895 as a guiding principle for the work of the "Commission for the treatment of legislation conflicts in the field of citizenship that no-one can have two citizenships simultaneously.[974]

Although multiple citizenship is increasingly common in reality today and corresponds to an international trend, that increasingly many people and even politicians have more than one citizenship – consider for instance the member of the European Parliament *Daniel Cohn-Bendit*, who in addition to German also has French citizenship; the former Czech Foreign Minister *Karel Schwarzenberg*, who along with his Czech citizenship is also Swiss; or in Germany the former Chief Minister of Lower Saxony, *David McAllister*, who is British and German – it is important to bear in mind that certain legal frictions associated with multiple citizenships can still occur. Given these frictions, multiple citizenship has traditionally been considered undesirable, but is becoming accepted.[975]

Since the *Expatriation Act* of 1907 and especially during the Cold War in the 1950s, dual citizenship was almost regarded as treason in the US, for example,[976] and was not allowed until the various relevant provisions of the *Nationality Act* of 1940, which were then[977] successively suspended in the nineteen-sixties by the US Supreme Court as unconstitutional.[978] Today, this "evil"[979] of multiple citizenship is becoming tolerated and the trend is clearly towards increased international acceptance of multiple citizenship.[980] In Canada, the UK, France, Switzerland, St. Kitts and

---

974 TOPAL (2010)

975 *Hansen/Weil* in HANSEN/WEIL (2002) p. 9; cf. also HERDEGEN (2010), cf. *supra*

976 HANSEN/WEIL (2001); cf. *Savorgnan v. United States et al.*, 338 US 49 (1950), *Perez v. Brownell*, 356 US 44 (1958); cf. also DONNER (1994)

977 Actually already in 1958 in *Trop v. Dulles*, 356 US 86 (1958), where the Supreme Court of the United States suspended a loss-of-nationality provision for the first time

978 According to *Trop v. Dulles* as interpreted in *Kennedy v. Mendoza-Martinez*, 372 US 144 (1963), *Schneider v. Rusk*, 377 US 163 (1964), and then, especially in *Afroyim v.* Rusk, 387 US 253 (1967), where the Supreme Court held that a US citizen has a constitutionally guaranteed right to remain a US citizen, "*unless he voluntarily relinquishes that citizenship*"

979 cf. "Evil doctrine" of BVerfGE 37, 217 (254), which corresponds to the traditional view that multiple nationalities were considered undesirable and should be avoided if possible

980 cf. KALEKIN-FISHMAN/PITKÄNEN (2007); KANAAN (2012); HAILBRONNER/RENNER/MAASSEN (2010); HOBE (2008); KÄLIN (2014)

Nevis, Malta and many other countries multiple citizenship are not an issue.[981]

Although countries are aware of the impact of multiple citizenship, a duty under public international law to prevent multiple citizenship cannot be recognised.[982]

On the contrary, there are now even some intergovernmental contracts which present multiple citizenship as desirable, in particular various treaties between Spain and Latin American countries or Portugal and Brazil.[983]

Multiple citizenship can moreover also intensify international relations: Spain has demonstrable positive experience of allowing multiple nationalities, which it uses to improve its foreign relations.[984] Likewise, countries that have Citizenship-by-Investment programmes almost always[985] allow the persons acquiring citizenship under their respective programme to keep their current citizenship since, of course, those programmes would not be attractive at all if multiple citizenship were not allowed.

Carens argues that multiple citizenship in principle does not pose a problem, because its prohibition does not much change the actual identity and views or loyalty of individuals.[986]

The *Council of Europe Convention on Nationality* of 1997, no longer intended to combat the emergence of multiple citizenship, is also generally value-neutral on this issue, leaving it to the States to determine their attitude towards multiple citizenship.[987]

---

981 cf. HANSEN/WEIL (2001)
982 HOKEMA (2002)
983 cf. DONNER (1994); and HAMPE (1960)
984 SALAHELDIN (2012)
985 Except for Russia, which in 2014 also introduced a Citizenship-by-Investment program, but one which oddly requires the applicants to relinquish their current citizenship if they want to become Russian
986 CARENS (1998)
987 KANAAN (2012)

13.1.9 Prohibition of abuse of rights (Article 15(2) UDHR) and withdrawal of citizenship

Further boundaries to the national government discretion in the area of citizenship law are thrown up by the international legal prohibition of abuse of rights, which nearly has the force of international customary law, and is expressly laid down in Article 15(2) UDHR. This provides that no one should arbitrarily have his citizenship revoked, or should be denied the right to change his citizenship. The history of the development of the prohibition of the abuse of rights is also rooted in the era of European Reformation and the Enlightenment.

Until the Thirty Years War (1618–1648) it was still common practice in many European regions that refusal to accept and observe a particular religion could result in the loss of certain rights and in extreme cases could mean that the person concerned could be declared an "outlaw", i.e. was excluded from the State community. The paradigm shift from *ius soli* to *ius sanguinis* started by the French Revolution of 1789 and the following years also led to the rejection of "*cuius regio, eius religio*" and changed the meaning of citizenship law from being an instrument of the objective State organisation to a subjective and individually enforceable right.

The term "arbitrary" within the meaning of Article 15(2) UDHR is thus justiciable as an indeterminate legal concept. The deprivation of citizenship without an objective reason is prohibited. What is meant by an objective reason is determined by the functions motivated as justifying the challenged action at its outset, and particularly by the *telos* of Article 15(2) UDHR, to prevent statelessness, which can remove all diplomatic and consular protection from the affected person, in the final analysis.

As Article 15(2) UDHR implies in its control structure that although a loss of citizenship due to a State sovereign act is conditionally permissible under public international law, the occurrence of statelessness is not, the wording of Article 15(1) UDHR – "right to *a* nationality" – underlines the hybrid nature of citizenship law on the one hand as a subjective human right, and as an (objective) function for State organisation on the other. Qualifying Article 15(2) UDHR exclusively as a subjective human right, the deprivation of citizenship even with a valid reason, i.e. an exclusion, is not permitted. Furthermore, Article 15(2) UDHR emphasises the subsidiary superposition of national and public international law.

In this regard Citizenship-by-Investment programmes can play an important role in that they offer people who have been unjustly deprived of their citizenship a means to acquire another citizenship, to acquire the "*right to have rights*".[988] Of course, Citizenship-by-Investment programmes are selective in that one has to have sufficient financial means to acquire citizenship through this route, but they at least offer a route for persons rendered stateless to re-acquire *a* citizenship.

13.1.10 Sufficient relationship or "genuine link" with the State

The rule that a State may not confer its citizenship to persons who have no relationship to it, is internationally recognised.[989] How close the required relationship must be is, however, controversial.[990] Following the French Revolution, the French parliamentarian *Lamourette* declared that Frenchness required no other bond than "philosophical consanguinity", and citizenship could therefore be generously granted to anyone who supported the revolution.[991] Archives of the British Home Office of the late Victorian era indicate that many public officials of that period where committed to a very liberal stance toward granting citizenship, in line with modern ultra-liberal citizenship theorists who assert that citizenship is nothing more than *a personal flag of convenience, to be deployed by individuals in accordance with their private interests in an ever-changing global economy.*[992]

A State may in any case not confer its citizenship to individual persons who demonstrate absolutely no attachment or who have "no relationship

---

988 Chief Justice Earl Warren in *Perez v. Brownell*, 356 US 44, 64 (1957)
989 MAKAROV (1962); DUBOIS (1955); HAILBRONNER/RENNER/MAASSEN (2010); KANAAN (2012)
990 KANAAN (2012); HOKEMA (2002)
991 *Rosanvallon*, cited in LABORDE (2004)
992 HARRIS (2004), with further citations

at all" to it, i.e. without at least the relevant person's consent[993] In the much-quoted *Nottebohm* decision of the ICJ,[994] a closer, effective relationship between the State and the person on whom citizenship is conferred is required. This decision, however, is mainly rejected in the literature and is furthermore related specifically and only to the question of diplomatic protection and related conflicts in the case of multiple citizenship.[995] This case, although often cited, can therefore not be used to draw further conclusions, let alone the fact that the decision is already more than half a century old and that meanwhile citizenship, and in particular the acceptance of multiple citizenship, has significantly progressed.

The acquisition of citizenship in accordance with the generally recognised *ius soli* principle is accepted under public international law, even if the birth merely happens to occur in the territory (the most significant example of this being the US), sometimes also referred to as "accidental citizenship" or "accidental citizens",[996] and can thus be totally arbitrary. Accidental citizens are moreover not unique to *ius soli* principle citizenship, but different techniques of making children into citizens produce their own unique accidents.[997] There is therefore no principle of "genuine link" or absence of arbitrariness which would also be decisive for the acquisition of citizenship by birth.[998] With respect to Citizenship-by-Investment, the voluntariness of the application for naturalisation can be determined in this context, and even the mere declaration of intent made by the applicant, i.e. her express desire to become a citizen and be part of the nation, presents in principle a sufficient connection for the granting of citizenship for the purposes of general public international law.[999] Invariably, however, the *ius doni* principle of acquisition of citizenship requires applicants to make specific investments in or economic contributions to the state, acquire real estate etc., and thereby establish

993 MAKAROV (1962); DUBOIS (1955); KANAAN (2012)
994 ICJ judgment of 6 April 1955, ICJ Rep. 1955 (*Nottebohm*)
995 cf. above, re diplomatic protection in general cf. FELTHAM (2006)
996 cf. NYERS (2009) p. 118
997 NYERS (2009) p. 133
998 KANAAN (2012); DAHM/DELBRÜCK/WOLFRUM (2002); cf. also HOKEMA (2002)
999 DUBOIS (1955); HOBE (2008); KANAAN (2012); RANDELZHOFER (1997)

further links with the respective country. Indeed, if one has made a substantial investment in a country, the links with that country can be significant,[1000] and will be significantly greater than if one has no further ties to a country than being accidently born there.

In conclusion, for a citizenship to be internationally recognised, there is no reasonable legal argument under international law or otherwise to require more "links" or a closer relationship to a state under the *ius doni* principle of acquisition, than the universally accepted *ius soli* principle of acquisition.

Furthermore, as already shown *supra*,[1001] in a European context, the logic of free movement and right of establishment within the EU is antithetical to the "genuine link" idea, and cannot allow EU member states not to recognise the citizenship of other EU member states – however acquired – using their free movement rights.[1002]

13.1.11 *Ultra vires* doctrine: binding of the national legislature to the purpose and functions of citizenship

The rule of law is closely linked with the principle of democracy, which characterises the constitutive principles of government in liberal-democratic nation States. The rule of law prohibits the national legislature from regulating something other than which can be understood from the perspective of the addressees of the text of the statute itself, the limits of which correspond to extremes of its permissible interpretation. To allow the constitutive people adequate control of laws, regulations etc. through their actions, the national legislature is also bound by both the purpose and the functions of citizenship in the area of citizenship law (*ultra vires* doctrine). An act of a person exercising State authority as an organ of State mandated by the constitutive people for this purpose, which exceeds the established limits, is unlawful as an application of the law *ultra vires*, and probably even invalid,[1003] because a nation State in

1000 cf. OCHOA (2014)
1001 cf. 6.3.5.6.
1002 KOCHENOV (2009)
1003 cf. DOEHRING (2004)

its capacity as a subject of public international law may not act outside of its statutorily or otherwise defined competencies.[1004]

The determination in citizenship law of the conditions under which citizenship can be acquired through naturalisation falls within the scope of action of the nation State legislature,[1005] though with the stipulation that "extraordinary economic contributions to the State" should apply as a criterion for direct naturalisation presents a less common way for the acquisition of citizenship. Nonetheless, in accepting this criterion, the national legislature is free to legislate and in no way acts *ultra vires*, because the fundamental purpose and function of citizenship are preserved; merely the mode of acquisition of citizenship is affected.

13.2 Other potential international legal barriers

Even if it is incumbent on each State to be responsible for the grant and withdrawal of citizenship in relation to citizenship of the respective State, not every State action in the area of citizenship law was and is recognised under public international law. At the latest since the conference in The Hague in 1930 on citizenship, it has been clear[1006] that other States are essentially just expected to recognise other national legislation, "*in so far as it is consistent with international conventions, international custom, and the principles of law generally recognised with regard to nationality*".[1007] However, the exact meaning of this is not clear, and there is no agreement on how this should be interpreted.

As has been shown *supra*, there is nothing in international law that would make a *ius doni* principle of citizenship acquisition look any more or less arbitrary than the *ius soli* principle of citizenship acquisition, at least in its pure form as still applicable in many countries, including the

---

1004 cf. DELBRÜCK/WOLFRUM (2002)
1005 cf. DONNER (1994)
1006 STILLER (2011)
1007 Article 1 of the Convention on Certain Questions Relating to The Conflicht ofNationality Laws, The Hague 12 April 1930

US, Canada and many others, or the various odd rules that states have practiced (cf. the citizenship of the Vatican City, the French Foreign Legion, etc.), and thus cannot in any way be held contrary to "*international conventions, international custom, and the principles of law generally recognised with regard to nationality*".

13.2.1 The nation State sovereignty reserve

As another angle from which to view and decide whether Citizenship-by-Investment is consistent with the applicable provisions of public international law, it should be recognised that the nation State scope for action in the area of citizenship law from the perspective of universal public international law – which is not tied to national ratification – is very broad but not unlimited. The remaining nation State sovereignty reserve represents the difference between the undiminished national sovereignty, international treaty law (Article 2(1)(a) Vienna Convention on the Law of Treaties (VCLT)),[1008] the binding international law (public international law *ius cogens*),[1009] and customary public international law.

A State which introduces a Citizenship-by-Investment programme is acting within its national sovereignty reserve because, given the very limited impact on third States,[1010] no international treaty law, public

[1008] According to this provision of the VCLT, these are international agreements between States, concluded in written form, irrespective of whether or not they are contained in one or more related documents, and whatever their particular designation

[1009] Mandatory norms of public international law within the meaning of Articles 53 and 54 VCLT are rules of a fundamental nature, from which no State may deviate by international agreement, cf. RESS (1989). They are legal principles which are accepted and recognised by the international community as a whole as norms, which may not be deviated from under any circumstances and which can be modified only by a subsequent norm of general public international law having the same character (Article VCLT 54(2)). Applicable norms, such as the principles listed in Article 2 UNC work *erga omnes* and apply readily also to States which are not directly linked to the VCLT, cf. *Vitzthum* in SIMMA (1991); absolute international legal principles notably include the guarantee of human dignity. Its complete primacy is in the interest of the whole community, so that it constitutes absolute obligations under public international law, cf. VERDROSS/SIMMA (1984)

[1010] Only a few thousand persons per year are naturalised through Citizenship-by-Investment worldwide – people who are *nota bene* wealthy, meticulously tested and thus not a burden on the community – as opposed to the hundreds of thousands who are

international law *ius cogens* or customary public international law is violated.

13.2.2 The right to a nationality (Article 15(1) UDHR)

According to Article 15(1) UDHR, every natural person has a subjective individual right to a nationality. Like the prohibition of wrongful deprivation of citizenship under Article 15(2) UDHR, Article 15(1) UDHR has a hybrid legal nature. In terms of subjective individual human rights, Article 15(1) UDHR should ensure that no one should be totally deprived of access to State benefits, such as the guarantee of diplomatic and consular protection, or indeed the issue of a national passport. Article 15(1) UDHR thus has a profound human rights dimension and, in my opinion, numbers among the principal rights of the UDHR. Its human rights dimension is in particular emphasised with the word "any", which underscores that any discrimination based on home, origin, creed, religion, gender, sexual identity etc., is not permitted. It is also emphasised by the fact that Article 15(1) UDHR, provides a special statutory specification of Article 1(1) UDHR, that all people are free and equal in dignity and rights. After all, every person born as a human being has the right to a nationality, by simply virtue of their humanity.

Since Article 15(1) UDHR does not speak of a "right to nationality", but rather only the right to a nationality, this provision as a legal record of the objective State law and "world constitutional law" is instrumental in obligating the nation States to exercise care, in particular in the form of coordination and allocation of diplomatic and consular protection they provide. By requiring a right to a nationality, Article 15(1) UDHR merely ensures a right to State protection *per se*, but does not provide a right to claim for the best possible outcome by simultaneously requiring the grant of citizenship in different States.

---

naturalised according to simplified naturalisation processes, such as, for example, those applying to people from former colonies of European countries (e.g. Spain or Portugal), ethnic groups (e.g. Hungary, Greece or Germany) or other similar arrangements

13.2.3 General prohibition of discrimination within the meaning of Article 14 ECHR

Based on international law, barriers to Citizenship-by-Investment could possibly be thrown up by the fact that nation States are obliged to honour the general prohibition of discrimination on the grounds of sex, race, skin colour, language, religion, political or other opinion, national or social origin, association with a national minority, property, birth or any other status in guaranteeing the rights and freedoms recognised in the ECHR (Article 14 ECHR). As a binding treaty of public international law and among the contracting States, the ECHR directly substantiates the obligations the jurisdictions of the contracting States have to secure for the persons subject to the Convention rights, which are directly created by the Treaty.[1011]

In this context, it will be recalled that Article 14 ECHR is not a self-standing provision and as such must be linked to another ECHR right. Given the scope of rights guaranteed by the ECHR it would be difficult to invoke Article 14 ECHR although such possibility should not be excluded *per se*. This is in particular because Article 14 prohibits such discriminatory measures which have no objective and reasonable justification rather than every difference in treatment. It should be also kept in mind that the CoE aims at *"greater unity between its members and that one of the methods by which that aim is to be pursued is the maintenance and further realisation of Human Rights and Fundamental Freedoms"*[1012] which provides for right to and change of nationality[1013] and not less the fact that the granting of citizenship is a field falling under an exclusive state competence.

Last but not least, granting citizenship on a basis of investment is not in its substance drastically different from other existing citizenship requirements such as the requirement for a minimum income or independence of the applicant from government welfare payments as a condition for

---

[1011] cf. MEYER-LADEWIG (2003)
[1012] Preamble of the ECHR
[1013] Article 15 UDHR

naturalisation.[1014] Such conditions could equally raise issues of discrimination. They are mainly concerned with promoting the sustainable integration of an applicant into the host country, which corresponds with the idea of the State community as a member-based collective, in which each individual – to a certain extent as a corrective to the principle of solidarity in the sense of a contractually based obligation of mutual care and protection – owes a certain contribution to the success of the whole. Citizenship-by-Investment, by ensuring upfront that the individual applicant has sufficient means and in addition, makes a substantial contribution to the State, which can be interpreted equally in the spirit of the principle of solidarity.

13.3 EU citizenship as a new supranational dimension to citizenship and limitation of national citizenship law

13.3.1 Overview

While the EEC Treaty in its original version only had the "market citizens"[1015] in mind, the Treaty on the EU since Maastricht also extends to a political "Union citizen".[1016] This was supplemented in the Amsterdam Treaty of 2 October 1997 and is now Article 20(1) TFEU: "*Citizenship of the Union is hereby established. Every person holding the nationality of a Member State shall be a citizen of the Union. Citizenship of the Union shall be additional to and not replace national citizenship*".

The legal nature of the Union citizenship and the place of this concept within the fabric of EU law is disputed. The opinions on this range from "*Fata Morgana*" to "*an unfinished concept of political affiliation*", a "*qualitative minus*" to citizenship, to a "*new, multiple citizenship on different levels*"[1017] and "*a citizenship of our time*".[1018]

[1014] For example, in Austria, cf. section 7.6.5.
[1015] The term "market citizen" was coined by the German European jurisprudence, see GRABITZ (1970), OPPERMANN (1999)
[1016] VON MÜNCH (2007); JOPPKE (2010)
[1017] These and the foregoing citations MÜNCH (2007)
[1018] JOPPKE (2010); cf. also KOCHENOV (2013)

In any case, European citizenship entails rights and obligations (especially rights) which not only relate to a person's State of citizenship, but they extend to other EU Member States.[1019] In reality, supranational citizenship is here.[1020] More than half a billion Europeans hold EU citizenship, and the residents of many regions in the EU have overlapping legal statuses: citizenship of a member state, citizenship of sub-national entities and EU citizenship.[1021] In any case, citizenship beyond the State is a definite reality and is starting to shape the legal position of individuals.[1022] Due to the fact that European citizenship is derived exclusively from the citizenship of the Member States (referred to by *Kochenov* as *ius tractum*, since the European citizenship status is purely derivative)[1023] and that there is no regulation or guidelines in the area of citizenship law within the EU, each EU Member State has potentially very far-reaching opportunities to influence the EU's composition.[1024] It may even be possible that if a Member State were to grant its citizenship to a large number of people of a non-EU third country, this could be challenged as a breach of EU law, in view of the obligations of solidarity among the Member States prescribed by Article 10 of the EU Treaty.[1025] The example of the UK however shows that even such steps on the part of a Member State, in this case mainly the differentiated citizenship law in the UK, relating to hundreds of thousands of people in the respective colonies and overseas territories, as occurred for example, in the case of Hong Kong, does not seem to come into conflict with EU law. The same would therefore have to apply to Citizenship-by-Investment, under which only a very small number of persons are naturalized every year.

An interesting aspect regarding naturalisation in the EU is that it raises the issue of the wide diversity of naturalisation rules in each individual EU Member State all leading to a single and common status of membership. This current situation of naturalisation regulation in the EU

[1019] cf. *Martiniello* in ALEINIKOFF/KLUSMEYER (2000)
[1020] cf. KOCHENOV (2010 II), with further references
[1021] cf. KOCHENOV (2012) p. 3; cf. also BELLAMY/CASTIGLIONE/SHAW (2006)
[1022] KOCHENOV (2013); but cf. also KOCHENOV (2010)
[1023] KOCHENOV (2009)
[1024] SCHÖNBERGER (2005); VON MÜNCH (2007)
[1025] *De Groot* in MÜLLER-GRAFF (2003)

Member States, whereby naturalisation rules are widely different from Member State to Member State, "*can be compared with establishing free movement of goods without putting a common customs tariff in place. This is nonsensical*".[1026] The diverse naturalisation regimes in the EU Member States are anachronistic, as the Member States maintaining stricter naturalisation requirements cannot thereby limit immigration flows.[1027]

13.3.2 Legal relationship to growth

Giegerich notably characterised EU citizenship[1028] as a legal relationship to growth, in the context of which the metamorphosis from mere "market citizens" or economic citizen (*bourgeois*) into the political subject (*citoyen*) occurs.[1029] To some extent, as a precursor of the EU's development from a supranational federation with its own legal capacity to a political union, Article 20(1) TFEU implemented EU citizenship. As its wording states, there is no original connection to an organised political community and this could not be made to happen given that the EU is not a State. It is a derivative construct[1030] that is intended to promote the formation of a transnational European identity.[1031] Union citizenship extends beyond a mere "market citizenship" but is, however, still far from a true European citizenship.[1032]

There is a substantial academic debate on EU citizenship law with many fundamental disagreements among scholars.[1033] Regarding the legal nature of a Union citizenship,[1034] the German Federal Constitutional

---

1026 KOCHENOV (2009) fn 92

1027 KOCHENOV (2009)

1028 For greater detail on Union citizenship: SCHÖNBERGER (2005), *De Waele* in TALANI (2012)

1029 cf. *Giegerich* in SCHULZE/ZULEEG/KADELBACH (2010) and *Hatje* in SCHWARZE (2009)

1030 cf. *Giegerich* in SCHULZE/ZULEEG/KADELBACH (2010); *Kaufmann/Bühler* in LENZ/BORCHARDT (2010); KOCHENOV (2009)

1031 The formation of an independent European identity was exposed for example, in the preamble to the EU Treaty. Thereafter, the process of an ever closer Union among the peoples of Europe, in particular the goal of securing peace, security and progress in Europe by strengthening the identity and independence of a united Europe

1032 cf. *Meyer* in MEYER (2011)

1033 cf. KOCHENOV (2012) and KOCHENOV (2013) for a very good overview

1034 For more detail on the legal nature of citizenship and its relation to the EU Member

Court emphasised in its decision of 30 September 2009, that even under the framework of the Treaty of Lisbon, a "*derived and national citizenship supplementary status*" (Article 20 and Article 9(3) TFEU) remains, which is not altered by the rights attached to Union citizenship.[1035] This is supported in addition to the wording of Article 20 TFEU, by the legal nature of the EU as a supranational union of States. As the Senate of the German Federal Constitutional Court further underlines, the Union's citizens are granted a right to participate in the democratic life of the EU (Article 10(3) and Article 11(1) TFEU), through which not just a "*necessary existing structural relationship between civic community and governmental authority*" is stressed, but the diplomatic consular protection of respective rights and also the legitimacy of documents is simplified.[1036]

Not only its regulatory purpose but also the wording and general scheme of Article 20 TFEU demonstrates that Union citizenship is subsidiary in nature and results from the citizenship of one or more Member States.[1037] Consequently, the loss of citizenship of an EU Member State automatically has additional consequences, including in principle the loss of EU citizenship and rights of all the consequences connected to that.[1038] Nevertheless, it constitutes a status on the basis of which the Union citizens are granted the specified additional protection and the rights contained in the treaties.[1039] These rights include especially the right to freedom of movement (Article 21 TFEU), the right of participation in local elections (Article 22(1) TFEU), the right to vote for the European Parliament (Article 22(2), TFEU), the right to diplomatic and consular protection (Article 23 TFEU), the right of petition (Article 24(1) TFEU), the right to apply to the Ombudsman (Article 24(2) TFEU) and the right to communication in an official language of choice (Article 24(3) TFEU).

State citizenship: *Kaufmann/Bühler* in LENZ/BORCHARDT (2010); *Pache* in SCHULZE/ZULEEG/KADELBACH (2010); *Stumpf* in SCHWARZE (2009)

1035 cf. HAILBRONNER (2011); *Kaufmann/Bühler* in LENZ/BORCHARDT (2010)

1036 *Federal Constitutional Court,* judgment of 30 June 2009, Case 2 BvE 2/08, www.lexetius.com, last accessed on 21 September 2012

1037 cf. *Hatje* in SCHWARZE (2009); KUNOY (2006)

1038 cf. *Kaufmann/Bühler* in LENZ/BORCHARDT (2010)

1039 cf. *Kaufmann/Bühler* in LENZ/BORCHARDT (2010)

Purely theoretically, it would be formally possible in a State organisation sense for the required decisions – similar to orders in most EU Member States – to be taken at the European level by the European Council (under Article 235 et seq. TFEU), to move to a directly democratically legitimate European parliament, creating a direct line between the "European sovereign" and European decision-making bodies, and establish thereby a stand-alone "European citizenship".[1040] However, given that in a democratically constituted community[1041] all State power has to come from the people, and democratic rule is always the result of an organically grown community whose identity emerges from common cultural beliefs, it would appear questionable whether such a solution would really be worthwhile and desirable in view of the functions of citizenship. In its present configuration, Union citizenship can contribute overcoming the disenchantment with politics, and the perceived distance between the sovereign and the political decision-making bodies, but cannot replace them.[1042]

Globally, States and political communities prove to be much more peaceful and stable if their common cultural values and beliefs emerged organically: i.e. were grown from within and not imposed from above by decree. In support of this thesis, the events in the former multi-ethnic State of Yugoslavia are recalled, where the suppression of organic development ended in a humanitarian catastrophe, whose cessation required the intervention of the international community. These findings suggest that citizenship should probably not only be defined as a formal link, as argued elsewhere herein, however worded – considering its basic functions (integration, peacekeeping, link between the State people and the domestic legal system) – but should possibly be ascribed a substantive meaning, which is closely oriented to its functions and objectives.

For an autonomous European citizenship in conjunction with a stronger European Parliament, capable of making major decisions in the context

---

1040 cf. HEINRICH BÖLL STIFTUNG (2012)

1041 See for example Article 1(2) ÖB-VG (*"Its law emanates from the people"*) or Article 20(2) (1) GC (*"All State authority emanates from the people"*) or the Swiss constitution

1042 On the practical implications of European citizenship and the State, in particular in the field of naming rights: NORDMEIER (2011)

of a European legislature and linking the European "constitutive people" with the European "State power", it would appear, in view of the continuing cultural heterogeneity of the constituent peoples of the EU Member States and despite the common origins of large parts of Europe in the Roman legal system, too early to be able to speak of an appetite for such a change, given the current depth of integration under the Treaty of Lisbon. With good reason, Article 20(1) TFEU does not constitute therefore an original, but merely a derivative citizenship: a EU citizen is one who possesses citizenship of one of the member states of the EU (Article 20(1) TFEU). The former European Commission president *Jacques Delors*, who was instrumental in the Maastricht Treaty,[1043] emphasised the developmental openness of the European integration process in the early nineties of the last century. An organically extending integration process, which reflects the various national cultural values and beliefs of the citizens in its State institutions, and not vice versa, and ultimately achieves the status of citizenship, is characterised by developmental openness and by the principle of subsidiarity. This should be born in mind in the design of the content of the future institution of EU citizenship.

13.3.3 Diplomatic and consular protection of EU citizens

The extraterritorial fiduciary duty of the State towards "its" nationals, given the close functional proximity of citizenship to human dignity, should be interpreted broadly and is concretised in particular in its obligation to provide diplomatic and consular protection.[1044] As an expression of effectively exercised State power, it is concerned with the comprehensive extraterritorial obligation to provide assistance,[1045] which is primarily engaged during acute emergencies such as urgent repatriation, assistance in cases of death and serious illnesses and accidents, assistance to victims of violent crimes, and the release of prisoners.[1046]

[1043] Consolidated version of the Treaty on EU of 24 December 2002 (Maastricht Treaty), OJEU C 325/7, published online at http://eur-lex.europa.eu/de/treaties/dat/12002M/pdf/12002M_DE.pdf, last accessed on 21 September 2012

[1044] For a good overview, cf. FELTHAM (2006)

[1045] cf. *Hatje* in SCHWARZE (2009); *Kaufmann/Bühler* in LENZ/BORCHARDT (2010); *Kluth* in CALLIESS/RUFFERT (2007); LOWE (2007)

[1046] cf. *Giegerich* in SCHULZE/ZULEEG/KADELBACH (2010); *Kaufmann/Bühler* in

Citizenship acts here in providing a formal element to the requirement to the exercise of State protection, as international law binds an individual to their home State, its sovereignty, and generally places them under its protection.[1047]

The granting of diplomatic protection concerns the international legal authority of the home country to take preventive steps with international legal means against threats of violations of international law, especially emanating from other countries, if these international contractual obligations towards the person concerned disregard or fall short of those required by general international law or minimum standards of alien law and in responding under international law to the treatment of its nationals by another State in case of damage. In contrast, the aim of consular protection is to provide advice and support outside of the State's territory, within the framework of public international law, by providing general support or promoting the interests of non-residents.[1048] The limits of such consular protection arise from general public international law.[1049] Its close association with citizenship, the holders of which can only be natural persons, and its anchoring in the guarantee of human dignity (Article 1 EU Charter), suggest that Article 23(1) TFEU should be restricted to natural persons,[1050] as they find themselves in an entirely different situation when compared to legal persons.[1051]

In a departure to some extent from the general principle that the extra-territorial fiduciary duty of the State covers only its own nationals, EU citizenship establishes different territorial limits under Article 355 TFEU to the personal relationship between individual Europeans and the EU or one of the Member States acting on its behalf,[1052] in that – based on the objective of the EU as a means of creating an identity of

LENZ/BORCHARDT (2010)

1047 cf. JÜRGENS (1987)

1048 cf. *Hatje* in SCHWARZE (2009); *Magiera* in MEYER (2011); and FELTHAM (2006)

1049 cf. *Magiera* in MEYER (2011); FELTHAM (2006)

1050 As a result, approvingly: *Magiera* in MEYER (2011); *Kaufmann/Bühler* in LENZ/BORCHARDT (2010), Article 23 TEU, MN 4, which is based on the fact that the fundamental freedoms of the Treaty shall also apply to legal persons

1051 cf. VERDROSS/SIMMA (1984)

1052 cf. *Giegerich* in SCHULZE/ZULEEG/KADELBACH (2010)

inward solidarity among its citizens with respect to the outside – Article 23 TFEU provides that any EU citizen in the territory of a third country in which the Member State he is a national of is not represented, may require protection from the diplomatic and consular authorities of any other Member State on the same conditions as their own nationals enjoy. To some extent this breaks with the personnel authority of the home country,[1053] which essentially has a monopoly in international law exclusively to provide diplomatic assistance to its nationals against other subjects of international law.[1054]

The basis for the enforcement of the law on extraterritorial care in a home country by another EU Member State in third countries[1055] for nationals of EU Member States with no diplomatic or consular representation in their country of residence, is created under Article 23(1) TFEU through the deputisation of diplomatic and consular protection, in the absence of permanent representation nor an accessible honorary consul to represent the home State in the country of residence.[1056] Member States have to adopt the necessary provisions and start the international negotiations required to secure this protection (Article 23(2) TFEU). Specifically, this means that Article 23 obliges EU Member States to undertake whatever international negotiations with third countries appear necessary to enforce the rights of EU citizens.[1057]

13.3.4 Petition right as an example of the content of EU citizenship (Article 20(2)(d) TFEU)

13.3.4.1 Containment of State power

The Lisbon treaty, in an effort to respond to the pervasive disenchantment with European policy and its much lamented remoteness, provides a European right of petition. This is not just another link between a citizen of a Member State but was founded on the principle of conferral of

[1053] cf. *Giegerich* in SCHULZE/ZULEEG/KADELBACH (2010)
[1054] cf. *Hatje* in SCHWARZE (2009)
[1055] cf. *Folz* in VEDDER/HEINTSCHEL VON HEINEGG (2012)
[1056] cf. *Giegerich* in SCHULZE/ZULEEG/KADELBACH (2010)
[1057] cf. *Folz* in VEDDER/HEINTSCHEL VON HEINEGG (2012)

powers, and is part of the process of the gradual transfer of powers from the nation State to the European level through relaxation of the formal bond between the Member State peoples and the Member State public authorities – especially when understood against the background that the European Parliament, despite its increased competences with the entry into force of the Lisbon Treaty, has at best limited decision-making powers and is only democratically engaged with once in five years. Petition serves to reinforce the principle of democracy and acts equally as a seismograph and "lightning rod" for public sentiment.

The Petitions Committee of the European Parliament, as the currently only directly and originally democratically elected representative body, is regulated in terms of its role, competence and procedure in Articles 191 to 193 of the Rules of Procedure of the European Parliament.[1058] Although the European Parliament, due to its self-organisation law[1059] (Article 232 TFEU) is empowered to organise itself as it wills and therefore requires no further explicit legal basis to regulate its petition procedure, the absence of a primary legal basis for authorisation for Articles 191–193 Rules of Procedure of the European Parliament does not detract from its additional underpinning (in terms of who benefits) provided under Article 44 EU Charter.

13.3.4.2 Expression of integral active citizenship

The right of petition to the European Parliament (Article 24 in conjunction with Article 227 TFEU) aims to promote an added proximity, to promotes the social legitimacy of the EU and complete the legal protection which is guaranteed by the Community jurisdiction.[1060] In view of the fact that the European Parliament (Article 223 et seq. TFEU) is the only original democratically elected body of the Community – according to Article 39(1) EU Charter, the Citizens of the Union[1061] in the

---

[1058] Rules of Procedure of the European Parliament of 7 March 2011, http://www.europarl.europa.eu/sides/getLastRules.do;jsessionid=5E26D54FB3A537F5E3E79A3859180121.node1?language=DE&reference=TOC, last accessed on 21 September 2012

[1059] *Bieber* in SCHULZE/ZULEEG/KADELBACH (2012)

[1060] cf. *Giegerich* in SCHULZE/ZULEEG/KADELBACH (2012)

[1061] On the status of citizenship, cf. *supra*

Member State in which they reside, have the active and passive right to vote in elections to the European Parliament under the same conditions as nationals of the Member State – the right to petition the European Parliament not only acts as a link between citizens of the Union, but it gives the executives in Brussels, Strasbourg, and Luxembourg regular feedback from the citizenry on their work performance.[1062] Accordingly, in order that the spatial distance between the citizens and the decision-makers in Brussels and Strasbourg should not become a substantive distance – i.e. leading behaviour characterised by aloofness – a constant line of communication between the democratic base and the European political establishment seems essential.

Petitions ensure constant contact between Parliament and the public, since they enable the Parliament on the one hand, to provide regular topical debate, and on the other hand, helps the EU appear reachable, as the right to petition in accordance with Article 227 TFEU opens in principle the possibility of direct influence on policy.[1063] This mechanism for the sustainable protection of the acceptance of the decisions taken at the European level, in my opinion, seems necessary for an EU which grew to 28 Member States in July 2013, and given the spatial distance between representatives and the represented at the European level, which is more pronounced even than at the national level, and which has in many Member States led to "Europe fatigue". The European right to petition thus underlies the idea of an "integrating active citizenship"[1064] – the mere possibility of being able to bring a petition in the European "policy operation" and to actually reach the Members of the European Parliament, counteracts the political centrifugal forces and has a system-stabilising effect.

13.3.4.3 Powers and procedures

Comparable with petition processes at the national level, Article 191 et seq. Rules and Procedure of the European Parliament provide that

---

[1062] cf. *Gaitanides* in HESELHAUS/NOWAK (2006)
[1063] cf. ECKHARDT (2010)
[1064] cf. Report on the petition system in the early twenty-first century, A5-0088/2001, p. 10

the Petitions Committee (Article 191(5) Rules and Procedure of the European Parliament) first examines the admissibility of a petition, and where admissible, considers its substantive contents. The Petitions Committee may decide to hear the petitioners, to set general hearings, to send findings of fact on the spot (Article 192(3) Rules and Procedure of the European Parliament) or the committee members may ask the European Commission to obtain information or documents (Article 192(4) Rules and Procedure of the European Parliament). *Expressis verbis*, the European Parliament primary legislation has no special powers such as a right to access documents. However, Article 13(2) TFEU, according to which the institutions must loyally cooperate, may be relied on as a general duty of cooperation on all EU institutions (Articles 223-309 TFEU), to provide each other with the support they deem necessary to meet their primary legal obligations.

The expression of this duty of cooperation is, in my opinion, also the principle of Community loyalty[1065] (Article 4(3) TFEU) which obliges all EU institutions and therefore also the European Commission (Article 244 et seq. TFEU) to support the Petitions Committee of the European Parliament in its findings.[1066] Article 4(3) TFEU is concretised in the commitment of all 28 Member States to take all appropriate measures to fulfil the EU's primary legal obligations.[1067]

Each petition found admissible is factually reviewed by the Petitions Committee of the European Parliament, which prepares a report or otherwise takes a position, in preparation for the European Commission's final decision on access to documents. Alternatively, it may request the President of Parliament to provide an opinion to the Commission or the Council – in the latter case the Speaker of Parliament informs the petitioner of the decisions taken and the reasons therefore in the respective language of the contract (Article 24(4) TFEU).[1068] In this context, it is ultimately in keeping with the constitutionally secured right to

1065 On the principle of Community loyalty: STREINZ (2003)
1066 cf. FRENZ (2009)
1067 cf. *Nelles/Tinkl/Lauchstädt* in SCHULZE/ZULEEG/KADELBACH (2010)
1068 cf. *Giegerich* in SCHULZE/ZULEEG/KADELBACH (2010)

good administration that any person may write to the institutions of the Union in one of the languages of the Treaties and can expect to receive an answer in the same language (Article 41(3) EU Charter).

13.3.4.4 Admission Requirements

All citizens of the Union and any person with a personal attachment, i.e. with permanent residence in a EU Member State, are entitled to petition.[1069] The right to petition is a subjective-public right of EU citizens, which is theirs in parallel to the primary rights of redress and – unlike, for example in Austria or during the Weimar Republic (1918-1933) – and is not bound to instance depletion. The right of petition allows this broad group to present their own interests and to consult the European Parliament on injustices or inequities so that a qualification as "individual constitutional right of EU citizens"[1070] does not appear presumptuous. Only EU citizens – and herein lies, in my opinion, the key difference to the petition right in most individual States – can claim the European right to petition.

The petition right presupposes the petitioner's concern in the, not necessarily legal, interests. It is sufficient if the petitioner outlines a "serious and real concern about his demand"[1071] or "the matter is of not negligible significance to the petitioner in an objective and verifiable manner".[1072]

13.3.4.5 "Specification"

Like at the national level, the European petitioner is also not entitled to a particular decision on the merits, but merely to receiving substantive examination and justified reasons, which he can enforce as a failure to act under Article 265 TFEU, if necessary.[1073] This underlined right of petition in the wording of Article 227 TFEU "*sent to the*

1069 cf. STREINZ (2008)

1070 cf. SCHNEIDER (2009)

1071 cf. *Giegerich* in SCHULZE/ZULEEG/KADELBACH (2010)

1072 cf. *Haag* in VON DER GROEBEN/SCHWARZE (2003)

1073 cf. FRENZ (2009); *Gaitanides* in HESELHAUS/NOWAK (2006); *Giegerich* in SCHULZE/ZULEEG/KADELBACH (2010); GUCKELBERGER (2004); *Schoo* in SCHWARZE (2009)

European Parliament" and the corresponding obligation of the European Parliament, however, do not justify any claim for relief in the matter. A duty on the European Parliament in principle to accept every petition received can be, however, deduced from the *telos* of Article 44 EU Charter, because the right to petition would otherwise be practically inoperable and would be reduced to a special form of the constitutional right to freedom of opinion and expression.[1074]

The above discussion shows the high level of protection of the rights of citizens beyond their national states. Indeed, citizenship "*can no longer be confined within the framework of national–statist communities*".[1075] In other words, citizenship protects the rights of EU citizens which are not granted by their states but by the Union itself, transcending national jurisdictions and state borders.[1076]

1074 cf. *Haag* in VON DER GROEBEN/SCHWARZE (2003)
1075 KOSTAKOPOLOU (1999) p. 391
1076 See in this context the analysis of Davies in AMTENBRINK/VAN DEN BERG (2010)

14

Evaluation of Citizenship-by-Investment – *ius doni*

14.1 Issues, Background and Objectives

According to the findings presented so far, citizenship law and its provisions on how citizenship may be granted can contribute to targeted investment and migration control or it can be used directly for these purposes. In addition, citizenship law could help to limit immigration, but also promote targeted immigration. The bases on which migration flows can be influenced, is subject to the public international law limits on the scope for action of national political decision-making bodies. A basis could therefore be to acquire highly-skilled workers to achieve a better balance in the labour market in a host country.[1077] The boundaries for a Citizenship-by-Investment programme are established in some of the reference States by the fact that citizenship is not merely legally defined as a formal bond between the citizens and the national legal order, but defined physically in the sense of factual preconditions whose primary objectives are demonstrating political integration and ensuring social cohesion.

14.2 Definition of *ius doni*

14.2.1 Naturalisation of investors as a policy to attract foreign direct investment

An investment can generally be defined as the transformation of resources which extends over a longer period and whose essence lies in its longer-term return: if the investor initially acquires an investment property, resources or rights, which requires expenditure or equivalent economic engagement, this is undertaken because the investor expects to benefit in the later stages from yields from the income from the investment property, resources or rights.[1078] An investment contributes to the establishment of performance potential, assets and capital.[1079]

Given the numerous economic and personal advantages associated with citizenship status,, through access to new markets, visa-free travel,

---

1077 See *Grossmann/Stadelmann* in CHISWICK (2011)
1078 cf. *Spremann* in KÖHLER/KÜPPER/PFINGSTEN (2007)
1079 cf. *Spremann* in KÖHLER/KÜPPER/PFINGSTEN (2007)

personal security, and the freedom of residence – for example in the EU[1080] – the granting of citizenship to foreign investors can serve as motivation for them to get involved economically in the host country, including beyond the initial investment, as the example of St. Kitts and Nevis has very successfully shown.[1081] In Citizenship-by-Investment programmes investors are prepared to make investments, in the sense as defined above, but additionally also in the form of non-refundable contributions to public institutions,[1082] thereby investing in the country of their new citizenship which they would otherwise – under normal conditions not involving the grant of citizenship (or residence) rights – not consider. This is made particularly clear where there are non-refundable contribution options to qualify under a programme,[1083] or even where such a non-refundable contribution is the major requirement under a programme.[1084]

1080 cf. ONG (2005); KÄLIN (2014)

1081 cf. KÄLIN (2014), INTERNATIONAL MONETARY FUND (2014); XU/EL-ASHRAM/GOLD (2015)

1082 Such as the contribution option in St. Kitts, where a non-refundable contribution to the Sugar Industry Diversification Foundation satisfies the investment requirement; or the equivalent option in Antigua and Barbuda, where such a contribution is possible to the National Development Fund; or under the program in Malta, where a contribution of at least EUR 650,000 to the National Development and Social Fund is required to qualify, cf. KÄLIN (2014)

1083 As in St. Kitts and Nevis, Antigua and Barbuda, Dominica and Grenada

1084 As in Malta

Inflows under Citizenship-by-Investment Programs[1085]

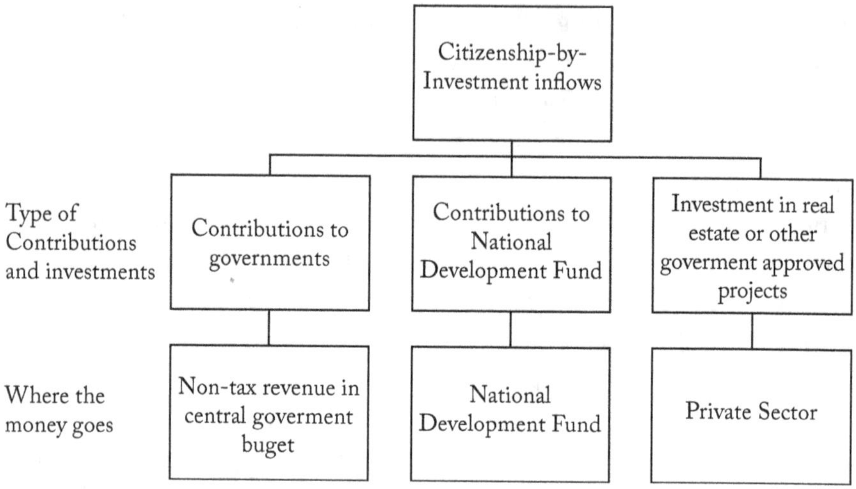

Therefore, states are able to attract through Citizenship-by-Investment programmes, investments into the country which would otherwise not occur. Such programmes, and the concept of *ius doni*, i.e. the grant of citizenship for an economic[1086] contribution to the state, can therefore be characterised as a foreign direct investment policy option, for states to attract additional foreign direct investment that they would otherwise not be able to attract, and "*the ability to employ discretionary, fast-tracked citizenship grants is a crucial addition to the policy toolbox of advancing the host country's stature, influence, and visibility in the world arena.*"[1087]

14.2.2 Requirement to make a significant contribution

Regardless of the country-specific features of a programme, the binding of citizenship acquisition to a particular investment or non-refundable contribution can be identified as a common defining characteristic of a Citizenship-by-Investment programme. From a comparative perspective,

---

[1085] *Source: IMF, 2015*

[1086] Or other contribution, as this should not be limited to economic contributions but could and should also include contributions of a cultural, scientific or other nature; however, this is not the subject here

[1087] SHACHAR (2011) p. 2095

a mere portfolio investment would not appear to be sufficient in most cases, but a direct investment in the host country or a non-refundable monetary contribution to the host country is required. In contrast to portfolio investments which are concerned with the best possible return on the invested capital and less with the long-term influence over day-to-day business management, let alone non-monetary returns such as the grant of citizenship, direct investments and contributions under Citizenship-by-Investment programmes are different in nature and are actually focused, as shown above in 13.2.1., more on the non-monetary aspects.[1088]

In general foreign direct investment policy, from the perspective of the host country, it should be borne in mind that an investor can decide after establishing a subsidiary in the country or a new business entity, or after obtaining a controlling majority[1089] in an existing entity, whether the administrative headquarters of the company should be or remain in the host country or be relocated to a third country, and thus may ultimately decide on which country benefits most from his economic commitment in the long term, by way of taxation, employment, profit generation etc. Given that more advantages in terms of freedom of movement and access to the market will be opened to an investor through the acquisition of the citizenship of the host country, it can hardly be disputed that the prospect of the acquisition of citizenship acts as an economic incentive to becoming economically more involved in the host country. In addition, the requirement to make a significant[1090]

[1088] cf. *Reinisch* in TIETJE (2009)

[1089] The shares of companies traded on an organised market are not always evenly distributed to the public. To influence business policy in their favour, individual shareholders sometimes seek to acquire control over a target company, through coordinated effort to acquire a sufficient stake to exercise decisive voting rights, and which can allow the beneficiary investors to replace an unpopular board through a hostile takeover. How many shares need to be acquired varies by jurisdiction – for instance, under the capital market laws of the Federal Republic of Germany, the definitive threshold between significant and insignificant participation for an equity investment is 30% (Section 15(1) German Securities Trading Act as amended by order on 9 September 1998 (Federal Law Gazette I 1998, p. 2708) and last amended by Article 2 of the Law of 26 June 2012 (BGBl. I 2012, s. 1375))

[1090] The determination of what constitutes significant in this context is of course country-specific and thus must remain with the legislature or government of the relevant country

contribution actually goes beyond the traditional foreign direct investment incentives normally employed by countries, and more directly and more immediately benefits the host country's economy and society. *Ius doni* therefore acts as a strong incentive that can be employed in foreign direct investment policy.

14.2.3 Comprehensive due diligence

Since the effects of a grant of citizenship following an extraordinary contribution lends it the appearance of naturalisation for "consideration", and because residence periods – and thus "observation periods" – are reduced to a minimum or even completely waived, due diligence is required on qualifying private-sector investment options under a Citizenship-by-Investment programme to ascertain that fair value is being obtained from foreign investors and to elucidate any latent investment risks. Due diligence and background verification is also required to clarify the reputation and personal and business background of the applicant.[1091] Given that the granting of Citizenship-by-Investment is a decision of considerable importance, it should only be granted according to normative decision theory[1092] on the basis of complete and error-free possession of the facts.[1093]

Due diligence is more generally referred to as a method of pre-purchase auditing of a company in connection with the completion of a business purchase agreement, during which a large amount of partly discretionary information about the target company is made accessible to the shareholders of the potential buyer, on the which basis of which not only is the target company evaluated, but the its risks and liabilities are ascertained.[1094] The concept of due diligence is, however, also used

[1091] cf. *Beldi* in BAUDENBACHER/KOKOTT (2011); GARNIER/MARTINEZ (2013)

[1092] Normative decision theory, which is mainly applied in business administration, concerns the question of how to define the optimality of a decision and effectively determine optimal decisions, whereby decision-making situations are classified according to the number of objectives, the information in the possession of the decision-maker regarding safety, risk and uncertainty, and the type of decision maker (individual, multiple decision makers, or decision-making body), cf. *Bamberg* in KÖHLER/KÜPPER/PFINGSTEN (2007)

[1093] LIEKEFETT (2005)

[1094] cf. *Beldi* in BAUDENBACHER/KOKOTT (2011)

as a generic term for the legal steps required to prepare for signature in the acquisition of a company.[1095] Essentially, it aims to elicit information and thereby improve the acquisition-decision quality, to access additional information about the object of purchase (screening)[1096] and to level existing information asymmetries (signalling).[1097] Corresponding information is usually provided for a certain period in a separate timeframe (the so-called data room).[1098]

According to the "*caveat emptor*" principle rooted in the US legal system, the transferee must first examine the target company in detail, in order to ascertain defects in the object of purchase, and to "be careful" – the meaning of "*caveat emptor*" – that the object of purchase meets expectations. According to this principle, which is also known under the maxim "let the buyer beware", it is exclusively the responsibility of the buyer to investigate the target company to ascertain its freedom from defects, to assess and evaluate the discovered defects immediately, or to secure the existence of any latent defects by the inclusion of assurances or warranties.

This general meaning of due diligence in business transactions could actually be a useful guide for the due diligence in the context of screening potential applicants under Citizenship-by-Investment programs: besides the requirement of thorough background checks along the lines of "Know Your Customer" banking best practice and with heightened background verification needs in certain cases,[1099] comprehensive due diligence in Citizenship-by-Investment programmes should also include an approach similar to the due diligence applied in corporate transactions: i.e. a comprehensive approach including an overall assessment

---

1095 *Beldi* in BAUDENBACHER/KOKOTT (2011)

1096 Screening can be defined as a strategy to overcome a lack of information on a company, which is pursued through continuous market research and market monitoring and can, for example, be aimed at assessing its potential customer's ability to pay, see *Kaas/Posselt* in KÖHLER/KÜPPER/PFINGSTEN (2007)

1097 Signalling is a marketing strategy, by which high quality providers can stand out from opportunistic competitors through characteristics of experience or credibility, see *Kaas/Posselt* in KÖHLER/KÜPPER/PFINGSTEN (2007)

1098 cf. VOLKART (2008)

1099 GARNIER/MARTINEZ (2013)

of possible risks and liabilities (in this case, for the country, its reputation,[1100] and the reputation of its Citizenship-by-Investment programme) vs. the benefits of naturalizing the applicant in question.

14.2.4 Two game modes of a similar strategy or two different animals?

On closer inspection, there appear, at first sight, to be two varieties of a similar strategy behind the concept of attracting new capital through the grant of citizenship, both of which target the acquisition of fresh capital and talent to the national economy for the benefit of the host country community.

Programmes in which the award of citizenship is tied solely to the supply of capital in the form of direct investment or non-refundable monetary contribution of a certain minimum amount without any additional or only minimal requirements – such as residence requirements – can be distinguished from those which facilitate the granting of citizenship on condition of a certain investment, but only after a period of residence and without sacrificing some of the traditional criteria for naturalisation.[1101]

Supported by the expectation that the investment in question will yield sustainable income to benefit their community in the form of welfare gains, States such as the UK, the US, Canada, Belgium, Australia and Singapore offer interested investors the possibility of simplified immigration based on investment, and subsequent naturalisation after a period of residence; however, these States still insist on a residence period to purportedly personally bind the investors to their local community in the medium to long term.[1102] Other countries grant citizenship directly without any residence requirement, such as St. Kitts and Nevis, Antigua and Barbuda, Austria and Cyprus.

[1100] For a good overview how the credibility of all passports issued by Tonga, the Marshall Islands, Nauru Samoa and Vanuatu was damaged through illegitimate or only partly legitimate, opaque programs with no or too little due diligence, cf. VAN FOSSEN (2007)
[1101] cf. DZANKIC (2012)
[1102] cf. DZANKIC (2012)

However, these two types of programmes differ substantially, as the grant of residence rights on the basis of investment, even with the subsequent possibility of acquiring citizenship as well, is fundamentally different in nature than the direct grant of citizenship under a Citizenship-by-Investment programme or *ius doni* provision in the law. These are not two game modes of a similar strategy but attract fundamentally different types of applicants. The investor immigration programmes must thus be distinguished from the Citizenship-by-Investment programmes based on *ius doni* provisions in the law. Investor immigration programmes give access to residence status, *ius doni* confers citizenship right without or with minimal, clearly defined residence requirements to the successful applicant. Investor immigration programmes give the possibility to apply for citizenship under generally the same conditions as other naturalisations, or slightly modified conditions, but in any case require substantial residence periods but generally no further investments to naturalize.[1103] Thus these must be distinguished from Citizenship-by-Investment programmes, where the award of citizenship is tied solely to the supply of capital in the form of direct investment or non-refundable monetary contribution of a certain minimum amount without any additional or only minimal requirements. This is what we can call the *ius doni* principle of citizenship acquisition, whereas the investor immigration programmes have actually little, if anything, to do with citizenship acquisition as they focus on attracting investment capital and investors to the country by offering residence or immigrant status.

14.2.5 *Ius doni* as a principle of citizenship acquisition

The *ius doni* principle that forms the basis of Citizenship-by-Investment programmes raises the question of whether a nation State may confer its citizenship on the sole basis that the applicant invests a large amount of money in the host country, i.e. to some extent "buys" into the host country: money in exchange for access to the national legal order and membership in the state. Citizenship-by-Investment concerns only the derivative acquisition of citizenship by way of naturalisation, in terms

[1103] Except e.g. in Bulgaria, which has a kind of a hybrid program

of which criteria must be met by the applicant so that she or he can be awarded the nationality of the host country. It is a special mode of acquisition by naturalisation, a new principle in citizenship acquisition.

Given its purpose is the acquisition of fresh capital for the host country as "consideration" for the granting of its citizenship, Citizenship-by-Investment has also been referred to as *ius pecuniae.*[1104] However, as it is a more precise term, it is preferable to refer to it here as citizenship acquisition by the principle *ius doni*:[1105] a new category of bond between the individual and the state and its national legal order, which exists is an addition to the traditional citizenship principles of *ius soli* and *ius sanguinis* and which is inspired by a view of the State community less than as a common destiny by God's grace, but more as an economically interpreted "club", [1106] which notably focuses on the contribution of individuals to the domestic polity. This identifies membership in the State, not membership in civil society.[1107]

There are undoubtedly various reasons arguing against the concept of Citizenship-by-Investment, but there are equally well-founded reasons supporting this concept. In any case, *ius doni* has become a reality in recent years with more and more states introducing such provisions, or activating existing provisions in their laws. Currently, there are more than 25 states[1108] which have *ius doni* provisions in their citizenship laws and where the government regularly makes use of them or even operates on that basis a formal Citizenship-by-Investment program. Thus, Citizenship-by-Investment is actually firmly established, *ius doni* is a reality.

In the following, the main arguments for and against *ius doni* or Citizenship-by-Investment will nevertheless be examined, with the aim to carefully weigh the various arguments against each other.

1104 DZANKIC (2012); STERN (2012)

1105 An alternative, a possibly even more precise term would be *ius subsidii rerum*

1106 According to the "Economic Theory of Clubs" by *Buchanan*, cf. BUCHANAN (1965); cf. also FREY/EICHBERGER (2011)

1107 cf. BEINER (1995)

1108 These include Antigua and Barbuda, Austria, Bulgaria, Canada, Croatia, Cyprus, Commonwealth of Dominica, France, Grenada, Slovakia, Montenegro, Malta, Singapore, St. Kitts and Nevis, Russia,Vanuatu and many Latin American countries

14.3 Arguments against *ius doni*

Malta's introduction of a Citizenship-by-Investment programme in late 2013 occasioned wide debate in several countries in Europe – especially Germany (where many politicians are fundamentally against the "sale" of citizenship) and the UK (which fears the endangering of its own investor immigration programme) – which was expanded EU-wide on 15 January 2014 in the European Parliament and has also led to a great variety of reactions by the authors who have addressed this issue from a legal, political and sociological perspective.[1109] The following sub-sections address the main concerns associated with the introduction of Citizenship-by-Investment programmes.

14.3.1 "Citizenship must not be for sale"

Rousseau contended that citizenship requires personal involvement, that public service should be the main business of the citizen and that as soon as this is no longer the case, as soon as citizens would prefer to serve with their money than with their persons, the state is not far from its end.[1110] Of course we have come a long way since *Rousseau*, however, the fundamental question is nevertheless to what extent monetary or economic considerations should play a role with regard to the status of citizenship or the acquisition of citizenship. It is also a question of to what extent the commercialisation of state sovereignty can and should go. Citizenship-by-Investment and the attraction of foreign capital in this way is comparable with the commercialisation of state sovereignty in other ways, such as by creating beneficial company incorporation laws which then compete with other jurisdictions, or more controversially, the creation of a tax haven or the licensing and hosting of online casinos.[1111]

1109 SHACHAR/BAUBÖCK (2014) provides a good overview of the spectrum of opinion
1110 ROUSSEAU (2006)
1111 On the commercialisation of state sovereignty, cf. SLEMROD (2008)

EU Commissioner *Reding* proclaimed[1112] "*Citizenship must not be up for sale*" following the introduction of a Citizenship-by-Investment programme in Malta, which prompted an outcry throughout Europe. Commission President *Jean-Claude Juncker* later stated "*As a matter of principle, nationality is not a product. Selling nationality is selling part of the dignity of a country. I am quite satisfied with the compromise that has been reached between the Maltese government and the European Commission, but I never understood this initiative. That is my personal point of view. I was Prime Minister for 19 years and I would never have sold Luxembourg's passports. Never*".[1113] *Sandel* more generally stated: "*the question of markets is really a question about how we want to live together. Do we want a society where everything is up for sale?*"[1114] However, there are many other things which are widely felt to be unsuitable for sale: land, sex, the avoidance of military service duty, babies - yet land can be bought, prostitution is often legal, commercial surrogacy is also often legal in many countries,[1115] some of the greatest art was sponsored by people who wanted to purchase salvation for themselves[1116] and military service in many countries now is no longer a civic duty for all but is left to those in society who have no other good options and "*who may be conscripted, in effect, by economic necessity*"[1117] – or to poor foreigners who buy citizenship in effect by risking their lives for the military, an ultimate form of *ius doni*.

Thus, to agree with Kochenov, "*To insist that citizenship is not for sale is to ensure that the perpetuation of the outright randomness of its conferral as well as hypocritical and self-righteous excuses lurking behind fundamental mechanisms of exclusion*".[1118]

Certain goods of course have value in ways that go beyond the utility

---

[1112] European Commission: SPEECH/14/18: Citizenship must not be up for sale, speech by the Vice-President of the European Commission Viviane Reding of 15 January 2014, published online at http://europa.eu/rapid/press-release_SPEECH-14-18_en.htm, last accessed on 18 January 2014

[1113] http://www.independent.com.mt/articles/2014-05-04/news/malta-will-play-an-important-part-in-the-ec-jean-claude-juncker-4841766916, last accessed 7 February 2015

[1114] SANDEL (2012) p. 203

[1115] cf. SANDEL (2014) p. 94 et seq.

[1116] KOCHENOV (2014) p. 2

[1117] SANDEL (2010) p. 82

[1118] KOCHENOV (2014) p. 3

they provide and "*how a good is allocated may be part of what makes it the kind of good it is*".[1119] Marketing a good can in fact also change its character.[1120] Furthermore, a good can be corrupted by being treated according to a lower standard of valuation than is appropriate to it. Is this the case when we "value" citizenship at a particular price, when we put a price tag on citizenship? If market reasoning is applied to certain domains in life, such as "*sex, procreation, child rearing, education, health, criminal punishment, immigration policy...it's less plausible to assume that everyone's preferences are equally worthwhile*".[1121] As *Paskalev* points out, the opposite can also be true, and can be the case with selective Citizenship-by-Investment practices: giving citizenship and a passport to a highly regarded person can make this citizenship and passport highly regarded, too.[1122]

Another approach to this point is to look at citizenship as an emanation of universal human rights and human dignity and to question its availability for consideration on that basis. The argument is that if citizenship is the status which grants access to many civil and political rights (such as the right to vote or to stand for election) and vast majority of economic and social rights (such as the right to education or health care), and as a protected right in itself – the "right to have rights" which cannot be revoked without the bearer's consent – its available for consideration creates an inequality among citizens and an inequality among the bearers of rights.[1123] Enabling the commodification of citizenship is felt to create levels of access to the rights it bestows,[1124] and to inequality among citizens and non-citizens, exacerbating the wrongs of statelessness.[1125] However, this approach to the issue conflates the political desire to cure the ills of statelessness and the unlawful denationalization practiced in some countries, such as Côte d'Ivoire,[1126] or the wrongs of unequal

[1119] SANDEL (2012) p. 33
[1120] HIRSCH (1976)
[1121] SANDEL (2012) p. 89
[1122] PASKALEV (2014)
[1123] See for instance NASH (2009) p. 1081; and SATZ (2010) pp. 100 et seq.
[1124] LAXER/SORON (2006) p. 30
[1125] HOWARD-HASSMAN (2015) pp. 27–30
[1126] HOWARD-HASSMAN (2015) p. 34

citizenship or discriminatory nationalisation rules, with concerns about the politically neutral provision of access to citizenship on an economic basis. Citizenship is indeed a status within a national legal order which will grant greater access to certain national, commonly held goods. However, where all a nation's citizen acquire their status on the basis of objective rules which treat all people equally, then there can be no question of inequality among citizens, regardless the route by which citizenship is acquired. Yet, to agree with *Hepple "the law is directed at only one element in the many causes of disadvantage, namely 'discrimination'. … Whether we rely on negative concepts like direct or indirect discrimination or a broader positive notion of 'equal' opportunity, or even 'fair opportunity', it would be illusory to believe that these can be translated into legal terms of art which will lead, without more, to the promised land of (transformative) equality. … Law is both too specific and too selective in its choice of the causes in the 'cycle of disadvantage' to be capable in itself, of delivering real substantive equal rights."*[1127]

Then, while the traditional assumption that citizenship rules are the preserve of a sovereign nation to determine has been mitigated by the public international law rules against the creation of statelessness or prohibiting discriminatory treatment of the recipients of rights,[1128] this is not to suggest that equal treatment as an aspect of human dignity requires the extension of all rights to all people,[1129] merely that all subjects of specific rights be treated equally. There is no essential relationship between Citizenship-by-Investment and inequality as a subject of rights, provided that the rules providing for such citizenship themselves treat individuals equally. In other words, provided that the state organising a Citizenship-by-Investment programme respects human dignity and the rule of law in the administration of its laws, including in the administration of the programme in question, then its grant bears no substantive differences from a rights and dignity perspective than the acquisition of citizenship by any other means.

[1127] HEPPLE (2014) p.227

[1128] WALTER/GÄRDITZ (2015) p. 27

[1129] WALTER/GÄRDITZ (2015) pp. 106–107

There seems to be a distinction between two kinds of goods: things which money cannot buy, like friends and Nobel Prizes, and things which money can buy but arguably should not, like kidneys and children.[1130] Citizenship clearly does not fall into the first category, but does it fall into the second? The answer to this question, really, is a political one, which must be determined by each country, by each society on its own. Be it sports, science, money or family, it is up to the national political process to determine the criteria for conferral of citizenship, and there is no ethical point to be made in arguing against money as a route to citizenship when loving a citizen, expensive education, hiring a good lawyer to prove your ancestry, or a talent in playing soccer will also work.[1131]

14.3.2 Limited or no requirements for integration

The presence of a large sum of money, owned by a natural person and which she intends to use or to invest in the receiving State, of course says nothing in itself about the person's willingness and ability to integrate into the local society. Citizenship-by-Investment as practiced for example in St. Kitts and Nevis, Austria or Malta – and also in other states which have extensive visa agreements with other States – promises virtually worldwide travel freedom and the ability to do business undisturbed worldwide, especially if the acquirer is not obliged to choose to reside in the host country, as well as personal security in knowing that one may "return" to the country of citizenship anytime. This is a very important factor if you are from a country that is politically and economically unstable, a dictatorship, or at war, or all of the above, and you are seeking a safe haven for you and your family. For example, since the nineteen-sixties the ethnic Chinese in Hong Kong and Southeast Asia "*have sought residence and citizenship rights in Western countries to escape political discrimination and anticipated upheavals that could disrupt businesses and threaten family security.*"[1132]

1130 SANDEL (2012)

1131 KOCHENOV (2014), re *"Olympic citizenship"* cf. SHACHAR (2011)

1132 ONG (1999) pp. 119–120, regarding dual citizenship among Hong Kong Canadians cf. *Preston/Siemiatycki/Kobayashi* in FAIST/KIVISTO (2007) pp. 203 et seq.

Very often, it is not membership but mobility which is at issue, and not only the rich but also the poor seek naturalisation for economic and security rather than civic reasons.[1133] Indeed, *"[T]he international mobility of people becomes possible primarily as a result of standardized paperwork (or plastic) an individual holds, …"*[1134] Citizenship-by-Investment offers the possibility to acquire such mobility and peace of mind through economic means, by making a contribution to a country and in return receiving citizenship of that country. However, in all the countries offering Citizenship-by-Investment programmes, there are no or only very limited "integration" requirements as is often the case with ordinary naturalisation procedures.

It is a fundamental normative question whether the condition of "integration" should be required in modern citizenship law. If this question is answered in the affirmative, it would be problematic in terms of the normative aspects of citizenship law to create conditions under which citizenship could be awarded based on investment of capital (or talent, for that matter) and not on what effective "integration" would involve, based on more traditional elements such as language, knowledge of the country or – unthinkable of course for liberal democratic states – even ethnic or religious affiliation. In Émile, *Rousseau* envisaged citizens as integrated in a network of spheres of concern which have their ultimate origin in shared ancestry and the bond of the family – the good citizen was the good father. However, this form of patriotic citizenship, which emerged from the golden age of nationalism cannot now hold true within today's pluralistic democracies. The protection which a state affords is not restricted to one specific group within a state, but to all legitimate participants in the state polity, which itself collectively regulates the conditions for access to itself. Some of these conditions may be related to the acquisition of a particular language or length of residence, but where states protect many nations, language groups, religions, tribes and cultures equally within their citizenry, integration into specific subsets must at best only be regarded as one route to citizenship.

1133 PASKALEV (2014); OCHOA (2014)

1134 SADIQ (2009) p. 173

An interesting case in point affecting a significant part of the world population, within the EU – where half a billion people have a citizenship with which they can exercise virtually the same rights in all EU member states without any integration requirements such as language etc. – this idea of "integration" as a requirement must be effectively ruled out or at least can no longer apply to other EU citizens.

As we have seen in this respect, depending on the approach taken in national citizenship legislation, citizenship is granted more as an incentive for or in recognition of successful integration or even assimilation.[1135]

Under the *ius doni* principle of citizenship acquisition, language skills, knowledge of the country or other appropriate means of demonstrating a certain minimum integration play no role at all or at most a very minor role, in what would at best be a particularly modified incentive to integration.

This limited explanatory power of social integration is therefore – at least outside the EU – a reasonable objection to a Citizenship-by-Investment approach, where "integration" should be normatively required as a condition for naturalisation or recognition, and over which opinions vary strongly, and understandably so.

14.3.3 Risk of abuse of political, economic and social rights?

Does Citizenship-by-Investment conceal the risk of abuse of political, economic or social rights? Each connection of an investing person to the domestic legal system of the host country created through the granting of citizenship, results in the recipient gaining access to political,[1136] economic and social rights. The latter would also be acquired by people who do not identify with the local laws in any way, which would not eliminate the danger of abuse of economic and social rights, if these people are able to exercise such rights. The question of political rights, however, is quite independent of the economic and social positions of

1135 On the assimilation model, which is particularly pronounced in France, cf. section 7.3.4.2

1136 In St. Kitts and Nevis, interestingly, such access is linked to five year's prior residence, the access to which is thus lawfully restricted for persons naturalised under the Citizenship by Investment program

the persons concerned.

The possible abuse of economic and social rights is in fact already occasioned by the granting of citizenships to persons who do not in any way identify with the local legal order, and who could derive personal benefit from these rights. This is also the case through the extreme application of the *ius soli* principle, for example in the US, Canada or previously in Ireland, where the exploitation of these rights acquired at birth, leads to "birth tourism".

This is also true of liberal ethno-nationalist citizenship laws, such as in Hungary, where several hundred thousand people of Hungarian descent in the surrounding countries, in Serbia and Romania for example, were granted Hungarian citizenship; or in Germany, where the "homecoming" law enabled over three million people, mostly from the former Soviet Union, to be granted German citizenship; or in Italy where hundreds of thousands of citizens from Argentina and other South American countries were given Italian passports.[1137] Most of these people pose a quite real risk toward abuse of social and other rights afforded to them by virtue of their EU citizenship that they acquired in this way.

What is the situation, on the other hand, of people who are naturalised under Citizenship-by-Investment programmes? Do applicants under Citizenship-by-Investment pose a similar risk toward abuse of social and other rights afforded to them by virtue of the citizenship that they acquired in this way? This is not so, because Citizenship-by-Investment programmes in all the States which offer them have already addressed this issue inherently due to the amount of the investment required and the checks applied within the application processes. In order for someone to invest funds of around USD 500,000 in St Kitts and Nevis, over EUR 1 million in Malta or even more in other States such as Cyprus and Austria, the relevant applicant must have extensive financial resources. Apart from the investment requirement itself, the application procedure requirements in all these States scrutinise carefully both the economic

1137 cf. data on EU Citizenship Observatory website, http://eudo-citizenship.eu, last accessed 25 January 2015

situation and the source of the funds relied upon, and other criteria such as good character etc., which ensures that the individuals are indeed wealthy individuals of good reputation.[1138] It can therefore be assumed that such persons actually pose no threat of abusing the new economic or social rights which they gain through the acquisition of citizenship based on their investments. On the contrary, experience has shown that such persons tend to be even less of a burden on public resources than the average citizen, as their children are often taught in private schools (paid for by them), they secure private health insurance to cover their costs in case of illness rather than use the public health system, and they are more likely to invest further funds and create jobs in the country rather than to have to rely on unemployment benefits.

As for the political rights, objections about the risks of possible abuse are also misguided: the value of access to a single vote is unlikely to justify investments of the level required by Citizenship-by-Investment programmes (over EUR 1 million in Malta, for instance). This is also illustrated by the consistent findings of extensive voter surveys in modern democratic States showing declining turnout in elections, and where the majority of the population is not (or no longer) interested in politics, with one reason commonly put forward being that they perceive their individual votes as having no impact on the outcome. And those who are interested can engage in politics even without having a formal status of membership, as the German citizen *Daniel Cohn-Bendit* showed in Paris in 1968.[1139] Furthermore, where a particular person is interested in political participation, there are various options open to wealthy persons without even having direct personal political rights (i.e. to be able themselves to vote as citizens or be voted for and hold public office), which can enable influence over policy, as clearly evidenced in many smaller States where large foreign investors and corporations hold indirect sway over government (or indeed in large states, such as in the UK, where the interests of an Australian-American media tycoon are felt to have directed the outcomes of national elections).[1140] Paradoxically,

[1138] cf. KÄLIN (2014)

[1139] KOCHENOV (2014)

[1140] Consider, for instance the only partly ironic headline of the Sun newpaper on 11

Citizenship-by-Investment programmes, if properly designed and managed, can help small states to become financially less dependent on single large foreign investors and thus be in a better position to fend off such undue influence in their political and economic affairs.

It is therefore clear that none of the political, economic nor social rights which are awarded by granting Citizenship-by-Investment are necessarily abused by those newly naturalised persons, so there is no specific danger in this regard.

14.3.4 Danger of a "sell-out of sovereignty"

If the only reason for the granting of citizenship is because an individual is investing a large sum of money in the host country, this is viewed sometimes as a "sell-out of sovereignty", as inappropriate money for citizenship exchange and fast-tracked access to the national legal order of the host country. If the granting of citizenship is practiced – such as in Austria – without the criteria of *ius doni* being clear and comprehensibly regulated by law, this can indeed raise questions of a possible abuse of rights, but does this amount to a sell out of sovereignty?

The fact that the risk of corruption and the abuse of rights cannot be dismissed easily was demonstrated in the case of the Austrian politician *Uwe Scheuch*. In the underlying case, a Russian investor was offered the prospect of Austrian citizenship as "consideration" for an investment worth EUR 5 million, with 5 to 10 percent of the estimated total investment to benefit *Scheuch's* political party. In January 2010 the Austrian Green party raised in parliament the question why Citizenship-by-Investment was only provided for under Section 10(6) ACA as a "discretionary policy" of the Austrian Federal Government

April 1992, *"It's The Sun Wot Won It"*, laying claim to the unexpected victory of the Convervative party over Labour in the national elections that year, following an intensive campaign directed against the Labour party leader, Neil Kinnock, by that newspaper, allegedly at the direction of Rupert Murdoch, the Chairman of the Sun's mother company, News International (evidence given by Rupert Murdoch to the Leveson Inquiry, 25 April 2012)

and not included in a statutory provision.[1141] This is a very good question. The Austrian Ministry of Interior stated on record that the Austrian Government had requested ministries to decide on a case-by-case basis, especially since there are now non-binding internal criteria to facilitate objective decision-making and at the same time ensure decision-making consistency.[1142]

The moral hazard resulting from the sale of citizenship does not therefore result from the transaction per se, but from opaque transactions which permit the inclusion of extraneous considerations. It is the possibility that an opaque transaction can be used to corrupt officials or politicians which can render a Citizenship-by-Investment programme corrosive to the status it purports to offer, but this is a problem with the system constructed, as this Austrian example illustrates. *Ius doni* on the basis of objective and published criteria backed by due diligence does not affect the sovereignty or integrity of the nation offering it any more than any other rules-based route to the acquisition of citizenship.

14.3.5 Possible violation of the *ultra* vires principle?

If you grant citizenship to achieve the aims discussed *supra* (incentive to integrate or recognition for integration), even the fact of regulating of Citizenship-by-Investment when assessed against the constitutional principle that the aim of regulation must be apparent from its statutory wording, or at least from its general framework, could possibly fall foul of the *ultra vires* principle. It is true that the main concern of citizenship regulation is traditionally migration control,[1143] not investment control or investment incentivisation. Citizenship law is primarily intended to be a means of achieving the best possible allocation of the world's population to nation States, and as an inclusion and exclusion mechanism, rather than a means of achieving the best possible allocation of global resources and of attracting foreign direct investment.

1141 cf. the description in the *Austrian Times*, published online, and DZANKIC (2014)

1142 Austrian Interior Ministry, Parliamentary Request, No 4270/J XXIV GP

1143 cf. *supra*

However, as has already been shown, although *ius doni* as a basis for direct naturalisation represents a different route to the acquisition of citizenship, the national legislator is free to adopt this criterion without acting *ultra vires*, given the fact that both the fundamental purpose and function of citizenship are preserved.

14.3.6 Limited correlation between "contribution" and "consideration"

The Citizenship-by-Investment model can present itself as economically viable and desirable. Given the nature of citizenship law, as a right closely interwoven with the principle of democracy and human dignity, Citizenship-by-Investment may appear, however, questionable from a legal theory perspective, because citizenship opens up access to political, social and economic rights, which from a theoretical perspective were generally not granted in return for monetary input of whatever kind but for the individual applicant's *personal* input: citizenship is granted, considering its traditional integration function, because the applicant "fits into" society, as assessed by the political decision-making body, based on the applicant's personal characteristics.[1144] It is traditionally not granted because the applicant contributes to the financing of the host country or its economic consolidation or other economic benefits provided to the country.[1145] If Citizenship-by-Investment is awarded to assist the host country in the financing of its general responsibilities, the enumeration and *numerus clausus* of the State's financial revenue sources may be taken into account. Due to their democratic constitutions, it is incumbent on the majority of the reference States to cover their responsibilities exclusively through their statutory sources of income, i.e. through taxes, fees, charges, levies and special levies. A monetary input in connection with

[1144] This is also argued by *Shachar* and *Hirschl* in particular, when comparing Olympic citizenship with Citizenship-by-Investment, cf. SHACHAR/HIRSCHL (2014): "*from a normative perspective it is important to distinguish between recipients of citizenship who are given specialized treatment on the basis of their* human *capital from those who gain citizenship merely in exchange for a hefty bank wire transfer*"

[1145] Having said that, however, traditionally in Switzerland the ordinary naturalisation of foreigners also involved consideration of their financial standing and contribution, and many Cantons required substantial sums of money to be paid as citizenship fees to the State – basically a Citizenship-by-Investment element

the granting of citizenship is thus questionable from this perspective and would have to be at least clearly established in primary legislation.

14.3.7 Rent-seeking and governance

Citizenship-by-Investment brings substantial inflows of capital into the domestic economy, and substantial revenues for governments, comparable to natural resources like oil or minerals. Citizenship can indeed be viewed like a natural resource in this regard. Such resources foster rent seeking behaviour, which can result in a failure in effective government will to use resources to improve economic performance or to benefit the citizenry at large. Furthermore, even for a government seeking to bring lasting economic benefit and sustainable long term increase in income from a resource windfall, this is a difficult task.[1146] There are indications of a link between the size of a country and corruption in the trade in "tokens of sovereignty", such as the sale of postage stamps for collectors, passports, or in the case of Tuvalu, its Internet domain name.[1147]

However, like the example of Norway with regard to natural resources shows, good government can achieve significant benefits for the country through the creation of suitable vehicles and processes to accumulate and distribute wealth created from resource windfalls.[1148] This means that while the issue of rent-seeking is a serious concern and may speak, *prima facie*, against Citizenship-by-Investment, with perceptions that they may promote narrow interests over general welfare,[1149] it really lies in the governance over Citizenship-by-Investment programmes whether this becomes a serious problem or can be avoided. As with some other forms of commercialisation of state sovereignty, in particular the operation of beneficial tax or incorporation regimes, governance actually proxies for a country's credibility[1150] and thus good governance is in any case a requirement for any successful Citizenship-by-Investment programme.

1146 On resource rents, cf. VENABLES (2010); cf. also BHAGWATI (1982)
1147 cf. SLEMROD (2008), with further references
1148 VENABLES (2010)
1149 cf. VAN FOSSEN (2007)
1150 cf. SLEMROD (2008), with further references

14.4 Arguments in favour of *ius doni*

Arguments in favour of *ius doni* also depend on the answer to the same fundamental question about what constitutes the ideal of citizenship today and how citizenship ought to be allocated. As the following sequence of reasoning shows, besides very fundamental considerations of global justice, if we adopt a market-oriented, non-political normative view of modern citizenship accepting the current system of nation states, the arguments in favour of the Citizenship-by-Investment concept seem strong.

14.4.1 Distributive Justice

On a most fundamental basis, the allocation of citizenship raises the question of distributive justice: whether a particular form of allocation of the rights and privileges of citizenship status is fair and just in comparison other forms of allocation – both globally and with regard to a particular state.

Questions of distributive justice are often viewed only within a particular state, which of course is protected from other states and their citizen's intrusion by that state's citizenship and immigration laws and policies. This however constitutes a moral dilemma that will *"remain a thorn in the flesh of liberal democracies"*.[1151] For citizenship and access rights are allocated in a completely arbitrary way, in a "birthright lottery"[1152] The immigration controls in place today involve coercive force through which state authorities directly structure the opportunities and interfere with the choices of those who want to cross borders, and this mainly promotes the interests of citizens of wealthy countries, who are anyway already privileged compared to the vast majority of the world's population who live in economically more or less deprived and unstable countries.[1153] Or as *Carens* put it, *"citizenship in the modern world is a lot like feudal status in the medieval world. It is assigned at birth; for the most*

[1151] *Bauböck* in SMITH (2011) p. 376
[1152] SHACHAR (2009)
[1153] *Bauböck* in SMITH (2011)

part it is not subject to change by the individual's will and efforts; and it has a major impact upon that person's life chances."[1154] This leads to a dilemma or an "immigration paradox":[1155] to what extent do we take into consideration the welfare of incumbent residents and citizens of a country, and to what extent do we take into consideration the welfare of citizens of other countries or all inhabitants of the world? Do we take a national view or a global view of distributive justice? Or perhaps, thinking of the EU here, do we take a regional view? *Beitz* and others have argued from a fundamental humanitarian perspective that a global view is required, that we should not understand national borders to have a fundamental moral significance and that principles of distributive justice must therefore apply globally.[1156] *Rawl's* "veil of ignorance"[1157] would need to be used for the entire world society, which would necessarily lead to very different ways of allocating or re-allocating the privileges of citizenship among the world's population than the citizenship allocation system we know today which is based on nation states that allocate citizenship mainly on birthright. Others do not believe the world should be seen as a "cooperative venture for mutual advantage" in a *Rawlsian* sense,[1158] and that therefore those principles of distributive justice do not apply. One argument also invokes the intergenerational perspective:[1159] that if we believe societies are meaningful as collectivities, they are interested in transferring their culture and know-how through generations and this is done through citizenship. This, however, is an argument akin to upholding the privileges of aristocracy in Britain to buy and sell land 100 years ago or to support the privileges in a feudal system: what is the worth of upholding a particular cultural tendency, if this is done in a profoundly inequitable way? One of the strongest arguments here is probably more that it is "*hard to understand the reasonableness of making people responsible for the welfare of others without also making them responsible for their governance.*"[1160]

1154 CARENS (1992) p. 26
1155 *Chang* in SMITH (2011)
1156 BEITZ (1999)
1157 RAWLS (1999)
1158 cf. *Macedo* in SMITH (2011)
1159 cf. e.g. *Bauböck* in SMITH (2011) pp. 358–364
1160 *Macedo* in SMITH (2011) p. 313

But whichever way this is looked at, we currently live in a global system of nation states, and citizenship is necessarily citizenship of one of the world's nation states. As we are concerned with the *ius doni* access to citizenship of a particular state, any questions of justice about the admission of citizens on this basis, i.e. in this case on the basis of investments that they have made in this particular state, are therefore necessarily to be viewed on the same level of how such allocation of citizenship compares to the allocation of citizenship on the basis of birthright, marriage, or periods of residence and other qualifications which that particular state otherwise requires. If distributive justice is to play any role with regard to the allocation of citizenship, then it would require entirely different ways of allocating citizenship globally, because accident of birth is obviously one of the world's most relevant yet most inequitable ways of allocating citizenship. In other words, from an external or global distributive justice viewpoint it cannot logically be argued that citizenship should "not be for sale", as this argument would require the premise that the allocation of citizenship among the world population as we have it today has been made according to global distributive justice principles, which is of course not the case. But if distributive justice is to play any role with regard to comparing the different possibilities of citizenship allocation of one particular state, i.e. if we are to compare *ius doni* to ordinary naturalisation, *ius soli* or *ius sanguinis*, then, from a distributive justice point of view, there likewise cannot be any logical argument that *ius doni* is in any way less desirable, less just or otherwise inferior to the other modes of citizenship allocation.

14.4.2 The liberal argument

Citizenship-by-Investment is essentially a liberal, market-driven approach to citizenship, and part of the appeal of markets is that they "*don't pass judgment on the preferences they satisfy. They don't ask whether some ways of valuing goods are higher, or worthier, than others...This non-judgmental stance toward values lies at the heart of market reasoning and explains much of its appeal*".[1161] Citizenship-by-Investment is based on

[1161] SANDEL (2012) p. 14

an individualistic, depoliticising liberal conception of citizenship that is formal, legalistic and without ties to a collective identity or membership in a particular community, as opposed to conservative – democratic conceptions of citizenship.[1162] This allows for a market-driven argument, based on the principle underlying a liberal conception to maximize individual autonomy and freedom of choice. The approach taken by economists such as *Gary Becker*[1163] which essentially maintains that the law of supply and demand governs the provision of all things, suggests that individuals should be free to buy and sell whatever they please, as long as they do not violate other people's rights. The "purchase" of citizenship should thus be allowed as long as it does not violate other people's rights. From a domestic point of view this is the case at least if it is not done in large enough numbers to influence the political process in a democracy; from an international point of view this is the case if it is not done in large enough numbers which may have adverse effects on other countries. For instance, one of the conclusions of the Independent International Fact-Finding Mission on the Conflict in Georgia was that *"The mass conferral of Russian nationality on persons living in neighbouring states risks violating the international legal principle of good neighbourly relations."*[1164] While the the situation assessed in that case was not triggered by any Citizenship-by-Investment program, the message of the Fact-Finding Mission is clear and equally applicable to any "passportization" policy.

Since market-oriented thinking has reached into domains of life which were traditionally governed by non-market values in recent decades – not least driven by many modern economists such as *Becker* who apply an economic approach to all spheres of life – increasingly we are putting a price on noneconomic goods, regardless of what the goods are.[1165]

1162 VAN FOSSEN (2007)

1163 BECKER (1976); Becker was awarded the 1992 Nobel Prize in Economics for "having extended the domain of microeconomic analysis to a wide range of human behaviour and interaction, including nonmarket behaviour"

1164 Report of the Independent International Fact-Finding Mission on the Conflict in Georgia' (2009), Vol 2, 174.

1165 SANDEL (2012)

14.4.3 The utilitarian view

Utilitarianism is an idea and philosophical concept going back to the ancient philosophers, but which in modern times was largely propounded by English philosophers and economists *Jeremy Bentham* and *John Stuart Mill*, who essentially maintained that an action is right if it brings *happiness* and wrong if produces the reverse of happiness,[1166] or that *"the highest principle of morality is to maximize happiness, the overall balance of pleasure over pain."*[1167] Maximizing utility is a principle not only for individuals but also for lawmakers; a government should decide to do whatever will maximize the happiness of the community as a whole, and citizens and lawmakers should thus ask themselves this question: if all of the benefits of this policy are added up, and all the costs are subtracted, will it produce more happiness than the alternative?[1168]

This provides another fundamental position in support of Citizenship-by-Investment. Open market transactions benefit both buyers (new citizens) and sellers (countries and their existing citizens) and thus improve the collective wellbeing or social utility. If I invest a significant amount of money to become a citizen of a particular country, that must be beneficial to me and make me better off, otherwise I would not "purchase" citizenship; likewise, a country earning significant additional foreign direct investment as a result of "selling" citizenship must make itself and its current citizens better off, otherwise it would not offer access to citizenship in this way. Both parties are better off and social utility is increased as a result of this exchange: an efficient allocation of goods by free markets.[1169] An underpriced good (citizenship) is made available to those most willing to pay for it.

Markets allocate goods based on the prices paid for those goods while queues allocate goods based on the ability or willingness to wait.[1170]

[1166] MILL/GERIANT (1993)
[1167] SANDEL (2010) p. 34
[1168] SANDEL (2010) p. 34
[1169] cf. SANDEL (2012) offers an interesting example with ticket scalping, which has somewhat similar characteristics to the citizenship by investment vs. citizenship by ordinary naturalisation options
[1170] SANDEL (2012)

Markets and queues are of course not the only ways of allocating goods, some are allocated by merit, others by need, lottery[1171] or chance. However, leaving aside birthright citizenship, citizenship acquired by ordinary naturalisation after years of residence closely corresponds to the queue-allocation of ability and willingness to wait, whereas Citizenship-by-Investment can be compared to the market allocation by the ability and willingness to pay a price. The utilitarian case for markets over queues is highly contingent,[1172] as there is no reason to assume that the willingness and ability to wait for citizenship is a better measure of its value to a person than the willingness and ability to pay for it, and likewise the willingness and ability of applicants to wait for citizenship is no better measure for a country and its existing citizens than the willingness and ability to make a significant investment or monetary contribution to the country. In fact, one could even argue the contrary with *Becker*:[1173] in his proposals regarding setting a price for the right to immigrate, he contends that immigrants willing to pay a significant amount would automatically have desirable characteristics, being skilled, ambitious, hardworking and unlikely to make use of welfare or unemployment benefits. Thus the willingness and ability pay for citizenship is probably an even better measure than the willingness and ability to wait for it. Indeed, as evidenced in many instances throughout Europe, where citizenship is granted to persons who become a burden to society rather than net contributors,[1174] it follows that from a utilitarian point

---

1171 The US Green Card Lottery is an interesting direct example of how the right to permanent residence in the United States (the "Green Card") is allocated by lottery rather than any other principle. Furthermore, a Green Card is a fairly direct route to citizenship following five years of residence in the US

1172 SANDEL (2012)

1173 BECKER (1997)

1174 One should mention here in particular the ethnic-nationalistic citizenship provisions in the laws of Hungary, Bulgaria, Romania, Spain, Italy and several other states which afford citizenship on the basis of ethnic or nationalistic motives regardless of whether the person in question will be a net contributor or rather a burden to society. Furthermore, many citizenship laws are heavily and unnecessarily biased toward "family" in that under the title of "family reunification" or on the basis of marriage there exists virtually unchecked access to citizenship. Italy is a good example, where two and a half years of marriage is enough to get a passport no matter what your financial situation or education or employment status is. If you do not have an Italian family and work or run a business there, it is however 10 years of uninterrupted residence with no recourse to public funds. (cf. *Italian Citizenship Act No. 91/92 of 5 February 1992, n. 91,* as amended by *Act No.*

of view, Citizenship-by-Investment should actually be given preference over other modes of non-birthright citizenship acquisition.

14.4.4 The cultural relativism argument

Cultural relativism[1175] is based on the two important premises of the existence of cultural diversity and the cultural origin of values.[1176] Cultural relativists would argue that citizenship has effectively already been sold for centuries and most cultures consider the practice acceptable. A more market driven model as in the form of Citizenship-by-Investment programmes is only a matter of the degree of the practice. The exchange of citizenship in return for economic contributions to the state has in fact been practiced since time immemorial, the attitudes of some citizens or political groups notwithstanding. As no absolute truths exist, from a cultural relativism point of view it is completely within ethical bounds given current societal values.[1177] Yet, the citizenship benefits going beyond economic activities of individuals must be also taken into account before making judgments. As testified by the EU citizenship, which was undoubtedly a product of an economic project as it was the construction of a *"single market (which was to) bind states together in a compact of mutual interest"*[1178], such benefits may largely affect people's lives. Emerging out of what was initially an economic project between states, EU citizenship offers its citizens a range of opportunities, including the *"possibility of choosing where to live their lives, which ultimately amounts to choosing friends, foes, and the law, by voting with their feet"*[1179] and enables them *"to live their lives as they, as opposed to a State where they were born and of which they are nationals, see fit, from work to marriage, from healthcare to education."*[1180]

94/2009). Interestingly, a number of EU Member States show clear positive bias towards unemployable people, while making it excessively difficult for the entrepreneurs to naturalize at the same time

1175 cf. SUMNER (1906), HERSKOVITS (1947) and NIELSEN (1966)

1176 BORNA/STEARNS (2002)

1177 BORNA/STEARNS (2002)

1178 WILLIAMS

1179 KOCHENOV (2013) p. 130

1180 KOCHENOV (2013) p. 130 (footnotes omitted).

14.4.5 Promotion of cross-border integration and convergence

Arguments in favour of Citizenship-by-Investment include also the fact that within the constraints of international law noted above, nation States must strive to achieve the best possible economic and social conditions for their State population. The levelling of intergovernmental prosperity is not only in the interests of the host country as affluence convergence mitigates transnational migration, but it also thereby reduces the intergovernmental frictional losses. Notwithstanding the concerns identified above arguing against Citizenship-by-Investment, it could play a significant role in helping promote cross-border integration, particularly, for example, in the case of a new EU Member State whose level of prosperity measured by GDP is below the EU Member State average, against the background of geopolitical power shifts, in particular with the rapid rise of emerging countries (Brazil, Russia, Turkey, India, China, but also Korea and Thailand et al). Greater investment in the host country's economy could help provide a multitude of people with jobs, thereby providing them with a steady income and greater personal autonomy. In so doing, they would thus contribute to the host country's economic and social stability.

From a purely economic perspective, the liberalisation of citizenship law for suitable applicants by Citizenship-by-Investment programmes is comparable with the unilateral liberalisation of international trade: if States unilaterally reduce their import barriers and welcome foreign goods, these countries benefit and their economic and political clout increases. The same applies if States unilaterally reduce their "import barriers" for highly skilled and wealthy people, and offer these people, in particular, the direct acquisition of citizenship. It is a fallacy to believe that States protect themselves by restricting immigration and access to citizenship. On the contrary, it is the reverse, States damage themselves by denying immigration and citizenship to suitable persons,[1181] as this represents a form of discrimination against desirable goods.[1182]

1181 While at the same time frequently admitting large numbers of less suitable persons

1182 cf. BECKER (1957)

14.4.6 Reduction of welfare differentials

Many nation States are losing their political autonomy as a result of globalisation, and supranational bodies such as the EU or the CARICOM are becoming increasingly important. The issue of social cohesion and integration is thus slowly moving from the national to the supranational level. Small EU Member States whose levels of prosperity are well below the average of the other EU Member States, as is currently the case with Greece or Bulgaria, could be helped towards increased prosperity convergence through a Citizenship-by-Investment programme, as explained above. Such programmes could play a significant role in the reduction of welfare differentials within the EU.

The legal rules as well as the design, set up and operation of such a system to the benefit of citizens and resident aliens cannot be realised without costs; however, once established the additional costs attributable to the new well-qualified citizens will be practically negligible.[1183]

14.4.7 Cosmopolitanism and global citizenship

The State borders within which we were born or from which we descended are no less arbitrarily imposed upon us than our other characteristics, such as skin colour, gender or our genetic makeup. Indeed, the citizenship which we receive at birth is completely arbitrary.[1184] As *Shachar* aptly pointed out, it amounts to a birthright lottery.[1185]

According to *Carens*, liberal democracies should therefore develop strategies which as far as possible would lead to a world without borders or reduce the impact of this arbitrary assignment of people inside and outside of State borders.[1186] We could also express this as an exhortation to promote global citizenship. In any event, as long as there remain nationals (citizens) and foreigners, ideal access criteria should be transparently

---

1183 cf. regarding this consideration in *Bauböck* in SMITH (2011)
1184 CARENS (1995); cf. also WALZER (1983) and SHACHAR (2009)
1185 SHACHAR (2009)
1186 CARENS (1995); and CARENS (2013)

formulated.[1187] Traditional models of migration have assumed "*migrants settle in one place and take on a new, singular political identity. But a more closely interconnected world means that the link between countries often remains continuous and can even be strengthened by migration*".[1188] Thus the traditional conception of citizenship is also "*increasingly at odds with the reality of modern life.*"[1189] Liberal states can no longer explicitly reproduce and reinvigorate particular nationhood through immigration and citizenship policy. The state now has to consider individuals for what they do, and not for what they are.[1190] For *Parsons*, individuals are now selected according to "achievement" and not "ascription",[1191] and this transition from ascription to achievement is the hallmark of modernisation. In this sense we could argue with *Joppke* that "*an immigration policy under the sign of skills and achieved individual characteristics, rather than primordial givens, has finally caught up with modernity*".[1192]

Citizenship-by-Investment fulfils exactly this function, by at least enabling those people who meet certain criteria, including also economic criteria, to obtain access to citizenship in a more interconnected world. Citizenship law should also generally and from its foundations be designed so that the foreign individuals who aspire to citizenship know precisely the conditions under which the citizenship can be obtained.[1193] This can be ensured not least by transparent Citizenship-by-Investment programmes in an exemplary manner: an accurate catalogue of criteria can be published, enabling whoever meets the requirements to expect to be naturalised. This leads to a new kind of cosmopolitanism,[1194] as, at least for wealthy people (and equally for the highly qualified in the immigration laws of most States today), the arbitrary limits are reduced or are removed.

1187 WALZER (1983)
1188 PICKUS (1998) p. 110
1189 PICKUS (1998) p. 110
1190 JOPPKE (2005)
1191 PARSONS (1971)
1192 JOPPKE (2005) p. 3
1193 BENHABIB (2004) pp. 139–140
1194 *Benhabib* aptly described cosmopolitanism as "*…the concern for the world as if it were one's polis*", BENHABIB (2004) p. 174; *Calhoun* describes cosmopolitan equally well as "*… belonging to all parts of the world; not restricted to any one country or its inhabitants.*", *Calhoun* in VERTOVEC/COHEN (2002) p. 102

This would also replace the monopoly exercised by any single State over its own citizens, at least in part, by a certain free market mechanism. This is only possible if viable alternatives exist,[1195] which is achieved already by the fact that globally already multiple Citizenship-by-Investment programmes have been established. Wealthy people who seek a transnational identity thus have choices and are able to avoid the obstacles of personal mobility and traverse borders in opportunistic ways.[1196] In the era of globalisation, the possibility of gaining and exchanging citizenships through Citizenship-by-Investment programmes, and in this respect not to be subject to any particular State monopoly, would appear to be a positive liberalising step towards a free cosmopolitism, comparable to the liberalisation of traditional State monopolies as the basis for a free national society.[1197] In this regard, on an international level it can even be argued that all states should make their citizenship available to anyone interested and willing to pay, so in effect a global market would exist for citizenships, and market forces would then determine the prices.

14.4.8 Individual freedom, mobility and security

The centralisation of State power within the individual State borders and partly within supranational borders (especially in the EU) leads to a restriction on the individual freedoms of citizens. Liberal thinkers therefore advocate for fundamentally decentralised State structures, and see the individual and not the State as the main focus.[1198] Citizenship is also closely linked to the monopolisation of loyalties by the modern nation State at the expense of local, ethnic or other existing national communities.[1199] Today there are also many international communities and affiliations for cosmopolitan, international people.

International mobility is a key element of individual freedom, but not all passports are equal, and citizens and passport holders of some countries

---

1195 cf. FRIEDMAN (1962)
1196 VAN FOSSEN (2007)
1197 cf. HAYEK (1944)
1198 *"[T]he liberal takes the individual, not the nation or citizen of a particular nation, as his unit"*, FRIEDMAN (1962); cf. also HAYEK (1944)
1199 GÜLALP (2006)

have vastly higher international mobility afforded to them. For a lot of people, in terms of citizenship it is mobility that is at issue, not membership.[1200] An industrialist from New York who wants to meet a business partner in Paris can do so within 12 hours, whereas a competitor from Botswana needs to apply for a visa, pay an administration fee and wait several days before finding out whether he will get his entry permit.[1201] And this only relates to travel mobility for business, study and leisure.

Due to the decentralised organisation of the world into nation States, which monopolise the authorisation of legitimate movement across and within their borders,[1202] individual freedom can, however, only ultimately be secured through migration and multiple affiliations.

This is first and foremost because the citizens are tied to their respective State through citizenship, subject to it and in fact severely restricted in many non-democratic States, even in their individual freedoms or rights. Currently, only about 60 percent of the world's countries are to some degree functioning democracies, where citizens have a realistic chance of deselecting an incompetent government at the ballots.[1203] Many Arab states are currently breaking apart.[1204] Many *de iure* citizens are *de facto* stateless, because they do not receive protection by their state of origin or enjoy substantive rights to return there.[1205] The recent conflict in Syria has led to the largest number of refugees since the Second World War.[1206] Since time immemorial, moving across borders in search of a better life has been a key driver behind the development of human civilisation.[1207] Indeed, many lives can be dramatically improved by leaving, and it is only recently that such migration started to be frowned upon, and now the "*generally accepted stance is that those unlucky enough to be born in miserable places offering no possible opportunities to lead decent lives or develop*

1200 PASKALEV (2014)
1201 BREVILLE (2014)
1202 VAN FOSSEN (2007)
1203 BELLAMY (2008) p. 3
1204 cf. "The rule of the gunman. Why post-colonial Arab states are breaking down", The Economist, 11 October 2014
1205 KOCHENOV (2014)
1206 UNHCR (2015)
1207 *Diamond* (1997), cited in KOCHENOV (2012)

one's talents should stay where they are without bothering richer nations by the constant attempts to improve their condition."[1208] The freedom to move away from or to find refuge in another, "better" State, is secured in the long term only by immigration rights and ultimately the acquisition of a second citizenship.[1209]

Only citizenship permits a "return" to a particular "home" country at any time: it is the only immigration status which is unconditionally recognised in public international law and in practically all national laws. Along with the right of emigration, which was formulated by the US Congress as long ago as 1868,[1210] a second citizenship offers an additional, crucial "one-way" option, to move to another country at any time.[1211] Citizenship-by-Investment programmes allow individuals and families who are exposed to potential hazards in their home countries – including political persecution and war and the deprivation of rights – to leave their home country and to enter a new State with the secure status as citizens (acquired by *ius doni*) at any time. This individual freedom and security offered by Citizenship-by-Investment – however flawed it may be as a solution only available to affluent individuals and families which excludes all those who are unable to pay the price – is an important aspect with an inherently humanitarian dimension, as it effectively enables people to acquire additional rights of movement, including the right to leave, which is only really secured if you have, in fact, somewhere to go to. Ultimately, this therefore also secures the right to have rights.[1212]

[1208] KOCHENOV (2015) p. 145

[1209] cf. KOCHENOV (2012); KOCHENOV (2015)

[1210] Expatriation Act of 27 July 1868, "*the right of expatriation is a natural and inherent right of all people, indispensable to the enjoyment of the rights of life, liberty and pursuit of happiness*". For modern Europeans, this principle is incorporated in Right to Exit of Article 4 of EU Directive 2004/38

[1211] *Bauböck* in SMITH (2011), about the fundamental importance of the right to leave any country, cf. KOCHENOV (2012)

[1212] Chief Justice Earl Warren in *Perez v. Brownell*, 356 US 44, 64 (1957), ARENDT (1968)

14.4.9 The myth of national homogeneity and the decoupling of nation and citizenship in the age of globalisation

The largest stated goal of nationalism, the dominant political ideology of the nineteenth and twentieth centuries, is the meeting or matching of nation and State, and the biggest myth of the nation State is that such a meeting or matching is not only possible, but that it exists objectively.[1213] Citizenship as a closed system based on nationality – on the matching of nation and State or nationality and citizenship – in the face of globalisation is an outmoded, outdated concept that creates tensions through the decoupling of nationality and civil rights.[1214] In this sense, globalisation seems to have ushered in a post-national era of citizenship.[1215]

14.4.10 *Ius doni* vs. *ius sanguinis* in ethnic nationalist citizenship regimes

The legal situation in Germany, where "ethnic Germans" automatically receive German citizenship on proof of their German roots upon arrival in Germany, leads to a confrontation between territory, culture and identity.[1216] Although the notion of a common German origin arguably does exist, the emigrants often do not have a grasp of the German language and are both culturally and politically less integrated than other immigrants, who can only acquire German citizenship after clearing the usual hurdles, even after years of legal residence. Germany has made several million people citizens in this way, mainly from the former Soviet Union.

In light of the large number of naturalisations, which comprises very significant numbers of people from origin countries which, in a Citizenship-by-Investment context, would raise eyebrows, we can rightfully conclude that *ius doni* not only creates far less of an issue in terms of absolute numbers, but also in terms of the qualification of the newly naturalised citizens, where people are selected to become naturalised through a highly selective process (main criteria: significant wealth and outstanding reputation).

1213 GÜLALP (2006)
1214 cf. SOYSAL (1994); ONG (1999)
1215 GÜLALP (2006); ONG (2006); cf. regarding America also SPIRO (2008)
1216 KASTORYANO (2006)

In Israel the *Law of Return*, introduced in 1950, offers every Jewish person and even their immediate family, no matter what their origin, not only the right to immigrate to Israel, but citizenship on arrival on Israeli soil.[1217] Beyond the single common element, "Jewish", there are no further conditions. Accordingly, Jews from the former Soviet Union are just as automatically naturalised as those from Yemen or South Africa or India. Likewise, it would seem appropriate to admit serious investors on the basis of a clean background and a serious investment or economic contribution to the country, without further conditions just like Jewish people are admitted without further conditions.

Such ethnic nationalist citizenship rules exist in many other countries, basing the selection criteria for admission to citizenship status on simple ethnic affiliation, and do not compare favourably with the equally simple selection criteria of *ius doni*. Ethnicity is a social construct which must be regarded as fundamentally arbitrary. It merely represents a social group selected and defined on the basis of some perceived shared experience – linguistic, historical, mythological or racial[1218] – which is both temporary, contentious and ultimately misleading, regardless that it may have assigned considerable value in a nations discourse for a period. Examples abound of the pernicious effect of ethnic and/or racist concepts being relied upon to define the criteria upon which a nation or citizenry is founded, as does evidence for the hollowness of the edifice upon which such concepts are built. One need only consider the recent scholarly debate over the origins of the earliest, or "most" indigenous populations of the Americas,[1219] a status which is privileged with additional rights in Venezuela.[1220] While the injustices visited upon the inhabitants of modern-day Venezuela by European colonists is beyond doubt and the

---

1217 cf. DIECKHOFF (2006); and BEN-PORAT/TURNER (2011)

1218 PEOPLES/BAILEY (2010) p. 289

1219 See for instance "Genetic Evidence for Two Founding Populations of the Americas", Nature (2015), accessed 21 July 2015: http://www.nature.com/nature/journal/vnfv/ncurrent/full/nature14895.html; contrast with "Genomic evidence for the Pleistocene and recent population history of Native Americans", Science (2015), accessed 21 July 2015: http://www.sciencemag.org/content/early/2015/07/20/science.aab3884.short?rss=1&ssource=mfr

1220 "A Promise Unkept", The Economist, 15 January 2009, accessed 21 July 2015: http://www.economist.com/node/12936585

desire to make amends understandable, might the few newly identified descendants of the more ancient Australasian-origin indigents not equally have a claim for even greater privilege over the now more numerous Asian-origin newcomers, who virtually wiped them out on their arrival around 15,000 years ago? Perhaps, alternatively, such indigents could be granted a right of return to their ancient motherland, Australia. Such an argument is obviously absurd, but so must be regarded the extension of German nationality to the Russophone bearers of Germanic surnames, or any other intrusions into citizenship of the idea of its grant by right of "blood". In practical terms, of course, the main difference is that *ius doni* has a significant positive impact in the host country, whereas often the opposite is the case with ethnic nationalist citizenship regimes. Provided that funds generated by *ius doni* naturalisations are used for the common good and in particular to benefit the least advantaged citizens, such as in Malta with its National Development and Social Fund, it would even satisfy *Rawl's* "difference principle", whereby social and economic inequalities are acceptable if they benefit the least advantaged members of society.[1221]

14.4.11 *Ius doni* vs. pure *ius soli*

The pure *ius soli* principle, which, for example is still practiced in the US[1222] and many other states, automatically grants every person born on a State's territory citizenship by simple virtue of his presence on the territory at birth, is becoming increasingly tenuous from the perspective of "sufficient connection to the State", in view of globalisation and the ever-increasing mobility of the world population.

If it is argued against *ius doni* that no sufficient or "genuine link" exists between the applicant for citizenship and the host state,[1223] even though that applicant is prepared to commit a substantial amount of his liquid assets for the benefit of his new country of citizenship, then what is the

1221 RAWLS (1999) p. 68; cf. also SANDEL (2010)

1222 cf. instead of many others SPIRO (2008)

1223 This was one of the main arguments put forward by the EU Commission against Malta's new Citizenship-by-Investment program.

quality of the link between those many who have become a citizen by accident, for example just because their mother happened to be in the US at the time of birth?[1224] *Ius doni* does in fact compare favourably to the pure *ius soli* principle, in that more often than not a closer connection, a more genuine link exists between the person and the state in question, than with accidental citizens by operation of *ius soli.*

14.4.12 Grant of citizenship in the common good

Every country has, in principle, the right to exclude whomever it wishes from entering and settling in its territory: likewise, every country has the right to regulate its naturalisation laws in accordance with the common good and to include whomever it wishes to admit to become a citizen.[1225] *Ius doni,* which could also be viewed as the grant of citizenship in the common good, is thus nothing less than the expression of the individual state's freedom to select and choose, in accordance with its ideas of the common good that prevail in the particular state's society, suitable individuals and families so that they may contribute to the economy and society and be admitted, on this basis, as citizens, in view of their contribution to the common good of that state.

This argument holds notwithstanding the criticisms levelled against such grants of citizenship (in the context of Olympic citizenship) as representing countries selfishly pursuing their good to the detriment of others.[1226] Again, these criticisms – which deplore competition among nations to attract talent or capital – while levelled at the citizenship rules which enable movement and which erode the idea that citizens must be meaningful members of a society in order to contribute to it,[1227] are actually confusing discomfort at the inequality among nations with arguments about national legal mechanisms. Provided that the access to citizenship offered by a Citizenship-by-Investment programme is allocated fairly

---

1224 As *Spiro* has aptly put it: "*The normative case for affording citizenship for life to the child of, say, a professional in the high-tech industry just because she was lucky enough to be born during Mommy's three-year stint in California seems weak*", SPIRO (2008) p. 23

1225 KESLER (1998) p. 16

1226 SHACHAR (2011) p. 2107

1227 SHACHAR (2011) p. 2102

and objectively, countries will be encouraged to compete to gain access to this resource for the furtherance of the national common good. With a level international playing field, there is no reason why such competition amongst states should be regarded as unfair.

14.4.13 *Ius doni* vs. *ius sanguinis* and *ius soli*: also a question of numbers

From a practical impact point of view it is important to compare the number of naturalisations which occur under typical Citizenship-by-Investment programmes through the application of *ius doni* principles, to the number of ordinary naturalisations.

In 2010, the last year where such statistics are available, the EU Member States granted citizenship to a total of not less than 810,000 persons.[1228]

In contrast, in a bit less than one year since the launch of Malta's new Citizenship-by-Investment programme, the Maltese government received some 400 applications for the highly successful programme.[1229] While this number relative to the large number of naturalisations throughout the EU represents the inclusion of a few, in many ways ideal new EU citizens, it will also result in some EUR 500 million in foreign direct investment for Malta, not counting any indirect effects and further investments resulting from the programme, in addition to significant other positive externalities. With an annual GDP of approximately EUR 8.5 billion (2013),[1230] this represents a significant inflow of capital for the country, while the number of applications are rather limited.

The number of applications under Austria's Citizenship-by-Investment provisions are not published, but are thought to be only a few dozen per year. In Cyprus, whose Citizenship-by-Investment programme has

---

1228 cf. http://ec.europa.eu/eurostat, last accessed 26 January 2015

1229 http://www.timesofmalta.com/articles/view/20150115/local/400-applications-for-maltese-passports-over-450m-in-foreign-investment-henley.552013, last accessed 26 January 2015

1230 ec.europa.eu/eurostat

undergone various modifications since its launch in 2011, numbers have only recently increased and while there is no public data available, estimates put the figure at currently about 100 applications per year.

If we also consider the few other countries in Europe which have *ius doni* provisions in their laws, such as Croatia and Slovenia, and if we round up the total to about 600 applications per year, this is in stark contrast to the over 800,000 persons naturalised or otherwise being granted citizenship in Europe in 2010. In fact, on the basis of these figures, less than one in a thousand of naturalisations in Europe are attributable to *ius doni*. These 0.01% however represent ideal EU citizens as they all, invariably (due to the stringent process and qualification requirements under Citizenship-by-Investment provisions) meet, or rather exceed, the requirements that the EU sets internally for EU citizens to avail themselves of the freedom of movement this status provides. Citizenship-by-Investment in Europe thus creates only extremely few additional citizens, who however are all highly qualified.

From an economic perspective, it is actually efficient to keep citizenship exclusive, and a citizenship admission policy can and probably should primarily be beneficial for existing citizens.[1231] In this respect, Citizenship-by-Investment ideally fulfils this stipulation as under this citizenship admission principle, only few new citizens who are, as a prerequisite, net contributors to society are admitted, thus creating a net benefit for the existing citizens of a country.[1232] Certainly, in practical terms, the number of citizens admitted under *ius doni* principles, in Europe at least, is entirely negligible and thus should not actually pose a real issue, legal[1233] or otherwise, regardless of the position one takes from a normative point of view.

[1231] STRAUBHAAR (2003)

[1232] Disregarding here the possible reputation risks of undesirable persons who have been admitted due to a lack of proper due diligence; however, assuming due diligence on applicants is done properly, these risks are actually minimal and definitely smaller than those presented by all other modes of citizenship acquisition

[1233] For example with regard to the principle of sincere cooperation in EU law (Article 4(3) of the Treaty on EU), cf. SHAW (2014)

Furthermore, if you consider the countries of origin of Citizenship-by-Investment applicants and those of ordinary naturalisations, and their respective numbers, we can quickly discern that many countries in the EU, for instance, have granted hundreds of thousands of citizenships to persons originating from countries which, in a Citizenship-by-Investment context, are considered "problematic" and where "heightened due diligence" should be called for.

Take for instance Germany, which naturalised thousands of people from Iran, Iraq, Afghanistan, Pakistan, Syria, as well as from Russia, Kazakhstan and other countries of the former Soviet Union. The following table shows the naturalisation statistics for Germany from 1990 until 2008. In light in particular now of the significant terrorist tourism we are experiencing, where naturalised citizens from Germany, France, the UK and other countries travel to Syria and other places to fight in brutal wars against the civilized world, it is timely to ask what heightened due diligence was and is being applied in these "normal" naturalisation procedures. The situation looks even worse if we consider the immigration to Europe from such countries, particular illegal immigration and the massive influx of refugees, which has resulted the ongoing infiltration of Islamist terrorists in Europe.[1234]

[1234] cf. US Department of State, Bureau of Counterterrorism, Country Reports on Terrorism 2013, Europe Overview, http://www.state.gov/j/ct/rls/crt/2013/224822.htm, last accessed 8 February 2015, and *Neue Zürcher Zeitung*, 21 January 2015: "Italien sorgt sich um seine Sicherheit. Mit den Massen von Kriegsflüchtlingen kommen auch gewaltbereite Islamisten nach Europa"

Naturalisation in Germany - Selected Countries of Origin

Nation	*1990*	*1991*	*1992*	*1993*	*1994*	*1995*
Romania	14,410	29,011	37,574	28,346	17,968	12,028
Russia	0	345	22,519	24,994	45,181	60,335
Soviet Union (former)	33,339	55,271	50,552	54,930	43,086	35,477
Turkey	2,034	3,529	7,377	12,915	19,590	31,578
Ukraine	0	1	1,089	1,746	2,610	2,894
Yugoslavia (former)	2,082	2,832	1,947	1,988	4,374	3,623
Morocco	212	389	1,137	2,363	2,888	3,397
Afghanistan	476	703	889	1,549	1,696	1,666
China	120	144	325	392	493	515
Iran	224	519	489	468	841	874
Iraq	186	249	343	472	487	364
Kazakhstan	0	3	8,002	19,745	63,496	101,393
Lebanon	293	405	585	543	562	595
Pakistan	388	455	597	670	340	167
Syria	334	393	475	626	678	602
Vietnam	1,454	2,118	1,928	1,815	2,572	3,430

Nation	*1996*	*1997*	*1998*	*1999*	*2000*	*2001*
Romania	9,777	8,668	6,318	3,819	2,008	2,026
Russia	60,662	62,641	65,868	39,082	4,583	4,972
Soviet Union (former)	21,457	8,966	3,925	535	n.a.	n.a.
Turkey	46,294	40,396	56,994	100,324	82,861	76,573
Ukraine	2,881	3,262	3,285	1,885	2,978	3,295
Yugoslavia (former)	2,967	2,244	2,721	3,444	n.a.	n.a.
Morocco	3,149	4,211	5,657	4,950	5,008	4,425
Afghanistan	1,819	1,475	1,200	1,355	4,773	5,111
China	602	510	667	644	1,467	1,556
Iran	649	1,005	1,272	1,610	14,410	12,020
Iraq	363	290	319	483	984	1,264
Kazakhstan	94,961	88,583	83,478	40,976	2,152	2,148
Lebanon	784	1,159	1,782	2,491	5,673	4,486
Pakistan	1,153	1,202	1,224	1,210	2,808	2,421
Syria	645	672	886	811	1,609	1,337
Vietnam	3,553	3,250	3,626	2,529	4,489	3,014

Naturalisation in Germany - Selected Countries of Origin[1235]

Nation	*2002*	*2003*	*2004*	*2005*	*2006*	*2007*	*2008*
Romania	1,974	1,394	1,309	1,789	1,379	3,502	2,137
Russia	3,734	2,764	4,381	5,055	4,679	4,069	2,439
Soviet Union (former)	n.a.	n.a.	n.a.	n.a.	n.a.	n.a.	n.a.
Turkey	64,631	56,244	44,465	32,661	33,388	28,861	24,449
Ukraine	3,656	3,889	3,844	3,363	4,536	4,454	1,953
Yugoslavia (former)	n.a.	n.a.	n.a.	n.a.	n.a.	n.a.	n.a.
Morocco	3,800	4,118	3,820	3,684	3,546	3,489	3,130
Afghanistan	4,750	4,948	4,077	3,133	3,063	2,831	2,512
China	1,336	1,311	1,133	952	1,036	1,092	1,172
Iran	13,026	9,440	6,362	4.482	3,662	3,121	2,734
Iraq	1,721	2,999	3,564	4,136	3,693	4,102	4,229
Kazakhstan	2,027	3,010	1,443	2,975	3,207	2,180	1,602
Lebanon	3,300	2,651	2,265	1,969	2,030	1,754	1,675
Pakistan	1,681	1,500	1,392	1,321	1,116	1,124	1,208
Syria	1,158	1,157	1,070	1,061	1,226	1,108	1,156
Vietnam	1,482	1,423	1,371	1,278	1,382	1,078	1,048

[1235] *Source: European University Institute/EUDO Citizenship Observatory, 2015*

In the light of the available citizenship statistics in Europe, Canada and the US alone, the number of naturalisations under Citizenship-by-Investment programmes pales in comparison with ordinary naturalisations. The same is true if we just consider naturalisations of people from countries which would normally attract heightened due diligence. In this respect, Citizenship-by-Investment programmes, which almost all today have most thorough due diligence applied in their processes, and which generally attract wealthy, well-educated entrepreneurs and investors, seem completely irrelevant from a statistical, demographic and a national security perspectives.

14.5 Definition of international standards and best practices

Recognising the fundamental principle that nation states are essentially free to determine who their citizens are and by what means they may acquire citizenship, the question of the compatibility of Citizenship-by-Investment with applicable international law should be explored, mainly to ensure that it does not adversely impact on the equality of the beneficiaries in their establishment and activities in third countries – as is mainly the case in the EU or CARICOM,[1236] but which can also be relevant with regard to short-term visa policy[1237] – which could restrict the beneficiaries' freedom of visa-free movement to more or fewer states. Because of the very limited but nonetheless actual impact of Citizenship-by-Investment on third States, it is desirable to create international standards on a multilateral basis. Appropriate international standards should support legal certainty and eliminate abuse – both by countries operating Citizenship-by-Investment programmes, and individuals applying for citizenship under such programmes.

[1236] Owing to their right of establishment and other rights afforded to EU citizens within the EU, and to CARICOM citizens within the CARICOM

[1237] An example is the removal of visa-free access for St. Kitts and Nevis citizens at the end of 2014 by Canada, citing security concerns: http://www.cic.gc.ca/english/department/media/notices/2014-11-21b.asp, last accessed 30 January 2015

Given Citizenship-by-Investment's overall objective to support global prosperity, and in view of the growing importance of capital as a prerequisite for State political action, and as the fundamental condition of the true sovereign equality of States,[1238] the fate of States and their political scope of action are increasingly decided by their financial resources – and the expected positive effect of Citizenship-by-Investment should not be undermined by the diversity of States and their autonomous scope for regulation in this area. States who do not adhere to best practice but let their respective programmes be loosely regulated or even corrupted have particular potential to undermine the Citizenship-by-Investment concept. Individual investors interested in applying under Citizenship-by-Investment programmes also have a keen interest to see States managing their respective programmes according to certain standards, as not doing so could undermine a programme's or even an entire country's reputation. A definition of international standards and best practice in this sector is therefore very important, as it is capable of having enormous positive effects on economies and societies if programmes are well-managed; for the states which introduce and manage such programmes; and for individual investors who are interested in applying under Citizenship-by-Investment facilities.

14.5.1 Transparency and accountability

One of the most important elements of good governance at all levels and all sectors relates to transparency and accountability.

Naturally, this is also and in particular true of Citizenship-by-Investment programmes, which should be designed and operated in an as transparent as possible manner.

The decision-making process within the relevant state institutions (government and parliament) with regard to the political decision to implement a Citizenship-by-Investment programme should also be as transparent as possible from the outset. Publicly recognised key questions

[1238] cf. Article 2(1) UNC.

in this process are: first, what goals shall be achieved with such a programme (attracting talented, highly skilled people? Attracting active companies? Attracting investments in the real estate sector? Establish a state fund for this or that reason?); and second, with what means shall these goals be achieved (how should a programme be structured on the investment requirements side?). The goals and means to achieve them should be communicated clearly internally (within the political system) and externally (to the wider public).

Considering Malta as an example, the Prime Minister consistently communicated from the very beginning that one of the goals of the Citizenship-by-Investment programme was to attract talent. That is very laudable. On the other hand, what was not communicated as clearly was in which projects the national fund to which contributions under the programme were made would be invested. So far, more than one year after launch of the Citizenship-by-Investment programme, no clear and measurable goals have been announced.

14.5.1.1 Clear structure and legislation

The governmental structures for operating a Citizenship-by-Investment programme and the underlying legislation should be as clearly established as possible. Legislation should provide for all relevant details of structure (i.e. which government authority should handle what part of the application processes, who will have oversight, etc.) and process (i.e. what exactly is required for an application, leaving minimal room for arbitrary interpretation by authorities and thus enabling consistent processing of applications).

Primary legislation should ensure that citizenship granted by Citizenship-by-Investment is of the same quality as citizenship granted under normal naturalisation procedures or citizenship obtained by birth.

Primary legislation should define clearly and definitely the reasons for which citizenship granted under a Citizenship-by-Investment programme may be revoked: ideally, these will be the same as those applicable under normal naturalisation rules.

14.5.1.2 Licensing and supervision of agents

If any private-sector agents are to be involved in sourcing applicants and mounting and lodging applications on behalf of applicants, then a framework should be established by primary legislation and more detailed regulation which provides for clear and transparent requirements for the licensing of such agents.

The agents should be qualified immigration consultants or companies specialised in this field with a proven track record (or whose principals are able to demonstrate a proven track record). Agents must adhere to and demonstrate capabilities in due diligence, in particular the background verification of potential applicants (their prospective clients), data protection, adherence to strict promotional guidelines set by government, etc.

Many countries which currently have such agents licensed to promote their respective Citizenship-by-Investment programmes and handling applications have illogical licensing requirements: for example, in St. Kitts and Nevis, any lawyer or corporate service provider or accountant (!) is *per se* qualified to act as an agent under the country's Citizenship-by-Investment programme. This practice leads on one hand to a large number of agents who are largely unspecialised and unqualified for the specific advisory and handling requirements of Citizenship-by-Investment applications, and on the other hand, to substandard or even problematic promotion activities by such agents.

Primary legislation should enable the government to suspend an agent's license at any time should such substandard promotion be detected,[1239] but also should it be found that an agent is not providing independent, clear and accurate advice to applicants, has insufficient knowledge of the application process and detailed requirements, including and in particular the due diligence requirements and a professional client onboarding process, does not actually fulfil the qualification requirements set by

[1239] An example of such provisions, albeit in secondary legislation, can be found in Art. 8 (1) and (2) of the St. Kitts and Nevis Citizenship-by-Investment Regulations, 2011

legislation, or which engages in any other undesirable practices. Likewise, an appeal board and a process should be established so that an agent whose license is suspended, withdrawn or not renewed can appeal this decision at an independent government body.

14.5.1.3 Approval and supervision of private sector projects

If a Citizenship-by-Investment programme includes the option of a private-sector investment (such as real estate, in particular), then a framework should be established by primary legislation and more detailed regulation which provides clear and transparent requirements for the approval and supervision of private sector projects.

Projects must, depending on the government's policy and overall strategy regarding their Citizenship-by-Investment programme, fulfil a clear set of criteria before they can be approved. Furthermore, it should remain in the government's prerogative only to approve a certain number of projects at a time in order to channel investments under the Citizenship-by-Investment programme optimally; safeguards should be enacted to avoid favouritism with regard to such limitation of approvals, and the decision-making process should therefore be transparent and public.

Ideally, a policy board would be established which, in cooperation with the Government sets the overall policy for private sector investments, and a process should be established whereby a private sector project promoter whose project is not approved, or whose approval is withdrawn, can appeal such decision.

14.5.1.4 Regular reporting and audit

Once a programme is operational, the responsible state body running the programme must periodically and publicly account for its business, including at least the number of applications lodged, processed, refused and completed, and information about the financial receipts obtained by government and in the private sector and/or the national development fund where the capital raised from the Citizenship-by-Investment programmes are directed. Independent external audit of these figures is a must.

Whether the names of applicants under Citizenship-by-Investment should be published is an interesting question. The initial decision of the Maltese government to amend legislation to avoid publishing applicants' names was criticised by the opposition party. However, looking internationally, the names of new citizens are not published in many countries, and for good reason: it respects and protects the privacy of these individuals. In some countries, legislation even provides specific protection in this regard.[1240] Therefore, the decision whether the names of applicants under a Citizenship-by-Investment programme should be made public is not straightforward and really depends on each country's legal and cultural tradition in privacy protection. Whether such names are published does not seem to have an actual impact on the governance and checks and balances built into such programmes, as these can be secured through other measures, as explained below.

14.5.1.5 Sovereign Wealth Funds as Beneficiaries under Citizenship-by-Investment Programmes

As the example of St. Kitts and Nevis shows, significant funds can be attracted through Citizenship-by-Investment programmes and channelled to sovereign wealth funds or quasi-sovereign wealth funds (as is the case with the Sugar Industry Diversification Foundation in St Kitts). This model has meanwhile been adapted by several further countries.[1241]

The IMF seems in fact to recommend the establishment of a Sovereign Wealth Fund (SWF) if foreign inflows of capital through a Citizenship-by-Investment programme are large and persistent, and if they encourage '*exploring the scope for sovereign debt reduction*'.[1242] SWFs need to be carefully structured with regard to their governance and accountability. The following diagram provides a good idea of what would be required for a SWF to comply with international best practice.

1240 E.g. in Austria
1241 Namely Antigua and Barbuda, Grenada and Malta
1242 XU/EL-ASHRAM/GOLD (2015)

Typical Governance Structure of Autonomous SWFs[1243]

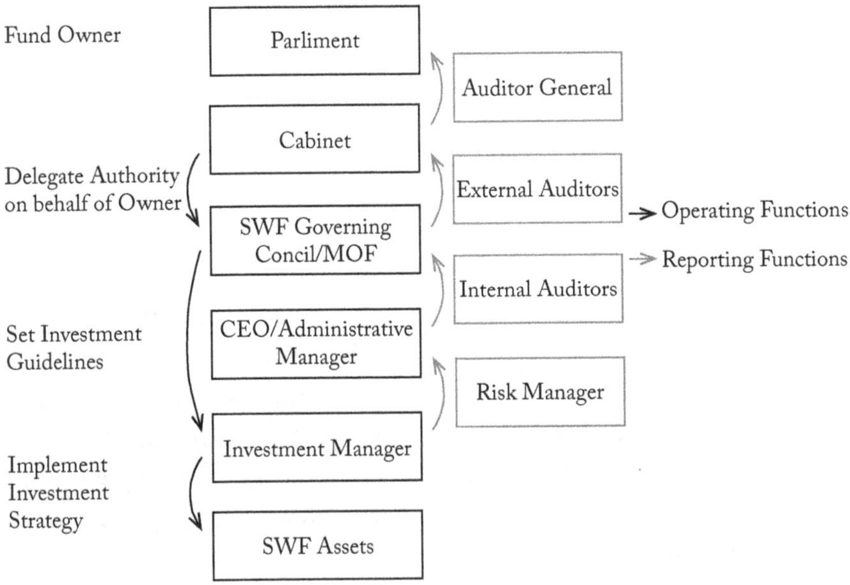

14.5.2 Efficiency and reliability of application process

Particularly from an applicant's perspective, but also in terms of the general good governance which should apply to all the activities of a public authority, the application process should be reliable and efficiently structured.

Primary or secondary legislation should provide clear timeframes for processing, to which the relevant Citizenship-by-Investment Unit or other government authorities handling applications must adhere.

For applications which are declined, there must either be a clearly defined process which enables a declined applicant to appeal so that his application is reviewed by an independent state body, or primary legislation must be clear that declined applications cannot be appealed. However, from a good governance and 'checks and balances' point of view it is much better and preferable to have an appeals process in place and clearly defined.

1243 *Source: IMF, 2015*

14.5.2.1 Documentation requirements

For most modern Citizenship-by-Investment programmes, documentation requirements are extensive and go into much detail. This may be quite onerous for the applicant, however it is necessary for government authorities to properly assess the profile and background of applicants and to make a well-informed determination of whether the applicant is suitable to be granted citizenship.

By way of example and to illustrate the details of documentary requirements, the following is a list of all the documents and forms that are currently required from an applicant under the Citizenship-by-Investment programme of St Kitts and Nevis.[1244] The Citizenship-by-Investment programme of St Kitts and Nevis is very advanced from a documentation requirement perspective and thus serves as a good example in this regard. This example illustrates what documentation such programmes currently require, and the level of detail.

1. Limited Power of Attorney to mandate a particular government-authorised agent to act on behalf of the client

Two copies are signed and dated (in blue ink) in duplicate by every applicant 16 years and older.

2. Citizenship Application Form

On this very comprehensive form, each question must be answered. One form must be completed for each person included in the application, also for children. In sections which are not applicable, applicants write "N/A" (e.g. employment history for minor children). If necessary, the applicant must supply additional details on separate sheets. All educational history (for adults, starting from High School) must be provided. Comprehensive information must be provided regarding source of funds in a special section. This section is reviewed carefully by the citizenship

[1244] Based on the *Henley & Partners:* Application Guide for Citizenship-by-Investment Program of St Kitts and Nevis, 2015

unit, so applicants need to be prepared to provide supporting evidence along with the application form (for example in support of real estate gains).

Both parents must sign the form on behalf of children who are below the age of 16, as their legal guardians.

3. Passport Application Form

A section of this form should be completed by an attorney or notary public as a recommender and this recommender's stamp must be placed in the space provided.

4. Photograph and Signature Certification Form

On this form, which serves to certify the identity of the applicant, the first section with personal details is completed by the applicant; the second section (certification) should be completed by either a Notary Public (provided along with an Apostille, except in the USA), an Attorney-at-law, or two Senior Officers of an internationally recognised bank. This section must also bear the original stamp or seal of the certifier. If the form is certified by a Notary Public, certification should be completed with an Apostille.

A photograph should be attached to this form in the box provided. It must be attached in such a way that it cannot be removed without tearing the photograph or the form.

5. Colour photographs

In addition to the photograph which the applicant attaches to the Photograph and Signature Certification Form, the applicant must submit a further six identical photographs. The photographs should be taken within six months of the date of submission, and conform to the following criteria: approximately 35 x 45 mm in size, in good quality colour and on high quality paper. The image should be clear, sharp and in focus on a white background and cannot have been altered in any way. They must contain a full front close-up view of the head and shoulders. The head should cover approximately 70–80% of the photograph. Clothing on the shoulders must be visible and should not be white. The expression must be neutral (not laughing or frowning) with the mouth closed. Sunglasses may not be worn. Tinted prescription glasses are acceptable, as long as the eyes remain visible. The applicant should be looking straight at the camera with eyes open. No hair should be in front of the eyes. The head should not be covered; however, headdresses may be worn, and should be black with the ears and hairline visible.

6. Certified Photograph

One of the photographs must be certified by the same individual who completed 'Section 9 – Recommender' on the Passport Application Form. The hand-written certification on the back of the photograph should appear as follows: 'I certify that this is a true likeness of the applicant …' [Signed]

7. Medical Certificate Form

One such form must be completed per applicant. A licensed medical doctor should complete Section B (Statement of Health) with an examination of each applicant. Each question should be answered and a final evaluation provided. If any of the answers provided in Section B are 'No', further explanation should be provided in the same box. The form should be signed, dated and stamped by a licensed medical doctor. It should not be older than six months at the time of submission.

8. HIV/AIDS Test results

Each applicant must provide original HIV test results from a qualified medical laboratory. It should be signed, stamped and dated by a member of the laboratory's staff (or the examining doctor). The HIV results must not be older than three months at the time of submission.

While the HIV test requirement might be problematic from an international law aspect,[1245] in particular from the aspect of upholding equality before the law without discrimination, the introducing of such requirement is not related to the Citizenship-by-Investment programmes but is rather a general application requirement of St. Kitts and Nevis and as such is applicable also to requests for citizenship by descent and citizenship by marriage,[1246] and also a global issue as practiced by large number of countries.[1247]

9.1 SIDF Investment Confirmation Form – For applicants applying through SIDF Contribution Option

The main applicant should complete and also sign this form if the SIDF option is chosen.

9.2. Real Estate sale and purchase contract and escrow agreement

Applicants applying through the Real Estate Investment option must arrange for the correct documentation to be completed in respect of the real estate purchase. A fully-executed original Sales and Purchase Contract and a fully-executed original Escrow Agreement will be required for submission with the application documents, in addition to the original copies kept by the applicant and the developer/real estate selling party.

10. Certified Passport Copy

The following must be submitted for each applicant included in the application:

- Passport picture page (showing name, nationality, date and place of issue, expiry date etc.)

1245 See e.g. Human Rights Watch, Discrimination, Denial, and Deportation: Human Rights Abuses Affecting Migrants Living with HIV (18 June 2009)

1246 See the application requrements of St. Kitts and Nevis at: http://www.stkittsnevis.org/citizen.html accessed 18 March 2016

1247 See restrictions of states in that respect at: http://www.hivtravel.org accessed 28 May 2016

- The relevant signature section (if different from the passport picture page)

Where children are included in the passport of a parent, these pages should also be included.

11. Certified Identity Card Copy

A certified copy of a national identity card (or other Government Issued ID card, such as a driving license) should be submitted for every applicant.

12. Certified Birth Certificate

Each applicant must submit two identical certified copies of either the complete birth certificate issued in the country of birth, or an equivalent document (such as a certified copy or original excerpt of the entry in the official family register, etc.). The name and other pertinent information should be drawn from the birth certificate for the completion of the Certificates of Registration so it is important to ensure that this document is accurate and corresponds with other identification documentation.

13. Original Police Certificate(s)

Each applicant aged 16 years and older must submit an original police certificate (an official criminal records check or certificate of good conduct) from the country of citizenship and from any country where he or she has lived more than one year over the past 10 years. Police certificates must be less than six months old at the time of submission.

In most countries police certificates are easily available upon request from a central police/government office.[1248] However, police authorities will only send the certificate directly to the foreign government requesting the certificate. In this case, the certificate should be sent directly to the Government's Citizenship-by-Investment Unit.

[1248] E.g. in the USA, http://www.fbi.gov/about-us/cjis/criminal-history-summary-checks

14. Certified Marriage Certificate (if applicable)

Applicants who are married must submit two identical certified copies of their marriage certificate. If husband and wife are included in one application package, only two identical certified copies are required.

15. Certified Divorce Certificate or Documentation (if applicable)

Applicants who have previously been divorced must submit a certified copy of their divorce certificate (or other divorce documents issued by the competent courts). One such copy is required for a man, and two identical copies are required of the divorce certificate for a divorced woman if she intends to revert to her maiden name on citizenship documents.

16. Certified Military Records (if applicable)

If any applicant has served in the armed forces, they must submit a certified copy of the relevant military record.

17. Certified Name Change Documentation (if applicable)

Where an individual's name has changed at any time other than by marriage, two certified copies of the documents/records of proof of change of name (i.e. deed poll, adoption papers, etc.) must be submitted.

18. Original professional reference

The main applicant must submit an original professional reference, issued by an attorney, notary public, chartered accountant, or other professional of similar standing.

The letter must be signed and dated, on official (office/company/institution) letter head and the following details should be included:

- Main applicant's full name, date of birth and passport information
- Period/length and type of relationship (longer than two years)
- Client's conduct

- The position the referrer has within the firm
- A statement that the referrer can be contacted further

This reference should be no older than six months at the time of submission.

19. Original bank reference

The main applicant is required to submit an original letter of reference from an internationally recognised bank, on official letter-headed paper. The letter must be typewritten and must be signed and dated by two senior bank officials. It should include the period/length of relationship, which should be longer than two years. This reference should not be older than six months at the time of submission.

20. Original document of evidence of residential address

The main applicant is required to submit one recent document of evidence of residential address, for example an original (or certified copy) of a recent utility bill or bank statement showing full name and residential address, or written confirmation from a bank or attorney. A credit card statement is not acceptable. One document cannot serve two purposes so applicants must ensure that a separate document is used for this requirement, i.e. the Bank Reference Letter cannot also act as the original document of evidence of residential address.

21. Original confirmation letter from institute of higher learning and sworn affidavit of support (if applicable)

Adult dependants aged between 18 and 25 years can be included in the same application if they are unmarried, fully financially supported by the main applicant and attending full-time an institution of higher education. In such cases, the main applicant must provide a sworn affidavit of support for each applicable dependent. This should be accompanied by an original enrolment letter from the relevant institution of higher education (i.e. university, etc.) and by current original transcripts of the courses or classes being attended (and grades which have been achieved to date).

22. Sworn affidavit of consent from spouse or ex-spouse relating to children

For applicants who are applying for citizenship and including their children, but who are not including their spouse, or if they wish to include children from a previous relationship, a sworn affidavit of consent is required from the spouse, ex-spouse or the children's mother indicating:

- Their relationship to the applicants
- The full names and passport numbers of each applicant
- That they have knowledge of the application
- That they give consent for each person in the file to apply for St Kitts citizenship
- That they have no need or interest in applying for citizenship now or at any time in the future

A certified copy of a government-issued picture ID (preferably the current passport data page of the consenting spouse) bearing the signature of the consenting parent, must also be included. Additionally, both parents are required to sign the Citizenship Application Form of the dependent minor's application. Where the main applicant has full legal custody of a dependent minor, or the non-applying parent is deceased, the main applicant must provide the relevant certified documentation in support of the particular circumstances.

23. Sworn affidavit of support relating to parents

For applicants who are applying for citizenship and including their parents, a sworn affidavit of support is required from the main applicant indicating:

- The relationship to the applicants, i.e. mother or father
- The full names and passport numbers of each applicant
- That the parents reside with (provide full address), are unemployed and are fully supported by the main applicant

24. Original bank statements

Original bank statements showing the applicant's assets and account balances, showing sufficient funds needed to invest in the Citizenship-by-Investment programme, are required from the main applicant.

25. Certified copies of degrees

Each adult applicant is required to provide certified copies of university degrees, if applicable. In cases where certified copies cannot be presented, a notarised statement from the university confirming the degree is required.

As can be seen from this list of documentary requirements (valid as of April 2015), the list is comprehensive and very detailed. The information submitted by applicants is checked and verified by independent due diligence agents, who also create an individual background verification report (BVR) on each applicant on behalf of the government authorities who evaluate the file.

14.5.3 Due diligence on applicants

One of the most important aspects in terms of internal good governance concerning the programme in question, and also from an international perspective in terms of the impact on other countries and the respectability and reputation of the programme and the country operating it, is the due diligence requirements and processes which applicants must undergo to pre-qualify under Citizenship-by-Investment programmes. The final qualification and decision are always a prerogative of the state authority, i.e. just because someone passed the required due diligence and background checks does not mean automatic grant of citizenship, but requires a further decision to grant or deny, following the successful screening and verification of the applicant's background.

Due diligence on applicants is a state function which should primarily be executed by state agencies, which also have exclusive access to numerous networks, including Financial Intelligence Units and Interpol. However, comprehensive due diligence which also involves background verification by private investigative firms – who check the information provided by applicants and who produce BVRs on the applicants – is also a critical element in a comprehensive modern due diligence process for investor immigration and Citizenship-by-Investment programmes.

Such background investigation must also ascertain that no part of the investment capital or other assets was obtained through criminal activities. An assessment should furthermore be made with regard to any 'high risk' indicators, such country of origin, country of major business interests or sources of income, and other factors. Applicants who are deemed 'high risk' may need to undergo additional, more in-depth due diligence investigations.

Specialised investigation firms who act on behalf of government authorities to execute such due diligence on applicants use many different public record resources to screen for any references or ties to negative indicators, including, but not limited to:[1249]

- Politically Exposed Persons
- Fraud
- Terrorism and terrorism financing
- Money laundering
- Other criminal activity
- Regulatory actions
- Litigation

[1249] cf. www.ipsaintl.com/Citizenship-by-Investment-Due-Diligence/, last accessed 14 May 2015

15

Ius doni in selected reference States

The following analysis of selected reference States considers the *ius doni* provisions in those states which have been chosen to enable the review and discussion of different aspects of how *ius doni* can be and is implemented in different national contexts.

Austria has been chosen as a well-established, wealthy EU country which has included *ius doni* provisions in its citizenship law since 1986 and has developed, if not a structured Citizenship-by-Investment programme, a rather well-established practice in this regard. Montenegro is part of the selection because it represents a European non-EU state which has, in its laws, *ius doni* provisions. They are regularly applied, and after an attempt to implement a more structured Citizenship-by-Investment programme some years ago, the discretionary grant of citizenship continues. St. Kitts and Nevis is part of this analysis as it represents the oldest Citizenship-by-Investment programme in modern times, established in 1984, one year after the country became independent from the UK. St. Kitts and Nevis also represents an extraordinary success story as the Citizenship-by-Investment programme has helped its economy survive the significant economic shocks that hit the Caribbean countries following the 2008–2009 financial crisis, cut in half its foreign debt and inject significant capital into the local economy thanks to this programme.[1250] All Citizenship-by-Investment programmes in the Caribbean region are now modelled after the Citizenship-by-Investment programme of St. Kitts and Nevis, as designed and implemented following its significant reform in 2006–2007, which was done with the advice and assistance of professional advisors.[1251] Finally, Malta features in this section because it has the newest and most advanced Citizenship-by-Investment programme in the world, designed to attract highest-calibre applicants. Malta has implemented the world's most stringent due diligence requirements and thus is a model also in this regard, setting a new standard internationally.

For each of these countries, all of which allow multiple citizenship (except Austria which allows multiple citizenship only if Austrian citizenship

1250 cf. XU/EL-ASHRAM/GOLD (2015)

1251 The Citizenship-by-Investment programme reform of 2006–2007 in St. Kitts and Nevis was executed with the advice and assistance of Henley & Partners

is acquired through its *ius doni* provisions, or a special permission is obtained prior to acquiring citizenship otherwise), different aspects will be looked at more thoroughly, to arrive at a good understanding of how *ius doni* provisions in citizenship law can operate in practice, including aspects which are important for policy decisions in this field.

15.1 Austria

15.1.1 State structural parameters

For a general introduction see 7.6.1. above. Austria was one of the first countries in recent history which introduced a modern *ius doni* provision in its citizenship law, with the amendments made to its citizenship act in 1986. Austria has never had a structured, formal Citizenship-by-Investment programme, but has rather developed an established practice to grant citizenship to suitable foreign investors.

15.1.2 Naturalisation statistics

In the years between 1990 and 2008, Austria naturalised between 9,198 and 45,112 persons per year, a total of more than 420,000.[1252] Of these, only a very small fraction are thought to be Citizenship-by-Investment naturalizations under Article 10 (6) ACA, according to press statements of between 33 and 41 per year in recent years.[1253] Actual figures are not officially published. This means that Citizenship-by-Investment naturalisations are less than 0.1% of total naturalisations per year. The naturalisation to population ratio is low at 0.2% per year – about the same as Malta after the introduction of its successful Citizenship-by-Investment programme, which doubled the number of naturalisations in the country following its introduction.

1252 cf. country database of citizenship acquisition for Austria on http://eudo-citizenship.eu, last accessed 26 January 2015

1253 cf. article in the Austrian daily "Die Presse" of 21 January 2010, accessed online at http://diepresse.com/home/politik/innenpolitik/534484/Staatsburgerschaft_Ein-Investment-reicht-nicht, last accessed 31 January 2015

15.1.3 Legal basis

As the legal basis of the Citizenship-by-Investment in Austria, either Section 10(6) of the Austrian Citizenship Act (*Staatsbürgerschaftsgesetz 1985*, BGBl 1985/311, as amended, hereinafter "ACA") or Section 11a(4)(4) ACA (granting citizenship on the basis of exceptional contributions) is engaged.

15.1.3.1 Section 10 (6) ACA as basis

Section 10(6) ACA is the pure *ius doni* provision, whereby the requirements of Section 10(1)(1) and (7) ACA do not apply if the Federal Government confirms that the granting of citizenship on the basis of prior and expected extraordinary contributions are in the particular interest of the Republic of Austria. As any administrative act of the Federal State would exceed the general attribution of competence of the Federation and the Federal States as defined by Article 11(1)(1) ÖB-VG, according to which the Federation is responsible for legislation and the Federal States for law enforcement – Section 10(6) ACA has been passed as a constitutional norm for these purposes in order to create a specific competence.[1254]

In addition to Section 10(6) ACA, according to Section 11a (4)(4) ACA, a foreigner is entitled to citizenship after a lawful and uninterrupted residence of at least six years in the Federal territory and under the conditions of Section 10(1)(2) to (8), 10(2) and (3), when the grant is in the interest of the Republic because of prior as well as expected outstanding contributions in the scientific, artistic and sports areas. Section 11a(4)(4) ACA requires evidence of delivered or expected extraordinary contributions that are of *particular* interest to the Republic of Austria, as required by Section 10(6) ACA.[1255] In contrast to Section 10(6), proof of German language skills is required in addition to the residence requirement, and any other citizenship must be renounced prior to acquiring Austrian citizenship.

[1254] cf. *Schober/Szymanski* in FESSLER/KELLER/POMMERENING (2006)
[1255] cf. DZANKIC (2012)

15.1.4 Discussion and opinion

The Austrian government does not publish figures on naturalisation processed under Section 10(6) ACA. According to a Parliamentary report[1256] of 21 January 2009, in 2009 alone, 34 persons were granted citizenship in Austria based on extraordinary contribution to the State.[1257]

The creation of a legal entitlement to the grant of citizenship by investment appears to be inconsistent with the history of the Austrian citizenship law[1258] and the consistent immigration practices in Austria, which are very restrictive and underpinned by concerns to prevent foreign incursion[1259] – in particular after the citizenship reform in 1998, which required "relevant knowledge of the German language" for citizenship (Section 10a ACA), but also through reform to the Aliens Act,[1260] which now also requires sufficient knowledge of the German language.

Given the omission of three crucial requirements for naturalisation, the award of the Austrian citizenship in accordance with Section 10(6) ACA can also be referred to as privileged citizenship, especially since the entry into force of the amendment to citizenship requirements in 2005, which introduced the requirement for command of the German language and proof of basic knowledge of the democratic order and historical foundations of Austria (Section 10a(1) ACA), with some exceptions, one of them naturalisations pursuant to 10 (6) ACA (Section 10a(2)(1) ACA).[1261] Only exceptional contributions rendered and yet to be rendered to the Republic of Austria would need to be demonstrated.[1262] Section 10(6) ACA already requires this cumulative coincidence of rendered and yet to be rendered contributions to the Republic of Austria, and in *Kleeber's* opinion, these actual and planned extraordinary

---

1256 http://www.parlament.gv.at/PAKT/VHG/XXIV/J/J_04270/fname_178160.pdf; last accessed on 21 September 2012

1257 For greater detail on the Citizenship by Investment in Austria: KLEEBER (2007)

1258 cf. KLEEBER (2007)

1259 cf. KLEEBER (2007)

1260 "*Niederlassungs- und Aufenthaltsgesetz*", BGBl 2005/100, which entered into force on 1 January, 2006

1261 cf. KLEEBER (2007)

1262 cf. KLEEBER (2007)

contributions to the State are enough to establish a sufficient close relationship to the domestic polity.[1263]

15.1.5 Discretion of the State and Federal Governments

The constituent elements of "extraordinary" and "in the particular interest" are concerned with vague concepts of law, which are not elaborated further in the ACA, and allow the Austrian State and Federal Governments a considerable discretion in deciding whether in their view the basic requirements for citizenship and the stipulations of the ACA and the relevant constitutional provisions are met. This includes finding the absence of a conviction (Section 10(1)(2) ACA) – in particular on grounds of a financial offence (Section 10(1)(3),(4) ACA); the non-impairment of the international relations of the Republic of Austria (Section 10(1)(5) ACA); that the grant in the interest of the Republic and preserves public peace, order and security (Section 10(1)(6) ACA); and the absence of relations with foreign States which would harm the interests of the Republic (Section 10(1)(8) ACA). On all these requirements the Federal Government has no competence to overrule the authority of the State Government. The Federal Government only decides on whether the granting of citizenship is ultimately in the interest of the Austrian Republic. Furthermore, the applicant must not have been refused residence, nor can there be a deportation order against her, nor should there be an affiliation to a criminal, extremist or terrorist group.[1264]

Under current Austrian citizenship law there is no individual right to the grant of Citizenship-by-Investment. By virtue of the connection to a positive confirmation of the State interest, the decision falls predominantly within the political scope of co-decision by the Federal Government. The applicant nevertheless has a subjective right to an error-free discretionary decision which results from the general principle of equality (Article 7(1)(1) ÖB-VG, although it is questionable as to whether this provision also applies to foreigners who are in the process

[1263] cf. KLEEBER (2007)
[1264] cf. KLEEBER (2007)

of applying for citizenship) and from customary Austrian administrative practice in this area. The classification of the confirmation as a decision and the possibility of legal recourse for the applicant thereby opened, contribute to disciplining the Austrian Federal Government to actually observe these most recently mentioned principles in individual cases, which is in the general public interest and justified by the constitution.

The constitution requires that an individual legal formative act must also be verifiable.[1265] According to the principle of unity of the legal system, the constitutional control mechanisms should not be undermined by unverifiable forms of action, at least not by the simple legislator.[1266] If the legislature enacts a standard for decision under federal constitutional law, to eliminate the possibility of its being overturned such a standard fit the basic constitutional order.[1267] Section 10(6) ACA transfers the competence to examine the naturalisation requirement of extraordinary contribution *ex lege* to the Austrian Federal Government and, in a case of affirmation, the other review to the relevant state government.[1268]

15.1.6 Analysis of central characteristics of the conditions

15.1.6.1 "Extraordinary"

A material condition for the grant of citizenship in Austria – equally the general requirements for naturalisation and those under *ius doni* provisions of Section 10 (6) ACA – is the absence of circumstances indicative of a lack of integrity or unreliable character on the part of the applicant. As a catch-all and general clause, Section 10(1)(6) ACA brings "public safety" into consideration, which as a general provision for all statutory Austrian legal rights, therefore also includes those of international and public international law ratified by the Republic of Austria and which are thus binding on all branches of public authority in Austria. As a result of the statutory reservation principle, Austrian citizenship "by investment"

1265 cf. KLEEBER (2007)
1266 cf. KLEEBER (2007)
1267 ÖVfGH, ÖVfSlg. 11.584, 11.756, 11.972
1268 cf. KLEEBER (2007); cf. *Thienel* in THIENEL/SCHULEV-STEINDL (2009); *Kucsko-Stadlmayer* in WALTER/MAYER/KUCSKO-STADLMAYER (2007)

may only be granted on the basis of a formal law and must not cause the violation of any legislative standards protected within the meaning of Section 10(1)(6) ACA. However, this condition has to be evaluated and decided on exclusively by the relevant state government.

The ACA uses a series of indefinite legal concepts which are (or used to be) specified by the Austrian Federal Interior Ministry (ÖBMI) in internal "policy" documents, but however, remain largely opaque to the public.[1269] Interpreted systematically, the term "extraordinary" within the meaning of Section 10(6) ACA can be taken to mean that the applicant must contribute something to the Republic of Austria, not required of him under the general requirements of ACA.[1270] According to the views presented here, it is not enough for the applicant to fulfil the general requirements for naturalisation in accordance with the ACA particularly well or better than average. Rather, there must be a contribution to an area which – bearing in mind that the Austrian Federal Government as part of the State executive is in particular bound by the principle of legal equality (Article 1 ÖB-VG) – clearly sets him apart from the majority of applicants and through this supports something felt to be essential to the Republic of Austria – which is supported by the wording of Section 10(6) ACA "in the *special* interest of the Republic", as well as Section 11a(4)(4) ACA, which simply provides for "interest". Against this background, only contributions which exceed those normally made by other people with the same level of wealth, talent and skills would be expected to qualify. It can be deduced from the judgments of the *Austrian Higher Administrative Court* (ÖVwGH)[1271] that a contribution is required which differs from those of other people. The other specific characteristics of qualifying extraordinary contributions are a matter for the representatives of the respective State governments to decide, given the undefined legal concepts of "extraordinary contribution" and the "special interest".[1272]

[1269] http://www.parlament.gv.at/PAKT/VHG/XXIV/J/J_04270/fname_178160.pdf; last accessed on 21 September 2012

[1270] cf. Section 7.6.5.

[1271] For example, ÖVwGH judgment of 27 August 1998, Case 93/13/0023; judgment of 15 December 1976, Case 2004/76

[1272] cf. KLEEBER (2007)

15.1.6.2 "In the interest of the Republic of Austria"

What "in the *special* interest of the Republic" means cannot be inferred alone from the wording of Section 10(6) ACA, and must therefore be deduced from the legislative context or the regulatory purpose of the ACA. Unlike, for example, in the citizenship law of St. Kitts and Nevis or Dominica (Commonwealth of Dominica), the criteria to acquire Citizenship-by-Investment are not legally specified – for a European country like Austria, surprisingly. Rather, they are left up to the ultimate discretion of the Austrian Federal Government.

As already mentioned, Section 10(6) ACA, through the use of the indefinite legal terms "extraordinary" and "of special interest" leaves substantial leeway for government action. The decision-making powers of the Austrian Government is equally derived from Article 11(1)(1) ÖB-VG, according to which citizenship or the definition of the relevant qualifying material criteria is a federal matter.

In light of the fact that no restrictions in its scope of application can be deduced from the formulation "decisions under this Federal Act" in Section 11 ACA, in the exercise of this scope the directive of Section 11 ACA should be observed, according to which, the overall behaviour of the foreigner in relation to the general good, the public interest and the extent of his integration should be taken into account (Section 11(1) ACA). In making this determination, the relevant Austrian state government is absolutely bound by the principle of statutory reserve and supremacy of law, which can be implied from Article 1 ÖB-VG, and which is directly expressed in Article 18(1) of the Austrian Federal Constitution. According to these principles, all public administration must be exercised only on the basis of the law. This includes, in particular, the orientation of foreigners in the social, economic and cultural life in Austria and the commitment to the fundamental values of a democratic European State and society (Section 11(2) ACA). Based on this directive, an extraordinary contribution within the meaning of Section 10(6) ACA is in the interest of the Republic of Austria, if integration and cohesion of the Austrian society are further through the generation of significant welfare gains – such as in the case of scientific or economic contributions – or if the general identification with the Austrian values and social order are strengthened – as in the case of artistic or athletic performance.

Considering that economic exposure can be so concentrated that the fate of entire cities or regions is dependent on the existence of a single company, which provides social facilities such as apartments and kindergartens and social security systems along with jobs, this could also apply to investment. This would be especially the case when a specific investment creates a significant number of new jobs, the establishment of promising new business models such as in the IT sector or biotechnology support (or sustaining those existing) which sustainably benefit Austria in the context of economic globalisation, or which help prevent the migration or the demise of a company which is of vital importance to a region, especially in its capacity as an employer, and systemically so if the economic survival of a significant number of additional companies are affected by its decline. For example, one skilled worker can play a key role, if her employer can demonstrate that without this worker it would be unable to fulfil its orders, resulting in a permanent reduction in its operations, with the subsequent release of labour.[1273]

According to the ÖVwGH, this would require the applicant to possess a particular skillset and/or position in a company's operations (decision-making responsibility etc.) with specific control over employment, permitting the inference of responsibility and a job-preserving function,[1274] allowing attribution of the total economic benefit from his employment, in particular in terms of the transfers of investment capital and/or the creation and safeguarding of jobs associated therewith (as provided for in a different context by Section 24 Alien Employment Act).[1275]

A teleological interpretation of the relevant provisions of the ACA is offered under the above premise: the general interest in social cohesion

---

1273 cf. LOIBL-VAN HUSEN (1999)

1274 ÖVwGH, judgment of 19 January 1995, Case 94/09/0389; ÖVwGH, judgment of 27 March 2003, Case 2000/09/0020

1275 "Ausländerbeschäftigungsgesetz"

and subsidiarity of the State can be given priority over the rule-of-law-motivated public interest in the uniform application of the requirements for naturalisation according to the ACA and a restrictive application of exceptional rules. Nevertheless, even under these conditions all relevant legal criteria, the constitutional postulates of democracy and rule of law (Article 1 ÖB-VG), the general principle of equality (Article 7 ÖB-VG, which generally however only applies to citizens) and the protection of minorities (Article 8 ÖB-VG) should be adequately taken into account and defined comprehensibly. Under these conditions, Citizenship-by-Investment as an "extraordinary contribution" includes conformity with the constitution, in accordance with Section 10(6) ACA.

15.1.6.3 Concretisation of the concept of extraordinary contribution

A possible criterion for the concretisation of the concept of extraordinary contribution, within the meaning of Section 10(6) ACA is provided by a regulation of the government of Burgenland. According to this, the applicant must make a contribution which promotes Burgenland's economy through investments, by establishing a company in Burgenland or investing in sporting events, which increase the attractiveness of Burgenland to tourists. Likewise, it may be sufficient that the applicant promotes folk festivals and the preservation of local traditions in Burgenland through donations. The award of citizenship on the basis of an investment can also be awarded under certain conditions. An example of such a conditional naturalisation is the Russian entrepreneur *Wolkow*, who was offered Austrian citizenship to settle in Burgenland, maintain his investment for five years and to attend sporting events in Burgenland.[1276]

15.1.6.4 Requirement for a qualified investment

Not every investment in Austria suffices for the acquisition of citizenship. It may be sufficient, however, that a foreign investor's contribution is in the form of technical innovations benefiting Austria, or that it creates

1276 http://www.uni-graz.at/verfrecht_fall_100203_poeschl.pdf; last accessed on 21 September 2012.

a substantial number of new jobs.[1277] Given the absence of a legislative definition, the specific number of new jobs required for the acquisition of Austrian citizenship cannot be quantified in absolute terms, as within the sense of the function of Citizenship-by-Investment, the value of jobs created also depends on the market segment they are created in, and their importance in the context of globalisation, so that in the high-technology and information technology segments, a much smaller number of new jobs may suffice, when compared for example to food retail or hotels. Furthermore, it is also possible to grant Austrian citizenship to an investor who does not establish a new company in Austria, but who saves an existing one from insolvency – especially in regions that are substantially dependent on the continued existence of ailing businesses, if the latter supports, for example, social institutions, or if a substantial pension liability were brought into question by the collapse of a company.

To acquire Austrian citizenship, the applicant can participate, for example, in a joint venture or make substantial direct investments which help create new jobs or to generate new export earnings.[1278]

It is worth mentioning, on the one hand that Austria requires multi-year residence in Austria as a supplementary condition of citizenship (Section 10(1)(1) ACA), and on the other hand offers a Citizenship-by-Investment facility which only requires a capital commitment, includes a considerable discretion for the Austrian state and Federal governments, and waives the usual legal requirements.[1279] The governmental discretion extends however only to the extent that the government may confirm that an application is in accordance with Section 10(6) ACA, while the justiciable administrative decision rests with the local state government,[1280] according to Section 39(1) and (2) ACA. The discretion must be exercised within the meaning of this Act (Section 130(2) ÖB-VG).

1277 cf. DZANKIC (2012)
1278 KLEEBER (2007); cf. also DZANKIC (2012); and KÄLIN (2014)
1279 KLEEBER (2007); DZANKIC (2012)
1280 KLEEBER (2007)

15.1.7 Formal requirements of Citizenship-by-Investment

15.1.7.1 Comprehensive obligation of openness on the investor

To ensure that the above material requirements for naturalisation are fulfilled in each individual case, and to prevent the practical problems that would arise from the revocation of citizenship from occurring, in addition to the presentation of the rather obvious documents such as an identity card and birth or marital certificates, it is particularly necessary that the applicant provides a certificate of good conduct, a detailed business or project plan, and good business references. Given that Citizenship-by-Investment is concerned with an absolute exception to the usual process for granting citizenship whose criteria are not defined by law in detail, the comprehensive binding of the Austrian public authority to the rule of law (Article 1 ÖB-VG) requires that the applicant must provide reliable written evidence in the original, which must be capable in the case of the business or project plan provided to communicate the feasibility and sustainability of the project offered without any further statements being required. The transmission of these documents by email may well be recognised as valid, if their submission is witnessed under a valid electronic signature, within the meaning of Section 2(3) of the Austrian Signature Act (ÖSiG).[1281]

15.1.8 Legal consequences of a successful application

15.1.8.1 Acquisition of unimpaired citizenship

On approval of an application for citizenship based on outstanding contribution, in accordance with Section 10(6) ACA, the applicant acquires the unimpaired status of Austrian an citizen – this is supported by Article 6(1) ÖB-VG, which provides for a uniform citizenship in the Republic of Austria, i.e. not graded by the extent of political or other rights, unlike in the UK for example.[1282]

1281 Federal Law on Electronic Signatures (Austrian Signature Act, ÖSigG); StF: BGBl. I Nr. 190/1999 (NR: GP XX RV 1999 AB 2065 p. 180; BR: AB 6065 p. 657), last amended by BGBl. I No. 75/2010 (NR: GP XXIV RV 750 AB 832 p. 73; BR: AB 8370 p. 787)

1282 For the citizenship law of The UK, cf. section 7.2.

15.1.8.2 Discretionary treatment

The constitutional right, not expressly regulated in the ÖB-VG on informational self-determination, has been written into law since the nineteen-seventies in a series of national, international and European legal instruments,[1283] such as in particular through the ÖDSG 2000.[1284] The latter regulations allow administrative bodies involved in the decision on the grant of citizenship based on extraordinary contribution, the discretionary handling of personal data. It is generally prohibited for the authority mentioned to publish or communicate the award of a nationality or the decision underlying it to other subjects of international law, because the right of informational self-determination includes objective components which create nearly universal protection. Unlike the *ius doni* provisions in the laws of e.g. St. Kitts and Nevis, Antigua and Barbuda, or Malta, Citizenship-by-Investment in Austria is characterised by far-reaching discretionary powers for the Federal Government partly to expose an act of investment-driven acquisition of citizenship to public scrutiny.[1285] This is, as already stated, not unproblematic from the perspective of the rule of law.

15.1.8.3 No requirement to relinquish current citizenships

Breaking with the principle that the award of Austrian citizenship presupposes renunciation of any previous citizenship, under the provisions of Section 10(6), this can be retained as an exception. On the one hand, this seems reasonable, because it would be practically much more difficult to channel direct investments to Austria under conditions of a compulsion to renounce other citizenships. On the other hand, the opportunity offered by Section 10(6) ACA for multiple nationalities in Austria, is questionable in relation to the general principle of equality (Article 7(1)(1) ÖB-VG) and the principle of non-discrimination laid down in the ÖB-VG (Article 1 ÖB-VG), because one of the chief principles of the Austrian legal system is to handle exceptions from the legal

---

[1283] cf. Austrian Commission of Jurists (2009) pp. 1 ff.
[1284] cf. Austrian Commission of Jurists (2009)
[1285] cf. KLEEBER (2007); DZANKIC (2012)

rules restrictively. On the other hand, it could be argued on the basis of the wording of Article 7(1)(1) ÖB-VG ("all citizens") that Austrian public authorities and therefore also the decision-making authorities responsible for citizenship, are only committed to equality of treatment to those who are already in possession of Austrian citizenship.

15.1.9 Discussion and evaluation

15.1.9.1 Worldwide travel, and freedom of trade and freedom of establishment in Europe

Foreign investors sometimes encounter considerable practical problems in meeting the extremely restrictive requirements of Austrian citizenship law, as presented in the introduction.[1286] In addition to the acquisition of citizenship, one of the outstanding benefits associated with the acquisition of Austrian nationality "by investment", is that the investor is entitled to an Austrian passport to travel visa-free worldwide, and to freely choose his/her place of residence both in the EU and in Switzerland. A compulsion to stay or to settle in Austria with the awarding of Citizenship-by-Investment is as little justified, however, as a commitment by the applicant to pay tax on her worldwide income in Austria. In the latter case, consequences only arise if she actually chooses his domicile or habitual residence permanently in Austria.[1287]

15.1.9.2 Exceeding the boundary between the State and private?

As a result of the extensive discretion the Austrian Federal Government has in the granting of citizenship pursuant to Section 10(6) ACA, it seems problematic that it is set apart from the usual statutory requirements for naturalisation. Insofar as Citizenship-by-Investment is also equated with other extraordinary contributions to the State, as Section 10(6) ACA allows, the boundary between public and private spheres

---

1286 http://www.uni-graz.at/verfrecht_fall_100203_poeschl.pdf; last accessed on 21 September 2012; cf. also KLEEBER (2007)

1287 cf. KÄLIN (2014)

could be exceeded, especially as the reputational gains from cultural, sports or academic achievements are not readily available for purchase.[1288] On the other hand, the naturalisation provisions of the ACA have constitutional status and permit the Austrian Federal Government to exercise this discretion, which has also been substantiated by the Ministry of Interior in an internal directive.[1289]

15.1.9.3 Breach of the principles of equal treatment and non-discrimination?

According to the view represented by *Dzankic*,[1290] which is unlike that of *Kleeber*,[1291] discretionary naturalisation under Section 10(6) ACA violates the constitutional principle of equal treatment in two instances (Article 7(1) ÖB-VG). This stipulates that all citizens are equal before the law (Article 7(1)(1) ÖB-VG). Yet, the beneficiary investors receive preferential treatment over other applicants with regard to the citizenship requirements needing to be met. In addition, they are allowed to retain their original citizenships, and they are thereby able to benefit from multiple citizenship. If *Dzankic* bases this view on Austrian constitutional law, it is countered by the fact that the wording of Article 7(1)(1) ÖB-VG speaks exclusively of "all citizens", but not "everyone", which emphasises the limitation of its personal scope to natural persons who are already Austrian citizens. Therefore, *Dzankic's* concerns regarding the acquisition criteria appear unconvincing: a general right of equal treatment for everyone can at best be deduced from international law in Article 2(1) of the UDHR, "*everyone has a right to the rights and freedoms in this Declaration, without distinction of any kind such as according to ...national ... origin*" read with the entitlement in Article 7 to equal treatment for any natural person (Article 7(1) UDHR) and equal protection against discrimination (Article 7(2) UDHR). While the UDHR was not intended be legally binding, being embodied in a declaration, it might have indeed become binding as customary law after being widely

---

1288 cf. DZANKIC (2012) (with reference to *Walzer*); and KLEEBER (2007)
1289 KLEEBER (2007)
1290 cf. DZANKIC (2012)
1291 cf. KLEEBER (2007)

accepted and consistently invoked by states for more than sixty years.[1292] Morover, the Preamble of the ECHR makes clear that this instrument has been adopted by taking into consideration the UDHR aimining *"at securing the universal and effective recognition and observance of the Rights therein designed"*.[1293] Unquestionably, the ECHR was intended to be consistent with the UDHR priciples and values.[1294] In addition and as already explained in the context of ECHR establishing discrimination might prove difficult given that not every difference in treatment constitutes discrimination but only such discriminatory measures which have no objective and reasonable justification.

15.2 Montenegro

15.2.1 State structural parameters

As a country located on the coast of the south-eastern Adriatic, Montenegro, with its capital Podgorica and its 21 (large) municipalities (*Opštine*) for which Article 113 et seq. of the Montenegrin Constitution (MC)[1295] provides the right of local self-government, borders the Balkan States of Croatia, Bosnia and Herzegovina, Serbia, Albania and Kosovo. Concerning its democratic self-conception, Article 1(1) MC stipulates that Montenegro is an independent and sovereign State with a republican form of government. The bearers of its sovereignty are the citizens of Montenegro (Article 2(1) MC) – currently numbering about 625,000 persons. State authority in Montenegro must be exercised directly and through freely elected representatives (Article 2(2) MC). Covering a total area of about 13,812 square kilometres, the Montenegrin territory places Montenegro in the group of small European States, and is united and inalienable pursuant to Article 3

1292 On the binding nature of UDHR see e.g. the Special Representative of the UN Commission on Human Rights, R. Gallindo Pohl's Report on the Human Rights Situation in the Islamic Republic of Iran (UN Doc. E/CN.4/1987/23) pp. 4-5

1293 UDHR Preamble

1294 GROVER (2010) p. 70

1295 The Constitution of the Republic of Montenegro (MC) and the Constitutional Law for the implementation of the Constitution of Montenegro, adopted on 19 October 2007; published online at http://www.comparativeconstitutionsproject.org/files/Montenegro_2007.pdf, last accessed on 21 September 2012

MC. Montenegro has a long and eventful history, which dates back to the Bronze Age.[1296]

The Republic of Montenegro respects and protects the rights and freedoms of its citizens (Article 6(1) MC), which are defined by Article 6(2) MC as inviolable and which should be respected by everyone (Article 6(3) MC). Among the aforementioned rights and freedoms, the express guarantee of human dignity in Article 28(2) MC is of significance. Montenegro was part of the Socialist Federal Republic of Yugoslavia and then of the common state with Serbia. Montenegro regained its former independence following a referendum on 3 June 2006. The right to request a referendum is exclusively that of the Montenegrin Parliament (Article 82(11) MC). The Constitution provides political participation in the form of elections and referendums (Article 45 MC). Its origin in the former Yugoslavia is, for example, reflected in the fact that the Serbian, Bosnian, Albanian and Croatian languages are officially recognised (Article 13(3) MC).

Concerning its citizenship,[1297] the regaining of its independence is reflected in the fact that all Montenegrin citizens who had other citizenships prior to 3 June 2006, are entitled to retain their existing nationality until a bilateral agreement with the respective State of origin enters into force, but not for longer than one year after the entry into force of the Montenegrin Constitution. (Article 12 of the Annex to the MC).

Montenegro is a candidate country for EU membership, and relatively advanced in its negotiations for accession. As such, it faces pre-accession conditionality[1298] pressures from the EU which have implications on its Citizenship-by-Investment practices.

[1296] For a history of Montenegro cf. ANRDIJASEVIC/RASTODER (2006)

[1297] For Montenegrin citizenship cf. http://www.mip.gov.me/en/index.php/Consular-functions/citizenship.html, last accessed on 21 September 2012, DZANKIC (2010); DZANKIC (2012); see also http://www.migration-online.de/data/publikationen_datei_1071768146.pdf, last accessed on 21 September 2012

[1298] For a discussion of EU enlargement and pre-accession conditionality, see KOCHENOV (2008)

15.2.2 Naturalisation statistics

Montenegro does not publish statistics on naturalisations. However, in 2011 and 2013, respectively, a Member of Parliament asked about naturalisation rates in a parliamentary session. The response from the Government[1299] indicated that between May 2008 and the end of 2014, a total of 25,705 persons were naturalised.[1300] There was no information provided on naturalisations on grounds of Article 12(1)(2) MNA specifically. Based on Article 12 MNA, from the beginning of its implementation until today, a total of 184 applicants have acquired Montenegrin citizenship – this is the total for all different categories defined in the Article 12 and there are no specific statistical data distinguishing between the categories mentioned in the Article. It is however thought that about 10 to 20 naturalisations per year occur under these *ius doni* provisions.

This means that, with a total population of about 620,000, *ius doni* naturalisations are in any event very low and also low in comparison to its normal naturalisation rate. The naturalisation to population ratio is low at 0.7% per year.

15.2.3 Constitutional determinants of citizenship

Under Article 12(1) MC, Montenegrin citizenship is applicable in Montenegro. The Republic of Montenegro protects the rights and interests of Montenegrin citizens (Article 12(2) MC). Accordingly, no Montenegrin citizen should be deported or extradited to another State, without international obligations under public international law expressly obliging Montenegro to this (Article 12(3) MC). In particular, Article 12(3) MC should be seen against the background that Montenegro is a Member State of the United Nations (UN), the World Trade Organisation (WTO), the OSCE and the Council of Europe, and a candidate country for EU membership and NATO. Montenegro

---

1299 Government replies to parliamentary questions of 22 July 2011 and of 18 March 2013

1300 http://www.mup.gov.me/biblioteka/izvjestaji?alphabet=lat, last accessed 11 February 2015

undertakes in this respect to maintain cooperative friendly relations with other States and to cooperate with regional and international organisations which follow the principles and rules of international law (Article 15(1) MC).

Article 1 of the Montenegrin Nationality Act (MNA)[1301] specifies the constitutional determinants of Montenegrin citizenship and defines these as the legal connection between a physical person and Montenegro, without regard to either his/her national or ethnic origin (Article 1(2) MNA). The MNA regulates the manner and the conditions for acquisition and loss of Montenegrin citizenship (Article 1(1) MNA). The various modes of acquisition of citizenship begin in Article 4 MNA with the acquisition of nationality by birth, which implies that *ius sanguinis* is the dominant Montenegrin principle for acquisition of citizenship.

15.2.4 General naturalisation requirements

The acquisition of Montenegrin citizenship by naturalisation is governed by Articles 8 et seq. MNA. According to this, an alien can acquire Montenegrin citizenship on application, if she meets the following requirements: she must first be 18 years old (Article 8(1) MNA); second, she must relinquish her previous citizenship (Article 8(2) MNA); third, she must have resided lawfully in Montenegro for an uninterrupted period of 10 years before applying (Article 8(3) MNA); fourth, she must earn a constant regular income in Montenegro which ensures her material and social security (Article 8(4) MNA); fifth, she must not have been sentenced in Montenegro or elsewhere to a minimum prison sentence of one year for a crime prosecuted *ex officio*, unless the conviction was overturned in the meantime (Article 8(5) MNA); sixth, she must demonstrate sufficient knowledge and basic command of the Montenegrin language (Article 8(6) MNA); and, seventh, she must have complied with all tax and other legal obligations (Article 8(7) MNA).

[1301] Nationality Law of the Republic of Montenegro – the Montenegrin Nationality Act (MNA) – published in the Official Gazette No. 13/2008; based on Article 95(3) of the Constitution of Montenegro, Podgorica entered into force on 14 February 2008, No. 01-288/2; published online at http://www.unhcr.org/refworld/pdfid/47e117082.pdf; last accessed on 21 September 2012

15.2.5 Conditions for naturalisation based on extraordinary contribution to the State

15.2.5.1 Article 12 MNA as the legal basis for Citizenship-by-Investment in Montenegro

Although a prior common practice existed, in June 2010 a more formal Citizenship-by-Investment programme was introduced in Montenegro, whereby citizenship could be acquired by investing in the Montenegrin economy or for "consideration", provided that the investment amount is in any case at least EUR 500,000.[1302] As certain EU countries threatened to reintroduce visas for Montenegrin citizens shortly after the launch of this "programme", it was announced that it would be suspended. However, it is understood that the government reverted to its discretionary Citizenship-by-Investment practice on a case-by-case basis as was done earlier, probably still guided by the decision published in 2010 and thus probably more carefully.

The legal basis for this Montenegrin Citizenship-by-Investment practice is Article 12(1)(2) MNA. In terms of a privileged naturalisation standard, Article 12 MNA provides for an exception to the above mentioned general conditions for naturalisation in Montenegro by determining that as a legal basis of Montenegrin Citizenship-by-Investment, a person of full age who does not fulfil the requirements of Article 8 MNA can be awarded the Montenegrin citizenship for contribution to the scientific, economic, cultural, sporting, national or other interest of Montenegro (Article 12(1) MNA).

15.2.5.2 Material conditions concerning Citizenship-by-Investment

Since Article 12(1) MNA does not further clarify the requirements of naturalisation on the basis of an investment in Montenegro, the naturalisation decision – unlike, for example in St. Kitts and Nevis or Malta – is predominantly within the political governmental scope

[1302] cf. DZANKIC (2012) and particularly DZANKIC (2010); Decree of Promulgating the Law on Montenegrin Citizenship (Official Gazette of Montenegro, No. 13/08 of 26 February 2008), Article 12.

of discretion. The decision on whether or not a contribution satisfies the requirements for a privileged citizenship is namely subject to discretionary decision by the Montenegrin Minister of the Interior, to whom the execution of the privileged naturalisation procedure is assigned.[1303] According to the view presented here, a subjective right of actual and potential investors can be derived from the constitutional right of access to information (Article 51 MC), under which at least the key criteria for decision should be disclosed, because a naturalisation process which is sufficiently fair and in keeping with the rule of law cannot otherwise be guaranteed. Just as in Austria, there is significant latitude for governmental action at the top political bodies in Montenegro, because Article 12(1) MNA is only very vague on the conditions of the grant and the interests of Montenegro.

It can be deduced, however, from the wording of Article 12(1) MC, that the contributions in question should serve the welfare of the Montenegrin community. Furthermore, Montenegrin Citizenship-by-Investment is not necessarily linked to physical presence such as a domestic residence – which is widely supported by the assumption that the domestic investment is in itself a viable basis for the robust anchoring of the investor to the domestic community.[1304] The applicant is not thereby bound to take up domestic residence but – as in Austria – is subject to the discretion of the Montenegrin Ministry of Interior regarding the final naturalisation decision.

In its decision of June 2010, the Montenegrin State Government affirmed (Article 100 MC) the substantive requirements for the privileged naturalisation in Montenegro.[1305] According to this, privileged Montenegrin citizenship is available to persons who invest in the Montenegrin economy or who bring substantial assets to the Republic of Montenegro.[1306]

[1303] DZANKIC (2010) p. 15
[1304] cf. DZANKIC (2012)
[1305] cf. DZANKIC (2010)
[1306] cf. DZANKIC (2010) pp. 15–16

According to Article 3 of the Government's 2010 decision, which however was suspended,[1307] this route was particularly open to proven investors with impeccable international reputation.

Furthermore, on the basis of Article 3 of the 2010 decision, the Montenegrin State Government has issued guidelines on the implementation of the criteria for capturing business and economic interests. According to this, a minimum investment of EUR 500,000 is required to qualify for privileged citizenship in Montenegro.[1308]

15.2.5.3 Formal requirements of Citizenship-by-Investment

The government should decide on the award of Montenegrin citizenship on the grounds mentioned in Article 12(1) MNA, after having obtained a binding decision or the opinion of the relevant administrative authority under Article 12 MNA (Article 12(2) MNA).

The amendments to the MNA which came into force in 2010 empowered the Montenegrin President (Article 11(5),(95) MC), the Prime Minister (Article 102(1)(1),(2) MC) and the Speaker of Parliament (Article 89(1) and (2) MC) to propose candidates for the grant of privileged citizenship.[1309] The Montenegrin Prime Minister thus represents the Montenegrin State Government and assumes its administrative authority (Article 102(2) MC). Nevertheless, the above-mentioned authorities are only authorised under applicable Montenegrin law to propose suitable candidates for naturalisation, while the final decision-making power, regarding the extent to which the contributions in question justifies the grant of Montenegrin citizenship, continues to remain with the Ministry of the Interior or the Secretary of the Interior.[1310] These decisions are also ultimately bound by any opinion requested of the Minister of Finance.[1311]

1307 cf. *supra*
1308 cf. DZANKIC (2010) p. 16
1309 cf. DZANKIC (2010)
1310 cf. DZANKIC (2012)
1311 cf. DZANKIC (2010)

As in Austria, the decision of the Government is binding on whether to grant Citizenship-by-Investment in Montenegro, i.e. the relevant authority may not grant privileged citizenship under Article 12(1) MNA, if the Montenegrin Government denies an interest in naturalisation. Article 12(2) MNA acknowledges the explicit duties of the various bodies involved in such decisions under the principle of separation of powers, as set out in Article 11 MC. According to Article 11(4) MC, the relationship between the State authorities should be balanced and should always be supported by a consistent mutual control.

15.2.6 Discussion and evaluation

With regards to Citizenship-by-Investment in Montenegro, the case of the naturalisation of former Thai Prime Minister *Thaksin Shinawatra* – who was suspected of corruption and is believed to have invested or promised to invest several million Euros in the Montenegrin tourist industry – is worth mentioning, a situation which only came to light following strenuous efforts by civil society organisations which demanded that the criteria for the award Montenegrin citizenships be published.[1312] The award of a Montenegrin passport and the granting of the privileged citizenship to *Shinawatra* generated lively debate, particularly in the Montenegrin mass media, NGOs and the interested public.[1313] A parliamentary spokeswoman announced that Montenegro would shortly adopt detailed rules, establishing a basis for predictable government decisions. This has however so far not been forthcoming.

15.2.7 De lege ferenda: requirement for increased investor due diligence

Since the import of capital is to some extent the key interest of the Montenegrin Government and the identity of the investor plays a rather subordinate role, and as there is no clear, thorough procedure in place to conduct appropriate due diligence on applicants for Citizenship-by-Investment, Montenegro is possibly also providing a loophole for people

[1312] cf. DZANKIC (2012)
[1313] cf. DZANKIC (2010); and DZANKIC (2012)

with dubious identities. *De lege ferenda* it would benefit the worldwide reputation of Montenegro, if the focus were not directed only on securing capital inflows in the form of direct investment, but also on in-depth due diligence and background verification of the investor. The *Shinawatra* case has shown that the public reputation of the State can be damaged by disregarding this eminently important aspect.

15.3 St. Kitts and Nevis[1314]

15.3.1 State structural parameters

With an area of approximately 270 square kilometres and a population of only around 50,000 inhabitants, 20,000 of whom alone live in the capital Basseterre, the Commonwealth State of St. Kitts and Nevis (official name: Federation of Saint Christopher and Nevis), belonging to the group of northern West Indies island states in the Caribbean, gained its full independence from the British colonial rule in 1983. Its form of government is a parliamentary monarchy in the Commonwealth. Ethnically, 94.3% of the inhabitants are Africans, 3.3% are mulatto, 0.9% Europeans and 1.5% other. With respect to faith, 34% of the inhabitants are Anglicans, 31% Methodists, 9% Moravians and 8% Catholics. Its official language is English.

15.3.2 Naturalisation statistics

In the years between 1990 and 2006, St. Kitts and Nevis naturalised or registered between 50 and 100 persons per year, a total of more than 2,000 and an average of about 75 per year. Of these, about 50% were from citizenship acquisitions by registration[1315] based on the *ius doni* provisions in the law.

Following the reform of the Citizenship-by-Investment programme in 2006–2007, the number of naturalisations under the programme

---

1314 The author was directly involved in advising the government of St. Kitts and Nevis with regard to the design and implementation of the 2006/2007 reform of its Citizenship-by-Investment programme and the introduction of the SIDF option at that time

1315 In St. Kitts and Nevis, oddly, Citizenship-by-Investment is based on citizenship by registration and not naturalisation

increased steadily every year, to reach a peak of about 1,000 citizenships granted in 2014.[1316] This means that, with a total population of about 50,000, Citizenship-by-Investment accounted for over 1,000% its normal naturalisation/registration rate. The naturalisation/registration to population ratio is very high at over 1.4 percent per year.

15.3.3 The Citizenship-by-Investment programme

15.3.3.1 Historical development lines and legal basis

St. Kitts and Nevis introduced its Citizenship-by-Investment programme (formerly known as the "Economic Citizenship Programme")[1317] in 1984, a year after gaining its independence from the UK. Worldwide, it is one of the oldest of its kind historically, and it followed the Caribbean nation's experience of extraordinary economic decline immediately after independence from the British mother country. An internationally very weak balance of payments, the barely existing competitiveness of its agricultural sector, and finally the fact that its domestic value creation was regularly affected by hurricanes, encouraged the political authorities in their decision to introduce specific programmes for direct investment in the domestic real estate sector and later in the sugar industry (Sugar Industry Diversification Foundation – SIDF).[1318] The legal basis of these programmes is the eighth Chapter of the St. Kitts and Nevis Constitution (SKN-C) and Section 3(5) of the St. Kitts and Nevis Citizenship Act, 1984, Cap. 1.05 (SKN-CA), as well as the St. Kitts and Nevis Citizenship-by-Investment Regulations, 2011 (Regulations), all as amended.

Oddly, in St. Kitts and Nevis, the *ius doni* provisions are dealt with as citizenship by registration and not naturalisation. Section 5 SKN-CA provides that "*a person registered under Section 3...shall be a citizen of St. Christopher and Nevis by registration as from the date on which he or she is registered*".

[1316] Henley & Partners estimates

[1317] For an authoritative treatment of the Citizenship by Investment Programme of St. Kitts and Nevis: http://ciu.gov.kn; KÄLIN (2014); cf. also DZANKIC (2012); and from an economic perspective, XU/EL-ASHRAM/GOLD (2015)

[1318] cf. http://ciu.gov.kn/?q=node/8, last accessed on 21 September 2012; DZANKIC (2012)

Naturalization is provided under a separate section (Section 6 SKN-CA) and unlike citizenship by registration, it requires that an oath of allegiance be sworn. Thus under the St. Kitts and Nevis Citizenship-by-Investment programme, no oath of allegiance is required.

15.3.3.2 Options for the applicant

The regulations promulgated based on the SKN-CA provisions provide for two options to choose from in order to earn the citizenship of St. Kitts and Nevis by investment, although legally there is also the option for Cabinet to grant citizenship by registration directly to someone who invests substantially in the country, directly based on Section 5(3) SKN-CA.

According to the regulations, suitable investments can be made under certain conditions either in the real estate sector or through a contribution to the SIDF. This must be viewed against the background that, as already mentioned, the State-run sugar factory, which once formed the economic backbone of the island State, had to be shut down in 2005 after decades of operating at a loss.

15.3.3.3 Promotion of domestic direct investments as a primary objective

The Citizenship-by-Investment programme provides significant relief to the usual requirements for naturalisation, in particular, the requirement for a continuous minimum stay of 14 years (Article 92 SKN-C). Anyone can be granted the citizenship of St. Kitts and Nevis, on application, if the Cabinet is convinced that they have or will invest "substantially"[1319] in St. Kitts and Nevis (Section 3(5) SKN-C). A direct investment to the value of USD 400,000[1320] in one of the country's State Government "approved investment projects" is required.[1321]

Unlike the comparable programmes in the US, Canada, Belgium, Australia and Singapore, the "Economic Citizenship Programme" not

---

1319 cf. http://ciu.gov.kn/?q=node/8, last accessed on 21 September 2012
1320 The official currency of St. Kitts and Nevis is the Eastern Caribbean dollar (XCD, or EC$)
1321 cf. KÄLIN (2014); KLEEBER (2007)

only waived the requirement of domestic residence, but has also derogated from the otherwise usual criteria for naturalisation such as mastery of the local language, or proof of knowledge of the State and/or its history, as the focus is on the import of capital.[1322]

15.3.3.4 Investment in the real estate sector

The overriding concern for the promotion of investment in the real estate sector by means of the Citizenship-by-Investment programme is to support the domestic tourism sector – as an economic factor, this is of paramount importance to island States which are undiversified and vulnerable to natural disasters – and for this reason the investor does not have a free selection of investment property: eligible projects are published by the Government in a regularly updated list[1323] and include, for example, tourist resorts, the expansion of the marina infrastructure and the construction of golf courses – all an expression of the public intention to make the Caribbean country, which was battered after the acquisition of its independence, into an attractive destination for tourists, thus providing it with a new economic basis.[1324]

15.3.3.5 The SIDF contribution option

Should the applicant opt for a non-refundable contribution to the SIDF of St. Kitts and Nevis (SIDF option), this can support the grant of citizenship under the predetermined minimum investment criterion, if it is channelled into this foundation– this is a public and quasi sovereign wealth fund institution, which supports unemployed former sugar industry workers and funds research and development for sustainable economic activity.[1325]

The "SIDF option", offered to interested investors since 2006, must be viewed against the background that St. Kitts and Nevis was under considerable pressure from both the EU and the World Trade Organisation

[1322] cf. DZANKIC (2012)
[1323] cf. www.ciu.gov.kn
[1324] cf. DZANKIC (2012)
[1325] cf. http://www.ciu.gov.kn/?q=node/13; last accessed on 21 September 2012

(WTO) in its sugar production, which ceased to be competitive in the world market due to high production costs.[1326]

The SIDF has seen a significant increase in deposits and assets in the years particularly between 2010 until 2013 when last data is available (estimates from the IMF). The total assets of the SIDF exceeded 15 percent of GDP in 2012.

SIDF Deposits and Assets (in percent of GDP)

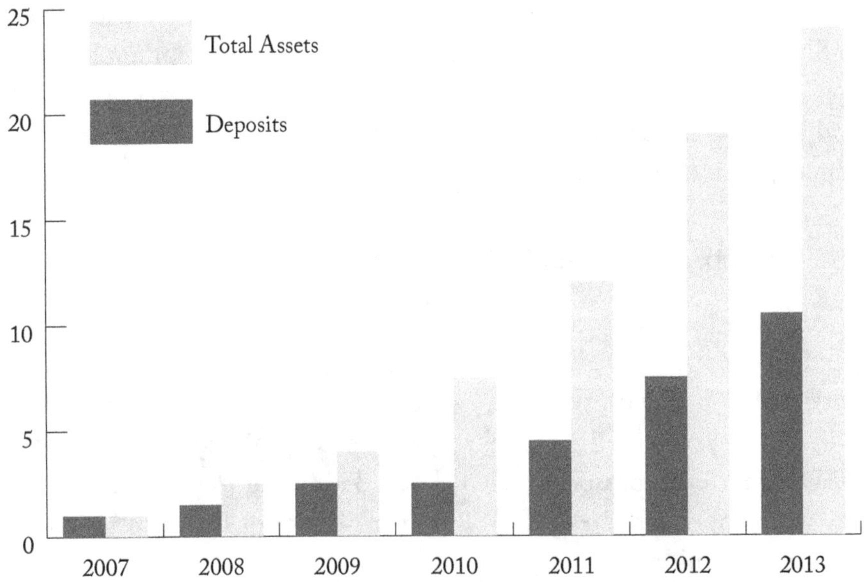

Sources: 2007-2011 data from SIDF financial statements, 2012-13 from authorities and IMF staff

15.3.3.6 Minimum investment amounts

While the investment in the real estate sector requires an investment of at least USD 400,000 per application (which can include a principal applicant and his family), the SIDF option requires a contribution of at least USD 250,000 (for a single applicant, and which, however – unlike the real estate option – includes all fees in connection with the

[1326] cf. DZANKIC (2012)

acquisition of citizenship).[1327] In the case of the SIDF option, the minimum contribution increases to USD 300,000 for up to three-member families, to USD 350,000 for up to five-member families, and to USD 450,000 for more than five-member families.[1328]

15.3.3.7 Application process

Citizenship-by-Investment must be applied for through one of the local service providers authorised by the government's *Financial Services Regulatory Commission*, which must have proven relevant experience (Section 2 of the Citizenship-by-Investment Programme Regulations of St. Kitts and Nevis).[1329] Applicants have to complete a comprehensive application form and answer detailed questions regarding their personal and business background, as well as provide numerous documents to support their applications.[1330]

15.3.3.8 Application costs

Apart from the investment-related costs, further fees, which include in particular a one-off registration fee, are charged for the granting of the Citizenship-by-Investment. As stated on the official website[1331] of the Government of St. Kitts and Nevis, the fee for registration is USD 47, USD 32 for each passport issued, USD 35,000 for the registration of the main applicant and USD 15,000 per person for the registration of spouse and children.

The other costs include the fees for the authorised local service provider's professional services, comprehensive due diligence[1332] – according to official government figures this amounts to USD 7,500 and another USD 4,000 for the acquisition of background information and handling charges for any other parties aged 16 and over.[1333] The due diligence of

[1327] cf. http://www.ciu.gov.kn/?q=node/13, last accessed on 21 September 2012
[1328] See KÄLIN (2014) and www.ciu.gov.kn
[1329] http://www.ciu.gov.kn/?q=node/14, last accessed on 21 September 2012
[1330] cf. *supra*
[1331] http://ciu.gov.kn/, last accessed on 21 September 2014
[1332] For the requirement of comprehensive investor due diligence cf. *supra*
[1333] http://www.ciu.gov.kn/?q=node/57, last accessed on 21 September 2014

potential new citizens, in view of the required investment amounts and the resulting risks, is very comprehensive.

15.3.3.9 Legal consequences in case of a successful application

Successful applicants receive citizenship of St. Kitts and Nevis, which comes with a number of privileges that result from the formal bond between the individual and the country of St. Kitts and Nevis associated with citizenship.[1334] Furthermore, as a CARICOM citizen a number of privileges are acquired that apply throughout CARICOM and in particular the OECS. Citizenship acquired by registration through the St. Kitts and Nevis Citizenship-by-Investment programme however is not equal to citizenship acquired through normal naturalisation or registration, as Section 3(5) of the SKN-CA does not afford voting rights if citizenship was acquired under the Citizenship-by-Investment program. Section 3(5) provides for citizens to be "*registered as a citizen of St. Kitts and Nevis without any rights of voting save under and in accordance with the provisions of any law governing the qualification of voters, if the Cabinet is satisfied that such person has invested substantially in St. Christopher and Nevis.*"

The successful applicant may apply for a passport, which in particular allows him visa-free travel in the British Commonwealth and many other countries – including Hong Kong and Switzerland – and the EU Member States.[1335] Following the 2009 Visa Agreement with the EU, nationals of St. Kitts and Nevis are entitled to enter one of the current Schengen Member States for up to three months within a period of six months. Article 1 of the Visa Agreement with the EU permits citizens of the EU and St. Kitts and Nevis visa-free travel for a maximum of three months in any six-month period in each other's territory.

1334 cf. DZANKIC (2012)

1335 http://www.ciu.gov.kn/?q=node/9, last accessed on 21 September 2014

15.3.4 Discussion and evaluation

15.3.4.1 Transparency and rule of law

Considered as a whole, the Citizenship-by-Investment programme of St. Kitts and Nevis seems detailed and mature when compared directly to similar programmes in e.g. Austria.[1336] The decision whether citizenship should be awarded on the basis of extraordinary contributions to the State in Austria, lies primarily at the Government's discretion, without a definition of the criteria which must be met by the applicant in law. The Citizenship-by-Investment programme of St. Kitts and Nevis distinguishes itself positively in terms of its transparency and certainty, from the point of view of the rule of law.

15.3.4.2 A safe haven for investors

On the one hand, it is no surprise that the Citizenship-by-Investment programme of St. Kitts and Nevis has now found recognition worldwide. No small token of this recognition is the Visa Agreement with the EU mentioned *supra*. Also in view of the domestic tax exemption and the relative stability of St. Kitts and Nevis, its geographic location and geopolitical non-relevance, the country represents a "safe haven" from the investor's perspective.

15.3.4.3 Economic impact and social return on investment

Given the excessive public debt created by many Western welfare states,[1337] which ultimately results from the shift in attitudes towards entitlement since the nineteen-sixties in wide sections of the population,[1338] it appears increasingly important under the conditions of economic globalisation, that the State can focus on its specific original core tasks, which include for instance providing an adequate supply of schools, police services and the administration of justice. Only a "lean State", which focuses on specific sovereign core tasks, but performs these

[1336] cf. DZANKIC (2012)
[1337] cf. MOYO (2011) for a view on the issues regarding the (Western) welfare states
[1338] See e.g. SPICKER (2002); STANDING (2005)

well, can also consistently remain a strong State. Each US dollar and Euro can only be spent once, and a large part of the funds obtained by government redistribution which should be used to fulfil core State functions or the realisation of social projects actually "remain" in the redistribution administration.

In view of the foregoing considerations, a State-initiated, targeted support of selected market sectors by attracting foreign direct investment can represent a step in the right direction, if this supports the State in the performance of non-core tasks and optional core tasks, which benefit the internal cohesion of the host country's society through support of the fulfilment of basic public needs or preventing the erosion of organic social structures. A tendency can be discerned not just in St. Kitts and Nevis, but also in the welfare states of advanced economies, not to distribute public funds to support economic development with a "watering can", but to ensure that selected projects benefit, which are hoped to have long-term prospects of profitability and provide a monetary return on investment for the investors involved, but also a "social return on investment"[1339] for the country or region as a whole through the number of people who thereby gain the opportunity to employ their individual skills and abilities in the service of "their" society to gain economic independence from government transfers and to make "their" contribution to the domestic tax revenue.

The "social return on investment" could ultimately mean that an initially aid-dependent government-supported market sector develops into a "cash cow", and that services of general interest such as the nationwide supply of nursery and kindergarten places or the expansion and maintenance of the public road networks – which were originally delivered by the State and due to changed conditions (national debt, excessive costs of government redistribution and bureaucracy, increased entitlement by a wider range of people etc.) can no longer be so maintained – in the medium to long term come to be provided by businesses: efficient, targeted and cost-effective.

[1339] cf. PENNEKAMP (2012)

St. Kitts and Nevis CBI Inflows and Fiscal Balance (in percent of GDP)

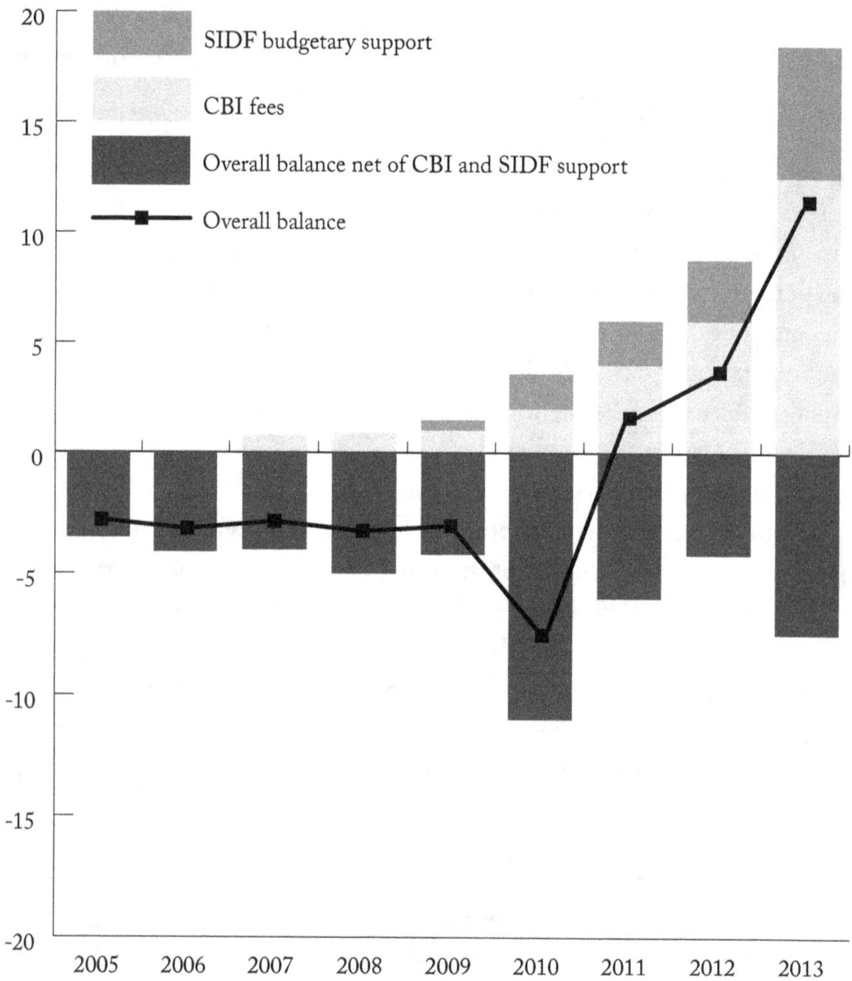

Sources: St. Kitts and Nevis authorities and IMF staff estimates

If the right objectives are chosen for promotion, companies can develop from individual, selfish and exclusively market participants into "clusters" within a modern civil society. With reasonable investor due diligence, development in this direction is in the public interest, because it means that apart from the direct beneficiaries, i.e. the employees of the beneficiary company, as St. Kitts and Nevis shows, an indefinite number of persons are also served by virtue of its socio-stabilising effect. Last but not least, attention should not only be directed to the import of capital as such, but also to the person of the investor, to avoid the influence of investors with dubious integrity. The ultimate aim is to assess both State and private power in terms of their social benefits (in welfare terms) and to adjust the boundary between the two spheres appropriately. As the significant positive macroeconomic impact of the Citizenship-by-Investment programme of St. Kitts and Nevis demonstrates,[1340] a "social return on investment" can be achieved, at least in small states. As more than half of the world's countries are small states,[1341] there is significant potential for such programmes to be implemented beneficially.

15.4 Malta[1342]

15.4.1 State structural parameters

Malta is an EU Member State with a population of 447,000, comprising seven islands in the Mediterranean covering 316 square kilometres. The main island is Malta where the majority of the population lives and where its capital, Valletta, is the political and cultural centre of the country. The other important island is Gozo, which is more rural and linked with Malta via an efficient ferry service. Malta was a British colony from 1800 until it became an independent state on 21 September 1964. Since independence it is a parliamentary republic. The overwhelming majority of the population is catholic, and Malta has one of the highest density of churches of any country. The two official languages are English and Maltese.

On becoming an independent nation, Malta introduced its first legal provisions for conferring and regulating Maltese citizenship.[1343] The Constitution of Malta contained provisions conferring Maltese citizenship that were typical of independence constitutions drafted by the UK for its colonies. The Constitution contained a section, chapter III, on

1340 International Monetary Fund (2014); XU/EL-ASHRAM/GOLD (2015)

1341 ALESINA/SPOLAORE (2005)

1342 The author has been directly involved in advising the government of Malta with regard to the design and implementation of the Malta Individual Investment Programme

1343 For overview of history of Maltese citizenship, cf. BUTTIGIEG (2013)

citizenship, that conferred Maltese citizenship automatically on all persons who were born in Malta and were citizens of the UK and Colonies before 21 September 1964, provided that one of the parents was also born in Malta: a combined application of the *ius soli* and *ius sanguinis* principles.[1344] Persons born in Malta during the period 21 September 1964 until 31 July 1989 acquired Maltese citizenship automatically at birth. As of 1 August 1989, Malta reintroduced *ius soli* and *ius sanguinis* principles to the acquisition of Maltese citizenship for persons born in Malta.

The constitutional citizenship provisions were complemented in 1965 by the enactment of the Maltese Citizenship Act. Indeed, following radical amendments in the year 2000, the Constitution, currently, only contains the principles as regards citizenship matters whilst the Act and its subsidiary legislation contains the implementing provisions that regulate all citizenship matters.

As from the year 2000 Malta abandoned its stance of being a single citizenship state and henceforth dual/multiple citizenship became permissible.

15.4.2 Naturalisation statistics

Between 1991 and 2013, Malta naturalised between 50 and 162 persons per year, a total of 2,372 and an average of about 108 per year.[1345]

In the first year of operation of the Malta Individual Investor Program (IIP), there have been nearly 450 applications registered. Assuming that the ordinary naturalisations remain at the same level, and assuming further that the initial levels of interest in this Citizenship-by-Investment programme will continue at about the same annual numbers, this will mean that Malta will see Citizenship-by-Investment naturalisations at about 400 percent its normal naturalisation/registration rate as a consequence of its programme. The naturalisation/registration to population

1344 BUTTIGIEG (2013)

1345 cf. country database of citizenship acquisition for Malta on http://eudo-citizenship.eu, last accessed 26 January 2015, and BUTTIGIEG (2013)

ratio is however extremely low at 0.025% per year, and including the *ius doni* naturalisations under the IIP, it would still raise to only 0.12%, which is low in international comparison.

15.4.3 The Individual Investor Programme

Citizenship law in Malta is regulated exclusively by the *Maltese Citizenship Act.*[1346] A newly elected parliament and government launched a Citizenship-by-Investment programme (the "Individual Investor Programme" or "IIP") in the spring of 2013, and by international advertisement, invited suitable specialised service providers to submit proposals for the design, implementation and operation of such a programme and to apply for the award of contracts in this regard. The successful bidder then worked out the detail of the programme with the Government in the latter half of 2013.[1347] After a confrontation with the parliamentary opposition, which was fully against the IIP, the necessary legislative changes were nevertheless adopted by Parliament and came into force in autumn 2013. Amendments to Article 10(9)(b) of the *Maltese Citizenship Act* provided that citizenship could be conferred

> *"to any person who is an applicant, or is a spouse or an eligible dependant of such applicant, under the individual investor programme of the Republic of Malta, and satisfies the requirements as prescribed in regulations made under this Act."*

The related *Regulations*, which provide for the mechanism to implement the programme, were adopted on 23 December 2013 and entered into force in January 2014.[1348] The said regulations were, however, amended following further controversy and the new regulations, which are currently into force, were published on the 4 February by means of Legal Notice 47 of 2014. On 14 February 2014 the accompanying application

---

[1346] Maltese Citizenship Act, 1965 (Chapter 188 of the Laws of Malta)

[1347] The author was part of the design and implementation team of the successful bidder, Henley & Partners, and continues to be closely involved with the IIP

[1348] LN 450/2013 Individual Investor Programme of the Republic of Malta Regulations, 2013

forms were then published and entered into force.[1349] In this context, it will be recalled that the introduction of the IIP lead to a wide debate in Europe,[1350] and also to the adoption of a resolution in the European Parliament[1351] and a review by the EU Commission.[1352]

15.4.3.1 Requirements for applicants

The IIP requires applicants to provide proof of a clean criminal record, proof of a comprehensive global health insurance policy, in addition to the submission of a comprehensive file containing information about the applicant's background, skills, career, source of assets, income and other personal details and to swear an *oath of allegiance* in Malta if the application is acceded to. This file is checked comprehensively and in detail, first by the government's concessionaire, which is the entity awarded with the public service concession contract to design, implement, and promote the programme, and/or by authorised agents, which are approved by Government to act as such and then by *Identity Malta*,[1353] which is the government agency entrusted with the responsibility for immigration and citizenship matters.

The investment requirements which must also be met by the applicant are provided in the *Regulations* as follows:

For the main applicant:

1 A non-refundable grant of EUR 650,000 to the National Development and Social Fund

---

[1349] http://justiceservices.gov.mt/DownloadDocument.aspx?app=lp&itemid=25885&1=1, last accessed on 17 January 2014

[1350] Covered by most major European newspapers, and accompanied by an extensive academic debate, cf. SHACHAR/BAUBÖCK (2014) for a good overview and spectrum of opinion

[1351] http://www.europarl.europa.eu/news/en/news-room/content/20140110IPR32392/html/EU-citizenship-should-not-be-for-sale-at-any-price-says-European-Parliament, last accessed on 3 February 2015

[1352] European Commission: Speech/14/18: Citizenship must not be up for sale, speech by the Vice-President of the European Commission Viviane Reding of 15 January 2014, published online at http://europa.eu/rapid/press-release_SPEECH-14-18_en.htm, last accessed on 3 February 2015

[1353] LN 269/2013, Identity Malta Agency (Establishment) Order, 2013

2 An investment of at least EUR 150,000 in an investment approved by the Government, and to be held for a minimum five year period

3 An investment of at least EUR 350,000 in property in Malta, which must be retained for at least five years, or alternatively the rental of a residential property in Malta for at least five years, the annual rent for which must not be less than EUR 16,000

If a spouse, children or parents are included in the citizenship application, the following additional contributions must be made:

4 For the spouse: a grant of EUR 25,000 to the National Development and Social Fund

5 For each child under 18: a grant of EUR 25,000 to the National Development and Social Fund

6 For each child over 18 but under 27, who remain unmarried and are wholly maintained by the main applicant: a grant of EUR 50,000 to the National Development and Social Fund

7 For each parent and/or grandparent over 55 who are wholly maintained by the main applicant and form part of the household: a grant of EUR 50,000 to the National Development and Social Fund.

15.4.3.2 Naturalisation costs

Apart from the investment-related costs, further fees are charged by the Government to cover the cost of undertaking due diligence, issuing passports and bank charges. No further costs other than those listed above are charged for the granting of citizenship under the Malta IIP.

15.4.3.3 Legal consequences in case of a successful application

Successful applicants receive full citizenship of Malta and a number of other rights that result from the formal bond associated with citizenship, between the individual and the state of Malta. By becoming a citizen of

Malta, furthermore, EU citizenship is acquired, and with it the various rights afforded to all EU citizens.[1354]

15.4.4 Compatibility with EU law

The debate over Malta's IIP has raised very interesting legal questions which aim at some of the fundamental aspects of the concept of EU citizenship and the principles on which the current EU treaties are based. It would therefore be remiss not to examine the key aspects, and to review some of the arguments, which have been brought forward in the debate surrounding the Malta Individual Investor Programme, or as one author put it, the "*Maltese Citizenship-for-Sale Affair*".[1355] The "agreement" reached between the Malta Government and the EU Commission also constitutes the first intrusion by the EU Commission into the exclusive competence of the Member States in the area of citizenship. The EU Commission has politically made use of the situation in Malta at the time of introduction of the IIP, namely the severe adverse position of the main political opposition party and of certain civil society groups, and the relative debate in the European Parliament which also came out with a (non-binding) resolution,[1356] and has thus been able to "agree" with the Malta Government on certain aspects of the Malta IIP.

15.4.4.1 The EU has no jurisdiction

The first and most fundamental question to ask is whether the EU actually has jurisdiction in the area of the citizenship law of the Member States.

As correctly stated by an EU Commission spokesperson in the initial public reaction to the launch of the Malta IIP, the EU has no jurisdiction in this matter and it is entirely up to the individual EU member states to regulate citizenship: indeed, a spokesperson for the European

---

1354 cf. KOCHENOV (2013)

1355 CARRERA (2014)

1356 http://www.europarl.europa.eu/news/en/news-room/content/20140110IPR32392/html/EU-citizenship-should-not-be-for-sale-at-any-price-says-European-Parliament, last accessed on 18 January 2014

Commission stated that "*member states have full sovereignty to decide to whom and how they grant their nationality.*"[1357]

The EU is based on the principle of conferral. The EU Treaties expressly state that all the powers which are not transferred to the EU remain with the individual member states.[1358] To understand which powers are conferred by the member states to the EU, it is necessary to find a legal basis to regulate a particular field in the EU Treaties. There is however no legal basis to regulate citizenship, and consequently, it remains in the exclusive domain of the Member States which are allowed virtually absolute freedom to decide who their citizens for the purposes of EU law are, as there is unsurprisingly no definition in EU law of "nationality of a Member State".[1359] The Member States are free even to limit their own body of citizenry (cf. Declaration of the United Kingdom of 31 December 1982 on the definition of the term "nationals") or extend it (cf. German Declaration on nationality made in 1957). Furthermore, from these Declarations appended to the Treaties, the intention of the Member States to retain full sovereignty in the area of citizenship is abundantly clear (cf. in particular the Danish Declaration on nationality made in 1957). In fact the entitlement to control citizenship laws is "*one of the most sacred cows in the division of competences between the Member States and the EU*".[1360] EU member states have been explicitly prohibited by the ECJ from questioning decisions of other Member States, which held that as long as a Member State acknowledges someone as its citizen, other Member States are not permitted to look past that decision.[1361] It is also settled case-law that the ECJ respects the unilateral determination of the scope of Member State citizenship for the purposes of EU law even if it splits the citizenry of the Member State.[1362] If the EU were to adopt any guidelines on citizenship, it would be acting *ultra vires* and breaching EU law.

1357 https://euobserver.com/justice/122101, last accessed 7 February 2015

1358 Article 4 and Article 5 TEU, in particular Article 5 (2), last sentence: "*Competences not conferred upon the Union in the Treaties remain with the Member States*"

1359 KOCHENOV (2015)

1360 CARRERA (2014) p. 1

1361 *See supra* ECJ C-369/90 (1992) (*Micheletti*) para. 10

1362 ECJ C-192/99 (2001) (*Kaur*) paras. 19 et seq.

15.4.4.2 There is no EU law to breach

Other than the above considerations that any harmonisation of citizenship law is prohibited by the Treaties, there is no applicable EU law that could possibly be breached. Articles 9 TEU and 20 et seq. TFEU do not establish rules on citizenship. They establish rules on EU citizenship, which is however derivative from the citizenship of the Member States established in national law, sometimes as clarified in the unilateral Declarations appended to the EU Treaties. All citizenship-related case law of the ECJ respects this point, as confirmed in *Rottmann: a derivative concept.*[1363] EU citizenship, on the other hand, does have an autonomous substance as far as rights are concerned. However, rights of EU citizenship are not the same as the rights conferred by the citizenship of a Member State.

It has also been argued that, both by the EU Commission on second thoughts after their initial, legally correct response, as well as by *Carrera*,[1364] that Malta's IIP is somehow in breach of the principle of sincere cooperation, which is formally enshrined in Article 4 (3) TEU. A possible infringement of this principle in the context of the granting of citizenship could be imagined in the case where a Member State would, without prior consultation, confer its citizenship to a large, disproportionate number of non-EU citizens.[1365] Apparently, however, not even the grant of German citizenship to over 3 million people mainly from the former Soviet Union who could claim some sort of German link, or the grant of Italian citizenship to over a million Argentineans with no real ties to Italy, or the handing out of Hungarian passports to hundreds of thousands of "Hungarians" living in Ukraine, Romania, Serbia and other countries, were sufficient to be regarded a violation of the principle of sincere cooperation. With regard to Malta, in that case, it must be quite difficult for the internal market to be disproportionately perturbed by the grant of a few thousand citizenships to applicants under the IIP.[1366]

[1363] ECJ C-135/08 (2010) para. 49

[1364] CARRERA (2014)

[1365] CARRERA (2014); see also opinion of *Advocate General Maduro* in *Rottmann* ECJ C-135/08 (2010)

[1366] cf. CARRERA (2014)

Carrera's argument, however, that qualitative effects may sometimes take precedence over quantitative ones, is difficult to understand, if not bewildering. He states that "*While the consequences of the Maltese IIP would be indeed marginal in pure numerical terms, the qualitative or substantive effects of the IIP seemed to be given far more weight*".[1367] It is argued that the main EU objective threatened by the Maltese IIP was the very status of citizenship in the EU. This argument however fails fundamentally, as it completely ignores the fact that there is no status of citizenship in the EU, as EU citizenship simply does not have independent existence but is purely derivative in nature and none of the EU institutions have the power to confer it.[1368] How could derivative EU citizenship be undermined by an additional mode of its indirect acquisition?

It is important to recall that the principle of sincere cooperation concerns the achievement of the goals of integration and genuine compliance with EU law. It could only seriously be argued to be breached if a Member State were to refuse to cooperate in implementing a law or updating a law to meet its outstanding challenges, or, if it were to create negative externalities for other Member States, even when acting within its own sphere of competences. Neither can be observed in the case of Malta's IIP. Sincere cooperation does not concern the use by the Member States of their own national competences in cases when such a use does not undermine the ability of the Union or other Member States to comply with EU law or to reach the goals of integration.[1369]

15.4.4.3 Internal Market and the "substance of the rights of EU citizenship" considerations

Article 4 TEU requires that Member States are not supposed to undermine the EU's achievements, in particular concerning the Internal Market and the substance of EU citizenship rights.[1370] As a consequence,

1367 CARRERA (2014) p. 25

1368 cf. *supra*

1369 cf. KLAMERT (2014)

1370 As noted by BRISIMI (2014) p. 176, the more recent case law on citizenship, cf. among others ECJ C-34/09 (2011) (*Zambrano*), "*confirm the heated debate as to the extension of EU residence and movement rights when there is no link to cross-border movement*"

any Member State that were to violate the rationale of EU citizenship and of the Internal Market would be potentially in breach of the law. The Internal Market and EU citizenship are a success, when any considerations of correlation between the citizenship of a Member State (i.e. strong ties - or shall we say genuine links - with a Member State of citizenship) and EU citizenship rights are removed. Indeed, Art. 18 TFEU established the principle of non-discrimination on the basis of citizenship, which expressly prohibits the Member States from taking any ties of EU citizens with their Member States of citizenship or residence into account. Residence or the exercise of any other rights of EU citizens in any Member State is not conditional on any cultural, linguistic or other considerations, stemming directly from Part II TFEU provisions, and are not subject to any restrictions. In fact, EU equality rules, when applied to EU citizens cover also those who do not have any cultural links with a Member State.[1371] Accordingly, even EU citizens born and permanently residing in the Caribbean possessions of the Member States which are not part of EU territory are thus fully covered by EU law, notwithstanding the fact that the Member State in question (the Netherlands) itself submitted during the hearings that these people had no links with it.[1372] Since 1992 ties with a Member State therefore do not matter at all, as otherwise the Internal Market would be undermined.[1373] The only link of relevance is that of the legal status of citizenship as established by the law of one of the Member States, as confirmed by the ECJ.[1374]

15.4.4.4 No harm to the EU or Member States

Importantly, in the case of the Malta IIP, no Member States let alone the EU, are being harmed. Moreover, the Malta programme is producing ideal EU citizens which by definition meet all the requirements of the key secondary legislation applicable in this field, thus excluding any possibility of harm.[1375] The due diligence on the applicant is extensive

1371 ECJ C-300/04 (2006) (*Eman and Sevinger*) para. 61
1372 ECJ C-300/04 (2006) (*Eman and Sevinger*) para. 60
1373 That would be a case of breach of sincere cooperation, Articles 4 and 5 TEU
1374 cf. supra ECJ C-369/90 (1992) (*Micheletti*) para. 10
1375 KOCHENOV (2015)

and exceeds the standards applied to ordinary naturalisations in EU countries by far, meaning that no argument about a negative impact on the EU or Member States in this respect can be supported either, not least because of the rather minimal numbers of naturalisations under the Malta IIP (a maximum of 1,800 applications have been set under the IIP by the Government of Malta against about 800,000 naturalisations and other grants of citizenship per year in EU Member States[1376] with varied degrees of due diligence applied, as the problem of the many terrorists with French, British, German, Belgian etc. passports dramatically illustrates).[1377]

Not only does Malta not harm the EU or any other EU member states through its programme, but on the contrary it is attracting significant investment and talent to the Union, attracting "ideal" EU citizens as defined by EU legislation itself.

15.4.5 Discussion and evaluation

15.4.5.1 Transparency and democratic control

Considered as a whole, Malta's "Individual Investor Programme" is more detailed and mature than the programmes in Antigua and Barbuda and St. Kitts and Nevis, and even more so in comparison with similar ones in Austria or Montenegro, as these have not yet acquired transparent structures and processes.

To achieve transparency in the running of the programme, the Maltese Citizenship Act, when providing for the Individual Investor Programme, was amended to include a provision for the appointment of an independent Regulator for the purposes of the correct implementation of the programme. Furthermore, the said Act establishes a high level committee to monitor the programme.[1378]

1376 http://ec.europa.eu/eurostat/statistics-explained/index.php/Migration_and_migrant_population_statistics, last accessed 16 February 2015

1377 cf. US Department of State, Bureau of Counterterrorism, Country Reports on Terrorism 2013, Europe Overview, http://www.state.gov/j/ct/rls/crt/2013/224822.htm, last accessed 8 February 2015

1378 Articles 25, 25A and B

15.4.5.2 A safe haven for investors in the EU

Despite initial adverse reaction from the political opposition and certain civil society groups associated with the opposition party, the Malta IIP has now achieved acceptance in the country and also worldwide. For international investors, Malta is a stable, neutral, efficient EU member state, representing an attractive "safe haven", which by operation of the EU treaties also confers EU citizenship entailing numerous rights and privileges throughout the EU and which, for international investors looking to apply under such a programme, is an important inducement, also from the perspective of their seeking safety and security. Malta in many ways offers the ultimate safe haven as its citizenship gives access and the right of establishment to more than 28 European countries, including several non-EU countries[1379] and its passport affords its holders extensive visa-free travel.[1380]

15.4.5.3 Social Return on Investment

Given the excessive public debt in many welfare States – which results ultimately from the shift in attitudes to one of entitlement in wide sections of their populations – it appears increasingly important under conditions of economic globalisation that the State only focuses on its specific original core tasks, which include for instance the adequate supply of schools, police services and the administration of justice. Only a "lean State" which focuses on these key areas will thrive in the increasingly competitive environment between countries in the future. Although Malta's debt situation and fiscal balance is one of the best in Europe, and not at all comparable to the other southern European states such as Portugal, Spain or Greece, this is also true for Malta. A programme like the IIP can and should have a significant social return on investment in the sense that the programme supports government funding of important projects, which the state could otherwise not, or

---

[1379] e.g. Switzerland, a traditional "safe haven" country par excellence

[1380] Malta ranks as having the 8th most attractive passport in the world in terms of visa-free travel; cf. HENLEY & PARTNERS (2014)

not sufficiently fund. The IIP is a very good example of a high-impact programme, due to its key characteristic of requiring a direct, non-refundable contribution to the National Development and Social Fund, and due to the fact that it is properly managed in all relevant respects.

15.4.5.4 Setting a new standard for Citizenship-by-Investment Programmes

With its introduction of an Individual Investor Programme, Malta has in many ways set a new standard for Citizenship-by-Investment programmes.

It is one of very few countries which have conducted a public tender to invite specialist firms to advise and assist with the design, implementation and operation of the programme. As with most other areas, the failures and successes of investor immigration and citizenship programmes show the need for expert advice. The Malta IIP sets a new standard in that a highly efficient, dedicated team within the Identity Malta Agency, i.e. outside the general government administration but still accountable to government as a government agency, works hand-in-hand with a concessionaire under a public services concession contract, to operate and strategically navigate the programme, and to manage the programme's international positioning. This is crucial as it allows the government to ensure tight controls over how the programme is promoted. Furthermore, a sophisticated, four-tier due diligence process has been designed and implemented, the most thorough due diligence process of any such programme in the world, and one in which Malta again sets a new standard.

16

Conclusions and Theses

1 The world's different languages and religions,[1381] cultures and societal conventions require a decentralised world order and its organisation into various individual states. The realisation of a global State, which would ensure law and order around the world, or the notion of a global citizenship to parallel state citizenship, is practically impossible,[1382] although the idea has persisted in human thought since ancient times.[1383] On the contrary, the breakup of colonial empires and the collapse of the USSR and the many nationalist secessions all over the world have led to a proliferation of new sovereign states in recent times: whereas in 1945 there were 74 independent countries, today there are about 200.[1384]

2 The legal concept of citizenship is "*one of our major practices of drawing lines*"[1385] and exists in the tension between (internal) inclusion and (external) exclusion,[1386] as the freedom of the citizens of a State can only be guaranteed by the curtailment of the freedoms or access of individuals not belonging to that State.[1387] The welfare, policies and culture of a community are protected through the restriction of access by individuals who do not belong to this community.[1388] A person's right to live and work in a given country are a critical determinant of that person's lifetime opportunities, and passports and visas are among the most important instruments of global social inequality, as they determine the opportunities of international mobility.[1389] These borders within which we happen to be born, and the documents we are entitled to, are no less arbitrary than other characteristics like skin colour, gender or the genetic strength we are endowed with.[1390]

1381 *Kant*, in describing nature states of its two means of dividing nations: language and religion, KANT (1995)
1382 cf. KANT (1795); KOLLER (1996)
1383 cf. HEATER (2002)
1384 ALESINA/SPOLAORE (2005)
1385 *Walker* (2001), cited in NYERS (2009) p. 1
1386 BRUBAKER (1992); cf. also BLOEMRAAD/KORTEWEG/YURDAKUL (2009)
1387 BOSNIAK (2006); cf. also *Kukathas* in SMITH (2011); HOWARD (2009); and CARENS (1995)
1388 WALZER (1983)
1389 SHACHAR (2003)
1390 cf. CARENS (2000); BENHABIB (2002); KOCHENOV (2012); PASKALEV (2014); SHACHAR (2009)

Citizenship has long been an important concept, not only in law but also in sociology[1391] and the political sciences.[1392] Indeed, the idea of citizenship figures centrally in constitutional and social theory, political philosophy, in cultural studies, and in law.[1393] It is one of the *"essentially contested concepts"*.[1394] Citizenship is without doubt a complex institution with various dimensions,[1395] and it is now central to many intellectual projects across disciplines.[1396] Its conception and definition ultimately depends a lot on the political viewpoint and is intimately linked to the kind of society and political community we want.[1397]

Citizenship, which can also be viewed as the legal counterpart of the sociopolitical concept of nationality,[1398] is not legally defined in the majority of States and its meaning is far from clear.[1399] From a legal perspective, citizenship (and previously the term subject) is mainly a classification criterion: it classifies natural persons as belonging to a particular State.[1400] State and citizens complement each other: citizens form the constituent people, one of the three constitutive components of the State according to *Jellinek's* three-element theory.[1401] As a legal institution, citizenship therefore precedes the national law and is established as a component of the States themselves.[1402] Regardless of whether one follows *Jellinek's* theory, it can be at least said that citizenship generates a legal bond, which links the individual to the national legal order and thereby gives them access to civil, political and social rights.

1391 JOPPKE (2010); cf. also MACKERT/MUELLER (2000)
1392 MAGNETTE (2005) p. 1; MILLER (2000)
1393 BOSNIAK (2006)
1394 GALLIE (1955) p. 167
1395 JOPPKE (2010)
1396 BOSNIAK (2006)
1397 MOUFFE (1992); cf. also SANDEL (2012)
1398 cf. MACKERT/MÜLLER (2000), although in modern legal English citizenship and nationality are usually used synonymously; the *European Convention on Citizenship*, Art. 2 a) on the other hand states *"For the purpose of this Convention, a "nationality" means the legal bond between a person and a State and does not indicate the person's ethnic origin."*
1399 KOCHENOV (2009)
1400 JELLINEK (1976); MAKAROV (1962); IPSEN (2004)
1401 JELLINEK (1976)
1402 KNOCKE (2005); cf. THEDIECK (1989)

There have also been many other attempts to arrive at a definition of citizenship,[1403] and international courts have coined varying definitions of citizenship in judgments relating to citizenship.

The legal essence of citizenship however is of a rather formal nature and consequently its acquisition may, at the discretion of the relevant State, be linked to nothing more than a simple formal declaration of intent to the competent national authority, and the acceptance of such intent by the competent national authority.

3 From a functional-teleological and similar genesis perspective, citizenship can be defined as a legal bond between a domestic natural person and the domestic legal system. With reference to the ICJ's ruling in *Nottebohm*, [1404] to support that bond, there needs to be a desire for this to be a "real" relationship between the individual and the domestic legal system ("*genuine connection*" or "*genuine link*") – but this applies only in the context of conflicts between multiple citizenships, or, as in *Nottebohm*, to assess the applicability of diplomatic protection.

The classical legal, economic and the sociological or political functions of citizenship can be distinguished.[1405] It would appear sensible given the diversity in political ideas circulating around the concept of citizenship and what it should contribute through (economic, but also cultural) globalisation and advanced information technology driven societies, to deduce that the relevant functions of the basic parameters of the nation State, which in view of progressive international investors, labour mobility and demographic change, impose a comprehensive territorial responsibility for the welfare not only of "own" nationals but all resident persons.[1406] With regard to their protective responsibilities a distinction can be made between, firstly, objectively State organisational and subjective-individual

[1403] For a good overview see KNOCKE (2005)

[1404] ICJ judgment of 6 April 1955, ICJ Rep. 1955 (*Nottebohm*)

[1405] cf. the Typology by *Marshall* in MARSHALL/BOTTOMORE (1992); which follows the well-known legal classification (HABERMAS (1992)); as well as MACKERT/MÜLLER (2000)

[1406] cf. SCHEUING (2003)

functions, secondly, between domestic and external functions, and thirdly, between traditional and modern functions.

4 Citizenship and citizenship law based on today's understanding has only been in existence since the formation of the modern nation States in the eighteenth and nineteenth centuries, and in particular since the French *Code Civil* of 1804, even though its historical origins[1407] – at least from the perspective of the Western countries dealt with here – extend back to ancient Greece.[1408]

In contrast to *Aristotle's* view of citizenship as a primarily political concept, the Roman jurists developed citizenship as a legal status, with various public and private rights and obligations.[1409] Through Roman law, medieval feudalism with the European Free States, the Renaissance and the Peace of Westphalia, to the French Revolution and the resulting nationalism,[1410] the further development of citizenship has not followed a single trajectory as it has played out very differently in various states.[1411]

The American and French Revolutions were critical for the modern conception of citizenship as it brought a closer tie between citizenship and the territorial unity of the States, which created a clear demarcation between citizen and non-citizen. This demarcation from the outside world created by modern citizenship resulted in the promotion of domestic homogenisation,[1412] modern nationalism and the nation State,[1413] which continue to affect the theory and practice of citizenship today.[1414] With the *Code Civil* of 1804 France opened the era of modern citizenship law.[1415] From then on citizenship law

1407 A study of other historical lines, e.g. from a Chinese or Indian point of view, has been omitted here, especially because the modern design of citizenship laws in virtually all States follow Western models

1408 cf. MANVILLE (1990)

1409 KLUSMEYER (1996) pp. 17–20; on Roman citizenship fundamental SHERWIN-WHITE (1973)

1410 MACKERT (2006); KLUSMEYER (1996); MAGNETTE (2005)

1411 BELLAMY (2004)

1412 MACKERT (2006); MILL (1993)

1413 cf. GOSEWINKEL (1995); MACKERT (2006); STILLER (2011)

1414 BRUBAKER (2004)

1415 WEIL (2004)

was clearly regulated and was based on the person: a person is or was a citizen because she descended from a citizen, a status which was conferred in a similar manner to the family name and which could not be lost if the person moved abroad.[1416] The groundbreaking developments in France in the eighteenth century extended beyond its State borders, and increasingly to almost all States with the mindset of the Revolution made "*le tour du monde*".[1417]

5 In the EU context, the logic of free movement within the area of freedom, security and justice is antithetical to the "genuine link" idea, as allowing EU member states not to recognize the citizenship of other EU member states using their free movement rights would introduce uncertainty in the application of EU law and making its uniform application throughout all EU member states impossible.[1418] Since non-recognition of citizenship of a different Member State would go against the core of the Internal Market principles, the ECJ prohibited taking *Nottebohm* rules on diplomatic protection within the EU into account.[1419] Thus since 1992 ties with a Member State do not matter at all, as otherwise the Internal Market would be undermined. The only tie of relevance is that of the citizenship as established by the law of one of the Member States.

Both the ECJ[1420] and the European Commission have made it clear that the matter of the acquisition of citizenship is in principle exclusively a matter of domestic law. The European Commission recalled that "*Member States have full sovereignty to decide to whom and how they grant their nationality*",[1421] in response to Malta's new Citizenship-by-Investment programme,[1422] but also that "*the principle*

1416 WEIL (2004)

1417 LIPOVANO (1935); cf. also WEIL (2004); STILLER (2011); BRUBAKER (1992)

1418 KOCHENOV (2009)

1419 ECJ C-369/90 (1992) (*Micheletti*)

1420 ECJ C-369/90 (1992) I-4239 (4262)

1421 Report on the position of the European Commission regarding Malta, published online at http://euobserver.com/justice/122101, last accessed on 1 December 2013

1422 cf. http://www.europarl.europa.eu/news/en/news-room/content/20140110IPR32392/html/EU-citizenship-should-not-be-for-sale-at-any-price-says-European-Parliament, last accessed on 18 January 2014

of sincere cooperation, which is inscribed in the EU Treaties (Article 4.3 of the Treaty on EU), should lead Member States to take account of the impact of decisions in the field of nationality on other Member States and the Union as a whole",[1423] even though it was also clearly established in the European Parliamentary debates that citizenship law remains a matter for individual Member States. Indeed, the Malta IIP discussions with the EU Commission represents a first direct incursion of EU institutions in a previously exclusive terrain of competence of the EU Member States, when "*one of the most sacred cows in the division of competences between the Member States and the EU is the entitlement to control citizenship laws.*"[1424] EU Member States have always been and also remain free to even establish special nationalities for their overseas regions or to create special groups of citizens upon whom they do not confer the right of abode.[1425] To what extent the EU law affects the national sovereignty of the EU Member States in the area of citizenship law is one of the most interesting questions in modern citizenship law and a "*true revolution in the modern understanding of citizenship*".[1426]

6 Whether the justification of the bond between the individual and the national legal order should be interpreted as a genuine link in the sense of a factual, ethical-normative or legal presence has never been decided conclusively on an international level or in any of the countries studied here. The traditional primary functions of citizenship – to support social cohesion, to achieve internal social peace, and to strengthen civil society structures instead of State subsistence – would suggest that a factual link is more likely needed, though not necessary. Thus, the majority of States require several years' domestic residence as a condition of naturalisation, which implies a certain minimum commitment on the part of the individual

---

1423 European Commission: SPEECH/14/18: Citizenship must not be up for sale, speech by the Vice-President of the European Commission Viviane Reding of 15 January 2014, published online at http://europa.eu/rapid/press-release_SPEECH-14-18_en.htm, last accessed on 18 January 2014

1424 CARRERA (2014) p. 1

1425 KOCHENOV (2011)

1426 KOCHENOV (2009) p. 171

to the domestic polity. However, this is not necessary and as long as the conferral of citizenship is not completely arbitrary, harmful to other countries, or done without the consent of the person concerned, nothing prevents nation states from deciding whom and how to grant citizenship to.

7 A fundamental first distinction can be drawn between the acquisition of citizenship at birth (of origin) and acquisition after birth. The types of acquisition at birth are distinguished into the *ius sanguinis* at birth and *ius soli* at birth. The types of acquisition after birth can be distinguished again into *ius sanguinis*[1427] or *ius soli*, acquisition based on family relations, by affinity (e.g. ethnic or religious affiliation) and naturalisation, including Citizenship-by-Investment.

8 In the original acquisition of citizenship, the principle of descent (*ius sanguinis*) competes traditionally with the territorial principle (*ius soli*), with numerous mixed forms being encountered in the practice of States. Both principles, which are universally accepted as valid principles for citizenship acquisition, can however lead to accidental citizens which essentially have no ties to the country of citizenship other than they are accidently born in the territory or born to a citizen parent outside the country.

The pure *ius soli* principle, which, for example is still practiced in the US[1428] and many other states, automatically grants every person born on State territory citizenship by simple virtue of his presence on the territory at birth, is becoming increasingly tenuous from the perspective of "sufficient connection to the State", in view of globalisation and the ever-increasing mobility of the world population.

9 In the course of economic globalisation, transnationalism and digitisation have resulted in a paradigm shift which can be observed against the background of increasing international and capital labour migration, which in the latter case has resulted in a growing

---

[1427] Which still should be considered as an original acquisition
[1428] cf. rather than many others SPIRO (2008)

divergence between domestic populations and State populations in some states. This divergence brings into question the legitimacy of democratic power and the self-determination of the peoples, which present itself as a collectivist expression of individual self-determination and thus of universal human dignity – at least in liberal democratic states, while large parts of the world are occupied by illiberal, non-democratic states meaning that for these countries such considerations must be viewed in a different light. It also raises the question of whether the allocation of the world's population to the nation States according to traditional citizenship concepts, remains appropriate.

10 The political attitude to multiple citizenship has changed, as now more than half of the countries in the world allow multiple citizenship, and every year more states follow in what is a global trend.[1429] Today, multiple citizenship is valued by States for its potential capacity for international influence.[1430] Beyond migration, this global trend is driven by geopolitical, economic and technological factors. Fears over the loyalty of citizens – the main argument used against dual citizenship – faded after the Cold War ended and increased international political cooperation calmed international relations. Unlike earlier migrants in the eighteenth and nineteenth centuries, who had little contact with those they left behind them, twenty-first century migrants communicate with their families on a daily basis, by phone, internet and email, they visit them on holiday and often go home to retire.[1431] A new class of "global citizens" has furthermore emerged which truly has multiple homes and bases and for whom multiple citizenship is the norm.[1432] A person who has more than one citizenship is in most cases more privileged than a person with only one, and can in many cases freely chose the more advantageous of two passports, two legal systems and two or more[1433] places of

[1429] BREVILLE (2014); *Hansen/Weil* in HANSEN/WEIL (2002) pp. 9–11
[1430] BREVILLE (2014); cf. also La Tribune, Paris 17 June 2011
[1431] BREVILLE (2014)
[1432] KÄLIN (2014)
[1433] In case of EU citizenship, 27 countries in addition to the country of citizenship

residence.[1434] However, multiple citizenship is still prohibited in many countries, while some only tolerate it in certain cases.

Multiple citizenship has undoubtedly somewhat eroded the strong bond between the individual citizens of a particular country and has led to the decoupling of citizenship status from the effective nationality. Having several citizenships means more options for the individual and a kind of citizenship of convenience: depending on the situation, one or the other passport can achieve the objective best (e.g. no visa is required to travel, faster entry at border checkpoints for instance for EU citizens entering from outside of the EU etc.). This does not mean however that you cannot maintain a meaningful relationship with several states, and indeed, with increased mobility and the transnational lives of global citizens, having multiple ties in different countries and even on different continents has become much more commonplace.[1435]

With regard to citizenship granted in the national interest – such as the granting of citizenship on the basis of extraordinary contribution to the State – it is actually desirable in most cases and also mostly unavoidable that the previous citizenship be retained. This has been recognised even in Austria, which generally still strictly requires the renunciation of previous citizenships as a condition of naturalisation, but in the case of naturalisation pursuant to Section 10(6) of the Austrian Citizenship Act, i.e. the acquisition of citizenship due to extraordinary contributions to the State – including economic contributions – interestingly allows the retention of previous citizenships.

11 If legal provisions specifically identify economic contributions as the main basis for the grant of citizenship, then this is most often referred to as Citizenship-by-Investment[1436] or what is referred to and introduced here as *ius doni*, as the investment in this context is

---

[1434] cf. KÄLIN (2014)

[1435] cf. KÄLIN (2014); RISSE (2010)

[1436] Or *Economic Citizenship*, or, with a view of the passport as its most important element for applicants, *Passports of Convenience*, cf. VAN FOSSEN (2007)

generally more of an economic contribution than an investment *sensu stricto*. This is true even in Citizenship-by-Investment programme types which require private sector investments, e.g. in real estate or a business venture, because in contrast to normal foreign direct investment, where the investment decisions are based on competitive rates of return and provide for a certain level of economic efficiency, investors in Citizenship-by-Investment programmes are generally willing to invest at less favourable rates of return or may acquire assets for more than their intrinsic value as the result of the inclusion of the passport asset in their investment decision.[1437]

12 Citizenship-by-Investment programmes allow individuals and families who are exposed to potential hazards in their home countries – including political persecution and war and the deprivation of rights – to leave their home country and to enter a new State with the secure status as citizens (acquired by *ius doni*) at any time. This individual freedom and security offered by Citizenship-by-Investment opportunities – however flawed it may be as a solution only for affluent individuals and families and excluding all who are unable to pay the price – is an important aspect with an inherently humanitarian dimension, as it effectively enables people to acquire additional rights of movement, including the right to leave, which is only really secured if you have somewhere to go to. Ultimately, this therefore also secures the right to have rights.[1438] Only citizenship permits "return" to a particular "home" country at any time: it is the only immigration status which is unconditionally recognised in public international law and in practically all national laws. Along with the right of emigration, which was formulated by the US Congress as long ago as 1868,[1439] a second citizenship offers an additional crucial "one-way" option to move to another country at any time.[1440]

1437 cf. XU/EL-ASHRAM/GOLD (2015)

1438 Chief Justice Earl Warren in *Perez v. Brownell*, 356 US 44, 64 (1957), ARENDT (1968)

1439 Expatriation Act of 27 July 1868, "*the right of expatriation is a natural and inherent right of all people, indispensable to the enjoyment of the rights of life, liberty and pursuit of happiness.*" For modern Europeans, this principle is incorporated in the Right to Exit of Article 4 of EU Directive 2004/38

1440 *Bauböck* in SMITH (2011), about the fundamental importance of the right to leave any

13 In light of the large number of ordinary routes to naturalisation and citizenship acquisition based on ethnic-nationalist provisions in the law, which covers very significant numbers of people from origin countries which, in a Citizenship-by-Investment context, would raise eyebrows, we can conclude that *ius doni*, where carried out through a highly selective process (with the main criteria being significant wealth and outstanding reputation), creates far less of an issue and potential problems.

In many countries (e.g. Germany, Spain, Hungary, Israel and Greece) ethnic nationalist citizenship rules exist, which base the selection criteria for admission to citizenship status on simple, formal ethnic or religious affiliation, however weak, and which do not compare favourably with the equally simple selection criteria of *ius doni*. The main difference is that *ius doni* has a significant positive impact in the host country, whereas often the opposite is the case with ethnic nationalist citizenship regimes.

14 If the argument that no sufficient or "genuine link" exists between the applicant for citizenship and the host state is levelled against *ius doni*,[1441] even though applicants are prepared to commit a substantial amount of their liquid financial resources for the benefit of their new country of citizenship, then what is the quality of the link between those many accidental citizens who have become citizens, for example just because their mother happened to be in the US at the time of birth? *Ius doni* in fact compares favourably with the pure *ius soli* principle, in that more often than not, a closer connection, a more "genuine" link exists between the person and the state in question, than with accidental citizens by operation of *ius soli*.

15 Every country has, in principle, the right to exclude whomever it wishes from entering and settling in its territory: likewise, every country has the right to regulate its naturalisation laws in accordance with the common good and to include whomever it wishes to admit

---

country, cf. KOCHENOV (2012)

[1441] This was one of the EU Commission's main arguments against Malta's new Citizenship-by-Investment Programme

to become a citizen.[1442] *Ius doni,* which could also be viewed as the grant of citizenship in the common good, is thus nothing less than the expression of the individual state's freedom to select and choose (in accordance with the ideas of the common good prevalent in the particular state's society) suitable individuals and families so that they may contribute to the economy and society and be admitted, on this basis, as citizens, in view of their contribution to the common good of that state.

16 From a practical impact perspective, it is important to compare the number of naturalisations which occur under typical Citizenship-by-Investment programmes through the application of *ius doni* principles with the number of ordinary naturalisations and grants of citizenship by ordinary application. In 2010, the last year for which such statistics are available, the EU Member States granted citizenship to a total of not less than 810,000 persons.[1443]

Moreover, if you compare the countries of origin of the Citizenship-by-Investment applicants and ordinary naturalisations granted, and their respective numbers, it is clear that many countries in the EU for instance (in particular Germany, Italy, Hungary, Portugal, Spain, Greece, Romania and Bulgaria) have together granted millions of citizenships to persons originating from countries which, in a Citizenship-by-Investment context, would be considered "problematic" and where "heightened due diligence" is called for. For instance, Germany naturalised thousands of people from Iran, Iraq, Afghanistan, Pakistan and Syria, and from Russia, Kazakhstan and other countries of the former Soviet Union. The situation looks even worse if we consider the immigration to Europe from such countries, particular illegal immigration and the influx of refugees, which has resulted in the ongoing infiltration of Islamist terrorists in Europe.[1444]

1442 KESLER (1998) p. 16

1443 cf. http://ec.europa.eu/eurostat, last accessed 26 January 2015

1444 cf. US Department of State, Bureau of Counterterrorism, Country Reports on Terrorism 2013, Europe Overview, http://www.state.gov/j/ct/rls/crt/2013/224822.htm, last accessed 8 February 2015, and *Neue Zürcher Zeitung,* 21 January 2015: "Italien

In contrast, in a little under a year since the launch of Malta's new Citizenship-by-Investment programme, the Maltese government has received some 450 applications under its highly successful Citizenship-by-Investment programme.[1445] While this number relative to the large number of naturalisations throughout the EU represents the inclusion of a few, in many ways ideal new EU citizens, those 450 applications will also result in some EUR 500 million in foreign direct investment for Malta, not counting any indirect effects and further investments resulting, in addition to significant other positive externalities. With an annual GDP of approximately EUR 8.5 billion (2013),[1446] this represents a significant inflow of capital for the country, while the number of applications are limited.

If we also consider the few other countries in Europe which have *ius doni* provisions in their laws, such as Austria, Cyprus, Croatia, Slovenia etc., and if we round up the total to an estimated 600 applications per year, this is in stark contrast to the over 800,000 persons naturalised in 2010 in Europe alone. In fact, on the basis of these figures, less than 0.01% of naturalisations in Europe are attributable to *ius doni*. These 0.01% however represent ideal EU citizens as they all, invariably (due to the stringent process and qualification requirements under Citizenship-by-Investment provisions) meet, or rather exceed, the requirements that the EU sets internally for EU citizens to avail themselves of the freedom of movement this status provides. Citizenship-by-Investment in Europe thus creates only extremely few additional citizens, who however are all highly qualified. The same is true in other parts of the world.

17 From an economic perspective, it is actually efficient to keep citizenship exclusive, and a citizenship admission policy should

sorgt sich um seine Sicherheit. Mit den Massen von Kriegsflüchtlingen kommen auch gewaltbereite Islamisten nach Europa"

[1445] http://www.timesofmalta.com/articles/view/20150115/local/400-applications-for-maltese-passports-over-450m-in-foreign-investment-henley.552013, last accessed 26 January 2015

[1446] ec.europa.eu/eurostat

primarily be beneficial for existing citizens.[1447] In this respect, Citizenship-by-Investment ideally fulfils this stipulation as under this citizenship admission principle, only few new citizens who are, as a prerequisite, net contributors to society are admitted, thus creating a net benefit for the existing citizens of a country.[1448] Certainly, in practical terms, the number of citizens admitted under *ius doni* principles is entirely negligible and thus should not actually pose a real issue, legal[1449] or otherwise, regardless of the position one takes from a normative point of view.

If we adopt a market-oriented, non-political normative view of modern citizenship, the arguments in favour of Citizenship-by-Investment are numerous, and they seem to prevail.

Citizenship-by-Investment is essentially a liberal, market-driven approach to citizenship, and part of the appeal of markets is that they "*don't pass judgment on the preferences they satisfy. They don't ask whether some ways of valuing goods are higher, or worthier, than others... This nonjudgmental stance toward values lies at the heart of market reasoning.*"[1450] Citizenship-by-Investment is based on an individualistic, depoliticising liberal conception of citizenship that is formal, legalistic and without ties to a collective identity or membership in a particular community, as opposed to conservative and democratic political conceptions of citizenship.[1451] This allows for a market-driven argument, based on the principle underlying a liberal conception to maximize individual autonomy and freedom of choice. Individuals should be free to buy and sell whatever they please, as long as they do not violate other people's rights.[1452] The "purchase" of citizenship should therefore

1447 STRAUBHAAR (2003)

1448 Disregarding here the possible reputation risks of undesirable persons who have been admitted due to a lack of proper due diligence; however, assuming due diligence on applicants is done properly, these risks are actually minimal and definitely smaller than those presented by all other modes of citizenship acquisition

1449 For example, with regard to the principle of sincere cooperation in EU law (Article 4(3) of the Treaty on EU), cf. SHAW (2014)

1450 SANDEL (2012) p. 14

1451 VAN FOSSEN (2007)

1452 BECKER (1976); *Becker* was awarded the 1992 Nobel Prize in Economics for "*having extended the domain of microeconomic analysis to a wide range of human behaviour and*

be allowed as long as it does not violate other people's rights. From a domestic perspective this is true at least if it is not done in large enough numbers to influence the political process in a democracy; from an international perspective this is true if it is not done in large enough numbers to create an unwanted influx of domestic citizens in other states where certain rights are conferred by the citizenship "purchased", such as in the EU for all EU citizens, or if such acquired citizenship is not used to circumvent visa restrictions.[1453] Since market-oriented thinking is increasingly reaching into domains of life which were traditionally governed by non-market values, we put prices on noneconomic goods, regardless what the goods are.[1454] This now also seems firmly established with regard to the acquisition of citizenship.

18 Utilitarianism[1455] provides another fundamental position in support of Citizenship-by-Investment. Open market transactions benefit both the buyers (new citizens) and sellers (countries and their existing citizens) and thus improve the collective wellbeing or social utility. If I invest a significant amount of money to become a citizen of a particular country, that must be beneficial to me and make me better off, otherwise I would not "purchase" this citizenship; likewise, a country earning significant additional foreign direct investment as a result of "selling" citizenship must be making itself and its current citizens better off, otherwise it would not offer access to citizenship in this way. Both parties are better off and social utility is increased as a result of this exchange: an efficient allocation of goods by free markets.[1456] A good (citizenship) is made available to those most willing to pay for it.

---

interaction, including nonmarket behaviour."

1453 Thus, in November 2014, Canada has implemented visa requirement on St. Kitts and Nevis to ensure that it *"will be able to properly determine the true identity of St. Kitts and Nevis passport holders and to deny entry to those who would otherwise be inadmissible to Canada."* (Notice of the Government of Canada, available at: http://www.cic.gc.ca/english/department/media/notices/2014-11-21b.asp, last accessed 18 March 2016)

1454 SANDEL (2012)

1455 cf. MILL/GERIANT (1993)

1456 cf. SANDEL (2012) offers an interesting example with ticket scalping, which has somewhat similar characteristics to the citizenship by investment vs. citizenship by ordinary naturalisation options

While markets allocate goods based on the prices paid for those goods *"queues allocate goods based on the ability and willingness to wait"*.[1457] Markets and queues are of course not the only ways of allocating goods, some are allocated by merit, others by need, lottery or chance. However, leaving aside birthright citizenship, citizenship acquired by ordinary naturalisation after years of residence closely corresponds to the queue-allocation of ability and willingness to wait, whereas Citizenship-by-Investment can be compared to market allocation by ability and willingness to pay a price. The utilitarian case for markets over queues is highly contingent,[1458] as there is no reason to assume that the willingness and ability to wait for citizenship is a better measure of its value to a person than the willingness and ability to pay for it, and likewise the willingness and ability of applicants to wait for citizenship is no better measure for a country and its existing citizens of the applicants suitability than their willingness and ability to make a significant investment or monetary contribution to the country. In fact, we could even argue the contrary with *Becker*:[1459] In his proposals regarding setting a price for the right to immigrate, he contends that immigrants willing to pay a significant amount would automatically have desirable characteristics, being skilled, ambitious, hardworking and unlikely to make use of welfare or unemployment benefits. Thus the willingness and ability to pay for citizenship is actually an even better measure than the willingness and ability to wait for it. Indeed, as evidenced in many instances throughout Europe where citizenship is granted to persons who ultimately become a burden to society rather than net contributors,[1460] it follows that from a utilitarian perspective,

---

1457 SANDEL (2012)

1458 SANDEL (2012)

1459 BECKER (1997)

1460 One should mention here the ethnic-nationalistic citizenship provisions in the laws of Hungary, Bulgaria, Romania, Spain, Italy and several other states which afford citizenship on the basis of ethnic or nationalistic motives regardless of whether the person in question will be a net contributor or rather a burden to society. Furthermore, many citizenship laws are heavily and unnecessarily biased toward "family" in that under the title of "family reunification" or on the basis of marriage there exists virtually unchecked access to citizenship. Italy is a good example, where two and a half years of marriage is enough to get a passport no matter what your financial situation or education or employment status is. If

Citizenship-by-Investment should actually be given preference over other modes of non-birthright citizenship acquisition.

19 The liberalisation of citizenship law for suitable applicants by Citizenship-by-Investment programmes is comparable to the unilateral liberalisation of international trade: if States unilaterally reduce their import barriers and welcome foreign goods, these countries benefit and their economic and political clout increases. The same applies if States unilaterally reduce their "import barriers" for highly skilled or for wealthy people and offer these people, in particular, the direct acquisition of citizenship. States do not in fact protect themselves by restricting immigration and access to citizenship. On the contrary, States damage themselves by denying immigration and citizenship to suitable persons,[1461] as this represents a form of discrimination against desirable goods.[1462]

20 The citizenship which we receive at birth is completely arbitrary.[1463] As *Shachar* aptly pointed out, it amounts to a birthright lottery.[1464] According to *Carens*, "*citizenship in the modern world is a lot like feudal status in the medieval world. It is assigned at birth; for the most part it is not subject to change by the individual's will and efforts; and it has a major impact upon that person's life chances.*"[1465] Liberal democracies should therefore develop strategies which as far as possible would lead to a world without borders or reduce the impact of this arbitrary assignment of people inside and outside of State borders.[1466] We could also express this as an exhortation to promote global citizenship. Inside and outside state borders is the crucial point in the argumentation with regard to human dignity as well as with regard to questions

you do not have an Italian family and work or run a business there, it is however 10 years of uninterrupted residence with no recourse to public funds. (cf. *Italian Citizenship Act No. 91/92 of 5 February 1992, n. 91*, as amended by *Act No. 94/2009*). Interestingly, a number of EU Member States show clear positive bias towards unemployable people, while making it excessively difficult for the entrepreneurs to naturalize at the same time

1461 While at the same time frequently admitting large numbers of less suitable persons

1462 cf. BECKER (1957)

1463 CARENS (1995); cf. also WALZER (1983); and SHACHAR (2009)

1464 SHACHAR (2009)

1465 CARENS (1992) p. 26

1466 CARENS (1995); and CARENS (2013)

of distributive justice on a global level, not just within one society: even *Rawls* considers questions of how goods should ideally be allocated, and what is the desert of such allocation, only within a particular society, a particular state – a state which is protected from other states and their citizen's intrusion by the exclusive nature of its citizenship laws, immigration laws, and the border police and other state authorities that enforces these laws, which represents a major moral dilemma for liberal democracies[1467]. Any questions of human dignity or questions of distributive justice about the merits of allocation of citizens on the basis of investments that they have made in the state are necessarily to be viewed on the same level of how such allocation of citizens compares to the allocation of citizens on the basis of birthright, marriage, or lengthy periods of residence. Very fundamentally, if arguments of human dignity and justice are to play any role with regard to allocation of citizenship, then we would need to avail ourselves of *Rawl's* "veil of ignorance"[1468] to look at the entire world society, which would necessarily lead to very different ways of allocating or re-allocating the privileges of citizenship among the world's population than the current citizenship allocation system we have today, for *Rawl's* tenet that "*[s]omehow we must nullify the effects of specific contingencies which put men at odds and tempt them to exploit social and natural circumstances to their own advantage*"[1469] would require entirely different ways of allocating citizenship, because accident of birth is obviously one of the world's most relevant and most blatantly unjust contingencies that allow people (and nations) to exploit it to their own advantage, with equally obvious dramatic consequences to human dignity and global justice. For "*[w]e do not deserve our place in the distribution of native endowments, any more than we deserve our initial starting point in society*"[1470]

21 In the face of this global injustice of citizenship allocation, at least *ius doni* allows all the people randomly allocated at birth citizenships

[1467] *Bauböck* in SMITH (2011)
[1468] RAWLS (1999)
[1469] RAWLS (1999) p. 118
[1470] Ibid.

that they feel are inadequate for them, the opportunity to seek actively an alternative citizenship on the basis of clear criteria, including the most universally accepted criteria which transcends all borders: money. Even though it could be argued that this excludes all those who cannot afford to pay the price set by states, it is in fact a less random, less arbitrary and less restrictive criterion than any other criteria for the allocation of citizenship.

22 As long as there remain nation states with nationals (citizens) and foreigners, at least ideal access criteria should be transparently formulated.[1471] Traditional models of migration have assumed "*migrants settle in one place and take on a new, singular political identity. But a more closely interconnected world means that the link between countries often remains continuous and can even be strengthened by migration*".[1472] Thus the traditional conception of citizenship is also "*increasingly at odds with the reality of modern life.*"[1473] Liberal states can no longer explicitly reproduce and reinvigorate particular nationhood through immigration and citizenship policy. The state now has to consider individuals for what they do, and not for what they are.[1474] Individuals are now selected according to "achievement" and not "ascription",[1475] and this transition from ascription to achievement is the hallmark of modernisation. In this sense it can be argued that "*an immigration policy under the sign of skills and achieved individual characteristics, rather than primordial givens, has finally caught up with modernity*".[1476]

Citizenship-by-Investment fulfils exactly this function, by at least enabling those people who meet certain criteria, in particular character and economic criteria, to obtain access to citizenship in a more interconnected world. Citizenship law should also generally and from its foundations be designed so that the foreign individuals who aspire to citizenship know precisely the conditions under which

---

[1471] WALZER (1983)
[1472] PICKUS (1998) p. 116
[1473] Ibid.
[1474] JOPPKE (2005)
[1475] PARSONS (1971)
[1476] JOPPKE (2005) p. 3

the citizenship can be obtained.[1477] This can be ensured not least by transparent Citizenship-by-Investment programmes in an exemplary manner: an accurate catalogue of criteria can be published, enabling whoever meets the requirements to expect to be admitted. This leads to a new kind of cosmopolitanism, as, at least for wealthy people (and equally for the highly qualified in the immigration laws of most States today), arbitrary limits are reduced or are removed. This would also replace the monopoly exercised by any single State over its own citizens, at least in part, by a certain free market mechanism. This is only possible if viable alternatives exist,[1478] which is achieved already by the fact that globally, many Citizenship-by-Investment programmes have already been established. Wealthy people who seek a transnational identity thus have choices and are able to overcome obstacles to personal mobility and traverse borders opportunistically.[1479] In the era of globalisation, the opportunity to gain and exchange citizenships through Citizenship-by-Investment programmes, and in this respect not to be subject to any particular State monopoly, would appear to be a positive liberalising step towards a free cosmopolitism, comparable to the liberalisation of traditional State monopolies as the basis for a free national society.[1480] In this regard, on an international level it can even be argued that all states should make their citizenship available to anyone interested and willing to pay, in effect creating a global market for citizenships, enabling market forces to then determine prices.

23 In international law nation States have a scope for action within their public international law sovereignty, within which they can direct the migration flows they confront, not only as a result of economic globalisation and cross-border labour mobility, but also as a result of demographic, climatic and geopolitical change. The remaining scope for action after the "deduction" of universal international law, customary international law and the international treaty law countries have ratified, corresponds to their scope for policymaking

1477 BENHABIB (2004) pp. 139–140
1478 cf. FRIEDMAN (1962)
1479 VAN FOSSEN (2007)
1480 cf. HAYEK (1944)

within which they can legislate autonomously in their capacities as subjects of public international law. Citizenship law remains principally in the *domaine reservé* of nation states, and thus also the freedom to regulate modes of acquisition of citizenship, including *ius doni.*

24 Conceptually, country-specific Citizenship-by-Investment programmes of various designs can be initiated and directed by a State for the acquisition of foreign direct investment, rendered in "consideration" for the granting of citizenship of the host country. The mere facilitation of naturalisation can be distinguished from partial waiver of the usual legal naturalisation requirements (domestic residence, mastery of a domestic language, basic knowledge of the host country and its history etc.), and naturalisation without further consideration, i.e. citizenship "in exchange for" investment. Insofar as naturalisation is based on the investor's personal economic contribution being the decisive criterion, this can be referred to as *ius doni.*

25 The largest economic benefits for a country are generated by programmes which require direct, non-refundable economic contributions to the government or to a national fund. There is no guarantee that the money will be wisely spent, however this model faces fewer problems related to the investments, is straightforward, and non-refundable contributions cannot be withdrawn.[1481] Significant positive macroeconomic impact can also be achieved by incentivising private sector investments, notably in the real estate sector. At the other end of the spectrum, we can find investor immigration programmes which merely ask for an investment in government bonds, which are repaid to the investor after a period, so that the actual impact in the destination country is minimal and raises the question whether such models actually make any sense for countries who wish to attract foreign investment and serious investors.[1482]

[1481] SUMPTION/HOOPER (2014); cf. also XU/EL-ASHRAM/GOLD (2015)

[1482] For a recent view regarding this and in particular the US EB-5 program, see *Eric*

26 Just like ordinary naturalisation, legal boundaries are drawn for Citizenship-by-Investment, which in liberally constituted States not only result from the principle of democracy ("no sale of sovereign rights"), but in particular from the prohibition of tying arrangements as a manifestation of the rule of law. Regardless the dogmatic classification of naturalisation, the "consideration" – here the direct investment – must be reasonable, all circumstances must be taken into account, and the decision must be within the competence of the relevant authority. The constitutional principle of legality in itself requires that the criteria for the granting of a Citizenship-by-Investment are adequately specified, based on the rule of law.

27 In terms of the reference States discussed, the Citizenship-by-Investment programmes of St. Kitts and Nevis and Malta are supported by more detailed legislative schemes than those of Austria and Montenegro, where the government has far-reaching discretionary latitude in terms of deciding whether to grant naturalisation to investors, without it being clear in the relevant laws under what conditions an investment will be considered as "sufficient consideration" for naturalisation. Theoretically, this limited legislative specification enables government decision-makers to better evaluate appropriate investors as part of a comprehensive due diligence process and to refuse naturalisation in case of doubt. However, practical experience, especially in Austria and Montenegro, has shown that discretion in decision making can invite corruption, bribery and other forms of crime. The criteria for Citizenship-by-Investment should therefore be enshrined in primary or secondary legislation, and precisely circumscribed, not least also from a general rule of law perspective.

28 Citizenship-by-Investment programmes open up opportunities for economically weaker States to catch up with wealthier States in terms of their economy, in particular if the investment made in the

---

Posner, http://www.slate.com/articles/news_and_politics/view_from_chicago/2015/05/eb_5_visa_program_for_immigrant_investors_this_path_to_citizenship_is_a.html, last accessed 17 May 2015

host country contributes, for example, to the emergence of industrial "clusters", which not only provide a wide range of people with a secure job and relieve the State community, but also support the public infrastructure (roads, schools, kindergartens etc.) of the host country and draw in other companies. The opportunities offered by Citizenship-by-Investment are very significant from an economic development perspective.

29 It would be farfetched to say that investment and migration flows between countries can be steered using Citizenship-by-Investment programmes (although the example of St. Kitts and Nevis impressively shows that this is very much possible, at least for a small State),[1483] but States can certainly influence investment flows using such programmes, assuming they are set up properly.

30 Over the last 200 years, citizenship and nationhood have been woven together, "*inextricably linked in defining political identity and place in the global landscape*".[1484] However, when the modern concept of citizenship crystallised following the American and French revolutions, people did not understand citizenship as we do today. Similarly, in the future, we will develop very different ideas of membership and belonging, of citizenship and of how citizenship can be acquired.[1485] "*The arrival of world citizenship is no longer merely a phantom, though we are still far from achieving it. State citizenship and world citizenship form a continuum that already shows itself, at least, in outline form*".[1486]

We are in the midst of a global trend of transformation of citizenship, which includes the advent of *ius doni*, an idea whose time has come. The future of citizenship, the conception of citizenship in the twenty-first century, will be very different indeed.

1483 cf. XU/EL-ASHRAM/GOLD (2015)
1484 JACOBSEN (1996) p. vii
1485 cf. PICKUS (1998)
1486 HABERMAS (1995) p. 279

Bibliography

Abderhalden Ursula/Ehrenzeller Bernhard: Aktuelle Entwicklungen im schweizerischen Ausländerrecht, ZAR 2008, pp. 216-223

Achermann Alberto/Achermann Christin/D'Amato Gianni/Kamm Martina/Von Rütte Barbara: Country Report: Switzerland, Eudo Citizenship Observatory, Florence 2013

Achermann Christian/Gass Stefanie: Staatsangehörigkeit und soziale Schliessung. Eine rechtsethnologische Sicht auf die Einbürgerungspraxis der Stadt Basel, Zurich 2003

Adams Walter: The Brain Drain, New York 1968

Aleinikoff T. Alexander: Between Principles and Politics: The Direction of US Citizenship Policy, Washington D.C. 1998

- id. -/Chetail Vincent: Migration and International Legal Norms, Washington D.C. 2003

- id. -/Klusmeyer Douglas: Citizenship Policies for an Age of Migration, Washington D.C. 1952

- id. -/- id. - From Migrants to Citizens: Membership in a Changing World, Washington D.C. 2000

- id. -/- id. - Citizenship Today: Global Perspectives and Practices, Washington D.C. 2001

- id. -/- id. - Relational Nationality: On Gender and Nationality in International Law, in: Aleinikoff T. Alexander/Klusmeyer Douglas B. (Eds.), Citizenship Today: Global Perspectives and Practices, Washington, D.C. 2001, pp. 89–124

- id. -/Martin David A./Motomura Hiroshi/Fullerton Maryellen: Immigration and Citizenship Process and Policy, 6th Edition, St. Paul MN 2008

Alesina Alberto/Spolaore Enrico: The Size of Nations, Cambridge Mass. 2005

Allan Trevor R.S.: The Sovereignty of Law: Freedom, Constitution and Common Law, Oxford 2013

Altmeier Peter: Vom nationalen Ausländerrecht zum europäischen Migrationsrecht, ZAR 2010, pp. 355–359

Amerasinghe Chittharanjan F.: Diplomatic Protection, Oxford 2008

Amrhein Saundra/Lindquist Ariana/Yale-Loehr Stephen/Danielson Laura: Green Card Stories, New York 2011

Andrijašević Živko M./Rastoder Serbo: The History of Montenegro: From Ancient Times to 2003, Podgorica 2006

Angeli Oliviero/Kolb Holger: Nicht nur effizienter, sondern auch gerechter? Ein Modell preisbasierter Zuwanderungssteuerung, ZAR 2011, pp. 254–258

Annoni Alessandra/Forlati Serena: The Changing Role of Nationality in International Law, Oxon/New York 2013

Arendt Hannah: Men in Dark Times, San Diego/New York/London 1968

- id. - The Origins of Totaliarianism, New York 1973

Argast Regula: Staatsbürgerschaft und Nation, Ausschliessung und Integration in der Schweiz 1848–1933, Göttingen 2007

Aristotle: The Politics and the Constitution of Athens, Everson Stephen (Ed.), Cambridge 1996

Armstrong Chris: The Price of Selling Citizenship, in: Shachar Ayelet/Bauböck Rainer (Eds.), Should Citizenship be for Sale? EUI Working Papers, Robert Schuhmann Centre for Advanced Studies 2014/01, European University Institute, Florence 2014, pp. 13–14

Aust Anthony: Modern Treaty Law and Practice, Cambridge 2007

Barbulescu Roxana: Global Mobility Corridors for the Ultra-Rich: The Neoliberal Transformation of Citizenship, in: Shachar Ayelet/Bauböck Rainer (Eds.), Should Citizenship be for Sale? EUI Working Papers, Robert Schuhmann Centre for Advanced Studies 2014/01, European University Institute, Florence 2014, pp. 15–16

Barnhill John H.: Brain Drain, in: Patrick Hayes (Ed.), The Making of Modern Immigration, Vol. 1, Santa Barbara/Denver/Oxford 2012, pp. 143–162

Barston R.P.: Modern Diplomacy, Harlow 2006

Bauböck Rainer: Transnational Citizenship: Membership and Rights in International Migration, Aldershot 1994

- id. - Political Community Beyond the Sovereign State, Supranational Federalism, and Transnational Minorities, in: Vertovec Steven/Cohen Robin (Eds.), Conceiving Cosmopolitanism: Theory, Context, and Practice, New York 2002, pp. 110–136

- id. - Expansive Citizenship: Voting Beyond Territory and Membership, Political Science and Politics (2005) 38, 683–87

- id. - Citizenship and Free Movement, in: Smith Rogers M. (Ed.), Citizenship, Borders, and Human Needs, Philadelphia 2011, pp. 343–376

- id. - What is Wrong with Selling Citizenship? It Corrupts Democracy!, in: Shachar Ayelet/Bauböck Rainer (Eds.), Should Citizenship be for Sale? EUI Working Papers, Robert Schuhmann Centre for Advanced Studies 2014/01, European University Institute, Florence 2014, pp. 19–21

- id. -/Ersbøll Eva/Groenendijk Kees/Waldrauch Harald: Acquisition and Loss of Nationality: Policies and Trends in 15 European Countries, Vol. 2: Country Analyses, Amsterdam 2006

- id. -/- id. -/- id. -/- id. - Policies and Trends in 15 European States, Workshop on Innovative Concepts for Alternative Migration Policies, Amsterdam 2006

- id. -/Perchinig Bernhard/Sievers Wiebke: Citizenship Policies in the New Europe, Amsterdam 2009

Baudenbacher Carl/Kokott Juliane: Current Developments in the European and International Business Law, Basel 2011

Bechthold Stefan: For the Economic Analysis of Law in Intellectual Property, GRUR Int. 2008, pp. 484–488

Becker Gary S.: The Economics of Discrimination, Chicago 1957

- id. - The Economic Approach to Human Behavior, Chicago 1976

- id. -/Becker Guity Nashat, The Economics of Life, New York 1997

Becker Ulrich: Staatsangehörigkeit und Aufenthalt als Anknüpfungspunkte für die Gewährung sozialer Rechte in der Europäischen Union: Thesen zur abgestuften territorialen Verantwortung der Mitgliedstaaten für den sozialen Schutz von Unionsbürgern, in: Muller-Graff Peter-Christian/ Schmahl Stefanie/Skouris Vasilios (Eds.), Festschrift for Dieter H. Scheuing Europäisches Recht zwischen Bewährung und Wandel, Baden-Baden 2011, pp. 480-492

Beiner Ronald: Theorizing Citizenship, Albany 1995

Beitz Charles R.: Politcal Theory and International Relations, Princeton 1999

Beldi Oliver: Die Auswirkungen der Due Diligence auf die Verkäuferhaftung beim Unternehmenskauf - Rechtsvergleichende Betrachtung Schweiz/ Deutschland/USA, in: Baudenbacher Carl/Kokott Juliane (Eds.), Aktuelle Entwicklungen des Europäischen und internationalen Wirtschaftsrechts, Basel 2011

Bellamy Richard: Citizenship: A Very Short Introduction, Oxford 2008

- id. -/Castiglione Dario/Santoro Emilio: Lineages of European Citizenship: Rights, Belonging and Participation in Eleven Nation-States, Basingstoke 2004

- id. -/Castiglione Dario/Shaw Jo: Making European Citizens: Civic Inclusion in a Transnational Context, Basingstoke 2006

Benhabib Seyla: The Claims of Culture: Equality and Diversity in the Global Era, Princeton/Oxford 2002

- id. - The Rights of Others, Cambridge 2004

Ben-Porat Guy/Turner Bryan S: The Contradictions of Israeli Citizenship: Land, Religion and State, Oxon/New York 2011

Berber Friedrich: Lehrbuch des Völkerrechts, Bd. 1: Allgemeines Friedensrecht, 2nd Edition, Munich 1975

Berens Wolfgang: Due Diligence in Mergers and Acquisitions, 5th Edition, Stuttgart 2008

Berezin Mabel/Schain Martin: Europe Without Borders: Remapping Territory, Citizenship and Identity in a Transnational Age, Baltimore 2003

Bergmann Wilfried/Ferid Murad/Henrich Dieter: Internationales Ehe- und Kindschaftsrecht mit Staatsangehörigkeitsrecht, Frankfurt am Main 2005

- id. -/Korth Jürgen: Deutsches Staatsangehörigkeits- und Passrecht, 1. Halbband: Staatsangehörigkeitsrecht, Cologne 1989

Berridge G.R.: Diplomacy, Theory and Practice, 3rd Edition, Hampshire 2005

Berton Raul Magni: Citizenship for Those who Invest into the Future of the State is Not Wrong, the Price is the Problem, in: Shachar Ayelet/ Bauböck Rainer (Eds.), Should Citizenship be for Sale? EUI Working Papers, Robert Schuhmann Centre for Advanced Studies 2014/01, European University Institute, Florence 2014, pp. 11–12

Bethge Philip/Brauck Markus/Müller Martin U./Rosenbach Marcel/ Schmundt Hilmar/Schulz Thomas/Tietz Janko: The Fantastic Four, Der Spiegel of 5 December 2011, pp. 70–81

Betten Rijkele: Income Tax Aspects of Emigration and Immigration of Individuals, Amsterdam 1998

Bhagwati Jagdish: Directly Unproductive, Profit-Seeking (DUP) Activities, Journal of Political Economy (1982), Vol. 90, 988–1002

Blitz Brad K./Lynch Maureen: Statelessness and Citizenship – A Comparative Study on the Benefits of Nationality – Cheltenham/Northampton 2011

Bloemraad Irene: Staatsangehörigkeit und Einwanderung: Assimilation, Multikulturalismus und der Nationalstaat, Berkeley 2006

- id. -/Korteweg Anna/Yurdakul Gökce: Citizenship and Immigration: Assimilation, Multiculturalism and the Nation State, Berlin 2009

Blumenwitz Dieter: Writings on Constitutional and International Law, Vol. 55, Würzburg 1992

- id. - Einführung in das anglo-amerikanische Recht, 6th Edition, Munich 1998

Borna Shaheen/Stearns James M.: The Ethics and Efficacy of Selling National Citizenship, Journal of Business Ethics (2002), Vol. 37, 193–207

Borstel Stefan von/Wisdorff Flora: Andere Prioritäten am Arbeitsmarkt – Erwerbslosenquote auf 20-Jahres-Tief. Grösse Aufgabe ist nun der Fachkräftemandel – DIE WELT of 1 December 2011, p. 11

Bosniak Linda: The Citizen and the Alien: Dilemmas of Contemporary Membership, Princeton 2006

Bratiloveanu Izabela: "Objektformel" – Eventual Acts of Damage to Human Dignity, AGORA International Journal of Juridical Sciences (2014), 19–26

Bréville Benoît: Pourquoi vous ne deviendrez jamais chinois, Le Monde Diplomatique, January 2014

Brisimi Vasiliki: The Interface between Competition and the Internal Market: Market Separation under Article 102 TFEU, Oxford 2014

Brockhaus: History – From the Eve of the First World War to the Present – Mannheim/Leipzig 2003

Brubaker William Rogers: Immigration and the Politics of Citizenship in Europe and North America, Lanham/New York/London 1989

- id. - Citizenship and Nationhood in France and Germany, Lanham/New York/London 1992

- id. - Nationalism Reframed, Nationalhood and the National Question in the New Europe, Cambridge 1996

- id. - Ethnicity Without Groups, Cambridge 2004

Buchanan James M.: An Economic Theory of Clubs, Economica Bd. 32 (1965), 1–14

Buttigieg Eugène: Country Report: Malta, EUDO Citizenship Observatory, Florence 2013

Cagaptay Soner: Passage to Turkishness. Immigration and Religion in Modern Turkey, in: Güalp Haldun (Ed.), Citizenship and Ethnic Conflict: Challenging the Nation State, Oxon 2006, pp. 61–82

Calder Gideon/Cole Phillip/Seglow Jonathan: Citizenship Acquisition and National Belonging: Migration, Membership and the Liberal Democratic State, Basingstoke, 2010

Calhoun Craig: The Class Conciousness of Frequent Travellers: Towards a Critique of Actually Existing Cosmopolitanism, in: Vertovec Steven/ Cohen Robin (Eds.), Conceiving Cosmopolitanism: Theory, Context, and Practice, New York 2008, pp. 86-116

Calliess Christian/Ruffert Matthias: Das Verfassungsrecht der Europäischen Union mit Europäischer Grundrechtecharta – Commentary, 3rd Edition, Neuwied/Kriftel 2007

Caplan Jane/Torpey John: Documenting Individual Identity – The Development of State Practices in the Modern World, London 2001

Carens Joseph H.: Aliens and Citizens: The Case for Open Borders, in: Beiner Ronald (Ed.), Theorizing Citizenship, Albany 1995, pp. 229-253

- id. - Membership and Morality: Admission to Citizenship in Liberal Democratic States, in: Brubaker William Rogers (Ed.), Immigration and the Politics of Citizenship in Europe and North America, Lanham and London 1989

- id. - Why Naturalization Should be Easy: A Reply to Noah Pickus, in: Pickus Noah M.J. (Eds.), Immigration and Citizenship in the Twenty-first Century, Lanham 1998, pp. 141-146

- id. - Migration and Morality: A Liberal Egalitarian Perspective, in: Barry Brian/Goodin Robert (Eds.), Free Movement: Ethical Issues in the Transnational Migration of People and of Money, University Park 1992, pp. 25-47

- id. - The Ethics of Immigration, Oxford 2013

Caroni Martina/Grasdorf-Meyer Tobias/Ott Lisa/Scheiber Nicole: Migrationsrecht, 3., stark überarbeitete Auflage, Bern 2014

Carrera Sergio: The Price of EU Citizenship: The Maltese Citizenship-for-Sale Affair and the Principle of Sincere Cooperation in Nationality Matters, CEPS Paper in Liberty and Security in Europe, (April, 2014), No. 64, Brussels 2014

Casalini Brunella: American Citizenship: Between Past and Present, in: Bellamy Richard/Castiglione Dario/Santoro Emilio (Eds.), Lineages of European Citizenship: Rights, Belonging and Participation in Eleven Nation-States, Basingstoke 2004, pp. 186-206

Castells Manuel: The Power of Identity, Oxford 1997

Chiswick Barry R.: The Economics of Immigration, Cheltenham 2005

- id. - High-Skilled Immigration in a Global Labor Market, Washington D.C. 2011

Cicero: Reden gegen Verres. Kommentar. Selection by Willibald Voigt Münster 1987

Cohn-Bendit Daniel/Schmid Thomas: Heimat Babylon: Das Wagnis der multikulturellen Demokratie, Hamburg 1992

Cornes Richard/Sandler Todd: The Theory of Externalities, Public Goods, and Club Goods, Cambridge 1996

Council of Europe: Definition and Development of Human Rights and Popular Sovereignty in Europe, Science and Technique of Democracy, No. 49, Strasbourg 2011

Craig Paul/de Bürca Grainne: EU Law: Text, Cases, and Materials, Oxford 2015

Crouch Colin: Kommerzialisierung oder Staatsbürgerschaft. Bildungspolitik und die Zukunft des öffentlichen Dienstes, in: Mackert Jürgen/Müller (Eds.), Moderne (Staats) Bürgerschaft. Nationale Staatsbürgerschaft und die Debatten der Citizenship Studies, Wiesbaden 2007, pp. 167-212

Dahlvik Julia/Fassmann Heinz/Sievers Wiebke: Migration und Integration – wissenschaftliche Perspektiven aus Österreich, Göttingen 2012

Dahm Georg/Delbrück Jost/Wolfrum Rüdiger: Völkerrecht, Band I/2: Der Staat und andere Völkerrechtssubjekte. Räume unter internationaler Verwaltung, Berlin 2002

Dahrendorf Ralf: Citizenship and Beyond: The Social Dynamics of an Idea, Social Forces (1974), Vol. 41, 673–701

D'Amato Gianni/Gerber Brigitta: Tagung Herausforderung Integration: Migrationspolitik für schweizerische und europäische Städte, Serie Sozialer Zusammenhalt und kultureller Pluralismus, Zurich 2005

Davies Gareth: The Humiliation of the State as a Constitutional Tactic, in: Amtenbrink Fabian/van den Berg Peter A. J. (Eds.), The Constitutional Integrity of the European Union, The Hague 2010, pp. 147–174

De Groot Gerard-René: Staatsangehörigkeitsrecht im Wandel: Eine rechtsvergleichende Studie über Erwerbs- und Verlustgründe der Staatsangehörigkeit, Köln 1989

Delbrück Jost/Wolfrum Rüdiger: Völkerrecht – Bd. I/3: Die Formen des völkerrechtlichen Handelns; Die inhaltliche Ordnung der internationalen Gemeinschaft, 2nd Edition, Berlin 2002

Denza Eileen: Diplomatic Law, Commentary on the Vienna Convention on Diplomatic Relations, 2nd Edition, Oxford 1998

Dershowitz Alan: Rights from Wrongs: A Secular Theory of the Origins of Rights, New York 2004

Despeux Gilles: Dual Nationality in France, StAZ 2001, pp. 129–137

Destination Canada: Reisen – Arbeiten – Auswandern – Leben in Kanada, http://www.destinationkanada.ca/auswandern/index.html, last accessed on 21 September 2012

DGB Bildungswerk e.V.: Staatsangehörigkeit – hier und anderswo: Bosnien und Herzegowina, Kroatien, Polen, Serbien und Montenegro, Türkei, in: Handreichung – Schriftenreihe Migration und Arbeitswelt, Vol. 19

- id. - Staatsangehörigkeit – hier und anderswo: Bulgarien, Deutschland, Slowakische Republik, Tschechische Republik, Ungarn, in: Handreichung – Schriftenreihe Migration und Arbeitswelt, Vol. 22

Dieckhoff Alain: The Nation in Israel: Between Democracy and Ethnicity, in: Güalp Haldun (Ed.): Citizenship and Ethnic Conflict: Challenging the Nation-State, Oxon 2006, pp. 83-98

Dietrich Marija: Staatliches Souveränitätsverständnis im Wandel der gesellschaftspolitischen Strukturen, Schriften zum internationalen und zum öffentlichen Recht, Vol. 95, Frankfurt am Main 2011

Doehring Karl: Völkerrecht: Ein Lehrbuch, 2nd Edition, Heidelberg 2004

Dolzer Rudolf/Vogel Klaus/Grasshof Karin: Bonner Kommentar zum Grundgesetz, 67 issue 1992, update, Heidelberg 2005

Donner Ruth: The Regulation of Nationality in International Law, 2nd Edition, Irvington-on-Hudson 1994

Downing Brian M.: The Military Revolution and Political Change: Origins of Democracy and Autocracy in Early Modern Europe, Princeton 1993

Dubois Bernhard: Die Frage der völkerrechtlichen Schranken landesrechtlicher Regelung der Staatsangehörigkeit, Bern 1955

Dummett Ann/Nicol Andrew: Subjects, Citizens, Aliens and Others: Nationality and Immigration Law, London 1990

Dynneson Thomas L.: Civism: Cultivating Citizenship in European History, New York 2001

Dzankic Jelena: Transformations of Citizenship in Montenegro: A Context-generated Evolution of Citizenship Policies, European Research Council, CITSEE Working Paper Series Nr. 2010/03, Edinburgh 2010

- id. - The Pros and Cons of Ius pecuniae: Investor Citizenship in Comparative Perspective, published by Robert Schumann Centre for Advanced Studies, EUI Working Papers No. 2012/14

- id. - Are All Animals Equal? Ethical Aspects of Investor Citizenship Programs, in: IFC Review (2014)

Eckhardt Saskia: Die Akteure des aussergerichtlichen Verfassungsrechtsschutzes in der Europäischen Union, Europäische Hochschulschriften Vol. 4938, Frankfurt am Main 2010

Eichenhofer Johannes/Hörich Carsten/Pichl Maximilian: "Ist Deutschland noch ein Einwanderungsland?" Bericht von der Vierten Herbsttagung des Netzwerks Migrationsrecht vom of 12 to 14 November 2011 in Stuttgart-Hohenheim, ZAR 2011, pp. 183–187

Eide Asbjørn: The Rights of "Old" versus "New" Minorities, in: Malloy Tove H./Marko Joseph (Eds.), Minority Governance in and Beyond Europe: Celebrating 10 Years of the European Yearbook of Minority Issues, Leiden/Boston 2014, pp. 23-38

Eilers Stephan/Rödding Adalbert/Schmalenbach Dirk: Unternehmensfinanzierung, Munich 2008

Emmerich-Fritsche Angelika: Sozialprinzip und Weltwirtschaftsverfassung am Beispiel von WTO und ULO, in: Hankel Wilhelm/Albrecht Schachtschneider Karl/Starbatty Joachim (Eds.), Der Ökonom als Politiker: Europa, Geld und die soziale Frage: Festschrift für Wilhelm Nölling, Stuttgart 2003, pp. 125-158

Erbguth Wilfried/Mahlburg Stefan: Steuerung von Offshore-Windenergieanlagen in der Ausschliesslichen Wirtschaftszone, in: DÖV 2003, S., 665–672

Erichsen Hans-Uwe/Ehlers Dirk: Allgemeines Verwaltungsrechtsrecht, 12th Edition, Berlin 2002

European Commission: Co-Creating EU Citizenship: A Policy Review, Brussels 2013

Fahrmeir Andreas: Citizen and Aliens: Foreigners and the Law in Britain and the German States, New York/Oxford 2000

- id. -/Faron Olivier/Weil Patrick: Migration Control in the North Atlantic World: The Evolution of State Practices in Europe and the US from the French Revoluion to the Inter-War Period, New York/Oxford 2003

Faist Thomas: Dual Citizenship as Overlapping Membership, Willy Brandt Series of Working Papers in International Migration and Ethnic Relations, Malmö 2001

- id. - Die transnationale soziale Frage. Soziale Rechte und Bürgerschaften im globalen Kontext, in: Mackert Jürgen/Müller (Eds.), Moderne (Staats) Bürgerschaft. Nationale Staatsbürgerschaft und die Debatten der Citizenship Studies, Wiesbaden 2007, pp. 285-307

- id. -/Kivisto Peter: Dual Citizenship in Global Perspective: From Unitary to Multiple Citizenship, Basingstoke/New York 2007

Faix Werner G./Kisgen Stefanie/Lau Alexander/Schulten Annette/Zywietz Tassilo: Praxishandbuch Aussenwirtschaft – Erfolgsfaktoren im Auslandsgeschäft, Wiesbaden 2006

Fehling Michael/Kastner Bertold/Wahrendorf Volker: Verwaltungsrecht – Administrative Procedures Act and Code of Administrative Procedure, 1st Edition, Baden-Baden 2006

Feltham Ralph G.: Diplomatic Handbook, Leiden 2006

Fessler Peter/Keller Christian/Pommerening-Schober Renate/Szymanski Wolf: Das neue österreichische Staatsbürgerschaftsrecht – Mit zahlreichen Anmerkungen, Verweisungen und grundlegenden Entscheidungen der Gerichtshöfe des öffentlichen Rechts, Wien 2006

Fine Robert/Cohen Robin: Four Cosmopolitanism Moments, in: Vertovec Steven/Cohen Robin (Eds.), Conceiving Cosmopolitanism: Theory, Context, and Practice, New York 2008, pp. 137-162

Fisch Jörg: Die Verteilung der Welt: Selbstbestimmung und das Selbstbestimmungsrecht der Völker, Journal of the College of History Vol. 79

Forsythe David P.: Human Rights in International Relations, 3rd Edition, New York 2012

Fortmann Anke: Mehrfache Staatsangehörigkeit – Eine Untersuchung der Verfassungskonformität des Optionsmodells, dissertation, European University Studies Vol. 4226, Frankfurt am Main 2005

Fossen Anthony van: Citizenship for Sale: Passports of Convenience From Pacific Island Tax Havens, Commonwealth and Comparative Politics (2007), Vol. 45 (2), 138–163

Fransman Laurie: Fransman's British Nationality Law, 3rd Edition, Hayward Heath 2011

Frenz Walter: Handbuch Europarecht, Vol. 4: European Constitutional Rights, Berlin/Heidelberg 2009

Frey Bruno S./Eichberger Reiner: The New Democratic Federalism for Europe: Functional, Overlapping and Competing Jurisdictions, Cheltenham/ Northampton, MA 1999

Friedman Milton: Capitalism and Freedom, Chicago/London 1962

Gallie William B.: Essentially Contested Concepts, Proceedings of the Aristotelian Society (1955), Vol. 56(1), 167–198

Galloway Donald: The Dilemmas of Canadian Citizenship Law, in: Aleinikoff T. Alexander/Klusmeyer Douglas (Eds.), From Migrants to Citizens: Membership in a Changing world, Washington D.C. 2000, pp. 82-118

Gardt Andreas Language and National Identity, in: Gardt Andreas/Hüppauf Bernd (Eds.), Globalization and the Future of German, Berlin 2004, pp. 197-212

Garnier Marine/Martinez Damien: Economic Citizenship: Country Competition for Citizenship, Thomson Reuters White Paper, Paris 2013

Gesemann Frank: Arbeitskräfte ohne Rechte: Migration im Nahen Osten, in: Dietrich Thränhardt/Uwe Hunger (Eds.), Migration im Spannungsfeld von Globalisierung und Nationalstaat, Leviathan Sonderheft 22/2003, Wiesbaden 2003, pp. 346-366

Giddens Anthony: The Nation-State and Violence, Cambridge 1985

Gidon Gottlieb: Nation against State, New York 1993

Giegerich Thomas/Zimmermann Andreas: Economic Social and Cultural Rights in the Global Era, Berlin 2008

Gimbel John Francesco: Science, Technology, and Reparations: Exploitation and Plunder in Postwar Germany, Stamford 1990

Gironda Vito: Die Politik der Staatsangehörigkeit. Italien und Deutschland im Vergleich 1800–1914, Bonn 2010

Göbel-Zimmermann Ralph: Die Neuregelung des Staatsangehörigkeitsrechts, Die Öffentliche Verwaltung (DÖV) 2000, pp. 95–103

- id. - Das neue Staatsangehörigkeitsrecht – Erfahrungen und Reformvorschläge, ZAR 2003, pp. 65–75

Göktürk Deniz/Gramling David/Kaes Anton: Germany in Transit: Nation and Migration, 1955-2005, London 2007

Gosewinkel Dieter: Die Staatsangehörigkeit als Institution des Nationalstaates. Zur Entstehung des Reichs- und Staatsangehörigkeitsgesetzes von 1913, in honour of Böckenförde, Berlin 1995

- id. - Einbürgern und Ausschliessen, Göttingen 2003

Government of Canada: Canadian Citizenship Act and current issues, prepared by Margaret Young, Law and Government Division 1997, revised 1998, published online at: http://publications.gc.ca/collections/Collection-R/LoPBdP/BP/bp445-e.htmzitiert:THE ACT(txt), last accessed on 21 September 2012

- id. - Citizenship and Immigration Canada – Backgrounders: New Federal Immigrant Investor Program will bring to Canada More Resources to Fund Economic Development and Job Creation Initiatives, published online at http://www.cic.gc.ca/english/department/media/backgrounders/2010/2010-11-10a.asp, last accessed on 21 September 2012

- id. - Citizenship and Immigration Canada – Entrepreneurs, published online at http://www.cic.gc.ca/english/immigrate/business/entrepreneurs/index.asp, last accessed on 21 September 2012

- id. - Citizenship and Immigration Canada – Investors, published online at http://www.cic.gc.ca/english/immigrate/business/investors/index.asp, last accessed on 21 September 2012

- id. - Citizenship and Immigration Canada – News Release: Canada Reopens Immigrant Investor Program, published online at http://www.cic.gc.ca/english/department/media/releases/2010/2010-11-10a.asp, last accessed on 21 September 2012

Government of Ontario (Canada): Business-related Immigration, published online at http://www.sse.gov.on.ca/medt/investinontario/ger/Pages/business_immigration_home.aspx, last accessed on 21 September 2012

Grabitz Eberhard: Europäisches Bürgerrecht zwischen Marktbürgerschaft und Staatsangehörigkeit, Cologne 1970

Graf Gerhard: Grundlagen der Finanzwissenschaft, 2nd Edition, Heidelberg 2005

Grawert Rolf: Staat und Staatsangehörigkeit, Berlin 1973

Gray Christopher Berry: The Philosophy of Law: An Encyclopedia, New York/Oxon 1999

Grossmann Volker/Stadelmann David: High-Skilled Immigration: The Link to Public Expenditure and Private Investments, in: Chiswick Barry R. (Ed.), High-Skilled Immigration in a Global Labor Market, Washington D.C. 2011, pp. 201-230

Grover Sonja C.: The European Court of Human Rights as a Pathway to Impunity for International Crimes, Berlin/Heidelberg 2010

Guckelberger Annette: Der Europäische Bürgerbeauftragte und die Petitionen zum Europäischen Parlament: Eine Bestandsaufnahme zu Beginn des 21. Jahrhunderts, Schriftenreihe der Hochschule Speyer, Vol. 162, Berlin 2004

Guineva Maria: Born Bulgarian – Priceless, for Everything Else, There's Diaspora Minister Bozhidar Dimitrov, published online at http://www.novinite.com/view_news.php?id=119343, last accessed on 21 September 2012

Gülalp Haldun: Citizenship and Ethnic Conflict: Challenging the Nation State, Oxon 2006

Habermas Jürgen: Die Krise der Europäischen Union im Lichte einer Konstitutionalisierung des Völkerrechts – Ein Essay zur Verfassung Europas, 1989

- id. - Staatsangehörigkeit und nationale Identität, in: Habermas Jürgen, Faktizität und Geltung, Frankfurt am Main 1992, pp. 632-660

- id. - The Crisis of the EU in the Light of the Constitutionalization of International Law – An Essay on the Constitution of Europe - ZaöRV (2012), Vol. 72, 1–44

- id. - Zur Verfassung Europas. Ein Essay, 4th Edition, 2012

Hagedorn Heike: Die Reform der Reform: neues Einbürgerungsrecht in Frankreich, Zeitschrift für Ausländerrecht and Ausländerpolitik Bd. 19/1999, S. 3–9

Hailbronner Kay: Nationality in Public International Law and European Law, in: Baubock Rainer/Ersboll Eva/Groenendijk Cornelis A./Waldrauch Harald (Eds.), Acquisition and Loss of Nationality: Policies and Trends in 15 European Countries, Volume 1: Comparative Analyses, Amsterdam 2006, pp. 35–104

- id. - Staatsangehörigkeit und Unionsrecht: zur EuGH-Entscheidung vom 2.3.2010, StAZ 2011, S. 1–6

- id. -/Renner Günter/Maassen Hans-Georg: Staatsangehörigkeitsrecht, 5th Edition, Munich 2010

Hainmueller Jens/Hangartner Dominik: Who Gets a Swiss Passport? A Natural Experiment in Immigrant Discrimination, American Political Science Review (2013), Vol. 107(1), 159-187

Hamburg Institute of International Economics (HWWI): Fokus Migration Nr. 8 (March 2007): Länderprofil Kanada, published online http://www.hwwi.org/uploads/tx_wilpubdb/LP_08_Kanada.pdf, last accessed on 28 January 2015

Hammar Tomas: Democracy and the Nation State, Aldershot 1990

Hampe Karl-Alexander: Das Staatsangehörigkeitsrecht von Spanien, Portugal und Irland, Frankfurt am Main and Berlin 1960

Hampshire James: Becoming Citizens: Naturalisation in the Liberal State, in: Calder Gideon/Cole Phillip/Seglow Jonathan (Eds.), Citizenship Acquisition and National Belonging: Migration, Membership and the Liberal Democratic State, Basingstoke 2010, pp. 74-90

Hansen Randall/Weil Patrick: Dual Nationality, Social Rights and Federal Citizenship in the US and Europe, London 2002

- id. -/- id. - Towards a European Nationality: Citizenship, Immigration and Nationality Law in the EU, New York 2001

Harris Jose: Nationality, Rights and Virtue: Some Approaches to Citizenship in Great Britain, in: Bellamy Richard/Castiglione Dario/Santoro Emilio (Eds.), Lineages of European Citizenship: Rights, Belonging and Participation in Eleven Nation-States, Basingstoke 2004, pp. 73-91

Hasse Edgar S.: Deutscher geworden – 1997 wurde Saitgazi Demirci offiziell Staatsbürger, WELT KOMPAKT of 17 December 2007

Hayek Friedrich A.: The Road to Serfdom: Text and Documents, in: Caldwell Bruce (Ed.), London 2007 (1944)

- id. - The Pure Theory of Capital, Indianapolis 2007

Hayes Patrick: The Making of Modern Immigration, Vol. 1, Santa Barbara/Denver/Oxford 2012

Heater Derek: World Citizenship: Cosmopolitan Thinking and Its Opponents, London/New York 2002

- id. - Citizenship: The Civic Ideal in World History, Politics and Education, Manchester 2004

Hecker Hellmuth: Mehrseitige völkerrechtliche Verträge zum Staatsangehörigkeitsrecht, Frankfurt am Main/Berlin 1970

Hegel Georg Wilhelm Friedrich: Grundlinien der Philosophie des Rechts oder Naturrecht und Staatswissenschaft im Grundrisse, herausgegeben von Eva Moldenhauer und Karl Markus Michel, Frankfurt am Main 2004

Heinrich Böll Stiftung: "Die Zukunft der europäischen Demokratie", Schriften zu Europa Bd. 7, published online http://www.boell.de/downloads/Zukunft_Europaeische_Demokratie.pdf, last accessed on 21 September 2012

Helbling Marc: Practising Citizenship and Heterogeneous Nationhood: Naturalisations in Swiss Municipalities, Amsterdam 2008

Henckel Elisa: "Zu viele Deutsche im Land", WELT KOMPAKT of 27 April 2012

Hengstschläger Johannes/Leeb David: Kommentar zum Allgemeinen Verwaltungsverfahren, Vienna 2009

Henley & Partners: Global Citizens: A Journey, New York/London/Zurich/Hong Kong 2013

- id. - The Henley & Partners Visa Restrictions Index 2014, Jersey 2014

- id. - Global Residence and Citizenship Report 2015, New York/London/Zurich/Hong Kong 2014

Hepple Bob: Equality: The Legal Framework, 2nd Edition, Oxford 2014

Herdegen Matthias: Völkerrecht, 9th Edition, Munich 2010

Hering Rita: Der philosophische Begriff der Staatsangehörigkeit in seiner theoretischen Entwicklung und dessen praktischer Umsetzung am Beispiel der Unionsbürgerschaft, Munich 2011

Hernández-Bretón Eugenio: Staatsangehörigkeit und Fremdenrecht in der Verfassung Venezuelas von 1999, StAZ (2003), 161–169

Herskovits Melville J.: The Science of Cultural Anthropology, New York 1947

Herzog Roman/Gerken Lüder: Von Roten Karten und stumpfen Schwertern – Eine Grundsatzkritik des EU-Verfassungsentwurfs, DIE WELT 19 June 2007, 4–5

Heselhaus Sebastian M./Nowak Carsten: Handbuch der Europäischen Verfassungsrechte, Munich/Vienna/Bern 2006

Hindess Barry: Neo-liberal Citizenship, Citizenship Studies (2002) Vol. 6(2), 127–143

Hirsch Fred: The Social Limits to Growth, Cambridge Mass. 1976

Hobbes: Thomas Leviathan: or The Matter, Forme and Power of a Commonwealth Ecclesiasticall and Civill London 1651

Hobe Stephan: Der offene Verfassungsstaat zwischen Souveränität und Interdependenz. Eine Studie zur Wandlung des Staatsbegriffs der deutschsprachigen Staatslehre im Kontext internationaler institutionalisierter Kooperation, Berlin 1998

- id. - Einführung in das Völkerrecht, Tübingen/Basel 2008

Hobsbawm Eric: Nations and Nationalism since 1780: Programme, Myth, Reality, 2nd Edition, Cambridge 1992

Hobsbawm Eric/Ranger Terence: The Invention of Tradition, Cambridge 1983

Hoffmann Christian: Integrationspolitik in Deutschland nach 1998: Staatsangehörigkeitsrecht, Green Card und Zuwanderungsgesetz, Hamburg 2009

Hofmann Rainer M./Hoffmann Holger: Ausländerrecht: AufenthG, FreizügG/EU/AsylVfG/StAG, Baden-Baden 2008

Hogan-Brun Gabrielle/Mar-Molinero Clare/Stevanson Patrick: Discourses on Language and Integration: Critical Perspectives on Language and Itegration, Amsterdam/Philadelphia 2009

Hollinger David A.: Nationalism, Cosmopolitanism, and the US, in: Noah M. J. Pickus (Ed.), Immigration and Citizenship in the Twenty-First Century, Lanham 1998, pp. 85-99

Holzer Wolfgang: Strukturfragen des Betriebsvereinbarungsrechts, Vienna 1982

Homeko Tido Oliver: Mehrfache Staatsangehörigkeit, Frankfurt am Main 2002

Hömig Dieter/Seifert Karl-Heinz: Grundgesetz für die Bundesrepublik Deutschland, 9th Edition, Baden-Baden 2010

Horn Karen Ilse: Die Soziale Marktwirtschaft – Alles, was Sie über den Neoliberalismus wissen sollten, Frankfurt am Main in 2010

Howard Marc Morjé: The Politics of Citizenship in Europe, Cambridge 2009

Howard-Hassman Rhoda E. /Walton-Roberts Margaret: The Human Right to Citizenship: A Slippery Concept, Philadelphia 2015

Hunger Uwe: Brain drain oder brain gain: Migration und Entwicklung, in: Thränhardt Dietrich/Hunger Uwe (Eds.), Migration im Spannungsfeld von Globalisierung und Nationalstaat, Leviathan Sonderheft 22/2003, Wiesbaden 2003, pp. 58-75

Hutchinson Dennis J.: More Substantive Equal Protection? A Note on Plyler v. Doe, Chicago, The Supreme Court Review (1982)

Ignatieff Michael: Blood and Belonging Journeys into the New Nationalism, New York 1993

Institute of the German Economy in Cologne (IW): MINT-Report 2011 – Zehn gute Gründe für ein MINT-Studium, published online http://www.iwkoeln.de/Portals/0/pdf/MINT-Report%202011%20 Statement.pdf, last accessed on 21 September 2012

International Monetary Fund (IMF): St. Kitts and Nevis: Ninth and Final Review Under the Stand-By Arrangement, Request for Waiver of Nonobservance of Performance Criterion, and Proposal for Post-Program Monitoring-Staff Report, IMF Country Report No. 14/297, Washington D.C. 2014

Ipsen Jörn: Staatsrecht I, Staatsorganisationsrecht, 23rd Edition, Munich 2011

Ipsen Knud: Völkerrecht, 5th Edition, Munich 2004

Isensee Josef/Kirchhof Paul: Handbuch des Staatsrechts der Bundesrepublik Deutschland, Vol. II, 3rd Edition, Heidelberg 2005

Isin Engin F./Turner Bryan S.: Citizenship Studies, Los Angeles/London/New Delhi/Singapore/Washington DC 2002/2011

Israel Ron: Global Citizenship, Lexington 2012

Jacobson David: Rights across Borders: Immigration and the Decline of Citizenship, Baltimore 1996

Janoski Thomas: The Ironies of Citizenship Naturalisation and Integration in Industrialised Countries, New York, 2010

Jarass Hans D./Pieroth Bodo: Grundgesetz für die Bundesrepublik Deutschland, 11th Edition, Munich 2011

Jellinek Georg: System der subjektiven öffentlichen Rechte, 2nd Edition, Aalen 1964

- id. - Allgemeine Staatslehre, Kronberg 1976

Jesse Eckard: Renaissance des Staates? Veröffentlichungen der Deutschen Gesellschaft für Politikwissenschaft (DGfP), (2011), Vol. 29

Joly Danièle: International Migration in the New Millenium, Aldershot, 2004

Jones-Correa Michael, Under Two Flags: Dual Nationality in Latin America and Its Consequences for Naturalization in the United States, in: Martin David A./Hailbronner Kay (Eds.), Rights and Duties of Dual Nationals: Evolutions and Prospects, New York 2002, pp. 303-333

Joppke Christian: Selecting by Origin: Ethnic Migration in the Liberal State, Cambridge Mass. 2005

- id. - Citizenship and Immigration, Malden 2011

Julcher Angela: Die Menschenwürde als Rechtsbegriff und ihre Bedeutung im österreichischen Arbeitsrecht – dissertation, Vienna 1999

Jürgens Thomas: Diplomatic Protection and Stateless Persons, writings on International Law, Vol. 85, Berlin 1987

Kahanec Martin/Zimmermann Klaus F.: High-Skilled Immigration Policy in Europe, in: Chiswick Barry R. (Eds.), High-Skilled Immigration in a Global Labor Market, Washington D.C. 2011, pp. 264-314

Kaiser Tobias: Weltbank kritisiert geringe Arbeitszeit in Europa – Die Produktivität der Alten Welt ist seit Mitte der 90er Jahre gegenüber Japan und den USA stark gesunken, DIE WELT of 26 January 2012, p. 10

Kalekin-Fishman Devorah/Pitkänen Pirkko: An Emerging Institution? Multiple Citizenship in Europe – Views of Officials, Berne 2007

Kälin Christian H.: The Global Residence and Citizenship Handbook, 4th Edition, New York/London/Zurich/Hong Kong 2014

- id. - The Future of Citizenship, in: Times of Malta, 30 January 2015

Kamann Matthias: Mehr Macht dem EU-Bürger – Juristen fordern europaweite Volksabstimmungen. Das Parlament in Strassburg soll weitere Befugnisse erhalten, DIE WELT of 10 February 2012, p. 5

Kanaan Salaheldin: Abkommen zur Mehrstaatigkeit: Europaratsabkommen und ihr Einfluss auf die Staatsangehörigkeitsgesetzgebung Deutschlands, Hamburg 2012

Kant Immanuel: Zum Ewigen Frieden: Ein philosophischer Entwurf, Königsberg 1795

Kaplan William: Belonging: The Meaning and Future of Canadian Citizenship, Montreal 1993

Kaser Max: Das römische Privatrecht – Erster Abschnitt: Das altrömische, das vorklassische und klassische Recht, Munich 1971

- id. - /Knütel Rolf Römisches Privatrecht, Munich 2008

Kastoryano Riva: Redefining German Unity. From Nationality to Citizenship, in: Güalp Haldun (Ed.), Citizenship and Ethnic Conflict: Challenging the Nation-State, Oxon 2006, pp. 19–38

Keppler Michael: Risiko ist nicht gleich Volatilität, Die Bank 1990, pp. 610–614

Kesler Charles R.: The Promise of American Citizenship, in: Pickus Noah M.J. (Ed.), Immigration and Citizenship in the Twenty-First Century, Lanham 1998, pp. 3–40

Khaochan Patarin: Thai Nationals with Dual Nationality Status, Chulalongkorn 2009

Khoja Sara: The European Union: An Area of Freedom, Justice and Security – But For Whom? An Examination of the Legal Status and Rights of Third Country Nationals Within the European Union and Their Possible Acquisition of European Union Citizenship, Berlin 2005

Kimminich Otto/Hobe Stefan: Einführung in das Völkerrecht, Tübingen 2008

Kirchner Hildebert/Butz Cornelie: Abkürzungsverzeichnis der Rechtssprache, 7. Auflage, Berlin 2011

Kiwan Dina: Naturalisation Policies, Education and Citizenship, Basingstoke/New York 2013

Klamert Marcus: The Principle of Loyalty in EU Law, Oxford 2014

Kleeber Gabriela: Die Erlangung der österreichischen Staatsangehörigkeit durch besondere, insbesondere wirtschaftliche, Leistungen für die Republik Österreich im Vergleich zu anderen Rechtsordnungen, PhD thesis, Vienna 2007

Klepper Irena: Diplomatisches Asyl – Zulässigkeit und Grenzen, Europäische Hochschulschriften Vol. 4814, Frankfurt am Main 2008

Klusmeyer Douglas B.: Between Consent and Descent: Conceptions of Democratic Citizenship, Washington D.C. 1996

- id. -/Aleinikoff T. Alexander: Citizenship Policies for an Age of Migration, Washington D.C. 2002

Kluth Winfried: Migrationsgerechtigkeit, ZAR 2011, pp. 329–335

Kluth Winfried/Dog Michael/Maassen Hans-Georg: Zuwanderungsrecht, Allgemeines Zuwanderungs- und Aufenthaltsrecht, Aufenthaltsrecht nach europäischem Recht, Baden-Baden 2008

Kneip Christoph: Tax Due Diligence – Steuerrisiken und Steuergestaltungen beim Unternehmenskauf, Munich 2005

Knocke Brigitte: Das Europäische Übereinkommen über die Staatsangehörigkeit als Schranke für die Regelung des nationalen Staatsangehörigkeitsrechts. Stand der Vereinbarkeit des Staatsangehörigkeitsrechts der Schweiz, der Bundesrepublick Deutschland, des Vereinigten Königreichs und Frankreichs mit den Vorgaben des Übereinkommens, Herdecke 2005

Kochenov Dimitry: EU Enlargement and the Failure of Conditionality: Preaccession Conditionality in the Fields of Democracy and the Rule of Law, Alphen aan den Rijn 2008

- id. - Ius Tractum of Many Faces: European Citizenship and the Difficult Relationship between Status and Rights, Columbia Journal of European Law (2009), Vol. 15, 169–237

- id. - Citizenship without Respect: The EU's Troubled Equality Ideal, Jean Monnet Working Paper 08/10, New York 2010

- id. - Regional Citizenships and EU Law: The Case of The Aland Islands and New Caldedonia, European Law Review (2010), 307–324; cited as KOCHENOV (2010 II)

- id. - EU Law of the Overseas. Outermost Regions, Associated Overseas Countries and Territories, Territories Sui Generis, Alphen aan den Rijn 2011

- id. – The Present and the Future of EU Citizenship: A Bird's Eye View of the Legal Debate, Jean Monnet Working Paper 02/12, New York 2012

- id. - The Essence of EU Citizenship Emerging From the Last Ten Years of Academic Debate: Beyond the Cherry Blossoms and the Moon?, International and Comparative Law Quarterly (2013), 97–136

- id. - The Right to Have What Rights? EU Citizenship in Need of Clarification, European Law Journal (2013), Vol. 19, 502–516, cited as KOCHENOV (2013 II)

- id. - Citizenship for Real: Its Hypocrisy, Its Randomness, Its Price, in Shachar Ayelet/Bauböck Rainer (Eds.), Should Citizenship be for Sale? EUI Working Papers, Robert Schuhmann Centre for Advanced Studies 2014/01, European University Institute, Florence 2014, pp. 27–29

- id. – The Right to Leave Any Country, Including One's Own, in: Plender Richard (Ed.), Issues in International Migration Law, London 2015

Köhler Richard/Küpper Hans-Ulrich/Pfingsten Andreas: Handwörterbuch der Betriebswirtschaft, 6th Edition, Stuttgart 2007

Kokott Juliane/Doehring Karl/Buergenthal Thomas: Grundzüge des Völkerrechts, 3rd Edition, Heidelberg 2003

Koller Peter: Moral Conduct Under Conditions of Moral Imperfection, in: Pauer-Studer Herlinde (Ed.), Norms, Values, and Society, Dordrecht/Boston/London 1994, pp. 93-112

- id. - Frieden und Gerechtigkeit in einer geteilten Welt, in: Merkel Reinhard/Wittman Roland (Eds.), "Zum ewigen Frieden" –Grundlagen, Aktualität und Aussichten einer Idee von Immanuel Kant, Frankfurt am Main 1996, pp. 213-238

Konrad Adenauer Stiftung (KAS): Türken in Deutschland, Konrad Adenauer Working Paper No. 60, Sankt Augustin 2002, published online http://www.kas.de/wf/doc/kas_201-544-1-30.pdf?040415180309, last accessed on 28 January 2015

Koopmans Ruud/Statham Paul/Giugni Paul/Passy Marco: Contested Citizenship: Immigration and Cultural Diversity in Europe, Florence 2005

Kopp Ferdinand/Ramsauer Ulrich: Verwaltungsverfahrensgesetz, 9th Edition, Munich 2005

Koser Khalid: International Migration: A Very Short Introduction, Oxford 2007

Kostadinov Petar: Fast-track Bulgarian Citizenship Should Not Be Limited to Athletes, published online at http://sofiaecho.com/2010/04/30/894944_fast-track-bulgarian-citizenship-should-not-be-limited-to-athletes-minister, last accessed on 21 September 2012

Kostakopoulou Theodora: Nested "Old" and "New" Citizenship in the European Union: Bringing out the Complexity, Columbia Journal of European Law (1999), 389–413

Kramer Alfred: Die Staatsangehoerigkeit der Altoesterreicher und Ungarn nach den Friedensvertraegen: Die staatsbuergerrechtlichen Bestimmungen der Friedensvertraege von Saint-Germain, Trianon, die Minderheitsschutzverträge sowie ihrer Annexe samt den Durchfuehrungsvorschriften d. Nachfolgestaaten mit bes. Beruecks. d. Republik Oesterreich, Vienna 1926

Krings Günter: Grund und Grenzen verfassungsrechtlicher Schutzansprüche: Die subjektiv-rechtliche Rekonstruktion der verfassungsrechtlichen Schutzpflichten und ihre Auswirkung auf die verfassungsrechtliche Fundierung des Verbrauchervertragsrechts, dissertation, Cologne 2003

Kuhnen Jan Drees: Die Zukunft der Nationen in Europa, Berlin 2009

Kukathas Chandran: Expatriatism: The Theory and Practice of Open Borders, in: Smith Rogers M. (Ed.), Citizenship, Borders, and Human Needs, Philadelphia 2011, pp. 324-342

Kumar Krishan: The Idea of Europe. Cultural Legacies, Transnational Imaginings, and the Nation State, in: Berezin Mabel/Schain Martin (Eds.), Europe Without Borders: Remapping Territory, Citizenship and Identity in a Transnational Age, Baltimore 2003, pp. 33-50

Kunoy Bjørn: A Union of National Citizens: The Origins of The Court's Lack of Avant-Gardisme in the Chen Case, Common Market Law Review, (2006), Vol. 43(1), 179–190

Kuttner Robert: Everything for Sale: the Virtues and Limites of Markets, New York 1998

Laband Paul: Das Staatsrecht des Deutschen Reiches, Vol. 1, 5th Edition, Tübingen 1911

Laborde Cécile: Republican Citizenship in France, in: Bellamy Richard/ Castiglione Dario/Santoro Emilio (Eds.), Lineages of European Citizenship: Rights, Belonging and Participation in Eleven Nation-States, Basingstoke 2004

Lämmermann Falk: Ein Jahrzehnt *Ius soli* – Bilanz und Ausblick – ZAR 2011, 1–8

Lasby Clarence G: Project Paperclip: German scientists and the Cold War, New York 1971

Lauterpacht Hersch: The Law of Peace, parts II–VI, International Law collected papers (edited by Lauterpacht Elihu), Vol. 3, Cambridge 1977

Laxer Gordon/Soron Dennis: Not for Sale: Decommodifying Public Life, Peterborough, Ontario 2006

Leavitt Neal: The Foreign Policy of John Rawls and Amartya Sen, Lanham, 2013

Lenz Carl Otto/Borchardt Klaus-Dieter: EU-Verträge: Kommentar nach dem Vertrag von Lissabon, Cologne 2010

- id. -/- id. - EU-Verträge – Kommentar nach dem Vertrag von Lissabon 5th Edition, Köln/Wien 2010

Lepsius M. Rainer: "Ethnos" oder "Demos": Zur Anwendung zweier Kategorien von Emerich Francis auf das nationale Selbstverständnis der Bundesrepublik und auf die Europäische Einigung, Kölner Zeitschrift für Soziologie und Sozialpsychologie (1986), Vol 38, 751–759

Leung Hon-Chu: Reiche Talente statt Arme Kinder. Bürgerrecht und Exklusion von Festland-Chinesen in Hongkong, in: Thränhardt Dietrich/Uwe Hunger (Eds.), Migration im Spannungsfeld von Globalisierung und Nationalstaat, Leviathan Sonderheft 22/2003, Wiesbaden 2003, pp. 293-312

Leyland Peter: The Constitution of the United Kingdom: A Contextual Analysis, Oregon 2012

Liekefett Kai Haakon: Due Diligence bei M&A-Transaktionen: Voraussetzungen und Grenzen bei Börsengängen, Fusionen, Übernahmen, Beteiligungskäufen, Private Equity und Joint Ventures, Berlin 2005

Liese Jens: Compliance in Due-Diligence-Fragelisten, BB-Special 4/2010, 27–30

Lipovano J. G.: L'Apatridie, Paris, 1935

Locke John: Two Treatises of Government, in: Laslett Peter (Ed.), Cambridge 1988

Loibl-Van Husen Susanne: Die Beschäftigungsbewilligung, Vienna 1999

Lowe Vaughan: International Law, Oxford 2007

Luhmann Niklas: Grundrechte als Institution. Ein Beitrag zur politischen Soziologie, Berlin 1965

Maassen Hans-Georg: Nationality Law Issues of Combating Terrorism, ZAR 2011, pp. 336–341

Maatsch Aleksandra: Ethnic Citizenship Regimes. Europeanization, Post-war Migration and Redressing Past Wrongs, Basingstoke 2011

Mackert Jürgen: Staatsangehörigkeitsrechtliche Fragen der Terrorismusbekämpfung, Wiesbaden 2006

- id. -/Müller Hans-Peter: Staatsangehörigkeit: eine Einführung, Wiesbaden 2000

Mackert Jürgen/Müller Hans-Peter:, Moderne (Staats) Bürgerschaft. Nationale Staatsbürgerschaft und die Debatten der Citizenship Studies, Wiesbaden 2007

Macklin Audrey: The Securitisation of Dual Citizenship, in: Faist Thomas/ Kivisto Peter (Eds.), Dual Citizenship in Global Perspective: From Unitary to Multiple Citizenship, Basingstoke/New York 2007

Magnette Paul: Citizenship: The History of An Idea, Colchester 2005

Makarov Aleksandr N.: Allgemeine Lehren des Staatsangehörigkeitsrechts, 2nd Edition, Stuttgart 1962

Mangoldt Hans v.: Ius-sanguinis-Prinzip, Ius-Soli-Prinzip und Mehrstaatigkeit: Umbrüche durch das Staatsangehörigkeitsreformgesetz, ZAR 1999, 243–252

Mangoldt Hermann/Klein Friedrich/Starck Christian: Das Bonner Grundgesetz – Kommentar, Vol. 1: Article 1–19 GG, 4th Edition, Munich 2001

Mankiv N. Gregory: Principles of Microeconomics, Mason, 2009

Manville Philip B.: The Origins of Citizenship in Ancient Athens, Princeton 1990

Marshall Thomas Humphrey: Citizenship and Social Class and Other Essays, Cambridge, 1950

Markou George P./Parthenis Christos Intercultural Education in Europe: The Greek Experience, in: Catarci Marco/Fiorucci Massimiliano (Eds.), Intercultural Education in the European Context: Theories, Experiences, Challenges, Farnham/Burlington 2015, pp. 167–202.

- id. -/Bottomore Tom: Citizenship and Social Class, London 1992

Martiniello Marco: Citizenship of the European Union, in: Aleinikoff T. Alexander/Klusmeyer Douglas B. (Eds.), From Migrants to Citizens, Washington D.C. 2000, pp. 342-382

Marx Karl: Das Kapital. Kritik der Politischen Ökonomie, nach der vierten, von Friedrich Engels herausgegebenen Auflage, Hamburg 1890

Masing Johannes: Wandel im Staatsangehörigkeitsrecht vor den Herausforderungen moderner Migration, Tübingen 2001

Matzka Manfred/Bezdeka Johann: Staatsangehörigkeitsgesetz Kurzkommentar, Vienna 2009

Mauch Christian: Vorsorgende Rechtspflege in Europa am Beispiel der GmbH – Lateinisches Notariat und seine Entsprechungen im common law, ZVglRWiss 2007, 272–298

Maunz Theodor/Dürig Günter: Grundgesetz - Kommentar – Vol. III: Article 16–22, 60, Munich, October 2010

Mayer Heinz: Das österreichische Bundes-Verwaltungsrecht – Short comment, 4th Edition, Vienna 2007

McAdam Jane: Climate Change, Forced Migration and International Law, Sydney 2011

McCrudden Christopher: Understanding Human Dignity (Proceedings of the British Academy), Oxford 2014

Meer Nasar/Modood Tariq: Diversity and Nationality: Contemporary Developments in Five European Citizenship Regimes, in: Kiwan Dina (Ed.), Naturalisation Policies, Education and Citizenship, Basingstoke/New York 2013, pp. 67-94

Meireis Rolf: The new German Citizenship Act, StAZ 2000, 65–72

Meloni Annalisa: Visa Policy within the EU Structure, Heidelberg 2006

Menger Christian-Friedrich: Deutsche Verfassungsgeschichte der Neuzeit, 7th Edition, Heidelberg 1990

Merkel Reinhard/Wittman Roland: "Zum ewigen Frieden" – Grundlagen, Aktualität und Aussichten einer Idee von Immanuel Kant, Frankfurt 1996

Meyer Jürgen: Charta der Verfassungsrechte der Europäischen Union, 3rd Edition, Baden-Baden 2011

Meyer-Ladewig Jens: EMRK – Konvention zum Schutz der Menschenrechte und Grundfreiheiten – Handkommentar, Baden-Baden 2003

Micklethwait John/Wooldridge Adrian: A Future Perfect: The Essentials of Globalisation, New York 2000

Midtbøen Arnfinn H.: Citizenship, Integration and the Quest for Social Cohesion: Nationality Reform in the Sandinavian Countries, Comparative Migration Studies (2015) 3(3)

Mill John Stuart: Considerations on Representative Government, New York 1862

- id. -/Geriant Williams: Utilitarianism, On Liberty, Considerations on Representative Government, London 1993

Miller David: Citizenship and National Identity, Cambridge 2000

Mogelson Luke: The Dream Boat, The New York Times Magazine, 17 November, New York 2013

Monazahian Daniel: Vergleich der UNO-Charta mit Immanuel Kant's "Zum ewigen Frieden" und John Rawls "Das Recht der Völker", Hamburg 2008

Morrison Sean: Foreign in a Domestic Sense: American Samoa and the Last U.S. Nationals, Hastings Constitutional Law Quarterly (2013) 41(1), 71–150

Mouffe Chantal, Dimensions of Radical Democracy: Pluralism, Citizenship, Community, London/New York 1992

Moyo Dambisa: How the West Was Lost: Fifty Years of Economic Folly – and the Stark Choices Ahead, Vancouver/Toronto 2011

Müller Jörg: Vermeidbare Kooperationsstrategie im Umweltbereich? Erfahrungen und Erklärungen am Beispiel des britischen Wasserrechts, ZfU 1991, 387–401

Müller-Graff Peter-Christian: Europäisches Integrationsrecht im Querschnitt. Europäische Verfassung, Nizza, Europäischer Wirtschaftsraum, Unionsbürgerschaft, Referenden, Gemeinschaftsprivatrecht, Baden-Baden 2003

Nash Kate: 'Between Citizenship and Human Rights' Sociology, (2009), Vol. 43(6), 1067–1083

Nevile Ann, Human rights and social policy: A comparative analysis of values and citizenship in OECD countries, Cheltenham 2010

Nielsen Kai: Ethical Relativism and the Facts of Cultural Relativity, Social Research (1966), Vol 33, 531–555

Noiriel Gérard: Le Creuset français. Histoire de l'immigration (XIXe–XXe siècles), Paris 1988

Nordmeier Friedrich: Unionsbürgerschaft, EMRK und Ankerkennungsprinzip: Folgen der namensrechtlichen EuGH-Rechtsprechung für Statusentscheidungen – Zugleich Besprechung der Entscheidung des Kammergerichts, StAZ 2011, 148, StAZ Nr. 5/2011, 129–140

Nowak Carsten: Europarecht nach Lissabon, Baden-Baden 2011

Nussbaum Martha C.: For Love of Country: Debating the Limits of Patriotism, Boston 1996

Nyers Peter (Ed.),: Securitisations of Citizenship, Abingdon/New York 2009

Nye Joseph S. Jr.: Soft Power: The Means To Success In World Politics, New York 2005

Ochoa Paulina: What Money Can't Buy: Face-to-Face Cooperation and Local Democratic Life, in Shachar Ayelet/Bauböck Rainer (Eds.), Should Citizenship be for Sale? EUI Working Papers, Robert Schuhmann Centre for Advanced Studies 2014/01, European University Institute, Florence 2014, pp. 23–24

OECD: International Migration Outlook 2013, Paris 2013

Okun Arthur: Equality and Efficiency: The Big Tradeoff, Washington, D.C., 1975

Ong Aihwa: Flexible Citizenship: The Cultural Logics of Transnationality, Durham and London 1999

- id. - (Re) Articulations of Citizenship, Political Science and Politics Bd. 38/4 (2005), 697–699

- id. - Neoliberalism as Exception. Mutations in Citizenship and Sovereignty, Durham/London 2006

Oppermann Thomas: Europarecht, Munich 1999

Palandt Otto: Civil Code, 71st Edition, Munich 2012

Parsons Talcott: The System of Modern Societies, Englewood Cliffs, 1971

Parusel Bernd/Schneider Jan: Zirkuläre Migration – Rechtsrahmen, statistische Erkenntnisse und Gestaltungsoptionen, ZAR 2011, 247–254

Paskalev Vesco: If You Do Not Like Selling Passports, Give Them For Free to Those who Deserve Them, in Shachar Ayelet/Bauböck Rainer (Eds.), Should Citizenship be for Sale? EUI Working Papers, Robert Schuhmann Centre for Advanced Studies 2014/01, European University Institute, Florence 2014, pp. 25–26

Pauer-Studer Herlinde (Ed.),: Norms, Values, and Society, Dordrecht/Boston/London 1994

Pennekamp Johannes: Weltverbesserer ohne Wollpullis, Frankfurter Allgemeine Zeitung (FAZ) v. 12/13 May 2012, C 1

Peoples James/Bailey Garrick.: Humanity: An Introduction to Cultural Anthropology, Boston 2010

- id. - Immigration and Citizenship in the Twenty-first Century, Lanham 1998

Peshkopia Ridvan: Conditioning Democratization: Institutional Reforms and EU Membership Conditionality in Albania and Macedonia, London/ New York (2015)

Pickus Noah: Trans-national America? Separating Rights from Belonging, Presentation at Law and Society Annual Meeting, Phoenix 1994

Pierik Roland/Wouter Werner: Cosmopolitanism in Context: Perspectives from International Law and Political Theory, Cambridge 2010

Plender Richard: Issues in International Migration Law, London 2015

Pohanka Reinhard: Dokumente der Freiheit, Wiesbaden 2009

Porch Douglas: The French Foreign Legion: A Complete History of the Legendary Fighting Force, New York 2010

Preuss Nicola: Europarechtliche Probleme der deutschen Notariatsverfassung, ZEuP 2005, 291–321

- id. - Kompetenzkonflikt zwischen Europäischer Union und Bundesrepublik Deutschland auf dem Gebiet des Notarrechts, GPR 2008, 2–10

Putsch Christian: Patient Erde, WELT KOMPAKT of 8 December 2011, 2–3

Randelzhofer Albrecht: Nationality, in: Encyclopedia of Public International Law (EPIL) III, 501 et seq., Amsterdam etc. 1997

Raschauer Bernhard: Allgemeines Verwaltungsrecht, Vienna 2009

Rawls John: A Theory of Justice, Cambridge, Mass. 1999

- id. - The Law of Peoples, Cambridge Mass. 2000

- id. - Justice as Fairness, Cambridge, Mass./London 2001

Reich Robert B.: The Work of Nations: Preparing Ourselves for Twenty-first Century Capitalism, New York 1991

Reichel David: Staatsbürgerschaft und Integration. Die Bedeutung der Einbürgerung für MigrantInnen, dissertation, Wiesbaden 2011

Reimann Mathias: Einführung in das US-amerikanische Privatrecht, Munich 1997

Renan Ernest: Qu'est-ce qu'une nation? Conférence faite en Sorbonne, le 11 mars 1882, Paris

Rengeling Hans-Werner: Die Verfassungsrechte des Grundgesetzes mit ihren europäischen Bezügen: Der von Klaus Stern und Florian Becker herausgegebene Verfassungsrechte-Kommentar, DVBl. 2011

Renner Günter: Streitpunkte: Erfahrungen mit dem neuen deutschen Staatsangehörigkeitsrecht, ZAR 2002, 265–269

- id. - Streitpunkte: Mehrstaatigkeit und Deutschkenntnisse, ZAR 2002, 339–348

Ress Georg: Verfassung und völkerrechtliches Vertragsrecht, in: Hailbronner Kay/Ress/Georg /Stein Torsten (Eds.), Staat und Volkerrechtsordnung, Festschrift fur Karl Doehring, Berlin/Heidelberg/New York/London/ Paris/Tokyo/Hong Kong 1989, pp. 803–852

Risse Thomas: A Community of Europeans? Transnational Identities and Public Spheres, Ithaca/London 2010

Rittstieg Helmut: Doppelte Staatsangehörigkeit im Völkerrecht, Neue Juristische Wochenschrift (1990) Vol. 43, 1401–1405

Robertson Craig: The Passport in America: The History of a Document, New York 2010

Roellecke Gerd: Staat und Tod, Paderborn 2004

Roudometof Victor: Collective Memory, National Identity, and Ethnic Conflict: Greece, Bulgaria and the Macedonian Question, Westport, CT (2002)

Rousseau Jean-Jacques: Du Contract social ou Principes du droit politique, Strasbourg 1791/2006

- id - Émile, ou De l'éducation, 1762

- id - The Government of Poland, 1835 /translated by Kendall Willmoore, Indianapolis 1985

Rowe Constance: Voltaire and the State, New York 1968

Rudan Delia Nationality and Political Rights, in Annoni Alessandra/Forlati Serena (Eds.), The Changing Role of Nationality in International Law, Oxon/New York 2013, pp. 117-134

Ruffner Markus: Die EG-Harmonisierungs- und Liberalisierungsrichtlinien – Blaupause und Regelungsstandard für das schweizerische Telekommunikationsrecht am Beispiel der Interkonnektion, in: Forstmoser Peter/von der Crone Hans Caspar/Weber Rolf H./Zobl Dieter (Eds.), Der Einfluss des europäischen Rechts auf die Schweiz, Schulthess, Zürich 1999

Sachs Michael: Grundgesetz – Kommentar, 5th Edition, Munich 2009

Sadiq Kamal: Paper Citizens: How Illegal Immigrants Acquire Citizenship in Developing Countries, New York 2008

Sagan Adam: Deutsches Arbeitsrecht im Zangengriff europäischer Verfassungsrechte, Frankfurter Allgemeine Zeitung of 28 March 2012, p. 19

Sahlins Peter: Unnaturally French, Foreign Citizen in the Old Regime and After, Ithaca/London 2004

Salter Mark B.: The Passport in International Relations, London 2003

Samtleben Jürgen: Brasilianisches Staatsangehörigkeitsrecht zwischen *ius soli* und *ius sanguinis*, StAZ 2009, pp. 268–271

Sandel Michael J.: Justice: What's The Right Thing To Do?, New York 2010

Sandel Michael J.: What Money Can't Buy: The Moral Limits of Markets, New York 2012

Sandkühler Hans-Jörg: Menschenrechte in die Zukunft denken, 60 Jahre Allgemeine Erklärung der Menschenrechte, Schriftenreihe des Zentrums für Europäische Rechtspolitik Vol. 56 (ZERP), Baden-Baden 2009

Sandler Todd/Tschirhart John T.: The Economic Theory of Clubs. An Evaluative Survey, in: Journal of Economic Literature, (1980) Vol. 18, 1481–1521

Sassen Saskia: Globalisation and its Discontents: Essays on the New Mobility of People and Money, New York 1999

Satz Deborah: Why Some Things Should Not Be for Sale: The Moral Limits of Markets, Oxford 2010

Saunders Peter: Staatsbürgerschaft in einer liberalen Gesellschaft, in: Mackert Jürgen/Müller Hans-Peter (Eds.), Moderne (Staats) Bürgerschaft: Nationale Staatsbürgerschaft und die Debatten der Citizenship Studies, Wiesbaden 2007, pp. 119-146

Schäfer Claus: "No Representation Without Taxation" – WSI-Verteilungsbericht 2011, WSI Mitteilungen 12/2011, S. 677 ff., published online at: http://www.boeckler.de/pdf/pm_wsimit_2011_12_schaefer.pdf, last accessed on 21 September 2012

Schattle Hans: The Practices of Global Citizenship, Lanham 2008

Schätzel Walter: De-facto Staatsangehörigkeit und De-facto-Staatenlosigkeit, in: Völkerrecht und rechtliches Weltbild: Festschrift for Alfred Verdross, Vienna 1960, pp. 217–227

Scheffler Eberhard: Die 115 wichtigsten Finanzkennzahlen – Hintergründe, Formeln und Aussagekraft, Munich 2010

Scheuner Ulrich: Die Reform der österreichischen Bundesverfassung vom Jahre 1929, veröffentlicht im Internet unter: http://www.zaoerv.de/02_1931/2_1931_1_a_226_251.pdf

Schick Rupert: Petitionen – Von der Untertanenbitte zum Bürgerrecht, 3rd Edition, Heidelberg 1996

Schick Stephanie: Kann man eine europäische Identität schaffen?, Marburg 2012

Schipke Alfred/Cebotari Aliona/Thaker Nita: The Eastern Caribbean Economic and Currency Union: Macroeconomics and Financial Systems, Washington D.C. 2013

Schlochauer Hans-Jürgen: Wörterbuch des Völkerrechts, Bd. 3. Rapallo-Vertrag bis Zypern, 2nd Edition, Berlin 1962

Schmidt Rainer: Auswirkungen des Zuwanderungsgesetzes auf den ius-Soli-Erwerb der deutschen Staatsangehörigkeit nach § 4 Abs. 3 StAG, StAZ 2005, pp. 65–72

Schmidt Sandra: Immigration Policy and New Ethnic Minorities in Contemporary Germany in Cordell Karl (Ed.), Cordell Karl Ethnicity and Democratisation in the New Europe, London/New York (1999), pp. 91–105

Schmidtke Oliver: Das kanadische Einwanderungsmodell: Wohlverstandenes Eigeninteresse und multikulturelles Ethos, in: Dietrich/Hunger Uwe (Eds.), Migration im Spannungsfeld von Globalisierung und Nationalstaat, Leviathan Sonderheft 22/2003, Wiesbaden 2003, pp. 205-226

Schneider Axel Rolf: Petitionen zum Europäischen Parlament mit Berücksichtigung des Bürgerbeauftragten, Schriften zum internationalen und zum öffentlichen Recht, Vol. 84, Frankfurt am Main 2009

Schönberger Christoph: Unionsbürger. Europas föderales Bürgerrecht in vergleichender Sicht, Tübingen 2005

Schöning Falk: Föderale Intervention als Instrument zur Bewahrung eines Bundesstaates – Rechtsvergleichende Analyse und völkerrechtliche Legitimation – Föderalismus-Studien Vol. 21, Baden-Baden 2011

Schröder Meinhard: Das Karlsruher Konzept der europäischen Integration – Bemerkungen zum Lissabon-Urteil des Bundesverfassungsgerichts vom 30. Juni 2009, in: Michaela Wittinger/Rudolf Wendt/Georg Ress (Eds.), Verfassung – Völkerrecht – Kulturgüterschutz, Festschrift für Wilfried Fiedler, Berlin 2011, pp. 675–690

Schuck Peter H.: Plural Citizenships, in: Pickus Noah M.J. (Eds.), Immigration and Citizenship in the Twenty-First Century, Lanham 1998, pp. 61-99

Schumacher Christoph/Barwig Klaus: Mehrstaatigkeit – Neuere Entwicklungen im Bereich des Europarates, ZAR 1989, 14–16

Schulte Beerbühl Margrit: War England ein Sonderfall der Industrialisierung? Der ökonomische Einfluss der protestantischen Immigranten auf die Entwicklung der englischen Wirtschaft vor der Industrialisierung, Geschichte und Gesellschaft (1995), Vol. 21, 479–505

- id. - Deutsche Kaufleute in London. Welthandel und Einbürgerung (1600–1818), Munich 2007

Schulze Reiner/Zuleeg Manfred/Kadelbach Stefan: Europarecht – Handbuch für die deutsche Rechtspraxis, 2nd Edition, Baden-Baden 2010

Schütze Robert: From Dual to Cooperative Federalism: The Changing Structure of European Law, Oxford/New York 2009

Schwarz Walter: Der gläserne Arbeitnehmer? Ein Beitrag zur Wahrung der Persönlichkeitsrechte im Betrieb, Vienna 1988

Schwarze Jürgen: EU-Kommentar, 2nd Edition, Baden-Baden 2009

Schweitzer Michael: Staatsrechts III: Staatsrecht, Völkerrecht, Europarecht, 9th Edition, Heidelberg 2008

Shachar Ayelet: Children of a Lesser State: Sustaining Global Inequality through Citizenship Laws, Jean Monnet Working Paper No. 2/2003, New York 2003

- id. - The Birthright Lottery: Citizenship and Global Inequality, Cambridge 2009

- id. - Picking Winners: Olympic Citizenship and the Global Race for Talent, The Yale Law Journal (2011), Vol. 120(8), 2088–2120

Shachar Ayelet/Bauböck Rainer: Should Citizenship be for Sale? EUI Working Papers, Robert Schuhmann Centre for Advanced Studies 2014/01, European University Institute, Florence 2014

- id. -/Hirschl Ran: On Citizenship, States, and Markets, in: Journal of Political Philosophy (2014), Vol. 22(2), 231–257

Shafir Gershon: The Citizenship Debates, Minneapolis/London 1998

- id. -/Peled Yoav: Being Israeli: The Dynamics of Multiple Citizenship (Cambridge Middle East Studies), Cambridge 2001

Shaw Jo: Law of the EU, Houndmills, 2000

- id. - Has the European Court of Justice Challenged Member State Sovereignty in Nationality Law? EUI Working Papers, Robert Schuhmann Centre for Advanced Studies 2011/62, European University Institute, Florence 2011

- id. - Citizenship for Sale: Could and Should the EU Intervene? in: EUI Working Papers, Robert Schumann Centre for Advanced Studies 2014/01, European University Institute, Florence 2014

Sherwin-White Adrian Nicholas: The Roman Citizenship, Oxford 1973

Sieyès Emmanuel Joseph: What Is the Third Estate?, translated by Blondel M., New York 1964

Simma Bruno: Charta der Vereinten Nationen – Commentary – Munich 1991

Sklair Leslie: The Transnational Capitalist Class, Oxford 2001

Slemrod Joel: Why is Elvis on Burkina Faso Postage Stamps?, Journal of Empirical Legal Studies (2008), Vol. 5, 683–712

Smith Adam: The Theory of Moral Sentiments (Dover Philosophical Classics edition), Mineola/New York 2006

Smith Rogers M.: Citizenship, Borders and Human Needs, Philadelphia 2011

Somin Ilya: Democracy and Political Ignorance, Stanford 2013

Sowade Kirsten: Markenschutz in den USA – Eine rechtsvergleichende Untersuchung aus der Sicht des deutschen Juristen – dissertation, Westfälische Wilhelms-Universität Münster 2002

Soysal Yasemin N.: Limits of Citizenship: Migrants and Postnational Membership in Europe, Chicago 1994

Spicker Paul: Poverty and the Welfare State: Dispelling the Myths, A Catalyst Working Paper (2002)

Spielvogel Jackson J. Western Civilization — Vol. II: Since 1500, 5th Edition, Belmont CA 2003

Spinner Bruno/Maritz Daniel, EG-Kompatibilität des schweizerischen Wirtschaftsrechts: Vom autonomen zum systematischen Nachvollzug, in: Forstmoser Peter/von der Crone Hans Caspar/Weber Rolf H./Zobl Dieter (Eds.), Der Einfluss des europäischen Rechts auf die Schweiz, Schulthess, Zürich 1999, pp. 127–138

Spiro Peter J.: Beyond Citizenship: American Identity After Globalisation, New York 2008

Spitta Juliane: Gemeinschaft jenseits von Identität? Über die paradoxe Renaissance einer politischen Idee, Bielefeld 2013

Stadler Max: Integration durch Recht, ZAR 2010, 351–354

Standing Guy: Promoting Income Security as a Right: Europe and North America, London 2005

Stasiulis Daiva/Ross Darryl: Security, Flexible Sovereignty, and the Perils of Multiple Citizenship, in: Nyers Peter (Ed.), Securitizations of Citizenship, Abingdon/New York 2009, pp. 94-117

Steiner Pascale/Wicker Hans-Rudolf: Paradoxien im Bürgerrecht, Zurich 2004

Stelkens Paul/Bonk Heinz-Joachim/Sachs Michael: Administrative Procedure Act, 7th Edition, Munich 2008

Stern Joachim: Ius Pecuniae – Staatsbürgerschaft zwischen ausreichendem Lebensunterhalt, Mindestsicherung und Menschenwürde, in: Dahlvik Julia/Fassmann Heinz/Sievers Wiebke (Eds.), Migration und Integration – wissenschaftliche Perspektiven aus Österreich, Göttingen 2012, pp. 55-74

Stern Klaus: The Constitutional Law of the Federal Republic of Germany, Vol. I: Basic Concepts and Principles of Constitutional law, Structural Principles of the Constitution – Munich 1977

Stiller Martin: An International Law History of Statelessness. Shown with selected examples from Europe, Russia and the US, Vienna 2011

Stone Lincoln: Immigration Options for Investors & Entrepreneurs, American Immigration Lawyers Association, Washington D.C. 2014

Straubhaar Thomas: Wird die Staatsangehörigkeit zu einer Klubmitgliedschaft?, in: Dietrich Thränhardt/Hunger Uwe (Eds.), Migration im Spannungsfeld von Globalisierung und Nationalstaat, Leviathan Sonderheft 22/2003, Wiesbaden 2003, pp. 76-89

Streinz Rudolf: Europarecht, 6th Edition, Heidelberg/Landsberg/Munich/ Berlin 2008

- id. - EUV/EGV – Vertrag über die europäische Union und Vertrag zur Gründung der europäischen Gemeinschaft, Munich 2003

Strohmeier Martin/Yalcin-Heckmann Lale: Die Kurden: Geschichte, Politik, Kultur, München 2010

Strunden Martin/Pasenow Michaela: Fachkräfte gesucht! – Ausländerrecht fit? Die Sächsische Initiative für gesteuerte Zuwanderung, ZAR 2011, 121–125

Studer Brigitte/Arlettaz Gérald/Argast Regula: Das Schweizer Bürgerrecht. Nationalität und Ordnung des Sozialen in der Schweiz von 1848 bis zur Gegenwart, Zurich 2008

Sturm Fritz: Statik und Dynamik im europäischen Staatsangehörigkeitsrecht – Eine rechtsvergleichende Analyse, in: Borchers Patrick J./Zekoll Joachim (Eds.), International Conflict of Laws for the Third Millennium: Essays in Honor of Friedrich K. Juenger, Ardsley/New York 2001, pp. 301–316

Stuurman Siep: Citizenship and Cultural Difference in France and the Netherlands, in: Bellamy Richard/Castiglione Dario/Santoro Emilio (Eds.), Lineages of European Citizenship: Rights, Belonging and Participation in Eleven Nation-States, Basingstoke 2004, pp. 167-185

Sumner William G.: Folkways, Boston 1906

Sumption Madeleine/Hooper Kate: Selling Visas and Citizenship: Policy Questions from the Global Boom in Investor Immigration, Washington D.C. 2014

Talani Leila Simona: Globalisation, Migration and the Future of Europe, Abingdon/New York 2012

Taylor Alan John Percivale: English History 1914–1945, Oxford 1965

Taylor Charles: Why Democracy Needs Patriotism, in: Cohen Joshua (Ed.), For Love of Country?, Boston 2002, pp. 119–121

Ternès Anabel: Fremd im eigenen Land: Aussiedler in Deutschland, Munich 2011

Thedieck Karl: Deutsche Staatsangehörigkeit im Bund und in den Ländern: Genese und Grundlagen der Staatsangehörigkeit in deutschlandrechtlicher Perspektive, public writings, Berlin 1989

Thiele Carmen: Das Verhältnis zwischen Staatenverantwortlichkeit und Menschenrechten, in: Archiv des Völkerrechts 4/2011, pp. 343–372

Thienel Rudolf/Schulev-Steindl Eva: Verwaltungsverfahrensrecht, Vienna 2009

Thränhardt Dietrich/Hunger Uwe (Eds.), Migration im Spannungsfeld von Globalisierung und Nationalstaat, Leviathan Sonderheft 22/2003, Wiesbaden 2003

Thürer Daniel: Werte in Europa – Werte in der Schweiz, in: Forstmoser Peter/ von der Crone Hans Caspar/Weber Rolf H./Zobl Dieter (Eds.), Der Einfluss des europaischen Rechts auf die Schweiz, Schulthess, Zurich 1999, 139–155

Tietje Christian: Internationales Wirtschaftsrecht, Berlin 2009

Tilly Charles: The Formation of National States in Western Europe, Princeton 1975

Tomandl Theodor: Die Schlichtung von Regelungsstreitigkeiten gem. § 97 Abs 1 Z 1 ArbVG, ZAS 1979, p. 203

Tombs Robert: The English and Their History, New York 2015

Tomuschat Christian: Völkerrecht, Collected texts, Baden-Baden 2009

Topal Utko: Staatsangehörigkeitsverlust und Mehrstaatigkeit – Eine verfassungsrechtliche Untersuchung zum Verlustgrund des Erwerbers einer ausländischen Staatsangehörigkeit, Munich 2010

Torpey John: The Invention of the Passport – Surveillance, Citizenship and the State, Cambridge 2000

Trachtman Joel P.: The International Law of Economic Migration, Michigan 2009

Triepel Heinrich: Internationale Regelung der Staatsangehörigkeit, Berlin 1929

United Nations High Commissioner for Refugees (UNHCR): Annual Appeal 2015 Update, Geneva 2015

Unterweger Josef: Staatsangehörigkeitsgesetz mit Kommentar, Vienna 2007

Uslucan Sükrü: Zur Weiterentwicklungsfähigkeit des Menschenrechts auf Staatsangehörigkeit: Deutet sich in Europa ein migrationsbedingtes Recht auf Staatsangehörigkeit an – auch unter Hinnahme der Mehrstaatigkeit, Berlin 2012

Vattel Emer de: Le droit des gens ou principes de la loi naturelle appliqués à la conduite et aux affaires des nations et des souverains. Deutsche Übersetzung von Wilhelm Euler, Tübingen 1959

Vedder Christoph/Heintschel von Heinegg Wolff: Europäisches Unionsrecht – EUV, AEUV, Verfassungsrechte-Charta, Handkommentar, Baden-Baden 2012

Venables Anthony J.: Resource Rents: When to Spend and How to Save, International Tax and Public Finance (2008), Vol. 17, 340–356

Verdross Alfred/Simma Bruno: Universelles Völkerrecht, Berlin 1984

Verstichel Annelies: Participation, Representation and Identity – The Right of Persons Belonging to Minorities to Effective Participation in Public Affairs: Content, Justification and Limits, Antwerpen/Oxford/Portland 2009

Vertovec Steven/Cohen Robin: Conceiving Cosmopolitanism: Theory, Context, and Practice, New York 2008

Vitzthum Wolfgang Graf von: Maritimes Aquitorium und Anschlusszone, in: Vitzthum Wolfgang Graf (Eds.), Handbuch des Seerechts, pp. 63–160, Munich 2006

- id. - Völkerrecht, 5th Edition, Berlin 2010

Volkart Rudolf: Corporate Finance – Fundamentals of Finance and Investment, 4th Edition, Zurich 2008

Von der Groeben Hans/Schwarze Jabob: Vertrag über die europäische Union und Vertrag zur Gründung der Europäischen Gemeinschaft, Bd. 1: Art. 1–53 EUV und Art. 1–80 EGV, Baden-Baden 2003

Von Mises Ludwig: Human Action. A Treatise on Economics, Auburn 1998

Von Münch Ingo: Die deutsche Staatsangehörigkeit. Vergangenheit – Gegenwart – Zukunft, Berlin 2007

Von Weizsäcker Richard: Von Deutschland aus – Reden des Bundespräsidenten, Berlin 1985

de Vries Karin: Integration at the Border: The Dutch Act on Integration Abroad and International Immigration Law, Oxford 2013

Wallerstein Immanuel: The Essential Wallerstein, New York 2000

Walter Anne: Familienzusammenführung in Europa – Völkerrecht, Gemeinschaftsrecht, nationales Recht –, Schriften zur europäischen Integration und internationalen Wirtschaftsordnung, 1st Edition, Baden-Baden 2009

Walter Christian /Gärditz Klaus Ferdinand: Der Bürgerstatus im Lichte von Migration und europäischer Integration, Kiel 2015

Walter Maja: Integrationsgrenze Verfassungsidentität – ZaöRV, (2012), Vol. 72, 177–200

Walter Robert/Mayer Heinz/Kucsko-Stadlmayer Gabriele: Bundesverfassungsrecht, Vienna 2007

- id. -/Kolonovits Dieter/Manz Gerhard: Verwaltungsverfahrensrecht, Vienna 2011

Walzer Michael: Spheres of Justice: A Defense of Pluralism and Equality, New York 1983

Ware Roger/Fortin Pierre/Paradis Pierre Emmanuel: The Economic Impact of the Immigrant Investor Program in Canada, Boston 2010

Weber Max: Wirtschaft und Gesellschaft, 5. Auflage, Tübingen 1972

Weil Patrick: Qu'est-ce qu'un français? Histoire de la nationalité française depuis la Révolution, Paris 2004

- id. - From Conditional to Secured and Sovereign: The New Strategic Link Between the Citizen and the Nation State in a Globalised World, International Journal of Constitutional Law (2011), Vol. 9, No. 3–4, 615–635

- id. - Zugang zur Staatsangehörigkeit – Ein Vergleich von 25 Staatsangehörigkeitsgesetzen, in: Conrad Christoph/Kocka Jürgen (Eds.), Staatsbürgerschaft in Europa. Historische Erfahrungen und aktuelle Debatten, Hamburg 2001, pp. 99–111

Weis Paul: Staatsangehörigkeit und Staatenlosigkeit im gegenwärtigen Völkerrecht, Berlin 1962

Weiss André: Traité Théorique et Pratique de Droit international privé – Tome premier: La Nationalité, Paris 1907

Weiss Yfaat: Deutsche und polnische Juden vor dem Holocaust. Jüdische Identität zwischen Staatsangehörigkeit und Ethnizität 1933–1940, Munich 2000

Wesel Uwe: Geschichte des Rechts – Von den Anfängen bis zur Gegenwart, 3rd Edition, Munich 2006

Wichmann Nicole: Reforming the Swiss Citizenship Act – Mission Impossible. SFM Discussion Paper, (May 2013), No. 29, Neuchatel

Wiener Antje: Europäische Bürgerschaftspraxis, in: Jürgen Mackert/Hans-Peter Müller (Eds.), Moderne (Staats) Bürgerschaft. Nationale Staatsbürgerschaft und die Debatten der Citizenship Studies, Wiesbaden 2007, pp. 261-283

Wiese Thomas: Die Bindungswirkung der tatsächlichen Verständigung, in: BB (1994), 333-336

Wiessner Siegfried: Die Funktion der Staatsangehörigkeit, dissertation Tübingen 1989

Williams Andrew: The Ethos of Europe: Values, Law and Justice in the EU, Cambridge 2010

Winter Elke: Descent, Territory and Common Values: Redefining Citizenship in Canada, in: Kiwan Dina (Ed.), Naturalisation Policies, Education and Citizenship, Basingstoke/New York 2013, pp. 95-122

Wittinger Michaela: Verfassungen, internationale Verträge und das Recht der Europäischen Union im Wandel: verfassungsrechtliche, völkerrechtliche und europarechtliche Betrachtungen zum Wandel mittels Auslegung, in: Michaela Wittinger/Rudolf

Wendt/Georg Ress, Verfassung – Völkerrecht – Kulturgüterschutz, Festschrift für Wilfried Fiedler, Berlin 2011

Wobbe Theresa: Die Koexistenz nationaler und supranationaler Bürgerschaft: Neue Formen politischer Inkorporation, in: Jürgen Mackert Jürgen/ Müller Hans-Peter (Eds.), Moderne (Staats) Bürgerschaft. Nationale Staatsbürgerschaft und die Debatten der Citizenship Studies, Wiesbaden 2007

Wolfrum Rüdiger/Philipp Christiane: Handbuch Vereinte Nationen, 2nd Edition, Munich 1991

Xu Xin/El-Ashram Ahmed/Gold Judith: Too Much of a Good Thing? Optimal Management of Citizenship-by-Investment Flows, International Monetary Fund Working Paper, 2015

Zachary G. Pascal: The Global Me – New Cosmopolitans and the Competitive Edge: Picking Globalism's Winners and Losers, New York 2000

Zimmermann Andreas: Staats- und völkerrechtliche Fragen der Reform des deutschen Staatsangehörigkeitsrechts, IPRax 2000, 180–185

Zimmermann Horst: Kommunalfinanzen – Eine Einführung in die finanzwissenschaftliche Analyse der kommunalen Finanzwissenschaft, Baden-Baden 1999

Zolberg Aristide R.: International Migrations in Political Perspective, in: Kritz Mary M./Keely Charles B/Tomasi Silvano M. (Eds.), Global Trends in Migration: Theory and research on International Population Movements, Staten Island, New York 1981, pp. 15-51

- id. - A Nation by Design: Immigration Policy in the Fashioning of America, Cambridge Mass., 2006

Legal Sources

ACA Law on Citizenship No. 311/1985, last amended by ÖBGBl. No. 111/2011

ArbMigrG Act on the labour market proper management of highly-skilled immigrants and to amend other residence status regulations of 20 December 2008 – ArbMigrG – announced in volume 2008 No 63 of 24 December 2008

BBG Federal Civil Service Act (FCSA) as amended on 5 February 2009, last amended by the Law of 21 July 2012, BGBl. I 2012 m.W.v. 26 July 2012

BeamtStG Law regulating the status law of the officials in the countries (Civil Servants Status Act) as amended 17 June 2008, as amended by Legal Services Restructuring Act of 5 February 2009

BgStbG Law on Citizenship No. 311/1985, as last amended by ÖBGBl. No. 54 of 31 May 2002

BILL C-18 The Citizenship of Canada Act, http://www.parl.gc.ca/About/Parliament/LegislativeSummaries/bills_ls.asp?lang=F&ls=C18&Parl=37&Ses=2& source=Bills_House_Government last accessed on 11 March 2012

Botschaft BüG Botschaft zur Totalrevision des Bundesgesetzes über das Schweizer Bürgerrecht (Bürgerrechtsgesetz, BüG) of 4 March 2011

Bulgaria Constitution Constitution of the Republic of Bulgaria of 12 July 1991 (BgVf.), as last amended by the Law of 6 February 2007 (Dărzacen Vestnik 2007, No. 12)

BVerfGG Federal Constitutional Court Act (Federal Constitutional Court) as amended by the publication of 11 August 1993 (Federal Law Gazette I 1993, p 1473), last amended by Article 3 of the Law of 12 July 2012 (BGBl. I 2012, p. 1501)

CaCA Canadian Citizenship Act (R.S.C., 1985, c. C-29), last amended by Bill C-24 on 19 June 2014, which has come into effect on 29 May 2015, published online at http://www.parl.gc.ca/LegisInfo/BillDetails.aspx?Language=E&Mode=1&Bill=C24&Parl=41&Ses=2, last accessed on 30 June 2015

CaCRF Canadian Charter of Rights and Freedoms, assented to 29 March 1982, published online at http://laws-lois.justice.gc.ca/eng/charter/page-1.html, last accessed on 10 March 2012

CaIRPA Canadian Immigration and Refugee Protection Act (S.C. 2001, c. 27), Act current to 20 February 2012, last amended on 6 June 2014, published online at http://laws.justice.gc.ca/eng/acts/I-2.5/, last accessed on 10 March 2012

CaSAA Canadian Social Assistance Act 1997 (CaSAA 1997)

CC Code Civil Francais, last amended by Action No.2006-399 4 April 2006, published online at CIVILCODhttp://195.83.177.9/code/liste.phtml?lang=uk&c=22E, last accessed on 21 March 2012

CRMN Convention on the Reduction of Multiple Nationalities and Military Service of Multi-State Learning) 6 May 1963 (BGBl. 1969 II, p. 1954)

Croatian Citizenship Act Croatian Citizenship Act 2001, Official Journal issues 53/1991, 70/1991, 28/1992, 113/1993, 4/1994, 130/2011

Cst Federal Constitution of the Swiss Confederation (Cst) of 18 April 1999 (1 January 2011), published online at http://www.admin.ch/ch/d/sr/101/index.html, last accessed on 24 March 2012

CwIA Commonwealth Immigrants Act 1962 (CwIA) 10 & 11 ELIZ. 2. CH. 21, published online at http://www.britishcitizen.info/CIA1962.pdf, last accessed on 21 September 2012

dGG Basic Law for the Federal Republic of Germany (Basic Law) as amended the Federal Law Gazette, Part III, section number 100-1, published streamlined version, as last amended by the Law of 11 July 2012 (Federal Law Gazette I 2012, S. 1478) dStAG Law on Citizenship 22 November 2011 (BGBl. I 2011, S. 2258)

dWpHG German Securities Trading Act (dWpHG) as amended by the publication of 9 September 1998 (Federal Law Gazette I 1998, p. 2708), last amended by Article 2 of the Law of 26 June 2012 (BGBl. I 2012, p. 1375)

ECHR Convention for the Protection of Human Rights and Fun-damental Freedoms (ECHR) of 4 November 1950, as amended by the new publication of 17 May 2002 (Federal Law Gazette II, p 1054), originally came into force on 3 September 1953

ECN European Convention on Nationality of 6 November 1997 (ECN), published online at http://conventions.coe.int/treaty/ger/Treaties/Html/166.htm, last accessed on 28 March 2012

EU Charter European Charter of constitutional rights (EU Charter), OJ. 2007 C 303, p. 1; as amended on 30 March 2010 (2010/C83/02), Abl. EU C 83/389

FCN Code de la nationalité française (FCN), consolidated ver-sion of 4 April 2006, published online at http://www.legifrance.gouv.fr/affichCode.do?cidTexte=LEGITEXT000006070721, last accessed on 21 September 2012

French Constitution Constitution of the Fifth French Republic of 10 April 1959 (French Constitution), as last amended by the revised version of 21 July 2008 Constitutional Act No. 2008-724 of 21 July, 2008

GBIA 1971 British Immigration Act 1971 (GBIA 1971), Chapter 77, Published online at http://www.legislation.gov.uk/ukpga/1971/77/pdfs/ukpga_19710077_en.pdf, last accessed on 13 May 2012

GBNA 1948 British Nationality Act 1981 of 30 July 1948 (GBNA 1948), 1948 Chapter 56 11 and 12 Geo 6, published online at http://www.legislation.gov.uk/ukpga/Geo6/11-12/56/contents, last accessed on 13 May 2012

GBNA 1981 British Nationality Act 1981 of 30 October 1981 (GBBNA 1981), 1981 Chapter 61, published online at http://www.coe.int/t/dghl/standardsetting/nationality/National%20legislation/UK%20British%20Nationality%20Act %201981.PDF

Hague Convention Hague Convention on certain questions to the Conflict of Nationality Laws of 12 April 1930 ("Hague Convention")

Maastricht Treaty Consolidated version of the Treaty on EU, of 24 December 2002 (Maastricht Treaty), OJ. EC C 325/7, Published online at http://eur-lex.europa.eu/de/treaties/dat/12002M/pdf/12002M_DE.pdf, last accessed on 13 May 2012

Montenegro Citizenship Act Citizenship Act of the Republic of Montenegro (MNA) – Montenegrin Citizenship Act – published in the Official Gazette No. 13/2008; on the basis of Article 95(3) of the Constitution of Montenegro, entered into force to Podgorica on 14 February 2008, No. 01-288/2; published online at http://www.unhcr.org/refworld/pdfid/47e117082.pdf, last accessed on 21 September 2012

Montenegro Constitution Constitution of the Republic of Montenegro (MnV) and constitutional law for the implementation of the Constitution of Montenegro, adopted on 19 October 2007, published on the Internet at http://www.comparativeconstitutionsproject.org/files/Montenegro_2007.pdf, last accessed on 21 September 2012

Montevideo Convention Montevideo Convention of 1933, LTNS No. 165, S. 19

ÖASVG Austrian General Social Insurance Act, ÖBGBl. No. 189/1955

ÖBV Austrian Federal Constitutional Law (ÖB-VG) ÖBGBl. No. 1/1930, as last amended by ÖBGBl. I No. 2/2008

ÖStGG Austrian State Basic Law of 21 December 1867 on the general rights of citizens represented at the Empire kingdoms and countries (Austrian Basic Law, öStGG), which entered into force on 23 December 1867, as amended by the insertion of a provision on the protection of the freedom of art (ÖBGBl. No. 262/1982), BVG of 29 November 1988 on the protection of personal freedom (ÖBGBl. No. 684/1988)

RL 2009/50/EG Council Directive 2009/50/EC of 25 May 2009 on the conditions of entry and residence of third-country nationals ("Blue Card Directive")

SCA /nSCA Federal Act of 29 September 1952 on the Acquisition and Loss of Swiss Citizenship, as amended; Swiss Citizenship Act

SKN-C St. Kitts and Nevis Constitution

SKN-CA St. Kitts and Nevis Citizenship Act, 1984

TEU Treaty on the EU of 7 February 1991, OJ. C 191 of 29 July 1992 as amended the Treaty of Lisbon of 13 December 2007, OJ C 306 of 17 December 2007.

TFEU Treaty on the Functioning of the EU, consolidated version of the Treaty establishing the European Community of 25 March 1957 (OJ EU. II 1957, S. 766), as amended by the Treaty of Lisbon of 13 December 2007 (OJ EU C 306 of 17 December 2007), in the publication of the publication of 9 May 2008, OJ EU C 115 of 9 May 2008, p. 47.

Treaty of Lisbon The Treaty of Lisbon amending the Treaty on the EU and the Treaty establishing the European Community of 13 December 2007 (Treaty of Lisbon) OJEU C 306 of 17 December 2007, published on the Internet at http://eur-lex.europa.eu/JOHtml.do?uri=OJ:C:2007:306: SOM:DE:HTML, last accessed on 13 May 2012

Two Plus Four Treaty Treaty on the final settlement with respect to Germany ("Two Plus Four Treaty") of 12 September 1990, BGBl. II 1990, 1318

UDHR Universal Declaration of Human Rights of 10 December 1948, Resolution 217 A (III) of the General Assembly of 10 December 1948

UNC Charter of the United Nations of 2606.1945 (Charter of the United Nations, UN Charta) came into force on 24 October 1945, last amended on the basis of Decision of 20 December, 1971, which came into effect on 24 September, 1973, published online at http://www.un.org/en/documents/charter/intro.shtml and http://treaties.un.org/doc/Publication/CTC/uncharter.pdf, both last accessed on 21 September, 2012

USC Constitution of the United States of America of 17 September 1787

VCLT Article 2, Paragraph 1 lit. b of the Vienna Convention on the Law of Treaties (VCLT), which entered into force on 27 January 1980 – in short: Vienna Treaty Convention

Abbreviations

a.a.	as amended
a.v.	amended version
AA	Administrative Act
ACA	Austrian Citizenship Act
AOL	and other locations
Art.	Article
AS	as such
ATT	Attorney
BB	Betriebsberater (Journal, year, and page)
BE	Buddhist Era
BGH	Bundesgerichtshof ("Federal Court" or a collection of its rulings in civil matters, Volume and Page)
CA	Citizenship Act
CaBImP	Canadian Business Immigration Program
CAD	Canadian dollar
CaDIC	Canada Deposit Insurance Company
CANIIP	Canada Immigrant Investor Program
CARICOM	Caribbean Community
CBI	Citizenship-by-Investment (Program)
CC	Civil Code
CDU	Christian Democratic Union (Germany)
cf.	see
CFRG	Constitution of the Federal Republic of Germany
CFSP	Common Foreign and Security Policy of the European Union

CIC	Canadian Ministry of Citizenship and Immigration
CIMM	Standing Committee on Citizenship and Immigration (Canada)
CJEL	Columbia Journal of European Law
CL	Case Law
CLMO	Canadian Labour Market Opinion
con.	Contentious
Dir.	Directive
e.g.	for example
EC	European Community
EC Treaty	the Treaty Establishing the European Community
ECHR	European Convention on Human Rights
ECJ	European Court of Justice
ECLC	European Constitutional Law Charter
Ed	Editor or edited by
Ed.	Edition
EEC	European Economic Community
EETL	European Economic and Tax Law (journal, date, and page)
EJBL	European Journal of Business Law (journal, date, and page)
ELJ	European Law Journal
EPIL	Encyclopedia of Public International Law
esp.	especially
etc.	and so on
et al.	and others
et seq.	and the following
EU	European Union
EUCL	European Union case law, Part I, Court of Justice (year and page)
Exp	Explanation

f.	and the following (note, page)
FCC	Federal Constitutional Court (of the Federal Republic of Germany)
ff.	and the following pages
FLG	Federal Law Gazette
fn	footnote
FS	Festschrift
GDP	Gross Domestic Product
GDR	German Democratic Republic
GG	Grundgesetz (German Constitution)
HRC	Higher Regional Court
HRSDC	Human Resources Skills Development Canada
Ibid.	ibidem, in the same place
i.e.	that is
ICJ	International Court of Justice
ICW	in conjunction with
id.	Idem
If apl.	If applicable
IIP	Individual Investor Program (Malta)
i.m.o.	in my opinion
IMC	Investment Migration Council
Impl	Implementation
infra	further down/below
Int	Introduction
L	Law
LC	Legal Case
Lit.	litera
LN	Legal Notice (Malta)

LZ	Law Journal
MN	Margin number
MNA	Montenegrin Citizenship Act
NGO	Non-Governmental Organisation
NJW	Neue Juristische Wochenschrift (journal, year and page)
NJW CLW	NJW Case Law Report
NN.	Nomen Nescio (without author, author unknown)
No.	Number
OECD	Organisation for Economic Cooperation and Development
OJEU	Official Journal (of the European Union)
par.	partially
Para.	Paragraph
PO	prevailing opinion
p.	page
pp.	pages
PR	Permanent Resident (Status)
Pre.	Rem Preliminary remark
Pub	Publisher/Publication (of)
pub.	published (by)
Reg.	Regulation
RIW	Recht der internationalen Wirtschaft (journal, year and page)
SC	so called
SCA	Swiss Citizenship Act
nSCA	new Swiss Citizenship Act, expected to come in force in 2015
SCst	Federal Constitution of the Swiss Confederation
Sec.	Section
SIDF	Sugar Industry Diversitication Foundation

SKN-C	St. Kitts and Nevis Constitution
SKN-CA	St. Kitts and Nevis Citizenship Act
Slg.	(Amtliche) Sammlung
StAZ	Zeitschrift für Standeswesen/Standesamt (journal, year, and page)
supra	further up
TFEU	Treaty on the Functioning of the European Union
TFW	(Canadian) Temporary Foreign Worker (s)
TWP	(Canadian) Temporary Work Permit
UAE	United Arab Emirates
UDHR	Universal Declaration of Human Rights of 10 December 1948
UK	United Kingdom
UN	United Nations
UNC	Charter of the United Nations
UNHCR	United Nations High Commissioner for Refugees
UNO	United Nation Organisation
US	United States
USC	United States Code or Code of Laws of the United States of America
USSR	Union of Socialist Soviet Republics; Soviet Union
WFR	with further references
WTMO	within the meaning of
WTO	World Trade Organisation
ZAR	Zeitschrift für Ausländerrecht and Ausländerpolitik (ZAR, year)
ZEuP	Zeitschrift für europäisches Wirtschaftsrecht (ZEup, year)
ZEuS	Zeitschrift für Europäische Studien (journal, date, and page)
&	and

Index

absolutism 33–6, 93, 108, 248–9, 395
abuse
international law 257–8, 325
political, economic and social rights, risk of abuse of 295–9, 325
accidental citizenship 259, 318
accountability *see* transparency and accountability
acquisition *see* principles of citizenship acquisition
active citizenship 15–16, 71, 89, 91, 94, 121, 195, 273–4
adaptation *see* assimilation and adaptation
agents, licensing and supervision of 328–9
AIDs/HIV test results 334
American Revolution 37–9, 107, 414
birth-right privileges, removal of 234
Constitution 37–8
Declaration of Independence 37–8
demarcation between citizen and non-citizen 395
natural rights 37–8
no taxation without representation 138
territorial unity 39, 395
Ancient Greece 30–1, 395
assimilation 31
common Athenian origin, myth of 31
cosmopolitanism 30–1
demes, assignment of 31
extraordinary contributions 210
human rights 31
nation States 106, 395
participation 30–1
restrictions of citizenship 30–1
separation of civil public sphere from family and clan 31
stoics 30–1
Antigua and Barbuda
criminal records 204
elections and voting 94
national interest, grant of citizenship in the 215
residence 286
apartheid 43, 244
appeals 183, 329, 331
application process
appeals 331
efficiency and reliability 331–40
documentation requirements 332–40
children 332–3, 339
transparency 331–40
arbitrariness *see also* birthright lottery
certainty, principle of 251
citizenship, concept of 3
contributions and investment 229, 235, 410
cosmopolitanism and global citizenship 410–11
family life, interference with 99
genuine links or connections 145
human dignity 409
ius sanguinis 225, 235
ius soli 225, 235, 259, 262
loss of citizenship 257
nationality 95, 98, 113
naturalisation 234–5
talent 218–19
Arendt, Hannah 21, 41–2, 46, 97, 245
Argentina 296, 384
arguments for and against *ius doni* 289–321, 405–6
Aristotle 30, 32, 34, 250, 395
Armstrong, Chris 218–19
ascription to achievement, from 311, 410–11
Assange, Julien 108
assignment of rights 96
assimilation and adaptation 31, 95, 173, 205, 249, 295
auctions 226
audits 329–30
Australia
aboriginals 317

all white policies 232
 citizenship tests 129
 detention camps 44
 immigration countries, definition of 116
 ius doni 13
 ius soli 8
 length of residence 203
 refugees, treatment of 44
 settler regimes 202
 welfare gains 286
Austria 345–59
 abuse of political, economic and social rights, risk of 297, 299
 acquisition of citizenship 197–8
 applications
  criteria and conditions 348–54
  legal consequences 355–7
 Burgenland 353
 character of applicants 349, 355
 citizenship, definition of 195
 coloniser regimes 201–2
 colours as a vehicle of national awareness 109
 Constitution 109, 193, 195–6, 349, 351, 356
 contributions and investment 85, 206, 227–8, 346–54, 357–8, 400
 corruption 413
 criminal records 198–9, 348
 criteria/conditions for citizenship 193–4, 198–200, 348–54
  central characteristics 349–53
  extraordinary contributions 85, 150, 206, 346–54, 357–8, 374, 400
  qualified investments, requirements for 353–4
  special interests of Austria 350, 351–3
 current citizenship, no requirement to relinquish 356–7
 custom 349
 democracy 353
 descent, citizenship by 197
 discretion 193, 196–8, 200, 299, 348–9, 351, 354, 356–8, 374, 413
 discrimination and equality 197, 247–8, 348, 350, 353, 356, 358–9
 documentation 355
 domicile or habitual residence 357
 due diligence 413
 Economic Theory of Clubs 228
 education, equality in 247–8
 EU 64, 344, 357
 extraordinary contributions 85, 150, 206, 346–54, 357–8, 374, 400
 financial position, existence of a secure 205
 formal requirements 355
 freedom of establishment 357
 freedom of trade 357
 gender equality 197
 Germany 192–4
 grant, citizenship by 197
 Habsburg Empire 192–3
 integration and cohesion 13, 195, 197, 293, 351–3
 international relations, non-impairment of 348
 ius doni 8, 345–59
 ius sanguinis 10, 122, 196–7
 ius soli 193–4
 job creation 354
 knowledge and commitment to values 197, 199, 347, 351
 language 171, 193, 203, 346–7
 legal basis 345–57, 413–14
 legitimation, citizenship by 197
 length of residence 193–5, 198, 203, 206, 346, 354
 marriage 206
 military service 195
 minority rights 194
 multiple/dual citizenship 150, 197, 206, 344–5, 356, 359, 400
 naturalisation 137, 150, 192–200
 oaths of allegiance 141
 passports 357
 private and State, boundary between 357–8
 privileged citizenship 347
 public interest 349, 351
 qualified investments 353–4
 redress, primary 276
 renunciation of previous citizenships 85, 200, 356, 400
 residence 193–5, 198, 286, 346, 354

rule of law 353, 356
science, artistic and sports talent 346, 351–2, 358
special interests of the Republic 350, 351–3
State structural parameters 192–5, 345
statistics 185, 319, 345–6, 404
subsidiarity 49, 353
sufficient connection 348
sufficient consideration 413
Switzerland 178, 180, 193, 196
talent 346, 350–2, 358
tax 357
technology 353–4
terminology 195
terrorist, extremist or criminal groups, affiliation to 348
transparency 355
Turks in Germany 194
tying arrangements 413
unimpaired citizenship, acquisition of 355
unity of legal system, principle of 349
Universal Declaration of Human Rights 358

authority and power of State
constituent people 11, 70, 261
constitutional and political dimensions of citizenship 104–6
culture 250
defence, right of 73
diplomatic or consular protection 97
elections and voting 100, 106, 250
EU 269, 272–6, 383
individual freedom of choice 245
language 109, 139
legal relationships 69–70
monarchy 152–3
nationality 70
petition, right of 272–3
prerogative of nation State, citizenship as 104
Roman law 67
territorial sovereignty 249
three-element theory 10–11, 44–5, 70–1, 105
totalitarianism 41
welfare 377

background verification reports (BVRs) 328, 340
Bank of Scotland, acquisition of shares in 211
banks
Know Your Customer banking best practice 285
references, certified 337
statements, originals of 339
Bauböck, Rainer 19
Becker, Gary S 225–6, 305–7, 407
Beitz, Charles R 303
Belgium
French Civil Code 166
language 110, 129
length of residence 203, 251
multiple citizenship 81
non-coloniser/occupier regimes 202
welfare gains 286
Benhabib, Seyla 97
Bentham, Jeremy 306
best practices 285, 325–6, 330
Bigot de Preameneu, Félix 165
Bill of Rights 1689 6
birth
accidental citizenship 259
after birth 118–20
at birth 118–21, 219, 229, 303, 317, 398, 408
certificates 335–6
discrimination and equality 234, 248–9
ius sanguinis 59, 118–21, 128, 179, 398
ius soli 59, 118–21, 128, 398
money 229, 410
privileges, removal of 234–5
tourism 296
birthright lottery 3, 408–10
cosmopolitanism and global citizenship 310, 409
distributive justice 303–4, 409–10
feudalism 219
human dignity 409–10
national interest, grant of citizenship in the 218–19
utilitarianism 307
Bitcoin 111
Black, Jeremiah Sullivan 80
blocked exchange versus market

approach 8, 10, 231–42
contributions and investment 232–3, 238–40, 407
ethics of the queue 238–40, 407
ius doni 238–40
market values 233, 234–8, 240
money 23, 232–3, 240
non-economic considerations 232–3, 406
political membership aspect of citizenship 238, 240–2
blue cards 51–3
Bodin, Jean 34
Boutros-Ghali, Boutros 20–1
brain drain 117
Buchanan, James M 223–4
Bulgaria
EU 236, 310
identity and democracy 236
Macedonia 236
Bush, George W 217
Canada
abuse of political, economic and social rights, risk of 296
Acts of Parliament 188
acquisition by naturalisation 189–91
armed forces engaged in conflict with Canada, persons in 185
birth tourism 296
British citizenship 185
British Empire 185
British population 187
certificates of citizenship 191
Charter of Rights and Freedoms 184–5, 186–7, 189
citizenship statistics 186
citizenship tests 129, 190–1
codes of practice, guidance notes and circulars 188
common law 187, 189
Commonwealth 161, 189
criminal records 185, 191
criteria/conditions for citizenship 189–91
de lege ferenda 192
delegated legislation 188
descent, citizenship by 185
discretion 191
exemptions and relief 191
freedom of assembly 186–7
freedom of association 187
freedom of conscience and religion 186
freedom of movement 189
freedom of thought, belief, opinion and expression 186
French population 187
immigration country, as 23, 117–18, 151, 185, 187
integration 151
Inuits 61
ius soli 8, 121, 188–9, 262
knowledge of country 190, 204
language 110, 141, 171, 187, 190
length of residence 189–90, 203, 206
loss of citizenship 189
loyalty 192
marriage 190, 206
multiculturalism 117–18, 187
multiple citizenship 185, 189, 191–2, 206, 256
naturalisation 137–8, 150–1, 184–92
oaths of allegiance 141, 191, 203
passports 189
personal status 206
point system model 54
political system, knowledge of 190
precedent 187–8
Quebec 187
restrictions 190
Roman law 187
settler regimes 202
Skilled Workers Programs 137–8
State structural parameters 184–6
statelessness 84
statistics 186, 325
structural features 186–8
talent 54
tax 190
United Kingdom 160–1, 185, 187
welfare gains 286
capitalism 40, 222
Carens, Joseph H 225, 227, 256, 303, 310, 408
CARICOM (Caribbean Community)
financial position, existence of a secure 205
freedom of movement 325

labour supply and demand 101
national interest, grant of citizenship in the 220
nationality 21
welfare differentials, reduction of 310
Carrera, Sergio 384–5
Catholic Church, influence of 107
certainty, principle of 250–2
character requirements *see also* criminal records
background verification reports (BVRs) 340
bank references, certified 337
naturalisation 204
Charter of Fundamental Rights of the EU 47, 73
Charter of the UN 2
children
documentation 332–3, 335, 338–9
parents, sworn affidavits of support relating to 339
passports 335
spouses or ex-spouses, sworn affidavits of consent from 338–9
China 117, 131
Chiswick, Barry R 225
citizenship, concept of
civil, political and social rights 393
classification 58, 66–71, 393
culture 75
declarations of intent 394
democracy 250
discrimination and equality 392
essentially contested term, as 393
EU 70–1, 76
functional-teleological perspective 394
internal inclusion/external inclusion 392
international courts 393
international law 64, 393
ius sanguinis 59
ius soli 59
legal relationship 66–70, 393
mobility, opportunities of 392
nationality 58, 62–71, 393
political community, membership of a 62–3
political sciences 393
restrictions 392
three-element theory 58–9, 393
traditional understanding of citizenship 75–8
citizenship tests 129, 190–1
city states 31, 147, 210
civil society 74–5, 90, 101, 121, 142, 382, 388, 397
classification of citizenship 66–71, 393
Cleisthenes 31
clubs *see* Economic Theory of Clubs
codifications and declarations 6
Cohn-Bendit, Daniel 255, 298
Cold War 255, 399
collective will 11, 15
colonialism 201–2, 392
colours as a vehicle of national awareness 109
common good, grant of citizenship in the 318–19, 403
Commonwealth 16–17, 151–3, 160–1
competition 222, 318–19
conditions for citizenship *see* criteria/ conditions for citizenship
conferral of powers, principle of 47–8, 176, 272–3, 293, 383
Congress of Vienna 1815 108
Conscription *see* military service
consistency principle 77–9
constituent elements of the State *see* three-element theory of constituent elements of the State
constituent people 10–12, 14–18
active citizenship 11, 15–16
authority of the State 11, 70, 261
belief in the nation 15
collective will 11, 15
congruence with State 91–2
constitutional and political dimensions of citizenship 105
custom and traditions 92
definition 15–16
democracy 91
digitalisation 14
elections and voting 106
EU 17–18, 269–70
functional significance of citizenship 91–2
identification points 14–16

imminent status 67
integration 91–2
ius sanguinis 92
legal relationship 70
nation States 10–12, 14–18
nationality 393
participation rights 16–17, 91
political community 14
resident population, incongruence with 14–18
status activus and *status negativus*, differentiation between 11
territorial element 15
three-element theory 10–11, 14–18, 44–5, 49, 89, 105, 393
Universal Declaration on Human Rights 16
voting rights 16–17
constitutional dimensions 103–14
authority of the State 105–6
colours as a vehicle of national awareness 109
constituent people 105
diplomatic and consular relations 105
discretion of nation State 111–14
discrimination and equality 264
elections and referenda 105
EU 47, 276
freedom of choice, respect for 245–6
historical development lines of the nation State, emergence of 107–8
human dignity 72–3
information age, nation State in the 110–11
international law 104–6
language as a vehicle of national awareness, national 109–10
nation State
Ancient Greece 106, 395
definition 106–7
discretion 111–14
historical development lines, emergence of 107–8
three-element theory 106–7
national citizenship laws 63, 104–5
petition, right of 276
population, limitation and control of State's 89
power, exercise of State 105–6
prerogative of nation States, citizenship as 104–6
resident and non-resident rights, differentiation between 97
self-determination 246
State sovereignty, citizenship as an expression of 104–6
territorial sovereignty 104–6
three-element theory 104–6
values, creation of a consistent community of 90
violence, State monopoly of 105
constitutional patriotism 288
consular protection *see* diplomatic or consular protection
consumer citizenship 84
contributions and investment 4, 12, 404–8
amount of contribution 297
blocked exchange versus market approach 23, 232–3, 238, 407
consideration 227–8, 300–1, 412–13
democracy 300
due diligence 238
Economic Theory of Clubs 222, 224–30, 412–13
ethics of the queue 238–40, 407
evaluation of *ius doni* 282–4, 300–1, 320, 326, 404–8
functional significance of citizenship 102
globalisation 233
human dignity 300
integration 300–1
investment, definition of 280
ius doni 8–9, 13, 400–1
national interest, grant of citizenship in the 215–19, 220
nationality 80
non-refundable contributions 412–13
portfolio investment 283
simplified investment 286
society, contributions to 300–1, 320, 326, 404–8
special contributions 76
stimulus principles 53
talent 52–3
transparency 54
ultra vires 299–300

utilitarianism 307
convenience, citizenship of 258–9, 400
Convention on Nationality 1997 (Council of Europe) 59, 64–5, 254, 257
convictions *see* criminal records
cooperation, principle of sincere 65, 384–5, 397
corruption 299, 301, 413
cosmopolitanism and global citizenship
ascription to achievement, from 311, 410–11
best practices 326
birthright lottery 310, 409
evaluation of *ius doni* 310–12, 410–11
free market 312
globalisation 411
historical development 30–1
immigration status and laws 411
liberalisation 312, 411
multiple citizenship 82, 399
nation State as an anachronism 19
Roman law 33
talent 53, 411
transparency 310–11
costs and fees 211, 226, 239, 372–3, 381
Côte d'Ivoire 292
criminal records 204, 340
criteria/conditions for citizenship 12–13 *see also* talent and highly-skilled people
certainty, principle of 251
cosmopolitanism and global citizenship 411
discretion 251
Economic Theory of Clubs 229
injustice 410
integration 251
modernity 410–11
naturalisation 128–30, 136–46
non-economic considerations 232–3, 406
rule of law 414
transparency 410
waiver 128
Croatia 8, 123, 320, 404
culture, traditions and values
authority of the State 250
citizenship, definition of 75
constituent population and State, congruence between 92
constitutional rights 90
creation of a consistent community of values 89–90
discrimination and equality 250
diversity 308
Economic Theory of Clubs 228
EU 51, 89–90, 129, 269–70
heterogeneity 270
human dignity 141
identification 14–15, 136, 141–3
integration 53
invention of symbols, traditions and theories of origin 40
ius sanguinis 122
language 110, 139, 141
market-based approach 233, 234–8, 240
military service 142–3
minority protection 141
multiculturalism 30, 117–18, 137
nationality 141
naturalisation 136–7
oaths of allegiance 141–2
privacy 330
protonationalism 35
relativism 308
residence 137
subsidiarity 90
tax 90, 142
custom
good faith 77
international law 147, 257, 262–3, 412
residence, law of place of 34
Cyprus
abuse of political, economic and social rights, risk of 297
ius doni 8
language 203
multiple citizenship 206
naturalisation 137
oaths of allegiance 203–4
property 253
residence 286
statistics 319–20, 404
de Gaulle, Charles 174
de Maleville, Jacques 165
declarations of intent 146, 148, 259–60,

394
defence of State 37
defence, individual's right of 73
degrees, certified copies of 339–40
Delors, Jacques 270
democracy
citizenship, definition of 250
constituent population and State, congruence between 91
contribution and consideration, limited correlation between 300
elections and voting 235, 250
EU 71
freedom of choice, respect for 245–6
human dignity 250
identification points 16
individual freedom, mobility and security 313
international law 250
ius doni 9
legitimacy 399
national citizenship laws 250
tying arrangements 413
ultra vires 260
demographics 76, 79, 102
Denmark 13, 129–30, 202
Descartes, René 165
descent, citizenship by 247–8 *see also ius sanguinis*
desirable goods, discrimination against 309, 408
developing countries 6, 19, 100, 117, 309
dignity *see* human dignity
Diogenes 30
diplomatic or consular protection
abuse of rights 257–8
constitutional and political dimensions of citizenship 105
discretion 111–12
EU 71, 396
functional significance of citizenship 96–7
genuine links or connections 112, 144–5, 259, 394
human rights 96
international law 96–7, 257–8
nationality, right to 263
stateless persons 96
disasters and emergencies 20, 101, 270
discretion 111–14, 215, 252, 257
discrimination and equality
Absolutism 248–9
apartheid 43, 244
barriers to citizenship 249–50, 264–5
birth 234, 248–9
citizenship, concept of 392
constitutional rights 264
culture, State authority over definition of 250
descent, based on 247–8
desirable goods, discrimination against 309, 408
Economic Theory of Clubs 225, 229
Enlightenment 248
equal opportunities 218–19
European Convention on Human Rights 264–5
evaluation of *ius doni* 292–3, 325
gender 43, 197, 263
general principle of equality 249–50
homeland, based on 247–8
human dignity 249
integration 265
international law 225, 247–50, 264–5
ius doni 264
language 247–9, 264
nation States, formation of 248
national citizenship laws 249–50
origin, based on 247–8, 264
political opinion 248–9
population, limitation and control of State's 89
race 43, 60, 244, 247–9, 264
religion 247–9, 264
rule of law 249
self-determination 264
social class 264
unity of citizenship 252
Universal Declaration of Human Rights 263
xenophobia 177
distributive justice 10, 302–5
birthright lottery 303–4, 409–10
EU 303
evaluation of *ius doni* 302–5, 409–10
feudal status, citizenship as equivalent to 303

human dignity 74
immigration controls 303
immigration paradox 303
intergenerational perspective 304
ius sanguinis 305
ius soli 305
naturalisation 305
veil of ignorance 303–4, 409–10
divergence/incongruence between populations 14–18, 23, 43, 91–2, 398–9
divorce certificates, certified 336
documentation requirements 332–40
see also **passports**
application forms 332–4, 339
background verification report (BVRs) 340
bank references, certified 337
bank statements, originals of 339
birth certificates, certified 335–6
children 332–3, 335, 338–9
colour photographs 333–4
degrees, certified copies of 339–40
divorce certificates, certified 336
education 332, 338, 339–40
higher learning, original confirmation letters from institutes of 338
HIV/AIDs test results 334
identity card copies, certified 335
marriage certificates, certified 336
medical certificate forms 334
military records, certificates, certified 337
name change documentation, certified 337
nationality 62–4
parents, sworn affidavits of support relating to 339
passports 333, 334–5
application forms 333, 334
certified copies 335
children 335
photographs
certified photographs 334
colour 333–4
signature certification forms 333
police certificates 336
powers of attorney 332
professional references 337
Real Estate sale and purchase contract and escrow agreements 335
residential address, original documents of evidence of 338
St Kitts and Nevis 332–40
SIDF Investment Confirmation Forms 335
signature certification forms 333
visas 3, 85, 223, 225, 230, 313, 325, 373, 389, 400, 406
domestic functions of citizenship 88–95, 395
Dominica 204
Donaldson, Mary 130
***Dred Scott v Sandford* decision (United States) 43**
dual citizenship *see* multiple/dual citizenship
Dubai 91
due diligence
agents, licensing and supervision of 328
background verification reports (BVRs) 328, 340
caveat emptor in US legal system 285
contributions and investment 238
EU 321, 325
evaluation of *ius doni* 284–6, 321, 325, 340–1, 403
Financial Intelligence Units 340
high risk indicators 340
Interpol 340
Know Your Customer banking best practice 285
latent defects 285
national interest, grant of citizenship in the 219
negative indicators 341
specialised investigation forms 341
State sovereignty 299
statistics 321, 325, 403–4
terrorism tourism 321
Dzankic, Jelena 358–9
economic and social rights, risk of abuse of 295–9, 325
economic crisis 89–90
economic function of citizenship 88, 394
economic globalisation *see* globalisation

economic structural deficits, control of 102
Economic Theory of Clubs 10, 221–30
auctions for admission 226
burden versus benefit 224–5
citizenship services 225
club goods 222–6
competition 222
consideration (contract) 227–8
contributions and investment 222, 224–30, 412–13
cultural contributions 228
discrimination and equality 225, 229
excludable benefits 223–4
factual connection 227–8
full members, eligibility criteria for 223
guests, eligibility criteria for 223
human capital 229–30
ius doni 222–9
loss of citizenship 223
maintenance of membership, fees for 226
migration policy 223
nation States, public goods provided by 222–3
public goods 222–4, 227
spectrum of opinion 222–6
tying arrangements 228–9, 413
value of citizenship 222–6
vote, right to 223
The Economist 53
education
degrees, certified copies of 339–40
documentation 332, 338, 339–40
higher learning, original confirmation letters from institutes of 338
elections and voting
active citizenship 15–16, 71, 89, 91, 94, 121, 195, 273–4
buying and selling 233
constituent people 16, 106
constitutional and political dimensions of citizenship 105
democracy and knowledge levels 235
democratic principle 250
Economic Theory of Clubs 223
EU 17, 71, 268–9
foreign citizens 16, 93–4
freedom of choice, respect for 246–7
human dignity 93–4
large and small countries, knowledge of issues in 235
national citizenship laws 45
passive citizenship 71, 89, 94, 121, 195, 273–4
power of State 100, 106, 250
referendums 179, 360
turnouts 297–8
emergencies and disasters 20, 101, 270
emerging economies 19, 100, 309
emigration countries, definition of 116–17
employment *see* job creation and employment
Engels, Friedrich 40
England *see* United Kingdom
Enlightenment 37–9, 107–8, 248
abuse of rights 257
birthright lottery 219
social contract 37
sovereignty, joint exercise of 37
watchman State, model of the 37
equality *see* discrimination and equality; equality of States
equality of States 114, 318, 326
L'Equipe 217
escrow agreements 335
ethics
evaluation of the *ius doni* 293
queue, of the 238–40, 407
ethnicity and race
all white policies 232
anti-Asian policies 232
apartheid 43, 244
discrimination and equality 43, 60, 244, 247–9, 264
ethno-national identity 24–5, 315–17
evaluation of the *ius doni* 315–17
ius sanguinis 59
liberal ethno-nationalist citizenship laws 296
multi-ethnic States 59–60, 123, 269
nationality 59–62
naturalisation 129–30, 146–7, 402
EU citizenship *see* European Union and EU citizenship
European Convention on Human

Rights 264–5
European Table Tennis Championship 217
European Union and EU citizenship 43–51, 265–77
Amsterdam Treaty 265
authority and power of the State 269, 272–6, 383
Charter on Fundamental Rights of the EU 47, 73
citizenship, definition of 44, 70–1, 76
competence-competence (implied powers) 49
competences 49–50, 65–6, 273, 382–3, 385, 397
conferral of powers, principle of 47–8, 176, 272–3, 293, 383
constituent people 17–18, 269–70
constitutional law protection 47
cooperation, principle of sincere 65, 384–5, 397
Court of Justice 47–8, 63, 65, 383, 386, 396–7
culture and values 51, 89–90, 129, 269–70
democracy 71
demographic changes 76
derived and national citizenship supplementary status 268
diplomatic or consular protection 71, 268, 270–2, 396
directives 46
discretion 111–14
distributive justice 303
due diligence 321, 325
economic crisis 90
elections and voting 17, 71, 268–9
equality of Member States 114
European Coal and Steel Community (ECSC) 45
European Commission 65, 275, 380, 382–3, 396–7
European Community (EC) 45
European Parliament 16–17, 268–9, 272–7, 289–91, 397
evaluation of the *ius doni* 281, 319–21, 325
financial position, existence of a secure 205
freedom of establishment 325, 388–9
freedom of movement 17–18, 44, 71, 78–9, 93, 260, 268, 320, 325, 396
freedom, security and justice, area of 146, 395
genuine links or contributions 146, 260, 396
globalisation 18
growth, legal relationship to 267–70
historical development 43–51
human dignity 71
institutions 48, 49, 65–6, 396–7
integration 44, 270, 295
internal market 385–6, 396
international law 265–77
job creation and employment 17–18, 78–9, 84, 99, 101
language 139–40, 268
legal nature of EU citizenship 267–8
legal subject status 44–7
liberal argument for *ius doli* 306
liberal ethno-nationalist citizenship laws 296
Lisbon Treaty 45–6, 47, 97, 268, 270, 272–3
local elections, right to participate in 268
loss or withdrawal of citizenship 46, 268
Maastricht Treaty 44–5, 47, 50–1, 265, 270
market approach 267, 406
mobility 17–18
national citizenship laws 46–7, 63, 65–6, 265–77, 396–7
national interest, grant of citizenship in the 220
nationality 21, 64–6, 70–1, 76, 397
naturalisation
number of 131
rules, differences in 266–7
object formula 97
Ombudsman, right of 268
overlapping citizenship 265–6
overseas territories 266
petition, right of 65, 268, 272–7
political subjects 267–9
proportionality 93
public authority exception 93

resident population, incongruence with 16–18
Rome Treaty of 1957 45
Schengen area 175
Second World War 45
social condition 76
State sovereignty 44–8, 65–6, 397
statistics 319–21, 403–5
subsidiarity 49–51, 93, 139–40, 270
supranational status 45, 47–9, 265–77
third countries, Member States extending citizenship to 266
three-element theory 44–5, 49, 70–1
transnational European identity, formation of 267
visas 325, 363, 373, 389, 400
welfare differentials, reduction of 310

evaluation of *ius doni* 279–341
abuse of political, economic and social rights, risk of 295–300, 325
acquisition, *ius doni* as a principle of 287–9
application process, efficiency and reliability of 331–40
arguments for and against *ius doni* 289–321, 405–6
best practices 325–6
common good, grant of citizenship in the 318–19, 403
contribution and consideration, limited correlation between 300–1
contributions and investment 282–4, 300–1, 320, 326, 404–8
contributions to society 300–1, 320, 326, 404–8
cosmopolitanism and global citizenship 310–12, 410–11
cross-border integration and convergence, promotion of 309
cultural relativism 308
definition 280–1
discrimination and equality 292–3, 325
distributive justice 302–5, 409–10
documentation requirements 332–40
due diligence 284–6, 321, 325, 340–1, 403
ethics 293
ethnic nationalist citizenship regimes 315–17
EU 281, 319–21, 325
freedom of movement 283
globalisation 315
highly-skilled workers 280
human dignity 292–3
human rights 292
individual freedom, mobility and security 312–14
inflows, table of 282
integration, limited or no requirements for 280, 293–5
international law 280, 292, 325–6
investment, definition of 280
issues, background and objectives 279
ius sanguinis 315–17, 319–21
ius soli 317–21
job creation 297, 309
liberal argument for *ius doli* 305–6
market-oriented approach 405–6
military service 291
money can buy, goods which 292–3
nation and citizenship, decoupling of 315
national homogeneity, myth of 315
naturalisation 280–2, 287–8
passports 291
rent-seeking and governance 301–2
residence 286–7
rule of law 293
sale, prohibition of citizenship for 290–3
significant contribution requirement 282–4
simplified investment 286
social cohesion 280
sovereign equality of States 326
standards, definition of 325–6
State sovereignty 290, 298–9
statelessness 292
statistics 319–21, 403–5
strategies, two game modes of 286–7
talent 286, 327
tax havens 290
transparency and accountability 326–41
types of contributions and investments 282
ultra vires, violation of principle of

299–300
utilitarianism 306–7, 406–8
welfare differentials, reduction of 310
welfare gains 286
external functions of citizenship 88, 395
external inclusion/internal inclusion 3, 19, 229, 392
external relations 11
extraordinary contributions
financial position, existence of a secure 128, 205
historical examples 210–12
multiple citizenship 400
naturalisation 128, 204 206
Facebook 111
family ties 98–9, 143 *see also* children
fast-track procedure, *ius doni* as 238
feudalism 30, 35, 121, 219, 303–4, 395, 408
fiduciary duties 71, 89, 244, 270–1
final point theory (adaptation and assimilation) versus incentive theory 95
Financial Intelligence Units (FIUs) 340
financial position, existence of a secure 12, 205
Finland 202
First World War 41
Fischer, Bobby 130
flag of convenience, citizenship as personal 258–9, 400
flexible citizenship 24
football clubs in Europe 226
foreign direct investment (FDI) *see* contributions and investment
France *see also* French Revolution
assimilation 249
adoption 174
assimilation 173–4
athletes, artists and *categories prioritaires* 172
burqa ban 173, 249
Catholicism 15
centre of vital interests 170–2
citizenship, definition of 168
citizenship tests 129
Code Civil 7, 38, 160, 165–6, 169–74, 395–6
Code de la nationalité française (CNF) 166, 169
coloniser regimes 201–2
consolidation of States 35
constituent people 15
Constitution 6, 7, 109–10, 164–5, 167–9, 173, 245–9
criminal records 170, 249
culture 110
declarations 174–5
discrimination and equality 173, 247–8
Edict of Fontainebleau of 1685 212
Edict of Nantes 212
elections and voting 15, 168
Enlightenment 165
EU law 64
extraordinary contributions 172–3, 212
February Revolution of 1848 108
final point theory 171
financial position, existence of a secure 205
French Foreign Legion 102
gender equality 173
Huguenots 7, 212
integration 171
ius sanguinis 8, 165–6, 168
ius soli 7–8, 10, 35, 165, 169–75
language 110, 140, 171–2, 174–5
legitimacy 168–9
length of residence 170–2, 203, 206
liberty, quality and fraternity 165, 168
list of selected countries of origin 167
loss of citizenship 169
marriage 174–5, 206
marriages of convenience 175
military service 102, 143, 171
Moroccan descent, citizens of 61
multiple citizenship 145, 175, 206, 256
national identity 237
nationalité d'origine principle 165–6
nationality 61, 67, 165–6, 168
naturalisation 137, 164–75, 201
ordinary naturalisation 170–1
overseas departments and regions 168
Paris riots 174
political opinion 248–9

religion and belief 165, 167, 247
residence 170
restrictions, trend towards 174
Roman law 67
secularism 165, 167
sovereignty of the people 245–6
special circumstances, naturalisation under 171–4
State structural parameters 164–6
statistics 166
structural features 167–8
Syria, travel to 321
Thirty Years War 212
treaties and agreements 168–9
United Kingdom 160, 164
use of force, monopoly on the 249
welfare versus loyalty 67
Franco, Francisco 232
François I, king of France 130
Frederick, Crown Prince of Denmark 130
free cities 34
freedom of choice, respect for individual 245–7, 312–13
freedom of establishment 325, 388–9
freedom of movement *see also* mobility
CARICOM 325
EU 17–18, 44, 71, 78–9, 93, 260, 268, 320, 325, 396
human rights 42–3
ius doni 401
labour 17–18, 78–9
visas 325
freedom of opinion and expression 277
freedom, security and justice, area of 146, 395
French-Guyana 168
French Polynesia 168
French Revolution 7, 10, 15, 37–9, 414
birth-right privileges, removal of 234
Code Civil of 1804 38
colours as a vehicle of national awareness 109
Constitution 38
Declaration of the Rights of Man 1789 38, 40
demarcation between citizen and non-citizen 39, 395–6
genuine links or connections 258
historical development 107
ius sanguinis 122
ius soli 39, 121
non-citizens and citizens, demarcation between 39
religion 257
territorial unity 39, 395
functional significance of citizenship 87–102, 394
assignment of rights 96
civil society 397
classical functions 88, 394
constituent population and State, congruence between 91–2
demographic, social and economic structural deficits, control of 102
differentiation 88
diplomatic and consular protection 96–7
domestic functions 88–95, 395
economic function 88, 394
external functions 88, 395
family ties, ensuring cross-border 98–9
features of citizenship concepts 101–2
final point theory versus incentive theory 95
foreign direct investment, promoting 102
globalisation 88, 394
information technology 394
integration through participation in policy-making 93–4
labour supply and labour demand, coherence between 101
legal function 88, 394
military personnel, recruitment of foreign 102
non-State functions 100–1
political function 88, 394
population, limitation and control of State's 88–9
public international law by individuals, effective suppression and sanctioning of violations by individuals of 100
public offices and functions, controlling access to 92–3
social cohesion 397

sociological function 88, 394
statelessness, avoidance of 97–8
subjective-individual functions 394–5
talent 102
traditional and modern functions, distinction between 395
values, creation of a consistent community of 89–90
welfare function 88, 96
Garriaud-Maylam, Joëlle 81–2
gender equality 43, 197, 263
genuine links or connections
birth 259
centre of interests 143
diplomatic or consular protection 112, 144–5, 259, 394
EU 146, 260, 396
factual presence 397
family ties 143
flag of convenience, citizenship as personal 258–9
habitual residence 143
ICJ 143–4
international law 143–5
ius soli 259–60, 398
knowledge of country 89
legal presence 397
loyalty 144
multiple citizenship 145, 259, 394
naturalisation 143–6
participation 143–4
population, limitation and control of State's 89
real and effective citizenship 144–5
sufficient link 258–60, 317–18, 398, 402
voluntariness 259–60
Germany
absolutism 107
British Empire 211
citizenship tests 129
colours as a vehicle of national awareness 109
Constitution 72, 123
culture 228
discrimination and equality 247–8
East Germans crossing into West Germany 68
Economic Theory of Clubs 228
eternity clause 72
ethnic nationalist citizenship regimes 315, 317
EU 267–8
family ties 99
French Civil Code 166
Germanic law 34
guest workers 99
historical development 107–8
integration 13, 315
ius sanguinis 53, 122–3
ius soli 53, 99, 122
language 140, 315
length of residence 203
Malta 289
military service 143
multiple citizenship 206
national identity 237
National Socialist Germany 41–2, 72
nationality 61–2
naturalisation 137, 151, 201, 322–4
non-coloniser/occupier regimes 202
Olympic citizenship 217
precedent 187
public officials 81
repatriates 232
return, law of 123
scientists and technicians after WWII, naturalisation of German 212–13
Soviet Union 384
statelessness 41–2
statistics 321–4, 403–4
Switzerland 177
Syria, travel to 321
terrorism tourism 321
territory, culture and identity, conflict between 315
Turks 67
xenophobia 177
Giegerich, Thomas 267
global citizenship *see* cosmopolitanism and global citizenship
global State, realisation of a 392
globalisation
contributions and investment 233
cosmopolitanism and global citizenship 411
EU 18

evaluation of the *ius doni* 315
functional significance of citizenship 88, 394
ius soli 121, 317, 398
market-based approach 411
migration State 12
multiple citizenship 80
nation States 19, 21–2, 55
national homogeneity, myth of 315
nationality 78–80
non-State function 100
oaths of allegiance 203
social changes 76
State control 17
State sovereignty 411–12
talent 55
technology 398–9
transnationalism 398–9
welfare differentials, reduction of 310
good faith 77
graduated citizenship 253
Greece 13, 310 *see also* Ancient Greece
Guadeloupe 168
Guantanamo Bay 96
Habermas, Jürgen 73, 288
habitual residence 143
Hague Conference of 1930 261
Hague Convention on Conflict of Nationality Laws 113
Haiti 81
Hambach Festival of 1832 108–9
heads of State 253
health
medical certificate forms 334
private health care 297
Hegel, Friedrich 38
Heinrich Böll Foundation 47
higher learning, original confirmation letters from institutes of 338
highly-skilled people *see* talent and highly-skilled people
Hirschl, Ran 230, 289
historical development of citizenship law 9–10, 30–51 *see also* American Revolution; French Revolution
absolutism 93, 108, 248–9
Ancient Greece 30–1, 210, 395
British Empire 210–11
Catholic Church, influence of 107
city states 31, 147, 210
codifications 6
constitutional and political dimensions 107–8
cosmopolitanism and global citizenship 30–1
development lines 107–8
Enlightenment 37–9, 107–8, 219, 248, 257
European Union 43–51
examples of *ius doni* 209–13
extraordinary contributions 210–12
Holy Roman Empire 35–6, 107
integration 42–4
Marxism 40–2
Middle Ages 33–6, 210–11, 395
nation States 107–8
nationalism 40–2, 395–6
naturalisation 150
post-war integration and European integration 42–4
Renaissance 33–6, 395
Roman law 32–3, 210, 395
totalitarianism 40–2
Hitler, Adolf 147
HIV/AIDs test results 334
Hobbes, Thomas 62
Holy Roman Empire 35–6, 107
homelessness 98
homogeneity
domestic homogeneity 39–40, 395
ethnicity 31
myth of national homogeneity 315
Hong Kong 266, 293
Howard's Citizenship Policy Indicator (CPI) 201
Huguenots 7, 212
human capital 219, 229–30
human dignity 10, 70–5, 300
autonomy 244–5
barriers to citizenship 244
birthright lottery 409–10
certainty, principle of 250–1
Charter of Fundamental Rights of the EU 73
constitutions 72–3
democracy 250
diplomatic or consular protection 270
discrimination and equality 249

distributive justice 74
EU 71
evaluation of the *ius doni* 292–3
fiduciary duties of States 244
final point theory versus incentive theory 95
freedom of choice, respect for 245–7
human rights 31, 72–3, 244–5
integration 94
international law 244–5
ius doni 74, 245
ius sanguinis 122
market values 234
national citizenship laws 74, 244, 250–1
nationality 70, 72–5
proportionality 244
religion 249
self-determination 73, 399
subsidiarity 244
supervision 244
universalism 244–5, 247, 250–1, 412
veil of ignorance 74–5
human rights
Charter on Fundamental Rights of the EU 47, 73, 273
civil, political and social rights 393
diplomatic or consular protection 96
European Convention on Human Rights 73, 264–5
human dignity 72–3, 244–5
integration 42–3
ius doni 8
multiple citizenship 80
national actions, limits on 23
nationality 71, 72, 263
self-determination 71
statelessness 97
subjectivity 263
universalism 42–3, 72, 292
humanitarianism 97, 303, 401
Hungary 296, 384
Iceland 130
identification points 14–16
identity cards 5, 335
Ignatieff, Michael 19
immigration and emigration countries 116–18
emigration countries, definition of 116–17
immigration countries, definition of 116–17
immigration status and laws 4, 51–5
ascription to achievement, from 311, 410
cosmopolitanism and global citizenship 411
desirable goods, discrimination against 309, 408
distributive justice 303
Economic Theory of Clubs 223, 229, 232–3
human dignity 74
illegal immigration 321, 403–4
immigrate, right to 307–8, 407
immigration paradox 303
international law 401
modern concepts 51–4
nation States 22
nationalism 41
political community, membership in a 63
post-war era and European integration 43
return, right to 401
imminent status 67–70
incentive theory versus final point theory 95
India 117
indigenous people 61, 316–17
individual freedom 245–7, 312–13
industrial clusters 414
industrialisation 41
Institut de Droit International (IDI) 255
integration
constituent population and State, congruence between 91–2
contribution and consideration, limited correlation between 300–1
cross-border integration and convergence, promotion of 309
culture 53
discrimination and equality 265
elections and voting 93–4
EU 42–4, 270, 295
final point theory versus incentive theory 95

functional significance of citizenship 93–4
historical development 42–4
human dignity 94
human rights 42–3
intergovernmental prosperity, levelling of 309
international law 42
knowledge of country 295
language 295
liberalisation of trade 309
limited or no requirements for integration 280, 293–5
migrant workers 52–4
mobility 294
money 232
national citizenship laws 205
national interest, grant of citizenship in the 215–16, 220
nationalism 294–5
naturalisation 136, 294
participation 93–4
political integration 53
population, limitation and control of State's 89
post-war integration and European integration 42–4
Refugee Convention 43–4
social integration 53, 295
State sovereignty 42, 43–4
target 51–3, 309
unity of citizenship 253
welfare differentials, reduction of 310
intergenerational perspective 99, 304
internal inclusion/external inclusion 3, 19, 229, 392
International Court of Justice (ICJ) 58, 111, 143–4, 259
International Monetary Fund (IMF) 330
international law and principles 4, 25, 243–77
abuse of rights, prohibition of 257–8, 325
assignment of rights 96
certainty, principle of 250–2
citizenship, definition of 64, 393
constitutional and political dimensions 104–6
customary international law 147, 257, 262–3, 412
democratic principle 250
diplomatic or consular protection 96–7, 271
discretion 112–13
discrimination and equality 225, 247–50, 264–5
equality, general principle of 249–50
EU 265–77
evaluation of *ius doni* 280, 292, 325–6
freedom of choice, respect for individual 245–7
genuine links or connections 143–5, 258–60
Hague Convention 113
human dignity 244–5
immigration law and status 401
individual freedom, mobility and security 314
integration 42
international courts 393
legal barriers 261–2
legal certainty 325
Middle Ages 36
minority protection 141
mobility 411–12
multiple/dual citizenship, prevention of 254–7
national actions, limits of 22–3
national citizenship laws 244
nationality 64–6, 100, 263
political opinion, religion, race or language, no undifferentiated connection to 248–9
standards, definition of 325–6
State sovereignty 100, 112–14, 262–3, 411–12
statelessness 97, 258
sufficient relationship or genuine links with State 258–60
suppression and sanction of individuals 100
treaty law 262–3, 412
ultra vires 260–1
unity of citizenship 252–3
universalism 244–5, 412
violence/use of force, State monopoly on use of 100

welfare 46, 257–8, 261
withdrawal of citizenship 257–8
international relations 63, 256, 399
Internet 110–11, 121
Interpol 204, 340, 388
investment *see* contributions and investment
Iran 61, 111, 321, 388, 403
Iraq 6, 61, 321, 403
Ireland
abuse of political, economic and social rights, risk of 296
birth tourism 296
emigration countries, definition of 117
ius sanguinis 123
language 129
non-coloniser/occupier regimes 202
subjects 161
Islamic countries 248
Islamists 321, 403–4
Israel
religion 129–30
return, law of 123, 129–30, 232, 316
Italy
Argentineans 384
emigration countries, definition of 117
language 129
liberal ethno-nationalist citizenship laws 296
non-coloniser/occupier regimes 202
ius doni*, evaluation of *see* evaluation of *ius doni
***ius sanguinis* 313–15, 317–21**
arbitrariness 225, 235
birth 59, 118–21, 128, 179, 398
after 118–20
at 118–21, 398
constituent population and State, congruence between 92
culture and traditions 122
distributive justice 305
ethnicity and race 59, 315–17
human dignity 122
ius soli 122, 124, 319–21, 398
mobility 122–3
national citizenship laws 10, 39
naturalisation 128
principles 118–24
subsidiarity 122
talent 52–3
ius soli 317–21
abuse of political, economic and social rights, risk of 296
accidental citizens 259, 318
arbitrariness 225, 235, 259, 262
birth 59, 118–21, 128, 398
after 118–20
at 118–21, 398
citizenship, definition of 59
classical *ius soli* countries 10
congruence, creation of 121
distributive justice 305
family ties 99
feudalism 35
genuine links or connections 259–60
globalisation 121, 317, 398
immigration countries, definition of 117
international law 262
Internet 121
ius sanguinis 122, 124, 319–21, 398
liberal laws 10
Middle Ages 35
national citizenship laws 39, 99
naturalisation 128
principles 117–24, 398
social cohesion 121
sufficient connection 317–18, 398
talent 52–3
Janoski, Thomas 201–2
Japan 117, 177, 202
Jellinek, Georg 10, 44–5, 49, 58, 88–9, 98, 104–7, 393
job creation and employment
abuse of political, economic and social rights, risk of 297
birthright lottery 3
blocked exchange versus market approach 239
blue cards 52–3
CARICOM 101
EU 17–18, 78–9, 84, 99, 101
evaluation of *ius doni* 297, 309
freedom of movement 17–18, 78–9
Germany 99
immigrate, right to 307–8, 407
industrial clusters 414
integration of migrant workers 52–4

intergenerational family ties 99
labour market 51, 53, 79, 101–2, 251, 280
MINT (mathematics, informatics, natural sciences and technology) occupations 52
mobility 17–20, 88, 101, 122–3
multinationals 111
policies 4
self-employed 78, 137–8
supply and demand 51, 53, 79, 101
talent 51–4, 280
Joppke, Christian 59, 62, 311
Josephinian Code of 1786 36
judicial review 252
Juncker, Jean-Claude 290
Kant, Immanuel 22, 43, 72, 107
Kelsen, Hans 195
Kennedy, John F 90
Kleeber, Gabriela 347–8, 358
Klusmeyer, Douglas 40
knowledge 12, 204–5
democracy, needed for a functioning 235
genuine links or connections 89
integration 295
Know Your Customer banking best practice 285
large and small countries, knowledge of issues in 235
mode of behaviour, citizenship as a 236–7
national knowledge 197, 199, 204–5
proof 204–5
Kochenov, Dimitry 147, 266
Konrad Adenauer Stiftung 91
Kosovo, conflict in 244
Kurds 61
Kuttner, Robert 232
Lamourette, Antoine-Adrien 258
language 12, 102, 128–30
constituent population and State, congruence between 92
constitutional and political dimensions 109–10
culture and values 110, 139, 141
discrimination and equality 247–9, 264
English 110
EU 139–40, 268
identification points 15
integration 295
military service 141
multilingual countries 110
naturalisation 128–30, 139–41, 203
petition, right of 275–6
regional languages 140
subsidiarity 139–40
latent defects 285
Latin America 8, 13, 116, 121, 202, 256
legal certainty 325
legal concept of citizenship 2–6, 24
exclusion 3–4
inclusion 3–4
legal relationships 66–70, 393
Roman law 32–3
legal function of citizenship 88, 394
legal sources, list of 455–9
legality, principle of 95, 413
legislation *see* national citizenship laws
length of residence
factual link 397–8
naturalisation 128–9, 203, 206
unity of citizenship 253
Liberia 130
liberalisation
cosmopolitanism and global citizenship 312, 411
discrimination against desirable goods 309, 408
international trade 309, 408
reversal 118
loans 239
Locke, John 37
loss of citizenship *see* withdrawal or loss of citizenship
lottery *see* birthright lottery
Louis IX, king of France 246
Louis XIV, king of France 34–5
Louis Philippe d'Orléans, King of France 108
loyalty *see also* oaths of allegiance
assignment of rights 96
genuine links or connections 144
multiple citizenship 254, 256, 399
nation State, monopoly of 312
naturalisation 136
petition, right of 275

population, limitation and control of State's 89
public offices and functions, controlling access to 92–3
welfare 67
Luther, Martin 6, 107–8
Luxembourg 13, 95, 179
McAllister, David 255
Macedonia 236
Machiavelli, Niccolò 34
Macklin, Audrey 83
McNeill, William H 31
Malaysia, ethnic Chinese in 42
Malta 8, 13, 377–90
abuse of political, economic and social rights, risk of 297
accountability 390
applications 379–81
legal consequences of successful applications 381
requirements 380–1
background of applicants 380
background to country 377
bank charges 381
children, spouses and parents 381
Constitution 228, 377–8
contributions and investment 23, 319, 380–1, 404
criminal records 380
democratic control 387–8
difference principle 317
discretion 413
documentation 379–80
due diligence 344, 381, 387–8, 390
elections and voting 15
equality and discrimination 386
EU 64–6, 319, 382–9, 404
breach, where there is no EU law to 384–5
compatibility of IIP with EU law 382–7
conferral of powers, principle of 383
Court of Justice 383, 386
equality and discrimination 386
EU citizenship, acquisition of 381–9
European Parliament 289
freedom of establishment 388–9
harm to EU or member States, no 387
harmonisation of law 384
internal market 385–6
jurisdiction 382–3
review of IIP by Commission 380, 382–3
sincere cooperation, principle of 384–5
substance of rights of EU citizenship 386
ultra vires 383
evaluation of *ius doni* 289–91
freedom of establishment 388–9
Germany 289
globalisation 389
Gozo 377
health insurance 380
Identity Malta 380
independence from UK 377
Individual Investor Programme 65, 228–9, 378–89
integration 293, 385
Interpol 388
ius doni 377–90
ius sanguinis 378
ius soli 378
language 203, 377, 386
launch of *ius doni* program 13
legal basis 48, 377–80, 396–7, 413
multiple citizenship 206, 256, 344–5, 378
National Development and Social Fund 317, 381, 389
national interest, grant of citizenship in the 215
naturalisation
costs 381
statistics 378–9
oaths of allegiance 141, 203, 380
passports 381, 387
Regulator, appointment of an independent 388
religion 377
reporting and audits 330
residence 386
risk assessment 388
safe haven for investors in the EU 388–9

sincere cooperation, principle of 384–5
Social Return on Investment (SRI) 389
standard for programmes, setting a new 389–90
State sovereignty 382–3
State structural parameters 377–8
statistics 319, 404, 378–9, 387
talent 327, 344
transparency 229, 327, 387–8
tying arrangements 228–9
United Kingdom 289, 377–8
visas 389
market-based approach
blocked exchange 10, 231–42, 406–7
contributions and investment 232, 238, 407
elections and voting 235
ethics of the queue 238–40, 407
evaluation of *ius doni* 405–6
EU 267, 406
globalisation 411
goods 307, 406–7
human dignity 234
knowledge and understanding 236–7
labour market 51, 53, 79, 101, 251, 280
liberal argument for *ius doli* 306
mode of behaviour, citizenship as a 236–7
money 232–3
national identity 236–8
non-economic considerations 232–3, 406
political membership aspect of citizenship 238, 240–2
underclass 235–6
universalism 234–5
utilitarianism 307, 406–7
values 233, 234–8, 240
marriage
certificates, certified 336
divorce certificates, certified 336
naturalisation 206
Marshall, Thomas H 58, 225
Martinique 168
Marx, Karl 38, 40
Marxism 40–2
mathematics, informatics, natural sciences and technology (MINT) occupations 52
Mayotte 168
medical certificate forms 334
Middle Ages 33–6, 395
city states 210
consolidation of States 34–5
customary law of the place of residence 34
extraordinary contributions 210–11
feudalism 35, 395
free cities 34
Germanic law 34
Holy Roman Emperor 35–6
international law 36
ius soli 35
participation 34
protonationalism 35
State sovereignty 34–6
military service
certified records 337
evaluation of *ius doni* 291
foreign personnel, recruitment of 102
freedom of choice, respect for 247
language 141
multiple citizenship 65, 81
national identity 237
naturalisation 141–3
Mill, John Stuart 15, 40, 306
Miller, David 15, 233
MINT (mathematics, informatics, natural sciences and technology) occupations 52
mobility *see also* freedom of movement
citizenship, concept of 393
international law 411–12
labour 17–20, 88, 101, 122–3
multiple citizenship 399–400
naturalisation 137
passports 312–13
residence 137
modern and traditional functions of citizenship, distinction between 395
Montenegro
access to information 364
acquisition of citizenship 361
background to country 359–60
background verifications 366–7

consideration 363
constituent determinants of citizenship 361–2
Constitution 359–60, 362, 364
contributions and investment 363–7
corruption 366, 413–14
criminal records 362
criteria/conditions for citizenship 362, 363–6
extraordinary 363–6
material conditions 363–5
de lege ferenda 366–7
discretion 344, 363–4, 413–14
due diligence 366–7, 413
elections and voting 359–60
European Union
foreign investment 363
membership 360, 361
formal requirements 365–6
general naturalisation requirements 362
human dignity 360
human rights 360, 361
independence 360
international law 361–2
international organizations, membership of 361–2
ius doni 359–67
ius sanguinis 361
languages 360, 362
legal basis 363, 413–14
loss of citizenship 361
multiple/dual citizenship 344–5
national and ethnic origins 361
naturalisation statistics 361
passports 366
privileged naturalisation 364–7
proposal of candidates 365
referendums 360
relinquishment of previous citizenship 362
residence 364
rule of law 364
Serbia 360
scientific, cultural, economic, sporting, national or other interests 363
State structural parameters 359–60
statistics 361
sufficient consideration 413
talent 363
tax 362
visas 363
Yugoslavia 360
money
appropriateness of what money can buy 233, 292–3
birth citizenship 229, 410
blocked exchange 23, 232–3, 240
elections, buying and selling 233
feudalism 210
human investments 219
integration 232
pollute, right to 232
utilitarianism 306
Montevideo Convention of 1933 11
morality *see* ethics
Morocco
Berbers 61–2
France, citizens of Moroccan descent in 61
multiculturalism 30, 117–18, 137
multinationals 55, 111
multiple/dual citizenship
acquisition of citizenship 254–7
boundaries to citizenship 254–5
Cold War 255, 399
conflicts of jurisdiction 254–5
consumer citizenship 84
convenience, citizenship of 400
cosmopolitanism and global citizenship 82
equality before the law 85
European Convention on Nationality 1997 254, 257
genuine links or connections 145, 259, 394
global citizens, class of 399
globalisation 80
human rights 80
intergovernmental contracts 256
international law 254–7
international relations 256
ius doni 256, 400–1
list of countries which prohibit/allow dual citizenship 82–3
loyalty 254, 256, 399
military service 65, 81

mobility 399–400
Multiple Nationality Convention (CoE) 254–5
national citizenship laws, design of 254–5
national interest, grant of citizenship in the 85, 215–16, 219
nationality 65, 80–6, 400
naturalisation 206
passports 399–400
political attitudes 8102
prevention 254–7
reserved domain of States 254, 412
return, right to 401
statelessness 84
technology 80
terrorism 84
Myanmar 60
name change documentation, certified 337
Napoleon Bonaparte 39
nation States *see also* State sovereignty; three-element theory of constituent elements of the state
anachronism, as an 18–22
consolidation of States 34–5
constituent people 10–12, 14–18
constitutional and political dimensions 106–8, 114–16, 395
cosmopolitanism and global citizenship 19
definition 111–14
de-nationalization 21
economic globalisation 19, 21–2
discrimination and equality 249
formation 248
globalisation 19, 21–2, 55
historical development 107–8
immigration law and status 22
information age 110–11
international law 262–3
loyalty 312
mobility of worker 19–20
multinationals 55
nationality 20–1
new States, proliferation of 2
prerogative of nation States, citizenship as 104–6
public goods 222–4, 227
re-nationalization 21
reserved domains 254, 312
three-element theory 106–7
transnationalism 19–20
use of force, monopoly on the 21
violence, State monopoly of 105
Westphalian sovereignty, end of 21
national actions through international law, limitations on 22–3
national citizenship laws *see also* immigration status and laws; individual countries
assimilation 205
clarity 327, 328
consistency principle 77–9
constitutional rights 63, 104–5
democracy 250
discrimination and equality 249–50
elections and voting 245
EU 45–7, 63, 65–6, 265–77, 396–7
freedom of choice, respect for 246–7
human dignity 74, 244, 250–1
integration 205
international law 244
ius sanguinis 39
ius soli 39, 99
multiple citizenship 400
nationality 58, 63, 65–9, 77–8
parliament 250
return, right of 401
traditional understanding of citizenship 75–6
treaties 63
ultra vires doctrine 79, 260–1, 300
national identity 24–5, 50, 236–8
national interest, grant of citizenship in the 215–20
birthright lottery 218–19
CARICOM 220
contributions and investment 215–19, 220
discretion 215
due diligence 219
economic benefits 215–19
equal opportunities 218–19
EU 220
integration 215–16, 220
ius doni 215–20
multiple citizenship 85, 400

naturalisation 215–16, 219
property development 215
proportionality 215
seed capital 215
State sovereignty 215
talent-for-citizenship 217–19

National Socialist Germany 41–2, 72

nationalism
culture 35
demarcation between citizen and non-citizen 395–6
First World War 41
historical development 40–2, 395–6
immigration law and status 41
industrialisation 41
integration 294–5
Marxism 40–2
nation States 6–7
national homogeneity, myth of 315
National Socialist Germany 41–2
nationality 40–1
naturalisation 402
patriotic citizenship 294–5
passports 41
protonationalism 35
religion 35
Second World War 41
Stalinist-Leninist Russia 41
statelessness 41–2
symbols, traditions and theories of origin, invention of 40
totalitarianism 41–2

nationality
authority of the State 70
belief in the nation 15
Canada, Inuits in 61
CARICOM 21
citizenship, definition of 58–9, 62–71, 75–8, 393
citizenship, versus 57–86
classification of citizenship 66–71, 393
concept of citizenship 13, 66–70
constituent people 393
Convention on Nationality 1997 (Council of Europe) 59, 64–5, 254, 257
criminal records 204
culture and values 141
demographic change 76, 79
demos and *ethnos*, merger of 40–1
diplomatic or consular protection 263
documentary citizenship 62–4
ethnicity 59–62
EU 21, 64–6, 70–1, 76, 78–9, 397
fiduciary and obligatory relationships, exclusive and indivisible 68
final point theory versus incentive theory 95
foreign direct investment 80
globalisation 78–80
good faith 77
human dignity and relevance to allocation of citizenship 70, 72–5
human rights 71, 72, 263
imminent status 67–70
international law 64–6, 100, 263
legal nature and legal classification of citizenship 66–71
multi-ethnic States 59–60
multiple citizenship 65, 80–6, 400
nation States 6–7, 20–1
national citizenship laws 58, 63, 65–9, 77–9
nationalism 40–1
nationality, definition of 59–61
political community, membership in a 62–3
proportionality 75
social changes 76, 79
special contributions 76
State sovereignty 62–3
territorial sovereignty 77
traditional understanding of citizenship, no obligation on national legislature to follow 75–8
transnationalism 78–80

natural resources 301–2

natural rights/law 30–1, 37–8

naturalisation, acquisition of citizenship by 127–48, 150–1
abuse of political, economic and social rights, risk of 297
citizenship tests 129
coloniser regimes 201–2
common good, grant of citizenship in the 318, 403
comparative approach 200–6

connection, citizenship as formal or material point of 146–8
contributions and investment 233
criteria/conditions for citizenship 128–30, 136–46
culture 136–7
distributive justice 305
ethnicity 129–30, 402
EU, differences in the 266–7
European countries, table of 132–5
evaluation of *ius doni* 280–2, 287–8
extraordinary contributions 128, 204, 206, 211
financial position, existence of a secure 128, 205
genuine links or connections 143–6
good character and lack of binding convictions 204
historical development 150
identification points 16
integration 136, 294
ius doni 128, 402
ius sanguinis 128
ius soli 128
knowledge, proof of national or historical 204–5
language 128–30, 139–41, 203
length of residence 128–9, 203, 206
loyalty 136
list of naturalisations 132–5
marriage 206
mobility 137
multiple/dual citizenship 206
nationalism 402
non-coloniser/occupier regimes 201, 202
number of naturalisations 130–1
oaths of allegiance 203–4
ordinary naturalisation 128–48, 403
own-earned income 137–8
personal status, effects of 206
religion 129–30, 402
residence 136–8
Roman Empire 33, 130
self-employed basis 137–8
settler regimes 201, 202
simplification 25
statistics 319, 403
sui generis naturalisation 128
talent 52, 320, 405
taxes and other contributions, payment of 138
ultra vires 261, 299–300
unity of citizenship 253
values, identification with fundamental national 136, 141–3

Netherlands
citizenship tests 129
coloniser regimes 201–2
Dutch Republic 36
Dutch Revolt 37
French Civil Code 166
integration 13, 141
language 141
restrictions, trend towards 174

New Zealand
all white policies 232
citizenship tests 129
immigration countries, definition of 116
ius doni 13
length of residence 203
settler regimes 202

non-economic considerations ***see also*** **culture, traditions and values; language; length of residence; talent and highly-skilled people**
blocked exchange versus market approach 232–3, 406
citizenship tests 129, 190–1
colours as a vehicle of national awareness 109
family ties 98–9, 143
society, contributions to 300–1, 320, 326, 404–8

non-intervention principle 36

non-liberal States
absolutism 33–6, 93, 108, 248–9, 395
divergence between populations 399
national identity 237
totalitarianism 40–2, 45, 237

non-refoulement **principle 43–4**

non-State functions 100–1

Nordic regimes 201, 202 ***see also*** **individual countries**

North Korea 237–8, 244

Norway 202, 302

notaries public 333

oaths of allegiance 141–2, 203–4
Okun, Arthur 219, 232
Olympic citizenship 226
Ombudsman 268
overseas territories 162, 168, 266, 397
Pakistan 117, 321, 403
parentage, citizenship by *see ius sanguinis*
parents, sworn affidavits of support relating to 339
parliaments
  bicameral parliaments 153
  European Parliament 16–17, 268–9, 272–7, 289–91, 397
  national citizenship laws 250
  ultra vires 260–1
Parsons, Talcott 311
participation *see also* elections and voting
  abuse of political, economic and social rights, risk of 298
  constituent people 16–17, 91
  genuine links or connections 143–4
  human dignity 94
  Middle Ages 34
  national identity 237–8
  residence permits 17
  underclass 235–6
  Universal Declaration of Human Rights 16
Paskalev, Vesco 291
passive citizenship 71, 89, 94, 121, 195, 273–4
passports
  application forms 333, 334
  benefits, rights and obligations, as expression of 5
  certified copies 335
  children 335
  evaluation of *ius doni* 291
  mobility 312–13
  multiple citizenship 399–400
  nationalism 41
  Universal Declaration of Human Rights 263
Paul the Apostle, Saint 210
Peace of Westphalia 34, 35–6, 108, 395
Pericles 31
persecution and war, escaping 401
Petition of Rights of 1628 138
petition, right of (EU citizenship) 268, 272–7
  active citizenship, expression of integral 273–4
  admission requirements 275–6
  Charter of Fundamental Rights 273
  conferral of powers, principle of 272–3
  constitutional rights 276
  containment of State power 272–3
  content of EU citizenship 272–7
  cooperation, duty of 275
  European Commission 275
  European Parliament 268, 272–7
    Rules of Procedure 273–5
    self-organisation 273
  freedom of opinion and expression 277
  languages 275–6
  Lisbon Treaty 272–3
  loyalty 275
  nationality 65
  Petitions Committee 273–5
  powers and procedure 274–6
  proximity 273
  specification 276–7
photographs
  certified photographs 334
  colour photos 333–4
  signature certification forms 333
Pierre and Miquelon 168
point system model 54
politics *see also* elections and voting
  abuse of political rights, risk of 295–9, 325
  citizenship, definition of 62–3
  EU 267–9
  function of citizenship 88, 394
  integration 53
  membership of community 14, 62–3, 103–14, 238, 240–2
  multiple citizenship 81–2
  opinion 248–9
  public offices and functions, controlling access to 93
  undue influence 298
pollute, right to 232
population, limitation and control of

State's 88–9
Portalis, Jean-Étienne-Marie 165
powers of attorney 332
precedent 153, 187–8
prerogative of nation States, citizenship as 104–6
principles of citizenship acquisition 115–24
immigration and emigration countries 116–18
ius sanguinis 118–24, 398
ius soli 117–22, 398
types of acquisition 118–20
privacy 330
private clubs *see* Economic Theory of Clubs
private sector projects, approval and supervision of 329
professional references 337
property
development 215
exclusion of foreigners from acquisition 35
multiple citizenship 85
naturalisation 128, 280
rights, security of property 37
proportionality 75, 93, 215, 244
Prussia 39
public interest
common good, grant of citizenship in the 318–19, 403
religion 249
public international law *see* international law and principles
public offices and functions, controlling access to 92–3
Qatar 217
race *see* ethnicity and race
Rawls, John 22, 42–3, 74–5, 218–19, 303–4, 317, 409
Real Estate sale and purchase contract and escrow agreements 335
Reding, Viviane 290
references 337, 355
Reformation 6, 257
refugees
detention camps 44
non-refoulement principle 43–4
Refugee Convention 43–4
State sovereignty 43–4
statistics 321, 403–4
Reich, Robert B 224–5
religion
Catholic Church, influence of 107
discrimination and equality 247–9, 264
French Revolution 257
human dignity 249
Islamic countries 248
Islamists 321, 403–4
naturalisation 129–30, 402
protonationalism 35
public interest 249
secularisation 107
State sovereignty 36
Renaissance 33–6, 395
Renan, Ernest 15
rent-seeking and governance 301–2
reporting and audits 329–30
residence
addresses, original documents of evidence of 338
culture 137
custom 34
evaluation of *ius doni* 286–7
habitual residence 143
mobility 137
naturalisation 136–8
permits 17
population, limitation and control of State's 89
resident and non-resident rights, differentiation between 97
resident population, incongruence with 14–18
return, right to 123, 129–30, 232, 316, 401
La Réunion 168
revolutions *see* American Revolution; French Revolution
Roman law 32–3, 187, 395
civitis Romana 32–3
Constitutio Antoniniana 33
cosmopolitanism and global citizenship 33
extraordinary contributions 210
imminent status 67
ius civile 32

legal status, citizenship as a 32–3
naturalisation 130
Romania 296, 384
Roosevelt, Theodore 80
Rousseau, Jean Jacques 7–8, 11, 37, 107, 165, 237, 289–90, 294
Russia *see also* Soviet Union
consolidation of States 35
nationalism 41
nationality 59–60
Stalinist-Leninist Russia 41
Rwandan genocide 244
Sadiq, Kamal 62–3
Saint-Barthélemy 168
St Kitts and Nevis
abuse of political, economic and social rights, risk of 297
agents, licensing and supervision of 328
applications
costs 372–3
legal consequences 373
process 372
background to country 367, 374
CARICOM 373
CBI inflows and fiscal balance 376
Commonwealth, visa-free travel in the 373
Constitution 228, 368
contributions and investment 368–72, 375–7
criminal records 204
discretion 413
documentation 332–40, 372
domestic direct investments as primary objective, promotion of 369–70
due diligence 372–3, 376
economic impact 374–7
elections and voting 94, 253
ethnicity 367
EU
SIDF 370–1
Visa Agreement 373, 374
extraordinary contributions 374
financial crisis 344
historical developments lines 368–9
independence 344, 367, 368
integration 293
ius doni 8, 54–5, 281, 367–77
knowledge of State, proof of 370
language 203, 367, 370
legal basis 368–9, 413
length of residence 203, 206, 369
marriage 206
multiple citizenship 206, 256, 344–5
national interest, grant of citizenship in the 215
naturalisation statistics 367–8
oaths of allegiance 369
Organisation of East Caribbean States (OECS) 373
passports 372
professional advisors 344
public interest 376
real estate sector, investment in 370
registration 367–9, 372–3
residence 286, 369–70
rule of law 374
safe haven for investors 374
service providers 372
social return on investment (SRI) 374–7
Sovereign Wealth Funds 330, 368–72
State structural parameters 367
statistics 367–8
Sugar Industry Diversification Foundation (SIDF) 330, 368–72, 376
Confirmation Forms 335
contribution option 370–2
deposit and assets 371
minimum investment amounts 371–2
talent 54–5
tax 374, 375
tourism 370
transparency 374
tying arrangements 228–9
UK, independence from 344, 367, 368
unity of citizenship 253
visas 373, 374
welfare stats 374–5
World Trade Organization 370–1
Saint Martin 168
Sandel, Michael J 232–3, 290
Scheuch, Uwe 299
Schwarzenberg, Karel 255

Scotland, Act of Union with 152, 160, 211
secession States 392
Second World War
EU 45
National Socialist Germany 41–2, 72
nationalism 41
scientists and technicians after WWII, naturalisation of 212–13
secularisation/secularism 107, 165, 167, 248
selection criteria *see* criteria/conditions for citizenship
self-determination
collectivism 399
constitutional rights 246
discrimination and equality 264
Enlightenment 7
freedom of choice, respect for 246–7
human dignity 73, 399
human rights 71
refugees 43–4
State sovereignty 247
self-employed 78, 137–8
self-interest theory 37
Senegal 131
Serbia 296, 384
services
agents, licensing and supervision of 328–9
Economic Theory of Clubs 225
State as the provider 237
settler regimes 201, 202
Shachar, Ayelet 217, 219, 229, 289, 408
Sieyès, Emmanuel Joseph 59
signature certification forms 333
Shinawatra, Thaksin 366–7
Simon, Julian L 226
sincere cooperation, principle of 65, 384–5, 397
Singapore 153, 286, 369–70
Slovenia 320, 404
Smith, Adam 37
soccer clubs in Europe 226
social class 264
social cohesion 121, 280, 397
social conditions
changes 12, 75–7, 79, 203, 251
convergence 309
discrimination and equality 3, 317
exclusion 235
globalisation 76
social contract 37
social identities 86
social networks 111, 233
social return on investment (SRI) 374–7, 389
social structural deficits, control of 102
social rights, risk of abuse of 295–9, 325
social security *see* state benefits
sociological function of citizenship 88, 394
Solon 31
South Africa
apartheid 43, 244
immigration countries, definition of 116
pass laws 43
Sovereign Wealth Funds (SWFs) 330–1
sovereignty *see* sovereignty of the people; State sovereignty
sovereignty of the people
elections and voting 113
freedom of choice, respect for individual 245–6
international law, violations of 100
international relations 63
joint sovereignty 37
nationality 40
Soviet Union
collapse 392
Germany 384
liberal ethno-nationalist citizenship laws 296
statelessness 41–2
Spain
Catalonia, status of 61
consolidation of States 35
Franco regime, right to return of people fleeing 232
intergovernmental contracts 256
nationality 61
Spiro, Peter J 141
standards 325–6
state benefits
family ties 99
freedom of choice, respect for 246
nationality 263

volunteer work 246
welfare states 3, 375, 389
State sovereignty 9, 290, 298–9
absolutism 34–5
abuse of rights 298–9
commercialisation 298–9
constitutional and political dimensions 104–6
discretion 111–14
due diligence 299
EU 44–8, 65–6, 397
globalisation 411–12
human dignity 74
international law 100, 112–14, 262–3, 411–12
joint exercise 37
Middle Ages 34–6
moral hazard 299
nationality 62–3
non-intervention principle 36
non-State function 100
refugees 43–4
regulation 4
religion 36
self-determination 247
sell-outs 298–9
tax 138
territoriality 10–11, 34, 77, 104–6
tokens of sovereignty 301
totalitarianism 42
treaty law 262–3
Westphalian sovereignty, end of 21
statelessness
constitutional rights, differentiation between resident and non-resident 97
de facto statelessness 313
diplomatic or consular protection 96
EU 97
evaluation of *ius doni* 292
functional significance of citizenship 97–8
homelessness 98
human rights 97–8
international law 97, 258
nationalism 41–2
three-element theory 98
***status activus* and *status negativus*, differentiation between 11**
Straubhaar, Thomas 226
subjectivity
citizenship as a right 7, 65, 67, 71, 257
consumer citizenship 84
defence, right of 73
family ties 99
nationality 258, 263
sincere cooperation, principle of 385
subsidiarity
EU 49–51, 93, 139–40, 270
family ties 98
final point theory versus incentive theory 95
human dignity 244
ius sanguinis 122
language 139–40
talent 54
tax 138
values, creation of a consistent community of 90
sufficient link 258–60, 317–18, 398, 402
Sugar Industry Diversification Foundation (SIDF) 368–72, 376
supranationalism 45, 47–9, 265–77
Sweden 129, 202
Switzerland 175–84
absolutism 249
adoption 179, 180
aptitude tests 184
Austria 178, 180
citizenship, definition of 178
citizenship tests 129, 184
conferral, principle of 176
Constitution 175–6, 178–84
criteria/conditions for citizenship 183–4
culture
diversity 176–7
knowledge 184
direct democracy 180, 183
elections and voting 15
ethnicity 176
EU 175–6, 179
family ties 99
financial position, existence of a secure 205
French Civil Code 166
Germany 176–8
identification points 15

individual and social responsibility, principle of 175–6
integration 13, 182–4
international law 175
international organisations 179
ius doni 184
ius sanguinis 10, 122–3, 179
knowledge of country 204
language 110, 176, 182, 184
legitimacy 179
length of residence 181–3, 203, 206
marriage 180, 182–4, 206
military service, compensation for avoiding 226
minimum requirements 180–1
multinationals 179
multiple citizenship 150, 180, 184, 206, 256
municipality and canton, combination of citizenship of 180–1
naturalisation 150, 181, 175–84
non-coloniser/occupier regimes 202
ordinary naturalisation 181
origin principle 180
paternity, declarations of 179
permanent residence permits 181–2
referendums 237–8
religion 249
responsibility for naturalisation 181
restrictions 177
Schengen area 175
simplified naturalisation 181–2
sovereignty of cantons 176
State sovereignty 36
State structural parameters 175–7
statistics 177
structural features 178–9
subjects 178
subsidiarity 176
suitability for naturalisation 183–4
xenophobia 177
will, nation by 15, 226

Syria
civil war 244
Kurds 61
statelessness 313
travel to Syria 321

talent and highly-skilled people 13, 51–5, 280
blue cards 51–2
competitiveness 51–2
coordination 51–4
cosmopolitanism and global citizenship 53, 411
discrimination against desirable goods 309, 408
economic criteria 52–3
evaluation of *ius doni* 286, 327
globalisation 55
integration 51–3
ius sanguinis 52–3
ius soli 52–3
labour market 51–4
modern immigration and citizenship concepts 51–4
multinationals 55
national interest, grant of citizenship in the 217–19
naturalisation 52, 320, 405
Olympic citizenship 102, 217–18, 226
reform of citizenship law 52, 55
reputation 233, 291
scientists and technicians after WWII, naturalisation of 212–13
subsidiarity 54
transparency 327
welfare losses 53–4

tax 239–40
contributions and foreign investment 138
culture and values 142
havens 290
no representation without taxation 138
State sovereignty 138
subsidiarity 138
values, creation of a consistent community of 90

technology and digitalisation
constituent people 14
functional significance of citizenship 394
globalisation 88–9
Internet 110–11, 121
ius soli 121
multiple citizenship 80
nation State 110–11

territoriality see also ius soli

constituent people 15
Roman law 33
sovereignty 10–11, 34, 77, 104–6
three-element theory 10–11, 44–5
unity 39, 395

terrorism
due diligence 321
Islamists 321, 403–4
multiple citizenship 84
Syria, travel to 321
tourism 321, 403–4

Thirty Years War 212, 257

three-element theory of constituent elements of the State 10–13, 104–7
authority of the State 10–11, 44–5, 70–1, 105
citizenship, definition of 58–9, 393
constituent people 10–12, 14–18, 44–5, 49, 89, 105, 393
constitutional and political dimensions 104–6
EU 44–5, 40, 70–1
national territory 10–11, 44–5
population, limitation and control of State's 88
statelessness 98

totalitarianism 40–2, 45, 237

traditional understanding of citizenship 75–8, 395

traditions *see* culture, traditions and values

transnationalism
divergence between populations 398–9
EU 267
functions of citizenship 96
globalisation 78–80, 233, 411
integration 309
international law 25
ius sanguinis 8
ius soli 8, 121
multiple citizenship 400
nation State as an anachronism 19–21

transparency and accountability
application process, efficiency and reliability of 331–40
clear structure and legislation 327, 328
cosmopolitanism and global citizenship 310–11
criteria/conditions for citizenship 54, 410
due diligence 340–1
evaluation of *ius doni* 326–41
licensing and supervision of agents 328–9
private sector projects, approval and supervision of 329
reporting and audit, regular 329–30
Sovereign Wealth Funds 330–1

treaty law 262–3, 412

Triepel, Heinrich 22

Tronchet, François Denis 165

Turkey
emerging country, as 100, 309
Kurds 61
Turkish Republic, Greeks and Armenians during formation of 42

Twitter 111

tying arrangements 228–9, 413

Ukraine 384

***ultra vires*, violation of principle of 299–300**
democracy 260
foreign direct investment 299–300
international law 260–1
national citizenship laws 79, 260–1, 300
naturalisation 261, 300
rule of law 260

underclass 235–6

United Arab Emirates (UAE) 91

United Kingdom 151–64
abode, right of 161
Act of Union with Scotland of 1707 152, 160, 211
allegiance to the Crown 159, 163
aristocracy 304
Bank of Scotland, acquisition of shares in 211
British citizenship 152, 162–4
British Empire 8, 150–2, 158–60, 163, 201–2, 210–11
British nationality 152, 158, 160–2
British Overseas Citizens 162
Canada 160–1
citizenship, definition of 150
citizenship statistics 153

common law 66–7, 152–3
Commonwealth 16–17, 151–3, 160–1
consolidation of States 35
constitutional monarchy 152–3, 159
culture 152
custom 152–3
decolonisation 160
dependent territories 162
discretion 164
English law 152
English within the UK 61
EU 64
extraordinary contributions 210–12
feudalism 304
France 160
genuine links or connections 258
Hong Kong 266
House of Commons 152–3
House of Lords 152
immigration countries, definition of 116
immigration status 161
ius doni 13
ius sanguinis 159, 163
ius soli 8, 35, 159–60, 162–4
King or Queen in Parliament, authority of 152–3
language 152
length of residence 162–4, 203, 206
list of selected countries of origin 154–9
London 210–11
loss of citizenship 163
loyalty 160
Malta 289, 377–8
marriage 206
Middle Ages 210–11
monarchy 150
multiple citizenship 164, 206, 256
nationality 61, 66–7
NATO 151
naturalisation 151–64
oaths of allegiance 163, 203
overseas territories 266
Parliament 152–3
partiality 161
passports 161–2
Poles 212
political system 152–3
precedent 153, 187
registration 163
Scotland 152, 160, 211
spouses 163–4
State structural parameters 151–3
statute law 153
statistics 153
structural features 158–63
subjects 158, 160–1, 178
Syria, travel to 321
UN Security Council 151
unwritten constitution 152
Victorian era 258
welfare gains 286
Westminster system 153
United Nations (UN) 2, 77, 151
United States *see also* American Revolution
abuse of political, economic and social rights, risk of 296
accidental citizens 259, 402
American Samoa 60
anti-Asian policies 232
birth tourism 296
caveat emptor 285
citizenship tests 129
Cold War 255, 399
Constitution 6
contributions and investment 226
criminal records 204
discrimination and equality 247
Dred Scott v Sandford decision 43
EB-5 immigration programme 226
elections and voting 15
emigration, right of 314, 401
exclusion of foreigners as a sovereign right 19
German scientists and technicians after WWII, naturalisation of 212–13
Guantanamo Bay 96
immigration countries, definition of 116–17
ius soli 121, 262, 317, 398
length of residence 203, 206
loans 239
marriage 206
military service 130
multiple citizenship 206, 255, 401

nationality 59–61
Native Americans 61
naturalisation 130–1, 239
oaths of allegiance 141, 163
Olympic citizenship 217
Project Paperclip 212–13
racism 43, 60
religion 249
residence permits 17
settler regimes 202
statistics 325
welfare gains 286
unity of citizenship 252–3
Universal Declaration of Human Rights (UDHR)
abuse of rights 257–8
constituent people 16
elections and voting 94
family ties 99
human dignity 31, 72–3
integration 42
nationality, right to 263
participation rights 16
statelessness 98
withdrawal of citizenship 257–8, 263
universalism
birth-right privileges, removal of 234–5
human dignity 244–5, 247, 250–1, 412
human rights 42–3, 72, 292
international law 244–5, 262, 412
market values 234–5
source-country universalism 117
use of force, State monopoly of 21, 100, 105, 249
utilitarianism 239, 306–7, 406–8
birthright lottery 307
foreign direct investment 307
market goods 307, 406–7
money 306
values *see* culture, traditions and values
van Gogh, Theo 141
Vatican City 147–8
Vattel, Emir de 38
veil of ignorance 74–5, 303–4, 409–10
Venezuela, indigenous population of 316–17
Vienna Convention on the Law of Treaties 262
violence, State monopoly of 21, 100, 105, 249
visas 3, 85, 223, 225, 230, 313, 325, 373, 389, 400, 406
Voltaire (François Marie Arouet) 7, 107, 165
voting *see* elections and voting
Waldrauch, Harald 118
Wallis and Futuna Islands 168
Walzer, Michael 17, 225, 232
Wartburg Festival of 1817 109
watchman State, model of the 37
Weber, Max 100
welfare
advancement and economic development, contributions to 8–9
assignment of rights 96
differentials, reduction of 310
functional significance of citizenship 88, 96
gains 286
globalisation 310
integration 310
loyalty 67
nation States 394
talent 53–4
welfare benefits *see* state benefits
Westphalian sovereignty, end of 21
Wikileaks 108
will, nations by 15, 226
Wilson, Woodrow 41
withdrawal or loss of citizenship
abuse of rights 257–8
Economic Theory of Clubs 223
EU 46, 268
individual freedom of choice 246
international law 46, 257–8, 261
multiple citizenship 84
national citizenship Laws 63
Universal Declaration of Human Rights 257–8, 263
Wolff, Christian 36
World Athletics Championship 217
World Bank 76, 79
World Economic Forum (WEF) (Davos) 20–1
World Trade Organization (WTO) 233, 361, 370–1

World War One 41
World War Two *see* Second World War
xenophobia 177
Yugoslavia
culture and values 269
former Yugoslavia 244, 269
Kosovo, conflict in 244
Montenegro 360
Zakaria, Fareed 21
Zavozin, Maxim 217
Zeno 30

www.ingramcontent.com/pod-product-compliance
Lightning Source LLC
La Vergne TN
LVHW011822200926
848484LV00005B/1277